# VOICE COMMUNICATION WITH
# COMPUTERS

## Conversational Systems

CHRISTOPHER SCHMANDT

VAN NOSTRAND REINHOLD
**New York**

Copyright © 1994 by Christopher Schmandt

Library of Congress Catalog Card Number 93-36404
ISBN 0-442-23935-1

I(T)P    Van Nostrand Reinhold is an International Thomson Publishing company.
         ITP logo is a trademark under license.

Printed in

Van Nostrand Reinhold                  International Thomson Publishing GmbH
115 Fifth Avenue                       Königswinterer Str. 418
New York, NY 10003                     53277 Bonn
                                       Germany

International Thomson Publishing       International Thomson Publishing Asia
Berkshire House, 168-173               221 Henderson Building #05-10
High Holborn, London WC1V 7AA          Singapore 0315
England

Thomas Nelson Australia                International Thomson Publishing Japan
102 Dodds Street                       Kyowa Building, 3F
South Melbourne 3205                   2-2-1 Hirakawacho
Victoria, Australia                    Chiyoda-Ku, Tokyo 102
                                       Japan

Nelson Canada
1120 Birchmount Road
Scarborough, Ontario
M1K 5G4, Canada

16  15  14  13  12  11  10 9 8 7 6 5 4 3 2 1

**Library of Congress Cataloging in Publication Data 93-36404**

Schmandt, Chris.
     Voice communication with computers / Chris Schmandt.
          p.     cm.
     Includes bibliographical references and index.
     ISBN 0-442-23935-1
     1. Interactive computer systems.   2. Natural language processing
(Computer science)   I. Title.
     QA76.9.I58S35   1993
     006.4'54—dc20
                                              93-36404
                                              CIP

*To Ava and Kaya for the patience to see me through writing this and helping me learn to hear the voice of the desert.*

# Contents

## Chapter 7.  Speech Recognition    132

# Speaking of Talk

As we enter the next millennium, speech unquestionably will become the primary means of communication between human beings and machines. By primary I mean the one most often used. The reasons are simple and go beyond our intuitive desire to use native spoken language, which comes naturally to us and accounts for so much of human-to-human discourse.

Namely, the value of speech is not just the use of "natural language," as such, but includes other valuable properties. Speech works in the dark. It allows you to communicate with small objects. It lets you transmit a message beyond arm's reach and around corners. It is a subcarrier of meaning through prosody, tone and, of course, volume.[1]

How does speech play into today's trends in computing?

Miniaturization is surely one such trend. I expect to have more computing on my wrist in ten years than I have on my desk today. Another is ubiquity. I expect computing to be woven into the entire fabric of my life.[2] Another is concurrence. More and more, I see the parallel use of our auditory channels, when our hands and eyes are occupied.[3] Finally, I anticipate the increasing use of computers "in passing." By that I mean the ability to voice a remark, pose a question, or give a

---

[1]Any parent knows that it is not what you say, but how you say it.

[2]In the literal sense, as well, I expect apparel to be part of my private area network: PAN.

[3]Schmandt illustrates this in Chapter 6 with his example of the Back Seat Driver.

salutation without bringing all of one's other faculties to a grinding halt, as we do now when we sit down to a session with our computer. Computer usage today is solely in the fovea of our attention, while tomorrow we will enjoy it equally at the periphery of thoughts, actions, and consciousness, more like air than headlines.

Consider these trends and the features intrinsic to the audio domain, and there is little question of where we are headed. Talk will be the most common means of interaction with all machines, large and small.[4]

This book is not only timely but different. Chris Schmandt brings a unique and important perspective to speech. Let me illustrate, with a story, the difference I see between his work and the work of others. The story is old and has gained some color with time, but illustrates an important point about breaking engineering deadlocks.

In 1978, the so-called Architecture Machine Group received the first working model of NEC's connected speech recognizer—the top of the line for its day, designed by Dr. Yasuo Kato, now a member of the Board of Directors of that same corporation. It was a continuous speech recognition system, speaker-dependent, and able to handle fifty utterances.[5]

In the celebrated program called Put-That-There (discussed in Chapter 8) this machine worked with unmatched elegance and became the objective and site for technical tourists from all over the world. But it had a problem; one that turned out not to be unique to that specific device but, in fact, quite general.

If a user of the system was tense or nervous, his or her voice would be affected. Although this condition was not necessarily audible to another human being, it was distinctly noticeable to the machine. This seemingly harmless feature turned into a disastrous bug, since the enormous importance of presenting one's results to sponsors often creates tension.

The Advanced Research Projects Agency (ARPA) makes periodic visits to MIT, frequently with very high-ranking military personnel. Of course, ARPA was very interested in this elegant prototype of the future of command and control systems.[6] The importance of these visits was so great that graduate students, sometimes Chris Schmandt himself, became sufficiently nervous that a perfectly working system (ten minutes before) functioned improperly in the presence of these august, easily disappointed, and frequently disbelieving visitors. There is something particularly frustrating and stupid looking about a speech recognition system when it does not work, which only exacerbates the problem and makes the person demonstrating the system even more anxious.

---

[4]I do not limit my remarks to computers, as we know them, but consider all machines: home appliances, entertainment equipment, telecommunication apparati, transportation machinery, engines for work, play, and learning—as well as some not yet imagined.

[5]The difference between a word and an utterance is crucial, as an utterance can be a part of a word or a concatenation of them (up to five seconds in this particular case).

[6]Command and control is deeply rooted in voice; my own limited experience in Army exercises witnessed a great deal of yelling.

The short-term fix was to train students and staff who demonstrated the system to be cool, calm, and collected and to ignore the stature of their guests. Guests were encouraged to wear blue jeans versus uniforms.

The longer-term solution resides in a different view of speech, as communication and interaction, not just as a string of words in the acoustic domain. This perspective results in a variety of ideas, of which one is to find the pauses in the speaker's speech[7] and judiciously issue the utterance "ah ha," taken from a suite of "ah ha's" ranging from the mousy to the elephantine. Namely, as one speaks to a system it should listen and, now and again, say "ah ha"—"ah ha"—"ah ha." The user will relax and the system's performance will skyrocket.

Discussions of ideas such as this have been highly criticized as yet another example of how members of the Media Lab are mere charlatans. How dare they give a user the false impression that the machine has understood when, in fact, it may not have?

The criticism is a perfect example of why computer science is so sensory deprived and getting duller by the day. Critics miss the point totally. Listen to yourself on the telephone. As someone is talking to you, you will naturally issue an "ah ha" every fifteen to thirty seconds. In fact, if you don't, after a while your telephone partner will be forced to ask, "Are you still there?" The point is that the "ah ha" *has no lexical value.* It is purely a communications protocol, no different from the electronic hand-shaking with which network architects are so familiar.

How did this escape researchers in the speech recognition community, itself a mature pursuit for over twenty-five years? The same question can be rephrased: Why was speech production and speech recognition so utterly decoupled?[8]

My answer is not popular with most members of the speech community, but it is at the root of why this book is so special. That is, the traditional speech recognition community was fundamentally disinterested in "communication." Its interest was in "transcription"; namely, transcoding from ASCII into utterances or spoken language into ASCII. It was not interested in the tightly coupled interaction of human dialogue, typical of face-to-face communication. That kind of speech, Schmandt's kind of speech, is filled with interruption, retort, and paralinguals (the "ah ha's"), wherein the verbal back-channel is no less important than speech output. This concept is what *Voice Communication with Computers* brings to the table.

*Voice Communication with Computers* is not just a textbook or tutorial, it is a perspective. Its point of view underscores the need to interact and communicate with computers in much the same way we communicate with human beings. Only when we are able to talk to machines the way we talk to people will the concept of "ease of use" be seriously addressed.

[7]We all pause, even those of us who speak like machine guns must come up for air.
[8]Literally, in almost all labs world-wide, researchers in speech production and speech recognition were in different groups, different labs, or different divisions.

Today "ease of use" means simple, direct manipulation, with little or no delegation. The future of computing is discourse and delegation and, for that, speech is mandatory—not a process of transcription but conversation. This is the area pioneered by Schmandt and reflected in the following pages.

Nicholas Negroponte
MIT Media Lab

# Preface

This book began as graduate class notes to supplement technical readings from a number of disciplines. Over the years as I have worked on various projects, I kept running against the question, "What can I read to better understand this?" Although materials are available, texts have been too focused and detailed and papers are spread across too many conference proceedings for either students or specialists in other areas to make good use of them. This book is meant to open the more specialized disciplines to a wider audience while conveying a vision of speech communication integrated with computing.

The primary message of this book is an approach to incorporating speech into computing environments; it is unique in its focus on the *user* of speech systems and interaction techniques to enhance the utility of voice computing. But a complete evaluation of speech at the interface is grounded in the understanding of speech technologies, the computational means of expressing linguistic and discourse knowledge, and the software architectures that support voice in multimedia computer environments.

This interdisciplinary approach is the most valuable asset of this book but simultaneously a limitation. I attempt to open technical doors for readers who span many fields and professions. For example, I discuss speech coding without reference to the standard notations of discrete time digital signal processing. This is a little bit like trying to teach high school physics to students who have not yet learned calculus: terribly inelegant in retrospect *if* one pursues studies in physics. But this is not a speech coding text; this book examines how and when to *use* speech coding, speech recognition, text-to-speech synthesis, computer-telephone interfaces, and natural language processing. Anyone trying to understand how to use voice in emerging computing environments should benefit from this information.

Technology has changed rapidly in the five years this book has been in progress. While it has been reassuring to see many of my expectations fulfilled—and technological developments only increase the potential for pervasive deployment of speech-capable applications—these changes have necessitated continual updating in this text. This pace of change almost guarantees that some portion of this book will be out of date by the time it appears in print. Five years ago speech technology was awkward, expensive, and difficult to integrate into work environments. Speech systems research almost invariably required interfacing to additional peripheral devices including complete components such as text-to-speech synthesizers or internal add-in hardware such as digital signal processors. No computer was equipped with a microphone back then, and while computer speakers usually were connected to tone-generating hardware to emit various beep sounds, these systems could not play a digital audio file. At that time, large-scale consumer access to digitized audio via the compact disc was only just beginning to make serious inroads on analog audio tape and vinyl LP music distribution.

Much has changed while I wrote and rewrote this book. Most computers are now audio capable, equipped with microphones and the ability to play back digital audio at qualities ranging from that of the telephone to that of the CD. The capacity of disk drives is now measured in Gigabytes, not Megabytes, minimizing the difficulty of storing audio data, which requires much more disk space than text. Some computers have been shipped with digital signal microprocessors included on the mother board. Others ship with digital-telephone network interfaces (ISDN) as standard equipment. The explosion of cellular telephony and palmtop computers has created a new community of potential computer audio users, who need the access and the means to communicate with computers as well as with other people while on the move.

Perhaps the most significant development, however, is the more than ten-fold increase in the speed of general-purpose processors found in all classes of computers. This speed now enables the majority of computers to perform basic real-time voice processing and simple speech recognition. The more powerful desktop workstations are capable of the highest quality text-to-speech synthesis, large vocabulary speech recognition, and sophisticated voice processing. Speech technology is rapidly becoming a commodity that can be distributed as shrink-wrapped software or included with a computer operating system.

During these five years, applications have also followed the enabling technology although with a frustrating lag. Basic speech recognition to control computer window systems is available in several products. A number of isolated applications allow voice annotations to spreadsheets and other text-oriented data. Several competing formats for voice attachments to electronic mail have also appeared, and now progress is being made to converge on a single standard format. Recently a new venture initiated a digital audio "radio" program distribution over the Internet. Speech recognition is now being used in the telephone network, to help complete collect call attempts, for example.

This is just the beginning of ubiquitous voice technology. Voice is so useful and such an important part of our lives that, by necessity, it will become pervasive in the ways computers are used. The trends of the last five years will continue only to accelerate over the next five. While we must accept that we are still a long, long way from the science fiction theme of the ever-present listening computer (with a pleasant voice as well!), we will find ourselves holding an increasing number of conversations with machines. Some of the readers of this book will be among those researchers or developers making this a reality.

# Acknowledgments

This book originated with sketchy class notes coauthored with Jim Davis, and Pascal Chesnais triggered our note-writing by encouraging us to give students almost anything. Jim wisely decided to complete his dissertation instead of joining me to write this book and graduated years ago.

I have had help from many people both in editing my technical writing as well as reviewing portions of this manuscript for accuracy. I have benefitted tremendously from their help; the errors that remain are my own. This list includes Barry Arons, Janet Cahn, Jim Davis, Kate Gordon, Harry Hersh, Lisa Stifelman, Ben Stoltz, Tony Vitale, and Nicole Yankelovich.

I have also benefitted tremendously from both editorial help as well as immeasurable assistance with the production of this book from Gayle Sherman and Elaine McCarthy. I think I would have given up months from completion without Gayle's help. Without the patience of Dianne Littwin at Van Nostrand Reinhold, I'm sure I would have backed out of this project years ago. And most important has been the support of my family, Ava and Kaya, who let me add the time to write this book to an already overly crowded work schedule.

This book includes descriptions of many research projects we have implemented at M.I.T, both at the Media Laboratory as well as one of its predecessors, the Architecture Machine Group. I would never have been in the position to create the group that performed this work without the unwavering support of my laboratory director, Nicholas Negroponte, for the last thirteen years. And I probably would have been unable to deal with the politics of a new laboratory without the comradeship of Walter Bender, even though we have worked on completely independent projects since jointly debugging network code a decade ago.

Finally and most importantly, my own ideas as well as these projects have evolved over years of interacting with students. They have written much of the software, helped me debug my class notes, and suffered through my attempts to put these thoughts into a coherent whole in my courses. Some have been friends, some have been peers; yet we have had plenty of disagreements. But our graduates are more valuable than anything else we do, and I have enjoyed working with them immensely. It would be impossible to rank-order their contributions, so I list them alphabetically: Mark Ackerman, Barry Arons, Derek Atkins, Lorne Berman, Jim Davis, Lorin Jurow, Debby Hindus, Angie Hinrichs, Chris Horner, Eric Hulteen, Andrew Kass, Kevin Landel, Eric Ly, Sanjay Manandhar, Mike McKenna, Atty Mullins, Sheldon Pacotti, Charles Simmons, Jordan Slott, Lisa Stifelman, Tom Trobaugh, Mark Vershel, Todd Wayne, Chi Wong, and Jim Zamiska.

During the course of writing this book I discovered the deserts of the American Southwest. Over the years I find myself repeatedly drawn back to their open spaces and infinite vistas. Although I have edited a significant portion of this book in their midst I have missed them badly while sitting at desks trying to put this project to rest. Although the two are somehow inextricably intermingled in my consciousness, I look forward to getting back to the purity of the desert without carrying this project along.

# Introduction

For most of us, speech has been an integral part of our daily lives since we were small children. Speech *is* communication; it is highly expressive and conveys subtle intentions clearly. Our conversations employ a range of interactive techniques to facilitate mutual understanding and ensure that we are understood.

But despite the effectiveness of speech communication, few of us use speech in our daily computing environments. In most workplaces voice is relegated to specialized industrial applications or aids to the disabled; voice is not a part of the computer interfaces based on displays, keyboards, and mice. Although current workstations have become capable of supporting much more sophisticated voice processing, the most successful speech application to date, voice mail, is tied most closely to the telephone.

As speech technologies and natural language understanding mature in the coming decades, many more potential applications will become reality. But much more than raw technology is required to bridge the gap between human conversation and computer interfaces; we must understand the assets and liabilities of voice communication if we are to gauge under which circumstances it will prove to be valuable to end users.

Conversational systems must speak and listen, but they also must understand, pose queries, take turns, and remember the topic of conversation. Understanding how people converse lets us develop better models for interaction with computers by voice. But speech is a very demanding medium to employ effectively, and unless user interaction techniques are chosen with great care, voice applications tend to be slow and awkward to use.

This book is about using speech in a variety of computing environments based on appreciating its role in human communication. Speech can be used as a method of *interacting* with a computer to place requests or receive warnings and notices. Voice can also be used as the underlying *data* itself, such as notes stored in a calendar, voice annotations of a text document, or telephone messages. Desktop workstations can already support both these speech functions. Speech excels as a method of interacting with the desktop computer over the telephone and has strong potential as the primary channel to access a computer small enough to fit in one's shirt pocket. The full utility of speech will be realized only when it is integrated across *all* these situations; when users find it effective to talk to their computers over the telephone, for example, they will suddenly have more utility for voice as data while in the office.

## CONTENTS OF THIS BOOK

This book serves different needs for different readers. The author believes that a firm grounding in the theory of operation of speech technologies forms an important basis for appreciating the difficulties of building applications and interfaces to employ them. This understanding is necessary if we wish to be capable of making any predictions or even guesses of where this field will lead us over the next decade. Paired with descriptions of voice technologies are chapters devoted to applications and user interaction techniques for each, including case studies to illustrate potential applications in more detail. But many chapters stand more or less on their own, and individual readers may pick and choose among them. Readers interested primarily in user interface design issues will gain most benefit from Chapters 4, 6, 8, 9, and 12. Those most concerned about system architectures and support for voice in multimedia computing environments should focus on Chapters 3, 5, 7, and 12. A telecommunications perspective is the emphasis of Chapters 10, 11, and 6.

A conversation requires the ability to speak and to listen, and, if the parties are not in close proximity, some means of transporting their voices across a distance. Chapter 1 discusses the communicative role of speech and introduces some representations of speech and an analytic approach that frames the content of this book. Chapter 2 discusses the physiology of human speech and how we perceive it through our ears; although later chapters refer back to this information, it is not essential for understanding the remainder of the book.

Voice interface technologies are required for computers to participate in conversations. These technologies include digital recording, speech synthesis, and speech recognition; these are the topics of Chapters 3, 5, and 7. Knowledge of the operations of the speech technologies better prepares the reader to appreciate their limitations and understand the impact of improvements in the technologies in the near and distant future.

Although speech is intuitive and seemingly effortless for most of us, it is actually quite difficult to employ as a computer interface. This difficulty is partially due to limitations of current technology but also a result of characteristics inherent in the speech medium itself. The heart of this book is both criteria for evaluating the suitability of voice to a range of applications and interaction techniques to make its use effective in the user interface. Although these topics are treated throughout this book, they receive particular emphasis in Chapters 4, 6, 8 and 12. These design guidelines are accentuated by case studies scattered throughout the book but especially in these chapters.

These middle chapters are presented in pairs. Each pair contains a chapter describing underlying technology matched with a chapter discussing how to apply the technology. Chapter 3 describes various speech coding methods in a descriptive form and differentiates coding schemes based on data rate, intelligibility, and flexibility. Chapter 4 then focuses on simple applications of stored voice in computer documents and the internal structure of audio editors used to produce those documents. Chapter 5 introduces text-to-speech algorithms. Chapter 6 then draws on both speech coding as well as speech synthesis to discuss *interactive* applications using speech output over the telephone.

Chapter 7 introduces an assortment of speech recognition techniques. After this, Chapter 8 returns to interactive systems, this time emphasizing voice input instead of touch tones. The vast majority of work to date on systems that speak and listen has involved short utterances and brief transactions. But both sentences and conversations exhibit a variety of structures that must be mastered if computers are to become *fluent*. Syntax and semantics constrain sentences in ways that facilitate interpretation; pragmatics relates a person's utterances to intentions and real-world objects; and discourse knowledge indicates how to respond and carry on the thread of a conversation across multiple exchanges. These aspects of speech communication, which are the focus of Chapters 9 and 13, must be incorporated into any system that can engage successfully in a conversation that in any way approaches the way we speak to each other.

Although a discussion of the workings of the telephone network may at first seem tangential to a book about voice in computing, the telephone plays a key role in any discussion of speech and computers. The ubiquity of the telephone assures it a central role in our voice communication tasks. Every aspect of telephone technology is rapidly changing from the underlying network to the devices we hold in our hands, and this is creating many opportunities for computers to get involved in our day-to-day communication tasks. Chapter 10 describes the telephone technologies, while Chapter 11 discusses the integration of telephone functionality into computer workstations. Much of Chapter 6 is about building telephone-based voice applications that can provide a means of accessing personal databases while not in the office.

When we work at our desks, we may employ a variety of speech processing technologies in isolation, but the full richness of voice at the desktop comes with the combination of multiple voice applications. Voice applications on the workstation also raise issues of interaction between both audio and window systems and operating system and run-time support for voice. This is the topic of Chapter 12. Speakers and microphones at every desk may allow us to capture many of the spontaneous conversations we hold every day, which are such an essential aspect of our work lives. Desktop voice processing also enables remote telephone access to many of the personal information management utilities that we use in our offices.

## ASSUMPTIONS

This book covers material derived from a number of specialized disciplines in a way that is accessible to a general audience. It is divided equally between background knowledge of speech technologies and practical application and interaction techniques. This broad view of voice communication taken in this book is by definition interdisciplinary. Speech communication is so vital and so rich that a number of specialized areas of research have risen around it, including speech science, digital signal processing and linguistics, aspects of artificial intelligence (computational linguistics), cognitive psychology, and human factors. This book touches on all these areas but makes no pretense of covering any of them in depth. This book attempts to open doors by revealing why each of these research areas is relevant to the design of conversational computer systems; the reader with further interest in any of these fields is encouraged to pursue the key overview references mentioned in each chapter.

Significant knowledge of higher mathematics as well as digital signal processing is assumed by many speech texts. These disciplines provide an important level of abstraction and on a practical level are tools required for any serious development of speech technology itself. But to be accessible to a wider audience, this book makes little use of mathematics beyond notation from basic algebra. This book provides an intuitive, rather than rigorous, treatment of speech signal processing to aid the reader in evaluation and selection of technologies and to appreciate their operation and design tradeoffs.

There is a wide gap between the goal of emulating conversational human behavior and what is commercially viable with today's speech technology. Despite the large amount of basic speech research around the world, there is little innovative work on how speech devices may be used in advanced systems, but it is difficult to discuss applications without examples. To this end, the author has taken the liberty to provide more detail with a series of voice projects from the Speech Research Group of M.I.T.'s Media Laboratory (including work from one of its predecessors, the Architecture Machine Group). Presented as case studies, these projects are intended both to illustrate applications of the ideas presented in each chapter and to present pertinent design issues. It is hoped that taken collectively these projects will offer a vision of the many ways in which computers can take part in communication.

# 1

# Speech as Communication

Speech can be viewed in many ways. Although chapters of this book focus on specific aspects of speech and the computer technologies that utilize speech, the reader should begin with a broad perspective on the role of speech in our daily lives. It is essential to appreciate the range of capabilities that conversational systems must possess before attempting to build them. This chapter lays the groundwork for the entire book by presenting several perspectives on speech communication.

The first section of this chapter emphasizes the *interactive* and *expressive* role of voice communication. Except in formal circumstances such as lectures and dramatic performances, speech occurs in the context of a *conversation,* wherein participants take turns speaking, interrupt each other, nod in agreement, or try to change the topic. Computer systems that talk or listen may ultimately be judged by their ability to converse in like manner simply because conversation permeates human experience. The second section discusses the various components or *layers* of a conversation. Although the distinctions between these layers are somewhat contrived, they provide a means of analyzing the communication process; research disciplines have evolved for the study of each of these components. Finally, the last section introduces the *representations* of speech and conversation, corresponding in part to the layers identified in the second section. These representations provide abstractions that a computer program may employ to engage in a conversation with a human.

## SPEECH AS CONVERSATION

Conversation is a process involving multiple participants, shared knowledge, and a protocol for taking turns and providing mutual feedback. Voice is our primary channel of interaction in conversation, and speech evolved in humans in response to the need among its members to communicate. It is hard to imagine many uses of speech that do not involve some interchange between multiple participants in a conversation; if we are discovered talking to ourselves, we usually feel embarrassed.

For people of normal physical and mental ability, speech is both rich in expressiveness and easy to use. We learn it without much apparent effort as children and employ it spontaneously on a daily basis.[1] People employ many layers of knowledge and sophisticated protocols while having a conversation; until we attempt to analyze dialogues, we are unaware of the complexity of this interplay between parties.

Although much is known about language, study of interactive speech communication has begun only recently. Considerable research has been done on natural language processing systems, but much of this is based on keyboard input. It is important to note the contrast between written and spoken language and between read or rehearsed speech and spontaneous utterances. Spoken language is less formal than written language, and errors in construction of spoken sentences are less objectionable. Spontaneous speech shows much evidence of the real-time processes associated with its production, including false starts, non-speech noises such as mouth clicks and breath sounds, and pauses either silent or filled ("... um ...") [Zue *et al.* 1989b]. In addition, speech naturally conveys intonational and emotional information that fiction writers and playwrights must struggle to impart to written language.

Speech is rich in interactive techniques to guarantee that the listener understands what is being expressed, including facial expressions, physical and vocal gestures, "uh-huhs," and the like. At certain points in a conversation, it is appropriate for the listener to begin speaking; these points are often indicated by longer pauses and lengthened final syllables or marked decreases in pitch at the end of a sentence. Each round of speech by one person is called a **turn; interruption** occurs when a participant speaks before a break point offered by the talker. Instead of taking a turn, the listener may quickly indicate agreement with a word or two, a nonverbal sound ("uh-huh"), or a facial gesture. Such responses, called **back channels,** speed the exchange and result in more effective conversations [Kraut *et al.* 1982].[2]

Because of these interactive characteristics, speech is used for immediate communication needs, while writing often implies a distance, either in time or space,

---

[1]For a person with normal speech and hearing to spend a day without speaking is quite a novel experience.

[2]We will return to these topics in Chapter 9.

between the author and reader. Speech is used in transitory interactions or situations in which the process of the interaction may be as important as its result. For example, the agenda for a meeting is likely to be written, and a written summary or minutes may be issued "for the record," but the actual decisions are made during a conversation. Chapanis and his colleagues arranged a series of experiments to compare the effectiveness of several communication media, i.e., voice, video, handwriting, and typewriting, either alone or in combination, for problem-solving tasks [Ochsman and Chapanis 1974]. Their findings indicated an overwhelming contribution of voice for such interactions. Any experimental condition that included voice was superior to any excluding voice; the inclusion of other media with voice resulted in only a small additional effectiveness. Although these experiments were simplistic in their use of student subjects and invented tasks and more recent work by others [Minneman and Bly 1991] clarifies a role for video interaction, the dominance of voice seems unassailable.

But conversation is more than mere interaction; communication often serves a purpose of changing or influencing the parties speaking to each other. I tell you something I have learned with the intention that you share my knowledge and hence enhance your view of the world. Or I wish to obtain some information from you so I ask you a question, hoping to elicit a reply. Or perhaps I seek to convince you to perform some activity for me; this may be satisfied either by your physical performance of the requested action or by your spoken promise to perform the act at a later time. "Speech Act" theories (to be discussed in more detail in Chapter 9) attempt to explain language as action, e.g., to request, command, query, and promise, as well as to inform.

The intention behind an utterance may not be explicit. For example, "Can you pass the salt?" is not a query about one's ability; it is a request. Many actual conversations resist such purposeful classifications. Some utterances ("go ahead," "uh-huh," "just a moment") exist only to guide the flow of the conversation or comment on the state of the discourse, rather than to convey information. Directly purposeful requests are often phrased in a manner allowing flexibility of interpretation and response. This looseness is important to the process of people defining and maintaining their work roles with respect to each other and establishing socially comfortable relationships in a hierarchical organization. The richness of speech allows a wide range of "acceptance" and "agreement" from wholehearted to skeptical to incredulous.

Speech also serves a strong social function among individuals and is often used just to pass the time, tell jokes, or talk about the weather. Indeed, extended periods of silence among a group may be associated with interpersonal awkwardness or discomfort. Sometimes the actual occurrence of the conversation serves a more significant purpose than any of the topics under discussion. Speech may be used to call attention to oneself in a social setting or as an exclamation of surprise or dismay in which an utterance has little meaning with respect to any preceding conversation. [Goffman 1981]

The expressiveness of speech and robustness of conversation strongly support the use of speech in computer systems, both for stored voice as a data type as well as speech as a medium of interaction. Unfortunately, current computers are capable of uttering only short sentences of marginal intelligibility and occasionally recognizing single words. Engaging a computer in a conversation can be like an interaction in a foreign country. One studies the phrase book, utters a request, and in return receives either a blank stare (wrong pronunciation, try again) or a torrent of fluent speech in which one cannot perceive even the word boundaries.

However, limitations in technology only reinforce the need to take advantage of conversational techniques to ensure that the user is understood. Users will judge the performance of computer systems employing speech on the basis of their expectations about conversation developed from years of experience speaking with fellow humans. Users may expect computers to be either deaf and dumb, or once they realize the system can talk and listen, expect it to speak fluently like you and me. Since the capabilities of current speech technology lie between these extremes, building effective conversational computer systems can be very frustrating.

## HIERARCHICAL STRUCTURE OF CONVERSATION

A more analytic approach to speech communication reveals a number of different ways of describing what actually occurs when we speak. The hierarchical structure of such analysis suggests goals to be attained at various stages in computer-based speech communication.

Conversation requires apparatus both for listening and speaking. Effective communication invokes mental processes employing the mouth and ears to convey a message thoroughly and reliably. There are many layers at which we can analyze the communication process, from the lower layers where speech is considered primarily acoustically to higher layers that express meaning and intention. Each layer involves increased knowledge and potential for intelligence and interactivity.

From the point of view of the speaker, we may look at speech from at least eight layers of processing as shown in Figure 1.1.

### Layers of Speech Processing

**discourse**  The regulation of conversation for pragmatic ends. This includes taking turns talking, the history of referents in a conversation so pronouns can refer to words spoken earlier, and the process of introducing new topics.

**pragmatics**  The intent or motivation for an utterance. This is the underlying reason the utterance was spoken.

**semantics**  The meaning of the words individually and their meaning as combined in a particular sentence.

**syntax**  The rules governing the combination of words in a sentence, their parts of speech, and their forms, such as case and number.

## speaker                                          listener

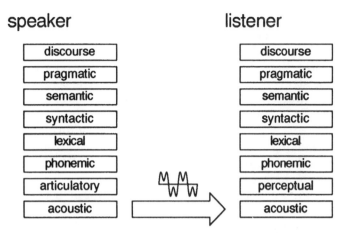

**Figure 1.1.** A layered view of speech communication.

**lexical**   The set of words in a language, the rules for forming new words from
affixes (prefixes and suffixes), and the stress ("accent") of syllables within the
words.

**phonetics**   The series of sounds that uniquely convey the series of words in the
sentence.

**articulation**   The motions or configurations of the vocal tract that produce the
sounds, e.g., the tongue touching the lips or the vocal cords vibrating.

**acoustics**   The realization of the string of phonemes in the sentence as vibrations of air molecules to produce pressure waves, i.e., sound.

Consider two hikers walking through the forest when one hiker's shoelace
becomes untied. The other hiker sees this and says, "Hey, you're going to trip on
your shoelace." The listener then ties the shoelace. We can consider this utterance
at each layer of description.

**Discourse** analysis reveals that "Hey" serves to call attention to the urgency
of the message and probably indicates the introduction of a new topic of conversation. It is probably spoken in a raised tone and an observer would reasonably
expect the listener to acknowledge this utterance, either with a vocal response or
by tying the shoe. Experience with discourse indicates that this is an appropriate
interruption or initiation of a conversation at least under some circumstances.
Discourse structure may help the listener understand that subsequent utterances refer to the shoelace instead of the difficulty of the terrain on which the conversants are traveling.

In terms of **pragmatics,** the speaker's intent is to warn the listener against
tripping; presumably the speaker does not wish the listener to fall. But this utterance might also have been a ruse intended to get the listener to look down for the
sake of playing a trick. We cannot differentiate these possibilities without know-

ing more about the context in which the sentence was spoken and the relationship between the conversants.

From a **semantics** standpoint, the sentence is about certain objects in the world: the listener, hiking, an article of clothing worn on the foot, and especially the string by which the boot is held on. The concern at the semantic layer is how the words refer to the world and what states of affairs they describe or predict. In this case, the meaning has to do with an animate entity ("you") performing some physical action ("tripping"), and the use of future tense indicates that the talker is making a prediction of something not currently taking place. Not all words refer to specific subjects; in the example, "Hey" serves to attract attention, but has no innate meaning.

**Syntax** is concerned with how the words fit together into the structure of the sentence. This includes the ordering of parts of speech (nouns, verbs, adjectives) and relations between words and the words that modify them. Syntax indicates that the correct word order is subject followed by verb, and syntax forces agreement of number, person, and case of the various words in the sentence. "You *is* going to . . ." is syntactically ill formed. Because the subject of the example is "you," the associated form of the verb "to be" is "are." The chosen verb form also indicates a future tense.

**Lexical** analysis tells us that "shoelace" comes from the root words "shoe" and "lace" and that the first syllable is stressed. Lexical analysis also identifies a set of definitions for each word taken in isolation. "Trip," for example, could be the act of falling or it could refer to a journey. Syntax reveals which definition is appropriate as each is associated with the word "trip" used as a different part of speech. In the example, "trip" is used as a verb and so refers to falling.

The **phonemic** layer is concerned with the string of phonemes of which the words are composed. Phonemes are the speech sounds that form the words of any language.[3] Phonemes include all the sounds associated with vowels and consonants. A grunt, growl, hiss, or gargling sound is not a phoneme in English, so it cannot be part of a word; such sounds are not referred to as speech. At the phoneme layer, while talking we are either continuously producing speech sounds or are silent. We are not silent at word boundaries; the phonemes all run together.

At the **articulatory** layer, the speaker makes a series of vocal gestures to produce the sounds that make up the phonemes. These sounds are created by a noise source at some location in the vocal tract, which is then modified by the configuration of the rest of the vocal tract. For example, to produce a "b" sound, the lips are first closed and air pressure from the lungs is built up behind them. A sudden release of air between the lips accompanied by vibration of the vocal cords produces the "b" sound. An "s" sound, by comparison, is produced by turbulence caused as a stream of air rushes through a constriction formed by the tongue and the roof of the mouth. The mouth can also be used to create nonspeech sounds, such as sighs and grunts.

---

[3]A more rigorous definition will be given in the next section.

Finally, the **acoustics** of the utterance is its nature as sound. Sound is transmitted as variations in air pressure over time; sound can be converted to an electrical signal by a microphone and represented as an electrical waveform. We can also analyze sound by converting the waveform to a spectrogram, which displays the various frequency components present in the sound. At the acoustic layer, speech is just another sound like the wind in the trees or a jet plane flying overhead.

From the perspective of the listener, the articulatory layer is replaced by a **perceptual** layer, which comprises the processes whereby sound (variations in air pressure over time) is converted to neural signals in the ear and ultimately interpreted as speech sounds in the brain. It is important to keep in mind that the hearer can directly sense only the acoustic layer of speech. If we send an electric signal representing the speech waveform over a telephone line and convert this signal to sound at the other end, the listening party can understand the speech. Therefore, the acoustic layer alone must contain all the information necessary to understand the speaker's intent, but it can be represented at the various layers as part of the process of understanding.

This layered approach is actually more descriptive than analytic in terms of human cognitive processes. The distinctions between the layers are fuzzy, and there is little evidence that humans actually organize discourse production into such layers. Intonation is interpreted in parallel at all these layers and thus illustrates the lack of sharp boundaries or sequential processing among them. At the pragmatic layer, intonation differentiates the simple question from exaggerated disbelief; the same words spoken with different intonation can have totally different meaning. At the syntactic layer, intonation is a cue to phrase boundaries. Intonation can differentiate the noun and verb forms of some words (e.g., conduct, convict) at the syntactic layer by conveying lexical stress. Intonation is not phonemic in English, but in some other languages a change in pitch does indicate a different word for the otherwise identical articulation. And intonation is articulated and realized acoustically in part as the fundamental frequency at which the vocal cords vibrate.

Dissecting the communication process into layers offers several benefits, both in terms of understanding as well as for practical implementations. Understanding this layering helps us appreciate the complexity and richness of speech. Research disciplines have evolved around each layer. A layered approach to representing conversation is essential for modular software development; a clean architecture isolates each module from the specialized knowledge of the others with information passed over well-defined interfaces. Because each layer consists of a different perspective on speech communication, each is likely to employ its own representation of speech for analysis and generation.

As a cautionary note, it needs to be recognized from the start that there is little evidence that humans actually function by invoking each of these layers during conversation. The model is descriptive without attempting to explain or identify components of our cognitive processes. The model is incomplete in that there are some aspects of speech communication that do not fit it, but it can serve as a framework for much of our discussion of conversational computer systems.

## REPRESENTATIONS OF SPEECH

We need a means of describing and manipulating speech at each of these layers. Representations for the lower layers, such as acoustic waveforms or phonemes, are simpler and more complete and also more closely correspond to directly observable phenomena. Higher-layer representations, such as semantic or discourse structure, are subject to a great deal more argument and interpretation and are usually abstractions convenient for a computer program or a linguistic comparison of several languages. Any single representation is capable of conveying particular aspects of speech; different representations are suitable for discussion of the different layers of the communication process.

The representation chosen for any layer should contain all the information required for analysis at that layer. Since higher layers possess a greater degree of abstraction than lower layers, higher-layer representations extract features from lower-layer representations and hence lose the ability to recreate the original information completely. For example, numerous cues at the acoustic layer may indicate that the talker is female, but if we represent the utterance as a string of phones or of words we have lost those cues. In terms of computer software, the representation is the data type by which speech is described. One must match the representation and the particular knowledge about speech that it conveys to the algorithms employing it at a particular layer of speech understanding.

### Acoustic Representations

Sounds consist of variations in air pressure over time at frequencies that we can hear. Speech consists of a subset of the sounds generated by the human vocal tract. If we wish to analyze a sound or save it to hear again later, we need to capture the variations in air pressure. We can convert air pressure to electric voltage with a microphone and then convert the voltage to magnetic flux on an audiocassette tape using a recording head, for example.

We can plot the speech signal in any of these media (air pressure, voltage, or magnetic flux) over time as a **waveform** as illustrated in Figure 1.2. This representation exhibits positive and negative values over time because the speech radiating from our mouths causes air pressure to be temporarily greater or less than that of the ambient air.

A waveform describing sound pressure in air is continuous, while the waveforms employed by computers are **digital,** or **sampled,** and have discrete values for each sample; these concepts are described in detail in Chapter 3. Tape recorders store analog waveforms; a compact audio disc holds a digital waveform. A digitized waveform can be made to very closely represent the original sound, and it can be captured easily with inexpensive equipment. A digitized sound stored in computer memory allows for fast random access. Once digitized, the sound may be further processed or compressed using digital signal processing techniques. The analog audiotape supports only sequential access (it must be rewound or fast-forwarded to jump to a different part of the tape) and is prone to mechanical breakdown.

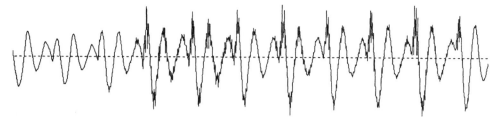

**Figure 1.2.** A waveform, showing 100 milliseconds of the word "me." The vertical axis depicts amplitude, and the horizontal axis represents time. The display depicts the transition from "m" to "e."

A waveform can effectively represent the original signal visually when plotted on a piece of paper or a computer screen. But to make observations about what a waveform sounds like, we must analyze it across a span of time not just at a single point. For example, in Figure 1.2 we can determine the amplitude ("volume") of the signal by looking at the differences between its highest and lowest points. We can also see that it is periodic: The signal repeats a pattern over and over. Since the horizontal axis represents time, we can determine the frequency of the signal by counting the number of periods in one second. A periodic sound with a higher frequency has a higher pitch than a periodic sound with a lower frequency.

One disadvantage of working directly with waveforms is that they require considerable storage space, making them bulky; Figure 1.2 shows only 100 milliseconds of speech. A variety of schemes for compressing speech to minimize storage are discussed in Chapter 3. A more crucial limitation is that a waveform simply shows the signal as a function of time. A waveform is in no way speech specific and can represent any acoustical phenomenon equally well. As a general-purpose representation, it contains all the acoustic information but does not explicitly describe its content in terms of properties of speech signals.

A speech-specific representation more succinctly conveys those features salient to speech and phonemes, such as syllable boundaries, fundamental frequency, and the higher-energy frequencies in the sound. A **spectrogram** is a transformation of the waveform into the frequency domain. As seen in Figure 1.3, the spectrogram reveals the distribution of various frequency components of the signal as a function of time indicating the energy at each frequency. The horizontal axis represents time, the vertical axis represents frequency, and the intensity or blackness at a point indicates the acoustic energy at that frequency and time.

A spectrogram still consists of a large amount of data but usually requires much less storage than the original waveform and reveals acoustic features specific to speech. Because of this, spectral analysis[4] is often employed to process

---

[4]To be precise, spectral or Fourier analysis uses mathematical techniques to derive the values of energy at particular frequencies. We can plot these as described above; this visual representation is the spectrogram.

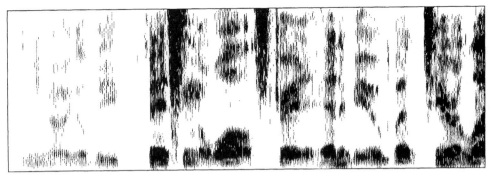

**Figure 1.3.** A spectrogram of 2.5 seconds of speech. The vertical axis is frequency, the horizontal axis is time, and energy maps to darkness.

speech for analysis by a human or a computer. People have been trained to read spectrograms and determine the words that were spoken. Although the spectrogram conveys salient features of a sound, the original acoustic signal cannot be reconstructed from it without some difficulty. As a result, the spectrogram is more useful for analysis of the speech signal than as a means of storing it for later playback.

Other acoustic representations in the frequency domain are even more succinct, though they are more difficult for a human to process visually than a spectrogram. **Linear Prediction Coefficients** and **Cepstral Analysis,** for example, are two such techniques that rely heavily on digital signal processing.[5] Both of these techniques reveal the resonances of the vocal tract and separate information about how the sound was produced at the noise source and how it was modified by various parts of the vocal tract. Because these two techniques extract salient information about how the sound was articulated they are frequently used as representations for computer analysis of speech.

## PHONEMES AND SYLLABLES

Two representations of speech which are more closely related to its lexical structure are phonemes and syllables. Phonemes are important small units, several of which make up most syllables.

### Phonemes

A **phoneme** is a unit of speech, the set of which defines all the sounds from which words can be constructed in a particular language. There is at least one pair of

---

[5]Linear prediction will be explained in Chapter 3. Cepstral analysis is beyond the scope of this book.

words in a language for which replacing one phoneme with another will change what is spoken into a different word. Of course, not every combination of phonemes results in a word; many combinations are nonsense.

For example, in English, the words "bit" and "bid" have different meanings, indicating that the "t" and "d" are different phonemes. Two words that differ in only a single phoneme are called a **minimal pair.** "Bit" and "bif" also vary by one sound, but this example does not prove that "t" and "f" are distinct phonemes as "bif" is not a word. But "tan" and "fan" are different words; this proves the phonemic difference between "t" and "f".

Vowels are also phonemes; the words "heed," "had," "hid," "hide," "howed," and "hood" each differ only by one sound, showing us that English has at least six vowel phonemes. It is simple to construct a minimal pair for any two vowels in English, while it may not be as simple to find a pair for two consonants.

An **allophone** is one of a number of different ways of pronouncing the same phoneme. Replacing one allophone of a phoneme with another does not change the meaning of a sentence, although the speaker will sound unnatural, stilted, or like a non-native. For example, consider the "t" sound in "sit" and "sitter." The "t" in "sit" is somewhat aspirated; a puff of air is released with the consonant. You can feel this if you put your hand in front of your mouth as you say the word. But in "sitter" the same phoneme is not aspirated; we say the aspiration is not phonemic for "t" and conclude that we have identified two allophones. If you aspirate the "t" in "sitter," it sounds somewhat forced but does not change the meaning of the word.

In contrast, aspiration of stop consonants is phonemic in Nepali. For an example of English phonemes that are allophones in another language, consider the difficulties Japanese speakers have distinguishing our "l" and "r." The reason is simply that while these are two phonemes in English, they are allophonic variants on the same phoneme in Japanese. Each language has its own set of phonemes and associated allophones. Sounds that are allophonic in one language may be phonemic in another and may not even exist in a third. When you learn a language, you learn its phonemes and how to employ the permissible allophonic variations on them. But learning phonemes is much more difficult as an adult than as a child.

Because phonemes are language specific, we can not rely on judgments based solely on our native languages to classify speech sounds. An individual speech sound is a **phone,** or **segment.** For any particular language, a given phoneme will have a set of allophones, each of which is a segment. Segments are properties of the human vocal mechanism, and phonemes are properties of languages. For most practical purposes, phone and phoneme may be considered to be synonyms.

Linguists use a notation for phones called the **International Phonetic Alphabet,** or **IPA.** IPA has a symbol for almost every possible phone; some of these symbols are shown in Figure 1.4. Since there are far more than 26 such phones, it is not possible to represent them all with the letters of the English alphabet. IPA borrows symbols from the Greek alphabet and elsewhere. For example, the "th" sound in "thin" is represented as "θ" in IPA, and the sound

| Phoneme | Example Word | Phoneme | Example Word | Phoneme | Example Word |
|---------|--------------|---------|--------------|---------|--------------|
| i | beet | p | put | č | chin |
| I | bit | t | tap | ǰ | judge |
| ɛ | bet | k | cat | m | map |
| e | bait | b | bit | n | nap |
| æ | bat | d | dill | ŋ | sing |
| α | cot | g | get | r | ring |
| ɔ | caught | f | fain | l | lip |
| ʌ | but | θ | thin | w | will |
| o | boat | s | sit | y | yell |
| U | foot | ʃ | shoe | h | head |
| u | boot | v | veal | | |
| ɜ | bird | δ | then | | |
| αj (αI) | bite | z | zeal | | |
| ɔj (ɔI) | boy | ž | azure | | |
| αw (αU) | bout | | | | |
| ə | about | | | | |

**Figure 1.4.** The English phonemes in IPA, the International Phonetic Alphabet.

in "then" is "δ."[6] American linguists who use computers have developed the **Arpabet,** which uses ordinary alphabet characters to represent phones; some phonemes are represented as a pair of letters. Arpabet[7] was developed for the convenience of computer manipulation and representation of speech using ASCII-printable characters.

To avoid the necessity of the reader learning either IPA or Arpabet, this book indicates phones by example, such as, "the 't' in bottle." Although slightly awkward, such a notation suffices for the limited examples described. The reader will find it necessary to learn a notation (IPA is more common in textbooks) to make any serious study of phonetics or linguistics.

A phonemic transcription, although compact, has lost much of the original signal content, such as pitch, speed, and amplitude of speech. Phonemes are abstractions from the original signal that highlight the speech-specific aspects of that

---

[6]Are these sounds phonemic in English?

[7]The word comes from the acronym ARPA, the Advanced Research Projects Agency (sometimes called DARPA), a research branch of the U.S. Defense Department that funded much early speech research in this country and continues to be the most significant source of government support for such research.

signal; this makes a phonemic transcription a concise representation for lexical analysis as it is much more abstract than the original waveform.

## Syllables

Another natural way to divide speech sounds is by the **syllable.** Almost any native speaker of English can break a word down into syllables, although some words can be more difficult, e.g., "chocolate" or "factory." A syllable consists of one or more consonants, a vowel (or diphthong[8]), followed by one or more consonants; consonants are optional, but the vowel is not. Two or more adjacent consonants are called a consonant **cluster;** examples are the initial sounds of "screw" and "sling." Acoustically, a syllable consists of a relatively high energy core (the vowel) optionally preceded or followed by periods of lower energy (consonants). Consonants have lower energy because they impose constrictions on the air flow from the lungs. Many natural languages, such as those written with the Arabic script and the northern Indian languages, are written with a syllabic system in which one symbol represents both a consonant and its associated vowel.

## Other Representations

There are many other representations of speech appropriate to higher layer aspects of conversation.[9] Lexical analysis reveals an utterance as a series of **words.** A dictionary, or **lexicon** lists all the words of a language and their meanings. The **phrase,** sometimes called a "breath group" when describing intonation, is relevant both to the study of prosody (pitch, rhythm, and meter) as well as syntax, which deals with structures such as the noun phrase and verb phrase. A **parse tree,** as shown in Figure 1.5, is another useful representation of the syntactic relationships among words in a sentence.

Representations for higher layers of analysis are varied and complex. Semantics associates meaning with words, and meaning implies a relationship to other words or concepts. A **semantic network** indicates the logical relationships between words and meaning. For example, a door is a physical object, but it has specific meaning only in terms of other objects, such as walls and buildings, as it covers entrance holes in these objects.

Discourse analysis has produced a variety of models of the focus of a conversation. For example, one of these uses a **stack** to store potential topics of current focus. New topics are pushed onto the stack, and a former topic again becomes the focus when all topics above it are popped off the stack. Once removed from the stack, a topic cannot become the focus without being reintroduced.

---

[8]A diphthong consists of two vowel sounds spoken in sequence and is considered a single phoneme. The two vowel sounds in a diphthong cannot be separated into different syllables. The vowels in "hi" and "bay" are examples of diphthongs.

[9]Most of the speech representations mentioned in this section will be detailed in Chapter 9.

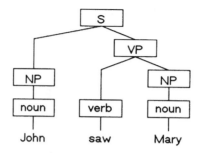

**Figure 1.5.** A parse tree.

## SUMMARY

The perspective of speech as a conversational process constitutes the foundation and point of view of this book. Conversations employ spontaneous speech and a variety of interaction techniques to coordinate the exchange of utterances between participants. Speech is our primary medium of communication, although writing may be favored for longer-lasting or more formal messages. Computer systems would do well to exploit the richness and robustness of human conversation.

But "conversation" is simply too rich and varied a term to be amenable to analysis without being analyzed in components. This chapter identified a number of such components of a conversation: acoustic, articulatory, phonetic, lexical, syntactic, semantic, pragmatic, and discourse. Disciplines of research have been established for each of these areas, and the rest of this book will borrow heavily from them. Each discipline has its own set of representations of speech, which allow utterances to be described and analyzed.

Representations such as waveforms, spectrograms, and phonetic transcriptions provide suitable abstractions that can be embedded in the computer programs that attempt to implement various layers of speech communication. Each representation highlights particular features or characteristics of speech and may be far removed from the original speech sounds.

The rationale for this book is that the study of speech in conversations is interdisciplinary and that the designers of conversational computer systems need to understand each of these individual components in order to fully appreciate the whole. The rest of this book is organized in part as a bottom-up analysis of the layers of speech communication. Each layer interacts with the other layers, and the underlying goal for conversational communication is unification of the layers.

# 2

# Speech Production and Perception

A basic knowledge of the physiology of speech production and its perception is necessary to understand both speech synthesis and speech recognition as well as compression techniques. This chapter provides an overview of the production and perception of speech. It briefly treats the organs of speech, i.e., the vocal tract and the auditory system. An articulatory model of speech is presented; this explains the different speech sounds of a language in terms of how they are produced. Finally, it introduces some basic findings of psychoacoustics that relate to the manner in which sound is perceived by the listener.

To distinguish the various types of sounds in English and the mechanisms whereby they are produced some signal processing terms are introduced. In this text, very simple and intuitive descriptions of such terms are given; more formal definitions may be found in texts on signal processing.

## VOCAL TRACT

The vocal tract is the set of organs that produce speech sounds; these organs are also used for eating, drinking, and breathing. As seen in Figure 2.1, the vocal tract includes portions of the throat, mouth, and nasal cavities. These organs, the **articulators,** are moved to various configurations to produce the different sounds that constitute speech. The primary topic of this section is the production of speech sounds in general; the next section classifies the sounds specific to English.

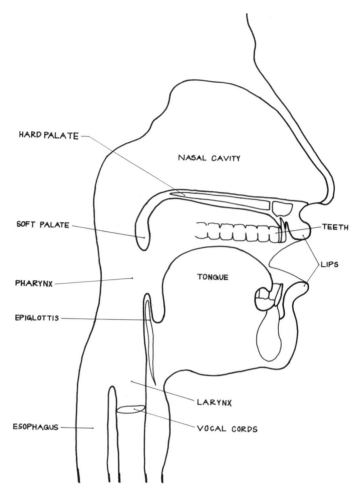

**Figure 2.1.** The major components of the vocal tract.

Sound is vibration in a medium, usually air, at frequencies that we can hear. In air, sound is carried as variations in pressure over time transmitted by the motion of air molecules. The air molecules create pressure variations by moving back and forth while not traveling a substantial distance. This variation is similar to the wave pattern generated when one end of a Slinky toy is moved back and forth. Some force must be created to cause this motion of molecules. In the vocal tract, this force is provided by air being expelled from the lungs by muscles in the diaphragm.

Without further modification, the air coming out of the lungs does not create a significant sound. If you open your mouth wide and exhale, you hear a little noise created as the air rushes out of the mouth, but this is usually not audible across a room. To become speech this air flow must be focused or concentrated in some way. Focusing is accomplished by one of two mechanisms, either vibration of the vocal cords to produce a periodic sound or turbulent air flow through a constriction to produce an aperiodic, or "noisy," sound.[1]

If the vocal cords are vibrating, the speech produced is termed **voiced.** The vocal cords are folds of tissue capable of opening and closing in a regular fashion as controlled by several sets of muscles and driven by the pressure of air being expelled from the lungs. In operation the vocal cords remain closed until the pressure behind them is strong enough to force them open. As the air rushes by and pressure is released, a partial vacuum (Bernoulli effect) helps pull the cords back together again to shut off the flow of air.

This opening and closing pattern occurs at a regular rate and results in a series of pulses at that frequency. This frequency, called the **fundamental frequency** of voicing, or **F0,** corresponds to the pitch that we perceive in speech. F0 is typically higher for female and young speakers and may be varied within a limited range by muscle tension. The waveform of this glottal pulse is roughly triangular (see Figure 2.2), which results in a spectrum rich in harmonics, i.e., higher frequency components. The energy of speech drops at about 12 dB[2] per octave from the fundamental. Figure 2.3 illustrates the spectrum of the sound produced by the vocal chords. The **spectrum** is a measure of the magnitude of all the frequency components that constitute a signal. Since the source is of a single frequency F0, energy is found at that frequency and at integral multiples of that frequency. For example, the author's typical fundamental frequency is at 110 Hz,[3] which means that energy will be found at 220 Hz, 330 Hz, 440 Hz, etc.

You can experience voicing directly for yourself. Place a finger at the front bottom of your throat, slightly above the level of the shoulders. Speak out loud, alternating making "s" and "z" sounds. During the voiced "z" you can feel the vocal cords vibrate with your finger.

Another source of sound in the vocal tract is turbulence as air rushes through a constriction. Turbulence is not periodic; it is caused by the continuous stream of air molecules bouncing around randomly. It is similar in nature to the sound made by a babbling brook or the wind blowing through trees or surf moving onto shore. Such sounds contain a relatively large amount of high frequency energy, or "hiss," because the acoustic waveform varies a great deal from moment to moment. Turbulence is characteristic of both continuous **frication** sounds, such as the phoneme "s," and sudden **plosive** ones associated with a quick opening of a closed vocal tract, as in the phoneme "p." This turbulence can take place at a number of locations in the vocal tract. In the fricative "s," it is at a constriction formed between the tongue and the roof of the mouth. With the plosive "p," it is

---

[1] A periodic signal repeats a pattern at a regular interval or frequency. Aperiodic signals do not exhibit such patterns. Wind instruments produce periodic sounds, while percussion instruments are generally aperiodic.

[2] 1 dB, short for decibel, corresponds to a just noticeable difference in sound energy.

[3] Hz, or Hertz, means cycles (or periods) per second. 1 kHz, or one kiloHertz, is one thousand cycles per second. 1 MHz, or MegaHertz, is one million cycles per second.

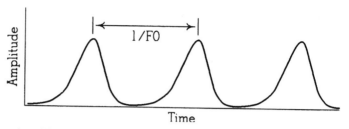

**Figure 2.2.** The glottal pulse is a roughly triangular-shaped waveform.

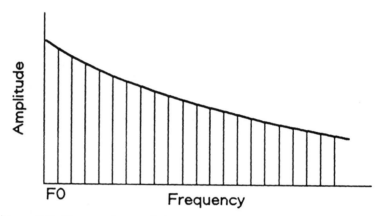

**Figure 2.3.** The spectrum of the sound produced by the vocal chords shows gradually decreasing magnitude with increasing frequency. This is properly a **line spectrum,** as energy is found only at multiples of F0, shown by the vertical line. The curve connecting the tops of these lines shows the **envelope,** or overall shape of the spectrum.

formed at the lips. The frication in "f" occurs around the lower lip making contact with the upper teeth.

There is more to classifying speech than identifying the source of the noise. The sound created by the noise source must then pass through the rest of the vocal tract that modifies it. These modifications are responsible for many of the distinguishing features of the different phonemes, or speech sounds. Even if the sound source is at the lips such that it does not have to pass through any further portions of the vocal tract, the size and shape of the oral cavity behind the lips affects the sound quality.

The vocal tract is usually analyzed as a series of **resonances.** A resonator is a physical system that enhances certain frequencies or range of frequencies. Resonators that amplify a very narrow range of frequencies are referred to as "high

Q",[4] and those which have a very broad band are "low Q" (see Figure 2.4). Because the vocal tract is composed of soft tissue, its resonators are rather low Q. In contrast, a very "clear" sound, such as a flute note, is produced by a high Q resonator.

The vocal tract is about 17 cm long and can be approximated as a series of joined tubes of varying diameters and lengths that add up to 17. One tube extends from the vocal cords up to the top of the mouth, the other, at approximately a right angle to the first, extends from there to the lips. The relative lengths of these tubes can be varied by the positioning of the tongue. If the tongue is low and flat (as in "ah"), then the front tube formed by the mouth is pronounced and the back tube is shorter. When the tongue is high in the mouth (as when saying the letter "e"), the front tube in front of the tongue is quite short, while the back tube is elongated.

If a column of air in a tube is excited by a source, it resonates at a characteristic frequency dependent upon the length of the tube. This is the principle upon which the flute is designed; opening the finger holes allows the air to escape at various points along the tube, thereby changing the length of the air column and thus its frequency. In the same way, the sound produced from the vocal cord vibration is enhanced at the frequencies corresponding to the length of the tubes in the vocal tract (see Figure 2.5). The frequencies at which these resonances occur are called **formants.** The lowest-frequency formant is labeled **F1** and called the first formant; the second formant is labeled **F2**, and so on. Most analysis stops at five or six formants. In the multitube model, each formant corresponds to a tube section.

Whichever the noise source, either voiced or turbulent, its spectrum is enhanced around the formant frequencies, which depend on the physical configuration of the vocal tract. Another part of the vocal tract that influences the noise source is the **nasal cavity,** a fairly soft region above the roof of the mouth and behind the nose. The passage from the back of the mouth to the nasal cavity can be closed by the **velum,** a small flap of tissue toward the top back of the mouth. When the velum is opened, the nasal cavity is physically connected and acoustically coupled with the vocal tract. The nasal cavity absorbs a significant amount of sound energy in the lower portion of the energy spectrum.

The radiation of the speech signal from the vocal tract into the surrounding air must also be considered. In addition to the mouth, sound is radiated from the cheeks, throat, and bony structure of the head and jaw, resulting in a signal that is much less directional than it would be otherwise with radiational patterns that are heavily frequency dependent. Flanagan [Flanagan 1960] measured sound energies of various frequencies at multiple locations about the head and found that at approximately 45 degrees (horizontally) away from the axis of the mouth

---

[4]Q, or Quality factor, is a measure of the difference between the higher and lower bounds of the frequencies amplified by the resonator, as measured at the point of half-power relative to the peak power at the center frequency. This number is divided by the center frequency; i.e., it is a factor of frequencies rather than a difference.

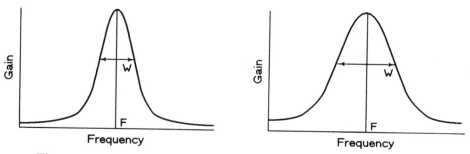

**Figure 2.4.** A high Q filter, left, and a low Q filter, right. F is the center frequency, and W is its bandwidth.

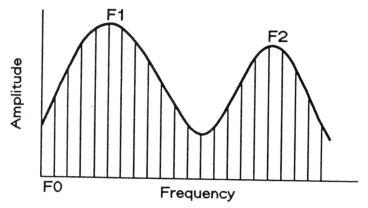

**Figure 2.5.** Resonances or formants of the vocal tract. The formants, labelled F1 and F2, are peaks in the vocal tract's filter function.

the signal was one half as strong, while directly behind the head the signal decreased by one order of magnitude less than in front of the head.

The noise source is referred to as the **source,** or **excitation,** signal. The manner in which the vocal tract enhances or diminishes the various frequencies of the signal as a function of its physical configuration is called its **transfer function.** A well-defined mathematical relationship allows computation of the signal that results from a source and a transfer function, but a detailed analysis of this relationship is beyond the scope of this book.

## THE SPEECH SOUNDS

Each language employs a characteristic set of phonemes or allophones to convey words. These speech sounds are generated by manipulating the components of the vocal tract into specific physical configurations. The set of sounds comprising the phonemes of a language must be distinctive because the listener perceives only the sound, not the vocal tract configuration that produces it. The classification of phonemes by the manner in which they are produced is referred to as an **articulatory model** of speech.

The three fundamental articulatory classifications are whether or not the phoneme is **voiced,** the **place** where the sound of the phoneme is made, and the **manner** in which it is made. The remainder of this section describes the various sounds of English according to their articulation.

## Vowels

Vowels are sounds produced by vocal cord vibration (voicing) and a relatively open vocal tract, i.e., the lips, tongue, or teeth do not close the passageway. In the English alphabet there are only five letters we call vowels, but in spoken English there are closer to 17 vowel phonemes. Vowels are steady state; after we begin speaking a vowel, we can continue it until we run out of breath. Because vowels are voiced, they are periodic as can be seen in Figure 2.6.

The vowels can be differentiated by the acoustical effect of the position of the tongue and lips during their pronunciation. We can distinguish three degrees of constriction of the vocal tract that indicate how close to the roof of the mouth the hump of the tongue gets (high, medium, and low). We can also differentiate three positions laterally where the hump of the tongue makes the greatest constriction (front, central, and back). In addition, vowels can be *nasalized* by moving the velum to open the air passage leading from the throat to the nose. English does not employ nasalization as a phonemic distinction; however, certain other languages such as French use nasalization as a distinguishing feature to contrast phonemes.

In English the vowels are distinguished solely by the position of the tongue, which changes the lengths of the two primary vocal tract tube sections. In other words, the first two formants form a set of distinctive features for the vowels. Although the typical positions of the formants will vary with gender and among speakers, they can generally be clustered together into regions in a space defined

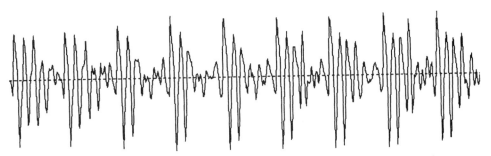

**Figure 2.6.** A waveform of the vowel in "but." The display shows amplitude mapped against time, over a 100 millisecond interval. Nine pitch periods can be seen; the frequency of voicing is about 90 Hz.

by F1 and F2 as illustrated in Figure 2.7. Such a diagram is sometimes called the "vowel triangle" because all of the vowels fit in a space that approximates a triangle in the chosen coordinate system of F1 versus F2.

Some vowels are **diphthongs.** Diphthongs are actually combinations of two vowel sounds with the vocal tract moving from one position to another during their production. The vowel sounds in "bay" and "boy" are examples of diphthongs.

**Consonants**

Consonants are characterized by constrictions in the vocal tract and can be differentiated by place of closure, manner (type or degree) of closure, and whether they are voiced.

Place refers to the location in the vocal tract of the closure associated with a consonant. **Labial** closure uses both lips as in "p" and "b" sounds. **Labial-dental** closure involves the lower lip and upper teeth as in "f" and "v" sounds. **Alveolar** closure involves the tongue and the gum ridge behind the front teeth as in "n," "d," "s," and "z" sounds. **Palatal** closure uses the tongue on the soft palate or roof of the mouth slightly farther back as in "sh" and "zh" sounds.

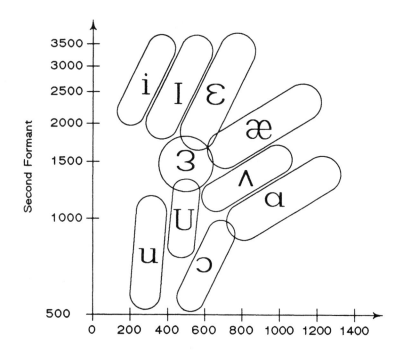

**Figure 2.7.** The vowel triangle displays English vowels mapped onto a Cartesian space defined by the the first and second formants. The IPA notation from Figure 1.4 is used for labeling.

**Velar** closure occurs at the back of the mouth, or hard palate, as in "g" and "k" sounds. Each of these places of closure results in a distinct sound as the shape of the vocal tract changes and consequently the frequencies of resonance vary. The closure divides the vocal tract into cavities in front of and behind the closure; these have different resonant frequencies depending on their size. For example, the position of the third formant is often a strong cue to the identity of a stop consonant.

Closure of the vocal tract is achieved in several different manners, each resulting in a different sound. **Stops** ("t," "b," "p," "d") involve a sudden and total cessation of air flow. Stop consonants are very dynamic. During the closure, no air flows through the vocal tract, resulting in silence. Noise resumes suddenly as the closure is released, and the air pressure from behind the closure may result in **aspiration** noise, such as in the "t" in "top." Stops are also called **plosives,** which focuses on the release rather than the closure of the consonant.

**Fricatives** ("s," "z," "sh," "zh") involve constriction to the point of producing turbulence and hence noise but not total closure. The partial closure for "s" is alveolar and that for "sh" is palatal. Because closure is incomplete the fricatives result in a continuous sound as air flows by. Sound created by air rushing through a small opening is aperiodic (see Figure 2.8) and dominated by high-frequency components. Combining these two traits, the characteristic acoustic feature of the fricatives is a moderate duration of high-frequency energy.

**Nasals** ("m," "n," "ng" as in "sing") are produced by closing the oral cavity but opening the velum to the nasal cavity. The nasal cavity absorbs a significant amount of low-frequency energy giving a distinctive cue to nasalization. The three English nasals are all voiced. The nasals are differentiated from each other by the place at which the vocal tract is closed, which is either labial ("m"), palatal ("n"), or velar ("ng").

Most of the consonant types mentioned so far have come in pairs, such as ("d," "t") and ("v," "f"). Both members of each of these pairs is produced with the articulators in the same place but are distinguished by the presence or absence of

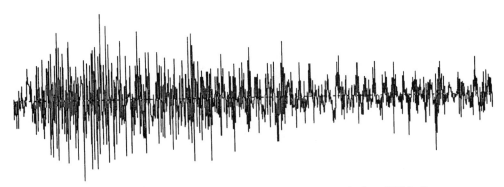

**Figure 2.8.** The aperiodic waveform of the consonant in "see." This figure also shows 100 milliseconds of speech. No periodicity is evident.

voicing. Voiced consonants thus have two noise sources: one at the place of articulation and the other at the periodic glottal pulses.

Whether or not a consonant is voiced depends on the type of consonant. In a stop there is no air flow so a stop is considered voiced if voicing resumes soon after the release; otherwise it is unvoiced. Air flow continues during a fricative so voicing is defined by whether the vocal cords are vibrating during the consonant itself.

### Liquids and Glides

A small class of special-case phonemes behave much like vowels. The **liquids** ("l," "r") invariably precede a vowel and are dynamic, involving a transition into the vowel. It is sometimes hard to identify "r" as a distinct consonant but rather to observe the effect, or **coloration,** of the vowel caused by the motion of the lips and the rise of the tongue in the middle of the mouth. The **glides** ("w," "y" as in "you") are similar to vowels except that the vocal tract is more constricted than for the vowels. According to another point of view, the glides are simply vowels that do not occur during the energy peak of the syllable.

### Acoustic Features of Phonemes

The methods used to articulate the various phonemes of a language must produce sounds with adequate acoustical cues to allow the listener to distinguish between possible phonemes in speech. Some examples of acoustical cues have just been mentioned: the distinctive structure of the first two formants in vowels, the energy at high frequencies that distinguish fricatives, the presence or absence of periodicity due to voicing, and the absorbing effect of the nasal cavity.

The listener can select from a multitude of cues occurring simultaneously to differentiate phonemes. In fluent speech the articulators often move only partially in the direction of target vocal tract configurations described above for each phoneme. The acoustical effect is still sufficiently pronounced to allow the listener to detect at least some of the cues and identify each phoneme.

## HEARING

Sound arrives at our ears as variations in air pressure. We can hear vibrations in the range of approximately 20 Hz up to 15 or 20 kHz; this figure varies among individuals, and the range decreases as we age. This sensory stimulus triggers neural activity through a complex but versatile mechanical transformation in the ear. There is a chain of processes whereby the physical sound from its source causes the auditory event of "hearing." In turn, these neural firings stimulate perceptual processing at higher levels of the brain. Although little is known about such processing from direct neural evidence, the domain of **psychoacoustics** studies our perception of sound by observing subjects' responses to acoustic stimuli.

**Auditory System**

The complement to the vocal tract is the auditory system. Although primarily designed to turn air pressure variations into corresponding neural signals, the ear also contains the **vestibular organs** that are used to maintain physical balance; we are not concerned with them here. The ear can be divided into three distinct sections. The outer ear directs sound toward the eardrum, the middle ear converts the pressure variations of sound into mechanical motion, and the inner ear converts this motion to electrical signals in the auditory neurons. The ear is shown in Figure 2.9.

The **outer ear** includes the **pinna** and the **ear canal,** which leads to the eardrum. The pinna consists of the fleshy protrusion on the side of the head and is what we usually refer to when we use the term "ear" (as in "Van Gogh cut off his ear"). The pinna with its various folds of cartilage around the ear opening serves primarily as a protective mechanism. The pinna provides some amplification of the sound by focusing it into the ear canal in much the same way that we may cup our hands behind our ears to better hear quiet sounds. It is directional at high frequencies and is used as a localization aid to find a sound source because it makes the ear more sensitive to sounds coming from in front of rather than behind the listener. In certain animals such as owls, the outer ear occupies a much larger surface area with respect to the head and is more fundamental to localization.

The ear canal is a tube about 1 cm wide by 2.5 cm long leading to the middle ear. It has a resonance of about 3000 Hz and therefore amplifies sound at this frequency. The length of the ear canal shields the middle ear from physical injury if the side of the head is struck.

The **middle ear** provides the linkage between the outer and inner ear; its function is to effectively convert variations in air pressure to mechanical motion of the liquid inside the inner ear. The **eardrum,** or **tympanic membrane,** covers the interior end of the ear canal. Vibrations in the air cause the eardrum to vibrate; thus it produces physical motion from the sound in the air. The middle ear is filled with air. The **eustachean tube** runs between the middle ear and the throat. When we yawn, the eustachean tube opens, allowing the air pressure to equalize across the eardrum. As experienced when descending rapidly in an airplane, this pressure balance is essential for effective transfer of sound across the eardrum.

The inner ear is filled with water. There is a large impedance mismatch between air- and water-like fluids. Water is much denser than air so air does not cause significant displacement in the liquid that it impinges; even a strong wind on a pond does not penetrate much deeper than to form surface ripples because of this mismatch. A series of three **ossicular bones** (the **malleus, incus,** and **stapes**) provide mechanical advantage (leverage) from the ear drum to the **oval window,** a membrane on the surface of the inner ear. As the eardrum is 17 times as large as the oval window, this difference in area provides further amplification. The size difference plus the mechanical advantage of the ossicular bones combine to provide a 22:1 amplification and thereby an impedance match for efficient transfer of acoustical energy to the inner ear.

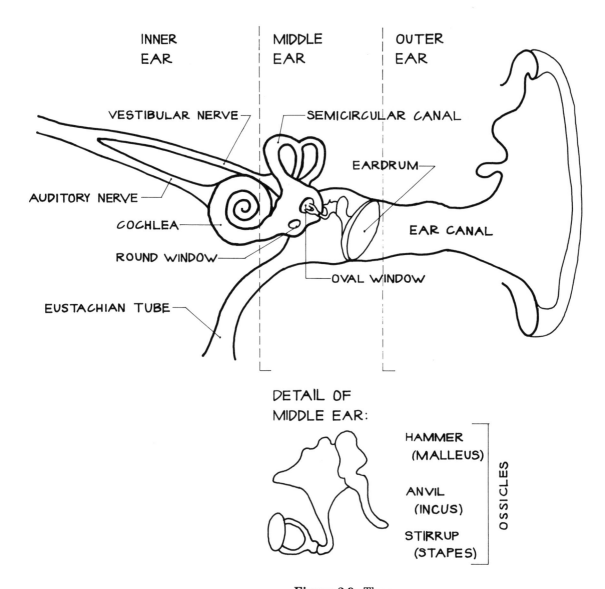

**Figure 2.9.** The ear.

The middle ear has several different modes of vibration that provide improved dynamic range without distortion (the goal of all good audio amplifiers). For loud sounds, the vibration mode is changed from pumping to a rotational action. In addition, for very loud sounds a reflex occurs in the muscles of the middle ear to damp the vibration and thereby protect the sensitive inner ear.

The **inner ear** is the transducer from mechanical to electrical energy. At its center is the **cochlea,** a spiral-shaped chamber looking somewhat like a snail shell and making 2⅝ turns. Sound-induced waves in the liquid medium of the cochlea cause vibration on the **basilar membrane.** Different portions of this tapering membrane vibrate in response to sound energy at specific frequencies. At the basal end it is thin and stiff, while at its apex it is flexible and massive.

The frequency dependent vibration of the basilar membrane induces motion in the microscopic hairs that penetrate the membrane. These hairs are linked to neurons to the brain that produce neural firings in response to the stimulus of the hairs' bending. Each neuron is connected to a small number of hairs in a particular location on the basilar membrane, and the basilar membrane responds to different frequencies along its length so the firing of a neuron corresponds to the presence of sound of the appropriate frequency. Because of this relationship between neural firings and basilar membrane vibration, an individual neuron is not very responsive to frequencies much higher or lower than its preferred one. Measurements of neural responses indicate that each acts as a bandpass filter and that all the neurons and associated hair cells exhibit a fairly constant Q.

Neural activity is highest at the onset of a sound and decays rapidly at first and then more slowly. This is known as **adaptation;** we are more sensitive to changing sounds than continual tones. Neurons fire more rapidly for louder sounds, reaching peak rates of up to 1000 firings per second for short periods. At frequencies below about 1 kHz, neurons tend to fire in phase with the vibration of the basilar membrane, i.e., every cycle of membrane motion induces one neural spike.

The ear's response to a sound is a series of neural spikes from many neurons simultaneously. The firing pattern of any particular neuron is a function of amplitude of the acoustic energy (at the basilar membrane) within the frequency range to which that neuron is sensitive. The pattern adapts over a short period of time and may be at least partially in phase with the acoustic signal. The neural firings are transmitted to a number of stages of processing in the central auditory system. At several points along the way are sites that are particularly sensitive to time or amplitude differences between signals arriving from each ear. Such differences are central to our ability to locate a sound spatially.

### Localization of Sounds

When we hear a sound, we perceive it as coming from some location in space outside of our head; this is known as **localization.** Much of our ability to localize sound depends on the differences in the sound that arrives at each of our two ears from a single source. These differences are due to the positions of the ears and hence their different distances from the sound source as well as the tendency of the head to partially block sound coming to an ear from the opposite side of the head.

We can localize a sound source within about 4 degrees in front of the head, 6 degrees behind the head, and only within 10 degrees at the sides. Localization is very frequency dependent and we are most sensitive to sounds at around 800 Hz.

Our hearing is about 100 times less sensitive to position than our visual system, but we can hear sounds behind our heads. We have a strong reflex to turn and look at a sound that occurs behind our heads. This moves the source of the sound into our field of view, which could aid survival, and places the source where we can better localize it. The motion of the head also provides cues to enhance localization as we seem to be especially sensitive to differences in location.

If a sound source is off to either side of our head, it takes the sound longer to reach the ear on the other side as it is further away (see Figure 2.10). In other words, when a sound begins one ear hears it before the other. But more importantly, while the sound continues the air vibrations will arrive at each ear out of phase with the other ear; this is defined as the **interaural phase difference.** The human head has a thickness of 21 or 22 centimeters, which means that it can take sound up to about 600 microseconds longer to reach the further ear. This phase difference becomes confused when it is greater than the wavelength of the sound so phase is most effective for localizing sound below 1500 Hz.

When a sound is off to one side, the mass of the head also blocks the direct path from the sound source to the opposite ear. This results in an **interaural intensity difference;** the sound is louder at the ear that has an unobscured path. This effect is most pronounced at frequencies above 10 kHz, as the head more effectively blocks small wavelengths.

The differences in phase and intensity of the sound arriving at each ear can help localize it to the left or right side but leave confusion as to whether the sound is in front of or behind the head. A sound in front of and to the left of the listener creates the same interaural phase and intensity differences as a sound the same distance behind and also to the left. The shape of the pinna interacts with incom-

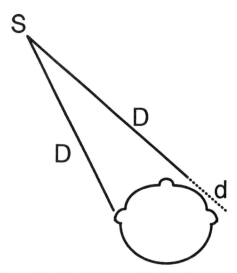

**Figure 2.10.** A sound on the left side of the head arrives at the right ear later than the left ear because it must travel further.

ing sound and provides front-back cues. Its amplification effect provides directionality through increased gain for sounds from the front. In addition, the folds of the pinna act as a complex filter enhancing some frequencies; this filtering is different for sounds from the front than from the back providing further front/back cues.

## Psychoacoustics

So far we have described the process whereby sound energy is converted to neural signals; we have not yet described how the listener perceives the sound characterized by such signals. Although more is known about higher-level processing of sound in the brain than we have mentioned in the brief overview above, there is still not sufficient knowledge to describe a model of such higher auditory processing. However, researchers can build an understanding of how we perceive sounds by presenting acoustical stimuli to subjects and observing their responses. The field of psychoacoustics attempts to quantify perception of pitch, loudness, and position of a sound source.

The ear responds to a wide but limited range of sound loudness. Below a certain level, sound cannot be perceived; above a much higher level, sound causes pain and eventually damage to the ear. Loudness is measured as **sound pressure level** (SPL) in units of **decibels** (dB). The decibel is a logarithmic scale; for power or energy, a signal that is X times greater than another is represented as $10 \log_{10} X$ dB. A sound twice as loud is 3 dB higher, a sound 10 times as loud is 10 dB higher, and a sound 100 times as loud is 20 dB higher than the other. The reference level for SPL is 0.0002 dyne/cm$^2$; this corresponds to 0 dB.

The ear is sensitive to frequencies of less than 20 Hz to approximately 18 kHz with variations in individuals and decreased sensitivity with age. We are most sensitive to frequencies in the range of 1 kHz to 5 kHz. At these frequencies, the threshold of hearing is 0 dB and the threshold of physical feeling in the ear is about 120 dB with a comfortable hearing range of about 100 dB. In other words, the loudest sounds that we hear may have ten billion times the energy as the quietest sounds. Most speech that we listen to is in the range of 30 to 80 dB SPL.

Perceived loudness is rather nonlinear with respect to frequency. A relationship known as the Fletcher-Munson curves [Fletcher and Munson 1933] maps equal input energy against frequency in equal loudness contours. These curves are rather flat around 1 kHz (which is usually used as a reference frequency); in this range perceived loudness is independent of frequency. Our sensitivity drops quickly below 500 Hz and above about 3000 Hz; thus it is natural for most speech information contributing to intelligibility to be within this frequency range.

The temporal resolution of our hearing is crucial to understanding speech perception. Brief sounds must be separated by several milliseconds in order to be distinguished, but in order to discern their order about 17 milliseconds difference is necessary. Due to the firing patterns of neurons at initial excitation, detecting details of multiple acoustic events requires about 20 milliseconds of averaging. To note the order in a series of short sounds, each sound must be between 100 and 200 milliseconds long, although this number decreases when the sounds have gradual onsets and offsets.[5] The prevalence of such transitions in speech may explain how we can perceive 10 to 15 phonemes per second in ordinary speech.

**Pitch** is the perceived frequency of a sound, which usually corresponds closely to the fundamental frequency, or F0, of a sound with a simple periodic excitation. We are sensitive to *relative* differences of pitch rather than absolute differences. A 5 Hz difference is much more significant with respect to a 100 Hz signal, than to a 1 kHz signal. An **octave** is a doubling of frequency. We are equally sensitive to octave differences in frequencies regardless of the absolute frequency; this means that the perceptual difference between 100 Hz and 200 Hz is the same as between 200 Hz and 400 Hz or between 400 Hz and 800 Hz.

The occurrence of a second sound interfering with an initial sound is known as **masking.** When listening to a steady sound at a particular frequency, the listener is not able to perceive the addition of a lower energy second sound at nearly the same frequency. These frequencies need not be identical; a sound of a given frequency interferes with sounds of similar frequencies over a range called a **critical band.** Measuring critical bands reveals how our sensitivity to pitch varies over the range of perceptible frequencies. A pitch scale of **barks** measures frequencies in units of critical bands. A similar scale, the **mel** scale, is approximately linear below 1 kHz and logarithmic above this.

Sounds need not be presented simultaneously to exhibit masking behavior. **Temporal masking** occurs when a sound masks the sound succeeding it (**forward** masking) or the sound preceding it (**backward** masking). Masking influences the perception of phonemes in a sequence as a large amount of energy in a particular frequency band of one phoneme will mask perception of energy in that band for the neighboring phonemes.

## SUMMARY

This chapter has introduced the basic mechanism for production and perception of speech sounds. Speech is produced by sound originating at various locations in the vocal tract and is modified by the configuration of the remainder of the vocal tract through which the sound is transmitted. The articulators, the organs of speech, move so as to make the range of sounds reflected by the various classes of phonemes.

Vowels are steady-state sounds produced by an unobstructed vocal tract and vibrating vocal cords. They can be distinguished by their first two resonances, or formants, the frequencies of which are determined primarily by the position of the tongue. Consonants are usually more dynamic; they can be characterized according to the place and manner of articulation. The positions of the articula-

---

[5]The onset is the time during which the sound is just starting up from silence to its steady state form. The offset is the converse phenomenon as the sound trails off to silence. Many sounds, especially those of speech, start up and later decay over at least several pitch periods.

tors during consonant production create spectra characteristic of each phoneme; each phoneme has multiple cues as to its identity.

Sound consists of vibrations in a medium (usually air) at a frequency we can hear. The variations in sound pressure are focused by the outer ear and cause mechanical motion in the middle ear. This mechanical motion results in waves in the liquid in the inner ear, which causes neurons to fire in response. Which neurons fire and the pattern of their firings is dependent on the spectral and temporal characteristics of the sound. We localize a sound based on interaural phase and intensity differences. Each ear receives a slightly different sound signal due to the position of the ears on either side of the head. The pinna enables us to distinguish between sounds in front and behind.

This chapter also discussed several topics in psychoacoustics and the frequency and temporal responses of the auditory system; what we perceive with our sense of hearing is as much due to the characteristics of our auditory system as to the qualities of the sounds themselves. These factors influence our perception of speech in particular as well as all sounds.

The next chapter explores methods to digitally capture, encode, and compress the speech signal for computer storage, analysis, or transmission. Data compression techniques for speech take advantage of temporal and frequency characteristics of the speech signal as well as the sensitivity of the auditory system to reduce the data rate without loss of intelligibility or perceived quality of the reconstructed signal.

## FURTHER READING

A concise overview of the human speech system can be found in Denes and Pinson and a more analytic and rigorous one in Flanagan (1972). Ladefoged offers an excellent treatment of phonetics. O'Shaughnessy covers many issues in speech production and hearing as a prelude to describing speech technologies. Handel offers an excellent overview of the perception of speech and music, while Yost is a more introductory text with superb illustrations.

# 3

# Speech Coding

This chapter introduces the methods of encoding speech digitally for use in such diverse environments as talking toys, compact audio discs, and transmission over the telephone network. To use voice as data in such diverse applications as voice mail, annotation of a text document, or a talking telephone book, it is necessary to store speech in a form that enables computer retrieval. Digital representations of speech also provide the basis for both speech synthesis and voice recognition. Chapter 4 discusses the management of stored voice for computer applications, and Chapter 6 explore interface issues for interactive voice response systems.

Although the use of a conventional analog tape recorder for voice storage is an option in consumer products such as answering machines, its use proves impractical in more interactive applications. Tape is serial, requiring repeated use of fast-forward and rewind controls to access the data. The tape recorder and the tape itself are prone to mechanical breakdown; standard audiotape is unable to endure the cutting and splicing of editing.

Alternatively, various digital coding schemes enable a sound to be manipulated in computer memory and stored on random access magnetic disks. Speech coding algorithms provide a number of digital representations of a segment of speech. The goal of these algorithms is to faithfully capture the voice signal while utilizing as few bits as possible. Minimizing the data rate conserves disk storage space and reduces the bandwidth required to transmit speech over a network; both storage and bandwidth may be scarce resources and hence costly. A wide range of speech quality is available using different encoding algorithms; quality requirements vary from application to application. In general, speech quality may be traded for information rate by choosing an appropriate coding algorithm.

Some formerly popular coding schemes, such as Linear Predictive Coding, made sizable sacrifices of quality for a low bit rate. While this may have been dictated by the technology of the time, continually decreasing storage costs and increasingly available network bandwidth now allow better-quality speech coding for workstation environments. The poorer-quality encoders do find use, however, in military environments where encryption or low transmitter power may be desired and in consumer applications such as toys where reasonable costs are essential.

The central issue in this chapter is the proposed trade-off between bit rate and intelligibility; each generation of speech coder attempts to improve speech quality and decrease data rate. However, speech coders may incur costs other than limited intelligibility. Coder complexity may be a factor; many coding algorithms require specialized hardware or digital signal processing microprocessors to run in real time.[1] Additionally, if the coder uses knowledge of the history of the signal to reduce the data rate, some flexibility may be lost in the encoding scheme, making it difficult both to edit the stored speech and to evaluate the encoded signal at a particular moment in time. And finally, although it is of less concern here, coder robustness may be an issue; some of the algorithms fail less gracefully, with increased sound degradation if the input data is corrupted.

After discussing the underlying process of digital sampling of speech, this chapter introduces some of the more popular speech coding algorithms. These algorithms may take advantage of a priori knowledge about the characteristics of the speech signal to encode only the most perceptually significant portions of the signal, reducing the data rate. These algorithms fall into two general classes: **waveform coders,** which take advantage of knowledge of the speech signal itself and **source coders,** which model the signal in terms of the vocal tract.

There are many more speech coding schemes than can be detailed in a single chapter of this book. The reader is referred to [Flanagan et al. 1979, Rabiner and Schafer 1978] for further discussion. The encoding schemes mentioned here are currently among the most common in actual use.

## SAMPLING AND QUANTIZATION

Speech is a continuous, time-varying signal. As it radiates from the head and travels through the air, this signal consists of variations in air pressure. A microphone is used as a transducer to convert this variation in air pressure to a corresponding variation in voltage in an electrical circuit. The resulting electrical signal is analog. An analog signal varies smoothly over time and at any moment is one of an unlimited number of possible values within the dynamic range of the

---

[1]A real-time algorithm can encode and decode speech as quickly as it is produced. A non-real-time algorithm cannot keep up with the input signal; it may require many seconds to encode each second of speech.

medium in which the signal is transmitted.[2] In analog form, the signal may be transmitted over a telephone circuit (as voltage) or stored on a magnetic tape (as magnetic flux).

All the sensory stimuli we encounter in the physical world are analog. For an analog signal to be stored or processed by a computer, it must first be transformed into a digital signal, i.e., **digitized.** Digitization is the initial step of signal processing for speech recognition. Speech synthesis algorithms also generate digital signals, which are then transformed into analog form so we can hear them.

A digitized signal consists of a series of numeric values at some regular rate (the sampling rate). The signal's possible values are constrained by the number of bits available to represent each sampled value—this simple representation is called **Pulse Code Modulation (PCM).** To convert an analog signal to this digital form it must be **sampled** and **quantized.**

Sampling assigns a numeric value to the signal in discrete units of time, i.e., a new value is given for the signal at a constant rate. The Nyquist rate specifies the maximum frequency of the signal that may be fully reproduced: a signal must be sampled at twice its highest frequency to be faithfully captured [Nyquist 1924]. In addition, when the analog signal is being recreated, it must be passed through a low-pass filter at one-half the sampling rate to remove audible artifacts of the sampling frequency.[3]

If these sampling rate conditions are not met, **aliasing** results. Aliasing is a form of distortion in which the high frequencies are falsely regenerated as lower frequencies. A rigorous description of aliasing requires mathematics beyond the scope of this book; nonetheless, the following example offers a degree of explanation. While watching a western film, you may have noticed that the wagon wheels sometimes appear to rotate backwards or in the correct direction but at the wrong rate; the same phenomenon occurs with airplane propellers, fans, etc. This is an example of aliasing. In actuality, the wheel is turning continuously, but film captures images at a rate of 24 frames per second. A repetitive motion that occurs at more than half this sampling rate cannot be captured correctly; when we view the film we perceive a motion that may be faster, slower, or of opposite direction.

Why does this happen? Consider the eight-spoked wagon wheel shown in Figure 3.1; as it rotates clockwise, the spokes move together. If the spokes move just a little in the $\frac{1}{24}$ of a second between frames (see Figure 3.2), they will appear to be moving forward at the correct speed. If the wheel moves exactly $\frac{1}{8}$ of a revolution between frames, the spokes will have changed position (see Figure 3.3); but since the spokes all look identical, the film audience will not see the spokes rotating even though they have moved forward. This is, of course, an illusion, as the stagecoach would be moving against the background scenery. If the wheel rotates slightly faster such that each spoke has traveled beyond the position originally

---

[2]An electric circuit saturates at a maximum voltage, and below a minimum level the voltage variations are not detectable.

[3]In practice, to ensure that the first condition is actually met during sampling, a similar filter at one half the sampling frequency is used at the input stage.

A

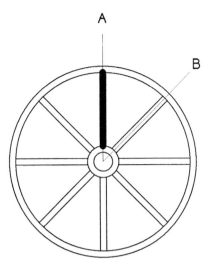

**Figure 3.1.** A wagon wheel with two spokes marked for reference points.

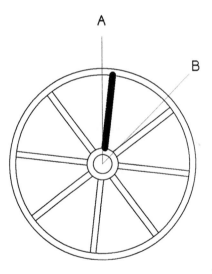

**Figure 3.2.** The wheel has rotated forward a small distance.

occupied by the next spoke (see Figure 3.4), the viewer will see a much slower motion identical to that depicted by Figure 3.2. Finally, if a spoke has moved most of the way to the next spoke position between frames (see Figure 3.5), it will appear that the wheel is slowly moving counterclockwise.

Except for the first case, these illusions are all examples of aliasing. The repetitive motion consists of identical spokes rotating into positions occupied by other

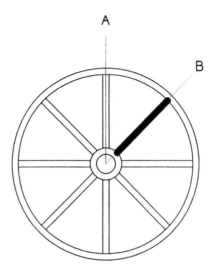

**Figure 3.3.** The wheel has rotated far enough that a spoke has moved forward to the position previously occupied by the next spoke.

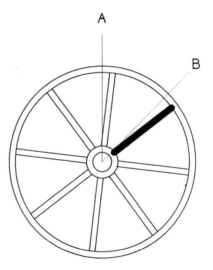

**Figure 3.4.** The wheel has rotated still further. Each spoke has moved just beyond the position formerly occupied by the next.

spokes in the time between frames. If aliasing is to be avoided, the sampling theorem suggests that this must happen at no more than one-half the sampling rate. This implies that each spoke must rotate no more than one-half the distance to the next spoke between frames; with eight spokes filmed at 24 frames per second, this corresponds to 1½ wheel revolutions per second. A characteristic

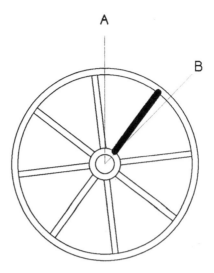

**Figure 3.5.** The spokes have moved almost to the position of the next spoke.

of aliasing is that frequencies above one-half the sampling rate appear incorrectly as lower frequencies. Identical aliasing artifacts also appear at multiples of the sampling frequency. The visual effects of the wheel moving a small fraction of the way to the next spoke, the distance to the next spoke plus the same small fraction, or the distance to the second spoke beyond plus the small fraction are all identical.

Another example provides a better understanding of sampling applied to an audio signal. Consider a relatively slowly varying signal as shown in Figure 3.6. If sampled at some rate **T,** a series of values that adequately capture the original

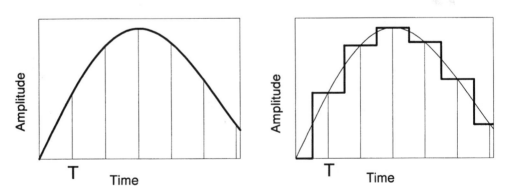

**Figure 3.6.** Sampling and reconstruction of a slowly varying signal. The continuously varying signal on the left is sampled at discrete time intervals T. The reconstructed signal is shown overlaid on the original in the right figure.

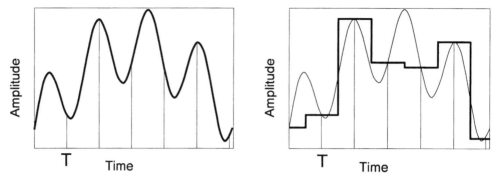

**Figure 3.7.** Inadequate reconstruction of a higher frequency signal. The original signal varies more rapidly than that in Figure 3.6, and the resulting reconstruction on the right shows gross errors.

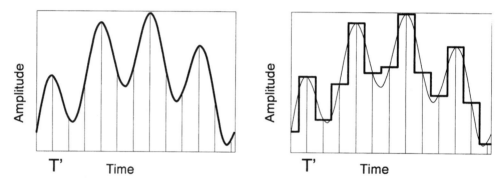

**Figure 3.8.** The higher frequency signal sampled at a higher rate, **T′**. The reconstructed signal now more accurately tracks the original.

signal are obtained. If the signal varies more rapidly (i.e., has components of a higher frequency), the same sampling rate may not correctly capture the signal (see Figure 3.7). Instead a higher sampling rate (smaller **T′**) is required to capture the more rapidly changing signal (see Figure 3.8); this signal has a higher **bandwidth.**

Bandwidth is the range of frequencies contained in a signal. For speech these span from a low frequency at the fundamental frequency of voicing (perhaps 100 to 400 Hertz—lower for men, higher for women, and higher still for children) to upwards of 15 kHz. The telephone network supports a voice bandwidth of approximately 3100 Hz (see Chapter 10 for more details); speech is sampled at 8000 Hz for digital telephone transmission.[4] Although this bandwidth is adequate for intelligibility, the transmitted voice is clearly of lower quality than face-to-face

---

[4]If ideal filters really existed, this sampling rate could be reduced to 6200Hz (twice 3100 Hz), but real filters have a gradual frequency cutoff as opposed to the discontinuous response of ideal filters.

communication. Compare this with a compact audio disc, which samples at 44.1 kHz giving a frequency response in the range of 20 kHz. Although the higher bandwidth is required more for the musical instruments than for the singers, the difference in voice quality offered by the increased bandwidth response is striking as well. Of course the compact disc requires a sampling rate five times greater than the telephone with the resulting increased requirements for storage and transmission rate.

Sampling rate is only one consideration of digitization; the other is the resolution of the samples at whatever rate they are taken. Each sample is represented as a digital value, and that number covers only a limited range of discrete values with reference to the original signal. For example, if 4 bits are allowed per sample, the sample may be one of 16 values; while if 8 bits are allowed per sample, it may be one of 256 values. The size in terms of number of bits of the samples can be thought of as specifying the fineness of the spacing between the lines in Figure 3.9. The closer the spacing between possible sample values, the higher the resolution of the samples and the more accurately the signal can be reproduced. In Figure 3.9, the **error,** or difference between the original and reconstructed signals, is shaded; higher resolution results in decreased quantization error.

The resolution of the quantizer (the number of bits per sample) is usually described in terms of a **signal-to-noise ratio,** or **SNR.** The error between the quantized sample and the original value of the signal can be thought of as noise, i.e., the presence of an unwanted difference signal that is not correlated with the original. The higher the SNR, the greater the fidelity of the digitized signal. SNR for PCM encoding is proportional to two to the power of the number of bits per sample, i.e., $\text{SNR} \approx 2^B$ where B is bits per sample. Adding one bit to the quantizer doubles the SNR.

Note that the SNR, or quantization error, is independent of the sampling rate limitation on bandwidth. The data rate of a sampled signal is the product of the sample size times the sampling rate. Increasing either or both increases

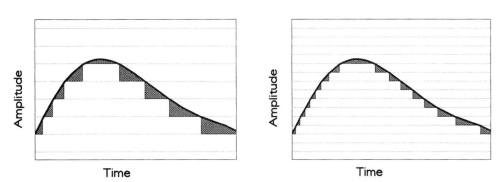

**Figure 3.9.** Low and high resolution quantization. Even when the signal is sampled continuously in time, its amplitude is quantized, resulting in an error, shown by the shaded regions.

the data rate. But increasing the sampling rate has no effect on quantization error and vice versa.

To compare the telephone and the compact audio disc again, consider that the telephone uses 8 bits per sample, while the compact disc uses 16 bits per sample. The telephone samples at 8 kHz (i.e., 8000 samples per second), while the compact disc sampling rate is 44.1 kHz. One second of telephone-quality speech requires 64,000 bits, while one second of compact disc-quality audio requires an order of magnitude more data, about 700,000 bits, for a single channel.[5]

Quantization and sampling are usually done with electronic components called **analog-to-digital** (A/D) and **digital-to-analog** (D/A) converters. Since one of each is required for bidirectional sampling and reconstruction, they are often combined in a **codec** (short for coder/decoder), which is implemented as a single integrated circuit. Codecs exist in all digital telephones and are being included as standard equipment in a growing number of computer workstations.

## SPEECH CODING ALGORITHMS

The issues of sampling and quantization apply to any time-varying digital signal. As applied to audio, the signal can be any sound: speech, a cat's meow, a piano, or the surf crashing on a beach. If we know the signal is speech, it is possible to take advantage of characteristics specific to voice to build a more efficient representation of the signal. Knowledge about characteristics of speech can be used to make limiting assumptions for waveform coders or models of the vocal tract for source coders.

This section discusses various algorithms for **coders** and their corresponding **decoders.** The coder produces a digital representation of the analog signal for either storage or transmission. The decoder takes a stream of this digital data and converts it back to an analog signal. This relationship is shown in Figure 3.10. Note that for simple PCM, the coder is an A/D converter with a clock to generate a sampling frequency and the decoder is a D/A converter. The decoder can derive a clock from the continuous stream of samples generated by the coder or have its own clock; this is necessary if the data is to be played back later from storage. If the decoder has its own clock, it must operate at the same frequency as that of the coder or the signal is distorted.[6]

### Waveform Coders

An important characteristic of the speech signal is its dynamic range, the difference between the loudest and most quiet speech sounds. Although speech has a

---

[5]The compact disc is stereo; each channel is encoded separately, doubling the data rate given above.

[6]In fact it is impossible to guarantee that two independent clocks will operate at precisely the same rate. This is known as clock skew. If audio data is arriving in real time over a packet network, from time to time the decoder must compensate by skipping or inserting data.

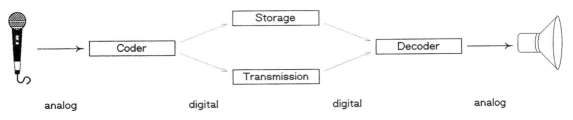

**Figure 3.10.** The coder and decoder are complementary in function.

fairly wide dynamic range, it reaches the peak of this range infrequently in normal speech. The amplitude of a speech signal is usually significantly lower than it is at occasional peaks, suggesting a quantizer utilizing a nonlinear mapping between quantized value (output) and sampled value (input). For very low signal values the difference between neighboring quantizer values is very small, giving fine quantization resolution; however, the difference between neighbors at higher signal values is larger, so the coarse quantization captures a large dynamic range without using more bits per sample. The mapping with nonlinear quantization is usually logarithmic. Figure 3.11 illustrates the increased dynamic range that is achieved by the logarithmic quantizer.

Nonlinear quantization maximizes the information content of the coding scheme by attempting to get roughly equal use of each quantizer value averaged over time. With linear coding, the high quantizer values are used less often; logarithmic coding compensates with a larger step size and hence coarser resolution at the high extreme. Notice how much more of the quantizer range is used for the lower amplitude portions of the signal shown in Figure 3.12. Similar effects can also be accomplished with adaptive quantizers, which change the step size over time.

A piece-wise linear approximation of logarithmic encoding, called μ-**law,**[7] at 8 bits per sample is standard for North American telephony.[8] In terms of signal-to-noise ratio, this 8 bits per sample logarithmic quantizer is roughly equivalent to 12 bits per sample of linear encoding. This gives approximately 72 dB of dynamic range instead of 48 dB, representing seven orders of magnitude of difference between the highest and lowest signal values that the coder can represent.

Another characteristic of speech is that adjacent samples are highly correlated; neighboring samples tend to be similar in value. While a speech signal contains frequency components up to one-half the sampling rate, the higher-frequency components are of lower energy than the lower-frequency components. Although the signal can change rapidly, the amplitude of the rapid changes is less than that of slower changes. This means that differences between adjacent samples are less than the overall range of values supported by the quantizer so fewer bits are required to represent differences than to represent the actual sample values.

---

[7]Pronounced "mu-law."
[8]A very similar scale, "A-law," is used in Europe.

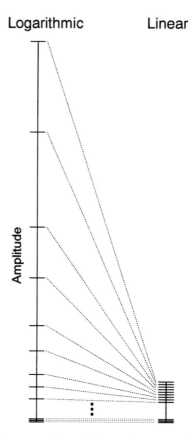

**Figure 3.11.** A comparison of dynamic range of logarithmic and linear coders for the same number of bits per sample. The logarithmic coder has a much greater dynamic range than a linear coder with comparable resolution at low amplitudes.

Encoding of the differences between samples is called **Delta PCM.** At each sampling interval the encoder produces the difference between the previous and the current sample value. The decoder simply adds this value to the previous value; the previous value is the only information it needs to retain. This process is illustrated in Figure 3.13.

The extreme implementation of difference coding is **Delta Modulation,** which uses just one bit per sample. When the signal is greater than the last sample, a "1" bit results; when less, a "0" bit results. During reconstruction, a constant step size is added to the current value of the signal for each "1" and subtracted for each "0."

This simple coder has two error modes. If the signal increases or decreases more rapidly than the step size times the sampling rate, **slope overload** results as the coder cannot keep up. This may be seen in the middle of Figure 3.14. To

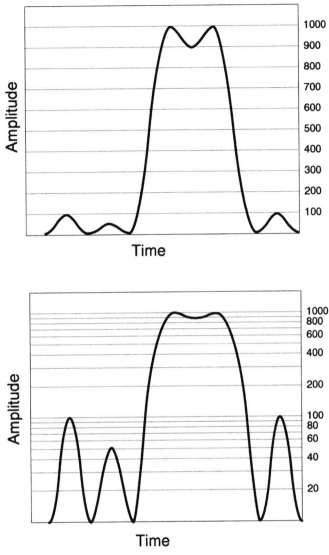

**Figure 3.12.** Use of a logarithmic scale disperses the signal density over the range of the coder. The top figure shows a linearly encoded signal; the bottom shows the same signal logarithmically encoded.

compensate for this effect, sampling rates significantly in excess of the Nyquist rate (e.g., in the range of 16 to 32 kHz) are usually used. The second error mode occurs when the delta-modulated signal has a low value such as in moments of silence. The reconstructed signal must still alternate up and down (see the right side of Figure 3.14) as the 1-bit coder cannot indicate a "no-change" condition. This is called **quieting noise.**

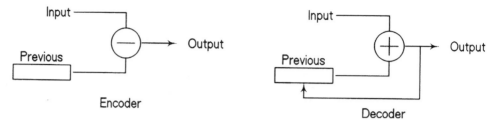

**Figure 3.13.** The Delta PCM encoder transmits the difference between sample values. The signal is reconstructed by the encoder, which always stores the previous output value.

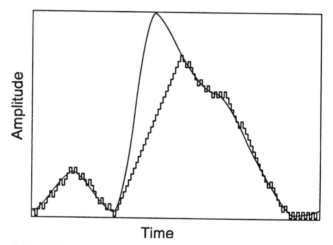

**Figure 3.14.** Delta Modulation. The jagged line is the delta modulated version of the smooth signal it encodes.

To compensate for these effects, **Continuously-Varying Slope Delta Modulation (CVSD)** uses a variable step size. Slope overload is detected as a series of consecutive "1" or "0" values. When this happens, the step size is increased to "catch up" with the input (see Figure 3.15). Note that the step size is increased at both the coder and the decoder, which remain synchronized because the decoder tracks the coder's state by its output; the sequence of identical bit values triggers a step size change in both.

After the step size increases, it then decays over a short period of time. Both the encoder and decoder must use the same time constant for this decay; they remain in synchronization because the decoder uses the incoming bit stream as its clock. Quieting noise is reduced by detecting the quieting pattern of alternating "0" and "1" values and decreasing the step size to an even smaller value while this condition persists.

CVSD is an example of *adaptive* quantization, so called because the quantizer adapts to the characteristics of the input signal. During periods of low signal

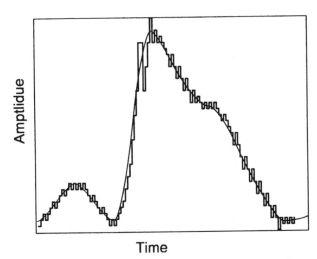

**Figure 3.15.** Quantizer step size increases for CVSD encoding to catch up with a rapidly increasing signal. The CVSD encoded version more closely tracks the original signal than does the delta modulation shown in Figure 3.14.

energy, a fine step size quantizer with a small range is employed, while a larger step size is substituted during higher amplitude signal excursions. In other words, at times when the signal is changing rapidly, there will be a larger difference between samples than at times when the signal is not changing rapidly. With CVSD these conditions are detected by monitoring the pattern of output bits from the quantizer.

A similar but more powerful encoder is **Adaptive Delta PCM (ADPCM),** a popular encoding scheme in the 16,000 to 32,000 bits per second range. ADPCM is a Delta PCM encoder in that it encodes the difference between samples but does so using a method in which the same number of bits per sample can sometimes represent very small changes in the input signal and at other times represent much larger changes. The encoder accomplishes this by looking up the actual sample differences in a table and storing or transmitting just enough information to allow the decoder to know where to look up a difference value from the same table.

When it samples the current input value of the signal, an ADPCM coder uses two additional pieces of internal information in addition to the table to decide how to encode the signal. This information is a function of the history of the signal, and therefore is available to the decoder even though it is not transmitted or stored. The first stored value is the *state,* which is just a copy of the last value output from the coder; this is common to all difference encoders. The second value is the *predictor,* perhaps more appropriately called an adapter, which directly compensates for changes in the signal magnitude.

The key component of the ADPCM decoder is its output table. Although the difference signal is encoded in only four bits (including a sign bit to indicate an increasing or decreasing output value), the table is much "wider." Each entry in

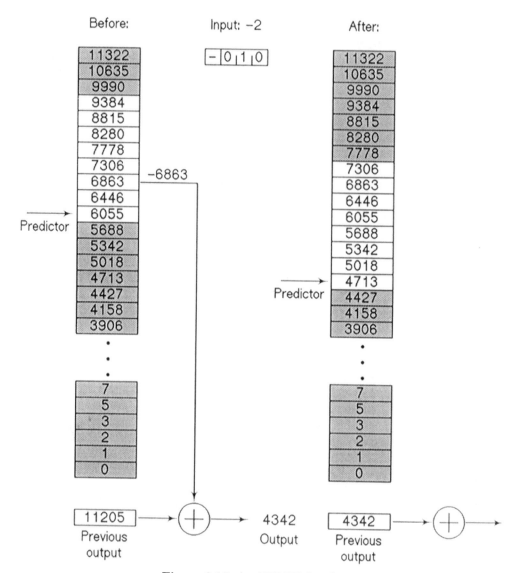

**Figure 3.16.** An ADPCM decoder.

the table may be eight or twelve bits giving a much larger dynamic range. At any moment, the three-bit difference value can be used to look up one of eight values from the table. These values are then added to or subtracted from the last output value giving the new output value. But the table has many more than eight entries. The predictor indicates where in the table the range of eight possible difference values should be chosen. As a function of the signal, the predictor can move to a coarser or finer part of the table (which is approximately exponential) as the signal amplitude changes. This movement within the lookup table is how adaptation occurs.

An ADPCM decoder is shown in Figure 3.16. For each input sample, the ADPCM decoder looks up a difference value that it adds to (or subtracts from) the previous output value to generate the new output value. It then adapts its own internal state. The difference value is found by table lookup relative to the predictor, which is just a base pointer into the table. This base pointer specifies the range of values which the encoder output can reference. Depending on the sign bit of the encoder output, the value found at the specified offset from the predictor is then added to or subtracted from the previous output value.

Based on another table, the input number is also used to look up an amount to move the base pointer. Moving the base pointer up selects a region of the lookup table with larger differences and coarser spacing; moving down has the opposite effect. This is shown on the right side of Figure 3.16 and is the adaptation mechanism for ADPCM.

Using an ADPCM encoding scheme with 4 bit samples at an 8 kHz sampling rate, it is possible to achieve speech quality virtually indistinguishable from that of 64,000 bit per second log PCM using only half of that data rate. Since many telephone channels are configured for 64,000 bits per second, ADPCM is used as part of a new approach to higher quality telephony that samples twice as often (16,000 times per second), thereby using the full digital telephone channel bandwidth to give a speech bandwidth of approximately 7.1 kHz. (The full algorithm is described in [Mermelstein 1975].) This has become an international standard because of its usefulness in telephone conference calls; the increased bandwidth is particularly helpful in conveying cues as to the identity of the speaker.[9]

In summary, waveform coders provide techniques to encode an input waveform such that the output waveform accurately matches the input. The simplest waveform coders are suitable for general audio encoding, although music sources place greater requirements on the encoder than speech. Due to the larger dynamic range of most music and its greater bandwidth, adequately digitizing music requires a larger sample size and a higher sampling rate. However, more sophisticated waveform coders take advantage of statistical properties of the speech signal to encode the signal in fewer bits without a loss of intelligibility. Because these methods depend on characteristics specific to speech, they are often not adequate for digitizing nonspeech audio signals.

**Source Coders**

In contrast to the waveform coders, that compress the speech signal by encoding the waveform, the source coders model the acoustical conditions that produced the signal. Source coders assume the sound was produced by the vocal tract and analyze it according to a source model. This model consists of an excitation component and a filter component corresponding to the vocal tract. Source decoders

[9]CCITT specification G.722. The **CCITT** is the International Telephone and Telegraph Consultative Committee, which defines international telecommunications standards.

then reconstruct the sound not by reproducing the waveform of the signal but rather by generating a different signal that has the same spectral characteristics as the original.

The most common source coder is **Linear Predictive Coding (LPC).** LPC analysis requires somewhat expensive processing for the encoder but the decoder is fairly simple. An input signal is analyzed to determine whether it is periodic (whether the speech is voiced or not) and, if so, its pitch is computed. The coder then examines the spectrum of the input signal and determines a fixed number of resonances as parameters of a filter bank. The filter is an "all pole" model, which means it can reproduce only the peaks of the spectrum of the vocal tract. These parameters are predictor coefficients, which indicate how a sample at any moment in time depends on the previous samples. An overall gain value is also computed from the average magnitude or energy of the input. The coder updates this set of values at a regular rate, typically every 20 milliseconds.

The decoder (see Figure 3.17) models the vocal tract to produce a steady stream of digital waveform values. The model consists of a sound source and a filter and is controlled by the parameters derived by the encoder including pitch, voiced/unvoiced switch, gain, and filter coefficients. The source may be periodic with a range of possible pitches or it may be aperiodic. To output a waveform value, a new value is read from the input and scaled by a gain factor; then it undergoes a filtering process that can be represented by the weighted sum of the current sample and the previous N samples, where N is the number of predictor coefficients. Note that this system left alone would produce a continuous stream of steady output; the parameters determine what the output sounds like. But the model is updated with each new set of vocal tract parameters frequently enough to make it sound like speech.

The LPC decoder requires significantly less computation than the encoder, which must perform sophisticated analysis of the speech signal. This assymetry may be useful in mass-market consumer applications, which store voice prompts

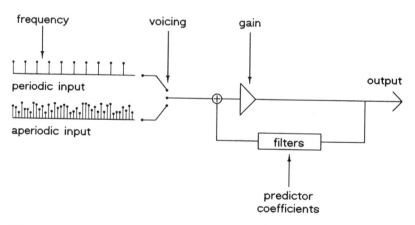

**Figure 3.17.** The LPC decoder models the vocal tract.

in read only memory (ROM). If the product need not encode speech but just play it, an expensive encoder is unnecessary. Such assymetry is not an advantage for bidirectional applications such as telecommunications. Digitization algorithms that employ such different encoders and decoders are sometimes called **analysis-synthesis techniques,** which are often confused with text-to-speech synthesis; this is the topic of Chapter 5.

Speech can be encoded intelligibly using LPC at around 2400 bits per second. This speech is not of high enough quality to be useful in many applications and with the decreasing cost of storage has lost much of its original attractiveness as a coding medium. However, since LPC compactly represents the most salient acoustical characteristics of the vocal tract, it is sometimes used as an internal representation of speech for recognition purposes. In addition, a related source coding algorithm may emerge as the standard for the digital cellular telephone system.

A number of techniques have been developed to increase the quality of LPC encoding with higher data rates. In addition to the LPC signal, **Residually Excited LPC (RELP)** encodes a second data stream corresponding to the difference that would result between the original signal and the LPC synthesized version of the signal. This "residue" is used as the input to the vocal tract model by the decoder, resulting in improved signal reproduction.

Another technique is **Multipulse LPC,** which improves the vocal tract model for voiced sounds. LPC models this as a series of impulses, which are very short-duration spikes of energy. However, the glottal pulse is actually triangular in shape and the shape of the pulse determines its spectrum; Multipulse LPC approximates the glottal pulse as a number of impulses configured so as to produce a more faithful source spectrum.

The source coders do not attempt to reproduce the waveform of the input signal; instead, they produce another waveform that sounds like the original by virtue of having a similar spectrum. They employ a technique that models the original waveform in terms of how it might be produced. As a consequence, the source coders are not very suitable for encoding nonspeech sounds. They are also rather fragile, breaking down if the input includes background noise or two people talking at once.

## CODER CONSIDERATIONS

The primary consideration when comparing the various speech coding schemes is the tradeoff between information rate and signal quality. When memory and/or communication bandwidth are available and quality is important, as in voice mail systems, higher data-rate coding algorithms are clearly desirable. In consumer products, especially toys, lower quality and lower cost coders are used as the decoder and speech storage must be inexpensive. This section discusses a number of considerations for matching a coding algorithm to a particular application environment.

## Intelligibility

The primary consideration in choosing a coding scheme is that of intelligibility—*everyone* wants the highest quality speech possible. Some coding algorithms manage to reduce the data rate at little cost in intelligibility by using techniques to get the most out of each bit. In general, however, there is a strong tradeoff between speech quality and data rate. For any coding scheme there are likely to be options to use less bits for each value or to sample the audio less frequently at the cost of decreased intelligibility.

There are actually two concepts to consider: signal **error** and **intelligibility.** Error is a mathematically rigorously defined measure of the energy of the difference between two signals on a sample-by-sample basis. Error can be measured against waveforms for the waveform coders and against spectra for the source coders. But this error measure is less important than intelligibility for many applications. To measure intelligibility, human subjects must listen to reproduced speech and answer questions designed to determine how well the speech was understood. This is much more difficult than comparing two signals. The discussion of the intelligibility of synthetic speech in Chapter 9 describes some listening tests to measure intelligibility.

A still more evasive factor to measure is signal **quality.** The speech may be intelligible but is it pleasant to hear? Judgment on this is subjective but can be extremely important to the acceptance of a new product such as voice mail, where use is optional for the intended customers.

A related issue is the degree to which any speech coding method interferes with listeners' ability to identify the talker. For example, the limited bandwidth of the telephone sometimes makes it difficult for us to quickly recognize a caller even though the bandwidth is adequate for transmitting highly intelligible speech. For some voice applications, such as the use of a computer network to share voice and data during a multisite meeting, knowing who is speaking is crucial.

## Editing

The ease with which a speech signal can be edited by cutting and splicing the sequence of stored data values may play a role in the choice of an encoding scheme. Both delta (difference) and adaptive coders track the current state during signal reproduction; this state is a function of a series of prior states, i.e., the history of the signal, and hence is computed each time the sound is played back. Simply splicing in data from another part of a file of speech stored with these coders does not work as the internal state of the decoder is incorrect.

Consider an ADPCM-encoded sound file as an example. In a low energy (quiet) portion of the sound, the predictor (the base pointer into the lookup table) is low so the difference between samples is small. In a louder portion of the signal the predictor points to a region of the table with large differences among samples. However, the position of the predictor is not encoded in the data stream. If samples from the loud portion of sound are spliced onto the quiet portion, the predictor will be incorrect and the output will be muffled or otherwise distorted as the wrong differences will be accessed from the lookup table to produce the coder output.

With coders such as ADPCM predictable results can be achieved if cutting and splicing is forced to occur during silent parts of the signal; during silent portions the predictor returns to a known state, i.e., its minimum value. As long as enough low value samples from the silent period are retained in the data stream so as to force the predictor down to its minimum, another speech segment starting from the minimum value prediction (just after silence) can be inserted. This precludes fine editing at the syllable level but may suffice for applications involving editing phrases or sentences.

Adaptation is not an issue with PCM encoding as the value of each sample is independent of any prior state. However, when pieces of PCM data are spliced together, the continuity of the waveform is momentarily disrupted, producing a "click" or "pop" during playback. This is due to changing the *shape* of the waveform, not just its value, from sample to sample. The discontinuity is less severe when the splice takes place during low energy portions of the signal, since the two segments are less likely to represent drastically different waveform shapes. The noise can be further reduced by both interpolating across the splice and reducing the amplitude of the samples around the splice for a short duration.

A packetization approach may make it possible to implement cut-and-paste editing using coders that have internal state. For example, LPC speech updates the entire set of decoder parameters every 20 milliseconds. LPC is really a stream of data packets, each defining an unrelated portion of sound; this allows edits at a granularity of 20 milliseconds. The decoder is designed to interpolate among the disparate sets of parameter values it receives with each packet allowing easy substitution of other packets while editing.

A similar packetization scheme can be implemented with many of the coding schemes by periodically including a copy of the coder's internal state information in the data stream. With ADPCM for example, the predictor and output signal value would be included perhaps every 100 milliseconds. Each packet of data would include a header containing the decoder state, and the state would be reset from this data each time a packet was read. This would allow editing to be performed on chunks of sound with lengths equal to multiples of the packet size.

In the absence of such a packetization scheme, it is necessary to first convert the entire sound file to PCM for editing. Editing is performed on the PCM data and then is converted back to the desired format by recoding the signal based on the new data stream.

## Silence Removal

In spontaneous speech there are substantial periods of silence.[10] The speaker often pauses briefly to gather his or her thoughts either in midsentence or

---

[10]Spontaneous speech is normal unrehearsed speech. Reading aloud or reciting a passage from memory are not spontaneous.

between sentences. Although the term "sentence" may be used fairly loosely with spontaneous speech, there are speech units marked by pauses for breath that usually correspond roughly to clauses or sentences. Removing these silences during recording can save storage space. Such techniques are commonly applied to almost any encoding technique. For example, silence removal is used with most voice mail systems regardless of the encoding scheme. The amount of storage space saved by silence removal is directly proportional to the amount of speech that was pauses.

A form of silence removal is actually used in many telephone networks. There is no need to keep a transmission channel occupied transferring the audio data associated with the frequent pauses in a conversation. By detecting these pauses, the channel may be freed to carry another conversation for the duration of the pause. When one of the parties starts speaking again, the channel must be restored to transmit the conversation. In practice, a small number of channels are used to carry a larger number of conversations; whenever a new spurt of speech occurs during one of the conversations, a free channel is assigned to it.

This channel-sharing scheme was originally implemented as an analog system known as **Time Assigned Speech Interpolation (TASI)** [O'Neill 1959] to carry an increased number of calls over limited-capacity, trans-Atlantic telephone cables. Today, digital techniques are employed to implement "virtual circuits," so called because the actual channel being used to carry a specific conversation will vary over time. The channel refers to a particular slot number in a digital data stream carrying a large number of conversations simultaneously. During silence, the slot associated with the conversation is freed and made available to the next conversation that begins. When the first conversation resumes, the slot it formerly occupied may be in use, in which case it is assigned to a new slot. These adjustments are transparent to equipment outside of the network. The number of channels required to carry the larger number of conversations is a property of the statistical nature of the speaking and silence intervals in ordinary conversations and is an important aspect of network traffic management.

During a telephone conversation, no time compression is achieved by silence removal; although audio data may not be transmitted across the network during silences, the listener must still wait for the talker to resume. In a recorded message with pauses removed, less time is required for playback than transpired during recording. Silence removal is generally effective, but some of the pauses in speech contain meaning; part of the richness of the message may be the indication of the talker's thought process and degree of deliberation implied by the location and duration of the pauses.

Several techniques can be used to reconstruct the missing pauses. Instead of simply removing the pauses from the stored data, a special data value may be inserted into the file indicating the presence of a pause and its duration. During playback this information indicates to the decoder to insert the right amount of silence. Since the ambient (background) noise of the recording is replaced by absolute silence, an audible discontinuity is noticeable. Another technique involves recording a small amount of the background noise and then playing it over and over to fill the reconstructed pauses. It is necessary to capture enough of the silence that the listener cannot easily hear the repetitive pattern during playback.

Another difficulty with silence removal is proper detection of the beginning, or onset, of speech after silence. The beginnings and endings of speech segments are often of low amplitude, which may make them difficult to detect, yet they contain significant phonetic information. Endings can be easily preserved simply by recording a little extra "silence" at the end of each burst of speech. Beginnings are harder; the encoder must buffer a small amount of the signal (several hundred milliseconds) so that when speech is finally detected this recently-saved portion can be stored with the rest of the signal. This buffering is difficult enough that it is often not done, degrading the speech signal.

## Time Scaling

Because speech is slow from the perspective of the listener, it is desirable to be able to play it back in less time than required to speak it originally. In some cases one may wish to slow down playback, perhaps while jotting down a phone number in a rapidly-spoken message. Changing the playback rate is referred to as **time compression** or **time-scale modification,** and a variety of techniques of varying complexity are available to perform it.[11]

Skipping pauses in the recording provides a small decrease in playback time. The previous section discussed pause removal from the perspective of minimizing storage or transmission channel requirements; cutting pauses saves time during playback as well. It is beneficial to be selective about how pauses are removed. Short (less than about 400 millisecond) **hesitation pauses** are usually not under the control of the talker and can be eliminated. But longer **juncture pauses** (about 500 to 1000 milliseconds) convey syntactic and semantic information as to the linguistic content of speech. These pauses, which often occur between sentences or clauses, are important to comprehension and eliminating them reduces intelligibility. One practical scheme is to eliminate hesitation pauses during playback and shorten all juncture pauses to a minimum amount of silence of perhaps 400 milliseconds.

The upper bound on the benefit to be gained by dropping pauses is the total duration of pauses in a recording, and for most speech this is significantly less than 20% of the total. Playback of nonsilent portions can be sped up by increasing the clock rate at which samples are played, but this produces unacceptable distortion. Increasing the clock shifts the frequency of speech upwards and it becomes whiny, the "cartoon chipmunk" effect.

A better technique, which can be surprisingly effective if implemented properly, is to selectively discard portions of the speech data during playback. For example,

---

[11]For a survey of time-scale modification techniques, see [Arons 1992a].

for an increase in playback rate of 20%, one could skip the first 12 milliseconds of every 60 milliseconds of data. This was first discussed by Maxemchuk [Maxemchuk 1980] who refined it somewhat by attempting to drop lower-energy portions of the speech signal in preference to higher energy sections. This technique is rather sensitive to the size of the interval over which a portion of the sound is dropped (60 milliseconds in the above example); this interval should ideally be larger than a pitch period but shorter than a phoneme.

Time compression by this method exhibits a burbling sound but can be surprisingly intelligible. The distortion can be somewhat reduced by smoothing the junctions of processed segments, by dropping and then increasing amplitude rapidly across the segment boundaries, or by performing a cross-fade in which the first segment decays in amplitude as the second segment starts up.

A preferred method of time compression is to identify pitch periods in the speech signal and remove whole periods. To the extent that the signal is periodic, removing one or more pitch periods should result in an almost unchanged but time-compressed output. The most popular of these time domain algorithms is **Synchronous Overlap and Add (SOLA)** [Roucos and Wilgus 1985]. SOLA removes pitch periods by operating on small windows of the signal, shifting the signal with respect to itself and finding the offset with the highest correlation, and then averaging the shifted segments. Essentially, this is pitch estimation by autocorrelation (finding the closest match time shift) and then removal of one or more pitch periods with interpolation. SOLA is well within the capacity of many current desktop workstations without any additional signal processing hardware.

Time compression techniques such as SOLA reduce the intelligibility of speech, but even naive listeners can understand speech played back twice as fast as the original; this ability increases with listener exposure of 8 to 10 hours [Orr *et al.* 1965]. A less formal study found listeners to be uncomfortable listening to normal speech after one-half hour of exposure to compressed speech [Beasley and Maki 1976].

## Robustness

A final consideration for some applications is the robustness of the speech encoding scheme. Depending on the storage and transmission techniques used, some data errors may occur, resulting in missing or corrupted data. The more highly compressed the signal, the more information is represented by each bit and the more destructive any data loss may be.

Without packetization of the audio data and saving state variables in packet headers, the temporary interruption of the data stream for most of the adaptive encoders can be destructive for the same reasons mentioned in the discussion of sound editing. Since the decoder determines the state of the encoder simply from the values of the data stream, the encoder and decoder will fall out of synchronization during temporary link loss. If the state information is transmitted periodically, then the decoder can recover relatively quickly.

Another aspect of robustness is the ability of the encoder to cope with noise on the input audio signal. Since the encoders rely on properties of the speech signal to reduce their bit rates, inputs that fail to obey these constraints will not be properly encoded. One should not expect to encode music with most of these encoders, for example. LPC is an extreme case as it is a source coder and the decoder incorporates a model of the vocal tract.


## SUMMARY

This chapter has discussed digitization and encoding of speech signals. Digitization is the process whereby naturally analog speech is sampled and quantized into a digital form amenable to manipulation by a computer. This may be likened to the previous chapter's description of how the ear transduces variations in air pressure on the ear drum to electrical pulses on neurons connected to the brain. Digitization stores a sound for future rote playback, but higher level processing is required to understand speech by recognizing its constituent words.

This chapter has described several current speech coding schemes in some detail to illustrate how knowledge of the properties of speech can be used to compress a signal. This is not meant to be an exhaustive list, and new coding algorithms have been gaining acceptance even as this book was being written. The coders described here do illustrate some of the more common coders that the reader is likely to encounter. The design considerations across coders reveal some of the underlying tradeoffs in speech coding. Basic issues of sampling rate, quantization error, and how the coders attempt to cope with these to achieve intelligibility should now be somewhat clear.

This chapter has also mentioned some of the considerations in addition to data rate that should influence the choice of coder. Issues such as coder complexity, speech intelligibility, ease of editing, and coder robustness may come into play with varying importance as a function of a particular application. Many of the encoding schemes mentioned take advantage of redundancies in the speech signal to reduce data rates. As a result, they may not be at all suitable for encoding nonspeech sounds, either music or noise.

Digital encoding of speech may be useful for several classes of applications; these will be discussed in the next chapter. Finally, regardless of the encoding scheme, there are a number of human factors issues to be faced in the use of speech output. This discussion is deferred to Chapter 6 after the discussion of text-to-speech synthesis, as both recorded and synthetic speech have similar advantages and liabilities.


## FURTHER READING

Rabiner and Schafer is the definitive text on digital coding of speech. Flanagan *et al.* [1979] is a concise survey article covering many of the same issues in summary form. Both these sources assume familiarity with basic digital signal processing concepts and mathematic notation.

# 4

# Applications and Editing of Stored Voice

The previous chapter described some of the basic techniques for digitizing and encoding speech for either transmission or storage but said little of its role as a computer data type. This chapter focuses on computer applications of stored speech with particular emphasis on the underlying system support they require, especially sound storage facilities and editing. First, a taxonomy of voice applications is described based on the usage characteristics of situations in which speech is digitized and played back. Next, one of these classes—speech in documents—is explored in some detail. Finally, this chapter presents underlying representations and a number of examples of speech editors, which are required to support sophisticated use of audio in documents. In the course of this discussion, many examples of research projects utilizing digitized speech are mentioned to illustrate the range of approaches that have been taken to applications of stored voice.

This chapter focuses on application areas, their associated system requirements, and the functionality they require for supporting voice digitization and playback. Discussion of many user interaction requirements and techniques is postponed until Chapter 6, which deals with user interface issues for interactive speech response systems that employ both digitized and synthesized speech. For the purposes of this chapter, it is assumed that each application runs in isolation; Chapter 12 discusses issues of voice as a data type, including visual representations and sharing of voice data among applications on a computer workstation.

## TAXONOMY OF VOICE OUTPUT APPLICATIONS

Stored voice is essential to a variety of applications such as these.

- Toys that play a small number of messages from read only memory.
- Dictation, in which voice is recorded for later transcription into text by another person.
- Voice mail, in which a message is recorded informally by a caller and is accessed once by the recipient over a telephone-based interface.
- Voice annotation of text or multimedia documents, which involve more careful authoring and often a visual user interface.

This section characterizes such applications according to the functionality that stored voice requires as differentiated by how users employ it in these classes of applications. Applications may emphasize either recording or playback, and the stored voice may be heard once or repeatedly. How the stored voice is to be used in a particular application determines the underlying system support required for both recording and playback as well as influences the choice of a particular speech coding technology and how it is stored as computer files.

### Playback-Only Applications

Stored voice can be employed in a variety of applications for which a small repertoire of utterances needs to be spoken. Depending on the application, varying degrees of speech quality may be acceptable. Applications at the low-end of voice output technology employ single integrated circuits for both the storage and decoding of the digitized speech. Examples of this simple technology are inexpensive consumer products such as talking toys (dolls, stuffed animals, etc.) and video games. Some answering machines use stored speech to record the time onto the answering machine tape at the end of each incoming message. Answering machines that store the caller's message digitally are also appearing as consumer products. Voice warnings are used in both commercial and military aircraft cockpits. Automobile manufacturers have used digitized speech for warnings, and some cash registers recite each item and its price; however, neither of these two applications has proven to be very popular.

In situations where only minimal quality speech output is needed, it may be economical to use an asymmetric combination of speech coder and decoder. It is practical to use a computationally intensive coding algorithm, such as LPC, if the decoder is simple and inexpensive. Only the decoder needs to be included in a product which supports playback only.

Higher quality speech is needed for recorded public announcements such as the recitation of station names on automated trains or periodic, repetitious announcements over airport public address systems (e.g., warnings about taking baggage carts down the escalator). Because it is important for the listener to understand the message, these applications demand higher quality speech. In

Japan such announcements are ubiquitous in public locations and are usually spoken in a stylized female voice.

A similar class of applications are the so-called **audio-tex,** or **interactive voice response (IVR)** telephone-based information services. To use such services, one dials a telephone number and selects topics with touch tones. Recorded speech is used both for the information to be played back after selection as well as for prompts and menus. Examples include services to hear a weather forecast for a particular city, to find out one's current bank account balance, and to access an airline's flight schedule. The stored voice for these applications needs to be of adequate quality to be easily understood over the telephone by infrequent users. Because the service is accessed over the telephone, the sound data is most conveniently stored digitally on magnetic disk at a single site. Interaction techniques for interactive voice response systems will be discussed in detail in Chapter 6.

For all the applications just mentioned, the stored speech is used as "read only" data as the purpose of the application is to play a fixed set of prerecorded sounds. There is no user interaction with the voice itself; the system simply plays it at the appropriate time in response to the user's input. There is no need for a speech editing capability or a visual representation of the recording on a display, and the speech may be stored in whatever format is most convenient for the output device.

The developers of such applications occasionally need to update the voice recordings, and may use an editor or speech development system to do so. This development system does not need to be distributed with the application since updating can be done at a single, central location on an infrequent basis and distributed in ROM (Read Only Memory), floppy disks, or digital tape. Even for the developers, however, "editing" often consists of simply rerecording the passage repeatedly until the desired diction is achieved.

Some applications make use of a limited repertoire of "canned" speech segments to compose sentences; this involves concatenating short segments of digitized sound. One example is the mechanized playback of telephone numbers from directory assistance. It is essential that the individual sounds be accessible quickly enough during playback to avoid a pause between segments. If the speech is stored in semiconductor memory, this is not an issue, but for slower media, access time may be problematic.

In most of these applications, voice is chosen because it is the best output medium available. Because voice broadcasts through the air, it can be used in situations where displays would not be appropriate or visible. It is chosen as a warning channel because it is effective when the user is doing something else with his eyes, such as watching where he is driving or flying. In the case of the telephone-based services, access is also a dominant issue; users of such services take advantage of the nearly universal availability of the telephone. These advantages will be discussed in more detail in Chapter 6.

### Interactive Record and Playback Applications

Voice mail is currently the most pervasive example of the class of application that involves frequent recording and playback of speech segments. Each time a call is received, a new message is recorded. Usually the recipient listens to the message only once but may replay parts of the message while transcribing information such as the caller's telephone number. Although voice mail systems are most often treated simply as elaborate answering machines (with which messages are recorded once and played once), they are functionally more powerful than the consumer products found in homes. For example, voice mail systems can be used within an organization to disperse voice memos to distribution lists specifying multiple recipients or to specify a future delivery date for a message. This verbal memo is recorded just like a telephone message, although the author may speak more carefully or rerecord the message several times because it will be heard by a wider audience.

Voice is slow and serial, and telephone-based voice mail interfaces do not offer the user the opportunity to save messages in a "folder" with a mnemonic name as do most electronic mail systems. Archiving old voice messages and recalling them later is tedious, and few users take advantage of such capability; consequently, recording and playback occur equally often, which eliminates the advantages of an asymmetrical encoder/decoder combination. Random access of the recorded speech file is necessary as well to support repeated listening to a portion of the message.

Because of the more casual nature of telephone-based voice messages over paper memoranda, editing capabilities need not be provided; it would be difficult to build an effective editor using an audio-only interface based on touch tones. Instead, the user may be offered the option of reviewing a message before sending it and perhaps may choose to rerecord it. This is in contrast to the system recordings provided by the voice mail vendor, which are recorded very carefully often, with the assistance of voice editing software.

During recording, **Automatic Gain Control (AGC)** may be employed in an attempt to record constant amplitude messages from variable quality telephone connections. AGC uses variable amplification during recording to normalize the level of the recorded signal independent of the source level but it has limitations. Boosting the gain for a quiet speaker in a noisy environment may not enhance intelligibility as both the signal and noise are amplified; a better strategy is to monitor recording levels and prompt the quiet talker to speak louder. Another problem with AGC is that it tends to increase the gain during quiet portions of the message, or pauses, which causes a "whoosh" as the background noise increases; this is evident on many home videotapes. AGC can be improved by normalizing the gain based on peaks in the speech signal averaging over a time period, but this technique is not in widespread use. Although each telephone call can have a different audio level, the level is usually consistent for the duration of a message. This allows gain to be applied after the recording by multiplying each sample by the same scale factor; this avoids the whoosh produced when the gain is varied during a recording.

## Dictation

Dictation is an application of stored voice in which recording capability is required by the user, but the stored voice is never meant to be heard by the ultimate recipient. Instead, a transcriptionist listens to the recorded voice and transcribes it into text, often as a letter, memo, or short report.

Dictation has a different set of interaction requirements than other voice applications. The originator of a dictation spends a significant amount of time thinking about content and so requires a start/stop control or push-to-talk button; this is somewhat in contrast to telephone messages, where the caller must speak all at once at the "beep." The transcriptionist uses a foot pedal to control playback. Transcribing requires the capability to repeatedly review a portion of the message to understand individual words, but minimal random access to jump or scan through large portions of the recorded voice. The ultimate recipient of the message reads the transcription, having no interaction with the stored voice.

Although dictation and transcription have traditionally been done using analog tape recorders, other methods are now available. Dictation in an office environment can be digitized with the transcriptionist using a computer to control playback (again using a foot pedal). Dictation can also be taken over the telephone. Although some companies market this as a special product, business travelers already frequently leave lengthy voice mail messages for their secretaries to transcribe.

Dictation is used to create text documents when users refuse to use keyboards or can afford the cost of transcription as offset by the faster speed of speaking over typing or writing. Digitized dictation can also be used as a temporary information storage medium while awaiting transcription. For example, a hospital's medical records system could apply such a hybrid system. Physicians usually dictate their reports, but hospital administrators as well as medical staff prefer medical records to be stored in computers for both easy access and archival storage. Once dictation tapes are transcribed the text is easily stored on line, but until then the information is inaccessible. If the dictation were stored as digital sound files, it could be accessed immediately from a voice-and-text workstation, even as transcriptionists slowly converted the sound files to text. But for the hospital staff accessing voice in the medical record before transcription, a user interface different from the transcriptionists' foot pedal is required; voice as a document type requires a greater degree of interactivity.

### Voice as a Document Type

The use of voice for announcements or in toys does not require any recording capability after the announcement has been created, while both voice messages and dictation are intended to be heard only a few times before being discarded. In contrast, voice can also be utilized as a medium for the creation of documents which are intended to be more permanent or to reach a larger audience. As a document type, voice may be used as a means of annotating text or it may itself be the primary medium. Voice documents may also include other media such as text and images. More care will be taken during recording voice documents as the stored speech is intended for more formal use than a telephone message. In many cases multiple listeners will hear the recording, especially if it is part of a presentation.

Computer workstation-based multimedia applications such as these have several additional requirements for stored voice not encountered in the classes of applications discussed thus far. The first requirement is a visual representation of the stored speech appearing in a document and a graphical user interface to control playback. Because of the longevity and larger audience for voice documents, more care is taken in their creation so the second requirement is a voice editor that provides a means to manipulate stored voice, including cutting, pasting, and recording new material for insertion. Editing has implications for sound file storage since it is likely to produce many small snippets of sound that result in fragmented files, and certain methods of file storage are more compatible with the internal data structures used by the editor to manipulate sound data.

## VOICE IN INTERACTIVE DOCUMENTS

The remainder of this chapter will focus on uses of stored speech as a document type. As mentioned above, voice may be used alone or composed with other media to form a document. This chapter focuses on composed multimedia documents employing a display and a graphical user interface. Chapter 6 treats the problems unique to audio-only documents accessed without any display. A voice editor is also usually provided to aid authoring of voice documents. Although voice may be imported into one application from another much as text is cut and pasted between windows, discussion of this capability is postponed to Chapter 12; here we consider only document creation and retrieval.

When both text and voice are available, the different media may be used for different types of messages. Voice is appropriate for casual and transient messages, while text is preferred for messages that the recipient will likely save as reference. Voice is also desirable for its expressiveness; voice can carry subtle messages far more easily than text. It is also faster to enter messages by voice. Nicholson reported the results of a usage study of a voice and text message system in [Nicholson 1985] that supports all these observations. Chalfonte *et al.* [Chalfonte *et al.* 1991] compared voice and text as a means of commenting on text for a collaborative writing task; they found that a greater proportion of voice annotations carried "deeper" comments on style and structure, while text markings related to surface features such as choice of words and syntax.

Voice may be used to annotate text documents; it overcomes some limitations of the two-dimensional page by allowing comments to be placed anywhere with a content-associated visual icon that requires less space than handwriting. Conversely, text may be used to comment on a voice recording such as appending text remarks to a voice mail message before forwarding it to another party. Applications to support voice and text require the creation and storage of voice and a user interface to access it while viewing a document.

The Diamond project at BBN (Bolt, Beranek, and Newman) [Thomas *et al.* 1985] was an early example of incorporating voice with text. Diamond was designed to support voice and graphics in both electronic mail and more formal documents. Nearly 10 years old, Diamond used LPC speech coding to minimize audio storage requirements. But the LPC coder was an external computer peripheral that was not readily available. This, combined with the low quality of LPC, limited the use of Diamond and it remained basically a prototype system. But many aspects of Diamond have reappeared in *Slate,* a multimedia mail system currently available as a product from BBN [Crowley 1991, Lison and Crowley 1989].

Slate documents can include a variety of media and Slate is designed to work in concert with a computer conferencing system, MMConf. Slate uses a commercially available speech coding card or the audio capabilities of the workstation itself. In addition to speech, Slate incorporates still images (bitmaps), geometric graphics (lines, curves, etc.), motion video, spreadsheets, and charts. Slate indicates the presence of voice in a document with a small icon that can include a line of text as shown in Figure 4.1. By default, the text contains the author's name and recording information, but the author can change the label. The reader clicks on the icon to play the associated stored voice. Slate supports a small voice editor to allow the author to modify a recording during its creation as shown in Figure 4.2.

Another example of voice annotation of text documents was Quilt at Bellcore (Bell Communications Research) [Leland, Fish, and Kraut 1988, Fish, *et al.* 1988]. Quilt was a tool to allow collaborative document creation, editing, and review. Multiple parties could add notes to the document being edited using a

 Remark by Harry Forsdick on 03/30/89, 8:37 am (10 seconds)

**Figure 4.1.** Slate shows an annotated icon to indicate speech in a document.

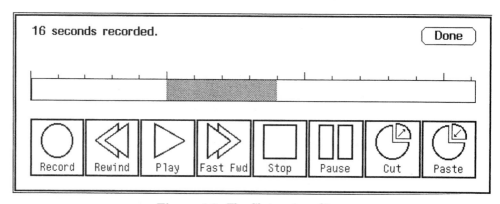

**Figure 4.2.** The Slate voice editor.

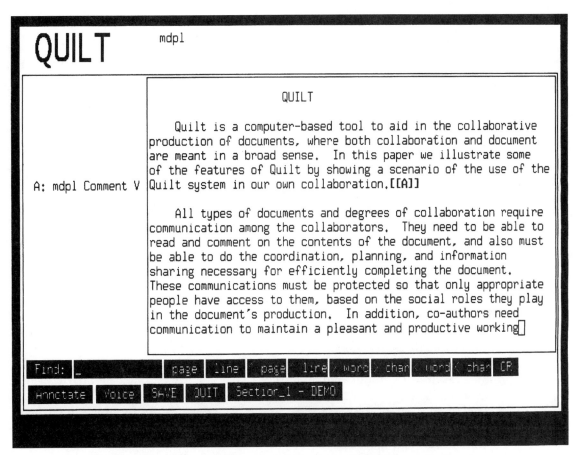

**Figure 4.3.** Quilt used **V** symbols to indicate the presence of voice comments in a text document.

simple voice annotation scheme. Voice recordings were indicated in the text with a "V" symbol as shown in Figure 4.3. Quilt was never widely deployed so it did not receive significant use, but it motivated preliminary studies with tape recorders that indicated that voice annotations were lengthier and more penetrating than text.

The Xerox PARC (Palo Alto Research Center) Etherphone project[1] supports voice annotation of text. It uses a "comic strip balloon" as an indicator of voice stored as part of a text document as shown in Figure 4.4. The capability to mix

---

[1]Etherphone is discussed in more detail in Chapter 11, and its voice editor is discussed later in this chapter.

---

**Sending Voice Messages**

Finch has to be running, too. Your Walnut sender will have four new buttons. Button *Record,* wait for the beep, then record your voice message. You can use the Etherphone's microphone if you wish (be sure to turn it on), but the quality will be better if you use the telephone handset instead. Button *STOP!* when you're done. Button *Play* to hear what you said.

After you record a voice message, notice the *VoiceFileID* field in the header of your Walnut Sender. If you choose not to send the voice

---

**Figure 4.4.** Voice is indicated by a "balloon" at Xerox PARC. (Copyright ©1986, Xerox Corporation. Reproduced with permission of Xerox Corporation.)

voice with text was extended by Zellweger to **scripted documents,** which sequentially play back (or display) portions of a multimedia document [Zellweger 1989]. A scripted document is a form of presentation with the management of time and sequence an added dimension of authoring; the script provides a single path through the document.

Stored speech is also used in multimedia documents that provide many paths for presentation under control of the "reader." For example, the MUSE system from M.I.T.'s Project Athena [Hodges *et al.* 1989] uses recorded video, audio, and textual annotation for the interactive presentation of educational material.[2] The student in a foreign language course may be asked to make decisions on the basis of a spoken dialogue played from a videodisc. Text may be employed during playback to define new vocabulary items. The student's response is indicated using the mouse, and the system responds with the next appropriate sequence.

An entirely different approach is taken in documents which consist only of voice, with nonvisual user interfaces. Muller defines an architecture for voice documents as a network of short audio segments and points out some of the timing issues with synchronizing user inputs with whichever segment is currently playing [Muller and Daniel 1990]. Resnick built a telephone-based groupware application, Hypervoice, that allowed callers to browse a community bulletin board of voice entries [Resnick 1992a]. Each entry consisted of a number of short voice recordings such as an event's time, description, and a contact person's telephone number; users navigated with touch tones. Arons' Hyperspeech used speech recognition to navigate a hypermedia database consisting of audio inter-

---

[2]MUSE is both the presentation system as well as the underlying language and editor used for creating the presentations.

views with five user interface researchers [Arons 1991b]. VoiceNotes is a user interface to a handheld digital audio storage device; users employ speech recognition and mechanical buttons to traverse and edit lists of reminders [Stifelman *et al.* 1993].

## VOICE EDITING

While adding voice to a document or presentation users will occasionally make mistakes and must correct them. To change a very short voice recording it is easy to simply record the speech again; an example is the outgoing message on an answering machine. Other applications, which use longer recordings, can benefit from the addition of a voice editor. An editor allows a user to delete or move portions of a recording and to insert new audio into an existing recording; these operations are controlled with a graphical user interface. An editor can also be used to extract a portion of sound from a longer voice recording to be used in another application. The rest of this chapter considers several architecture issues for voice editors and illustrates editor user interfaces with a number of examples.

### Temporal Granularity

Audio editors may provide different levels of temporal granularity for specifying the position within a sound at which a sound manipulation operation is to occur. The granularity of an editor is determined both by the application's requirements as well as by the nature of the stored sound to be edited. The temporal granularity also places requirements on the editor for display of the sound being edited.

A **fine-grained** editor allows edit operations to be performed at any point in the sound. It makes no assumptions about the content of the sound and gives the user complete control of editing. Fine-grained editors usually display sound as a waveform (see Figure 4.5) or **average magnitude** (see Figure 4.6). Average magnitude is the sum of the absolute value of some number of audio samples divided by the number of samples; samples are taken over a large enough window to average multiple pitch periods. A mechanism may be provided to zoom in and out of the sound view for local or global editing; the zooming changes the ratio of pixels to time for display purposes.

A fine-grained editor is most useful for studio work such as producing music or motion picture sound tracks. In these situations a great deal of flexibility is required as a variety of sounds may be manipulated and very careful edits are needed. For example, the Sound Droid digital audio editing system [Snell 1982] was used in the motion picture industry and emulated existing analog studio equipment both in user interface as well as basic functionality.

A **coarse-grained** editor provides much less temporal control but abstracts sound into "chunks" based on periods of speech and silence. Coarse granularity is more suitable for editing speech because speech consists of a series of semanti-

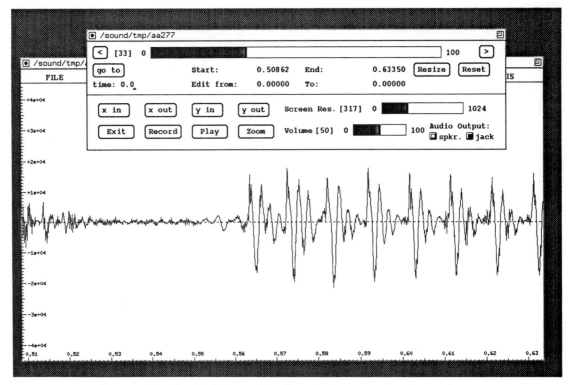

**Figure 4.5.** The MixView audio editor displays sound as a waveform.

cally meaningful phrases; a coarse-grained editor facilitates the user's identifying phrases and editing them as units. The abstraction of sound into speech and silence intervals also allows more succinct visual representations with reduced screen space requirements.

The coarse-grained editor is well suited to removing spurious remarks, cleaning up false starts from a recording, and replacing a sentence; it is not suited to modifying individual words. In a study of users of an early voice editor, Allen noted that subjects desired to edit individual words frequently [Allen 1983], but in practice it is nearly impossible to modify a single word in a sentence without having the result sound broken, with very unnatural prosody. Since users will not be able to perform successful fine-grained editing of voice, coarse-grained editors make no attempt to support this function, and use a simple binary representation to simplify the user interface.

### Manipulation of Audio Data

An audio editor must manipulate stored sound data in response to the user's commands. As users are likely to make changes and review them several times before achieving the desired result, it is useful if the editor allows preview before com-

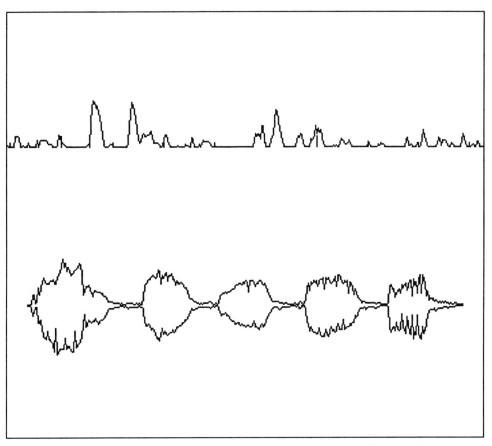

**Figure 4.6.** Average magnitude display of a sound (top) and an envelope display showing both positive and negative peaks (bottom).

mitting the changes to the original sound file. Although this could be done simply by editing a copy of the sound file, most editors instead operate on an internal representation of the sound that allows users to edit and review without changing the file at all. When finished the user may choose to save the edited sound at which point the file is changed. Many text editors employ similar techniques.

More importantly, editing an in-memory representation of the file offers significant performance improvements over editing a file directly. For example, if the user deletes the first character of a text file or the first 100 milliseconds of an audio file, it is time consuming to move the entire remainder of the file.[3]

---

[3]Under some operating systems this requires copying the entire file as well.

Instead, the editor just modifies its description of the sound to note that the very beginning of the file should be skipped over during playback. At the end of the editing session the disk file can be changed in a single operation avoiding slow file operations during editing. This is even more important in the editing of sound than in text as sound files are much longer than most text files. A chapter of this book may takes roughly 40,000 bytes of text storage, but for many speech coding algorithms this would represent less than 10 seconds of sound.

An audio editor may represent a sound being edited as a **buffer** or **playback list.** This can be implemented as a linked list where each entry in the list points to a sound file and indicates start and end points. Figure 4.7 shows how such a representation is employed during editing. When a file is initially read into a buffer (shown in the top portion of the figure), the buffer includes the entire sound. The edit list contains a single entry with a start point of zero and stop point at the end of the file; duration is represented by shading in the figure. A "cut" operation removes a portion of the sound (shown in the middle of the figure). Now the buffer list has two entries. The first entry points to the initial part of the file at offset zero and extending up to the beginning of the cut section. The second buffer entry points to the same file but starts after the cut section and extends to the end of the sound. When the edit is reviewed, the editor plays the first chunk of the file and immediately skips the middle part of the file to play only the final segment. When the buffer is then written out to a file, a single homogeneous file is created by merging the two sections of sound (shown in the bottom of the figure).

To insert a new sound into the middle of a buffer, the buffer must be split into two list entries with the new sound added to the list in between them as shown

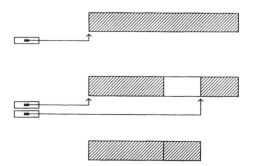

**Figure 4.7.** Edit buffers. At the top, a single buffer node points to an entire file. In the middle, after removing a portion of the sound, two buffer nodes are required to point to the two segments of the file. At the bottom is the correct representation after the buffer has been written to a file; the two portions of the original file have been merged into a single continuous file.

in Figure 4.8. With each edit operation performed by the user, one or more entries are likely to be added to the buffer list. After a number of operations, the resulting representation is complex (see Figure 4.9), but it is hidden completely from the user. Depending on how sound is stored in disk files, the complexity may be largely hidden from the editing program as well; some sound file systems

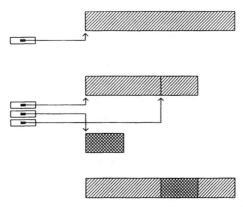

**Figure 4.8.** Edit buffers showing insertion of a new sound into an existing sound. The original sound at the top must be divided into two segments, each with its own buffer node and a new node inserted in their midst. The resulting buffer in the middle may then be written to a single file at bottom.

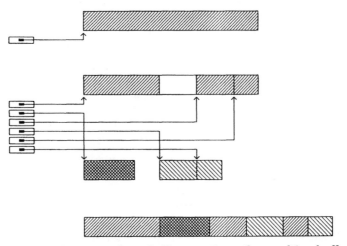

**Figure 4.9.** After a number of edit operations, the resulting buffer may become rather complicated.

provide transparent sequential access to chunks of sound stored in different locations on the disk.

## EXAMPLES OF VOICE EDITORS

All sound editors include a user interface to the editing functions. These functions include selection of a sound file for editing, playback of the sound, deleting part of the sound, and inserting new sound. The appearance of the user interface depends on the window system, graphical toolkits, and style conventions for the particular operating environment in which it runs. The editor may be modeled after existing tools with which users are familiar, such as text editors for the office and audio equipment for the studio.

One of the earliest voice editors was built by Maxemchuk at Bell Laboratories as part of an experimental speech storage facility [Maxemchuk 1980]. This editor had a primitive interface based on an alphanumeric terminal; a subsequent version used a more sophisticated display. This section briefly describes a number of more recent audio editors; they exhibit a wide range of user interfaces and sound representations yet share many aspects of underlying software architecture.

### Intelligent Ear, M.I.T.

The Intelligent Ear was an early voice editor from the Architecture Machine Group (M.I.T.) [Schmandt 1981]. It displayed a sound as an amplitude envelope using average magnitude to modulate both height and brightness as shown in Figure 4.10. The entire sound was displayed on the screen; long sounds were shown with less temporal detail than short sounds because of the compression required to fit them on the screen. The Intelligent Ear also used speech recognition to attempt to detect keywords in the sound and displayed these as text with brightness indicating the degree of certainty with which the word was recognized.

This editor used a touchscreen for input. When the user touched a location on the sound display, a cursor moved to that location. When the *play* button was touched, playback began at that point and the sound display changed color while the cursor moved in synchronization with playback. This motion was provided to aid the user's mental mapping of the visual cue of average magnitude to the actual contents of the sound. Other editing functions included *delete* and *record,* which enabled the user to specify an insertion point at which to record additional speech. Edit operations were buffered in that they did not change any sound file data, but this buffering was only one operation deep. After an insertion or deletion the user could play through and listen to the result; only after accepting this result was the sound file actually changed on disk. An edit operation was either accepted or rejected by touching a red or green button which appeared after the edit, but the user was not able to make multiple edits and preview the result without modifying the file.

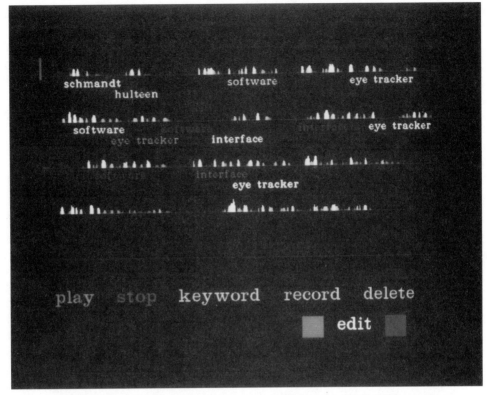

**Figure 4.10.** The touch-sensitive user interface to the Intelligent Ear editor.

The Intelligent Ear was a demonstration project which saw only limited internal use by its authors to edit voice prompts in later research projects. It was novel in its early use of a color graphical interface and touchscreen for voice editing.

### Tioga Voice, Xerox PARC

The Tioga Voice audio editor at Xerox PARC was modeled after the Tioga text editor's user interface and underlying data representations with the intention of making editing voice similar to editing text [Ades and Swinehart 1986]. Tioga Voice was designed to support audio in a variety of applications and could be used as a listening tool as well as an editor.

The Tioga Voice user interface shown in Figure 4.11 supported a number of features. Portions of speech and silence were displayed by a binary representation in a small bar (or "capillary tube" as described by its creators), and text annotation could be added as well. On a color screen, recent changes or additions appeared brighter than older sound segments. During recording the display changed dynamically showing the new sound as a string of arrows both to keep a sense of

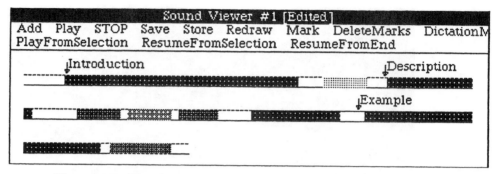

**Figure 4.11.** The Tioga Voice editor. (Copyright ©1986, Xerox Corporation. Reproduced with permission of Xerox Corporation.)

its relationship to the whole recording as well as to remind the user that the recording was still in progress. During playback, a marker moved across the sound bars indicating the current play position.

To facilitate the manipulation of sound files, Tioga Voice kept track of the current *selection,* i.e., the piece of sound most recently referenced. During dictation mode, the selection corresponded to the most recent portion of speech recorded to allow for quick review or cancelling erroneous input. If the user began recording, coughed, and then stopped recording, this audio segment could be deleted by a single mouse click.

Tioga Voice was built on top of the Etherphone system, which provided sound storage and voice services through server processes running on other computers. Although voice segments were stored as sequential files on disk, they were accessed through the file server as a list of segments referred to as a *voice rope* [Terry and Swinehart 1988]; text was stored in a similar fashion, also referred to as a *rope.* A complete sound consisted of the rope database plus raw sound storage (see Figure 4.12). The voice ropes were similar to the edit buffer schemes described above except that they were saved on disk as part of the storage mechanism provided by the server for all sound access. Each rope represented a path through portions of one or more sound files; editing simply created more ropes. Because editing simply created more ropes instead of actually modifying the underlying sound files, periodic garbage collection was required to recover unreferenced disk files.

### PX Editor, Bell Northern Research

Another example of a sound editor is that which was developed for the PX (Personal eXchange) project at Bell Northern Research's Computer Systems Research Laboratory [Kamel, Emami and Eckert 1990, Bowles *et al.* 1991]. PX is discussed in greater detail in Chapter 11; in this section we consider only its sound editor.

The PX editor, shown in Figure 4.13, ran on Apple Macintosh computers with an external hardware interface for speech input. This editor supported several

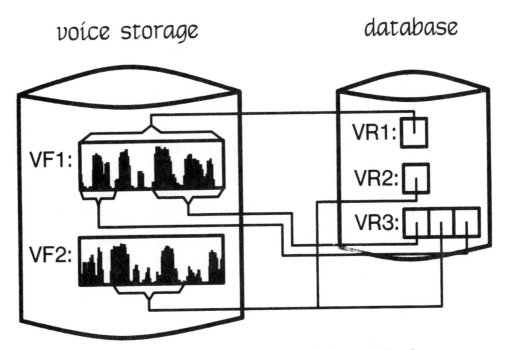

**Figure 4.12.** Voice ropes, showing the rope database which references portions of linear sound files. (Reprinted with permission from *Transactions on Computer Systems* ©1988, ACM.)

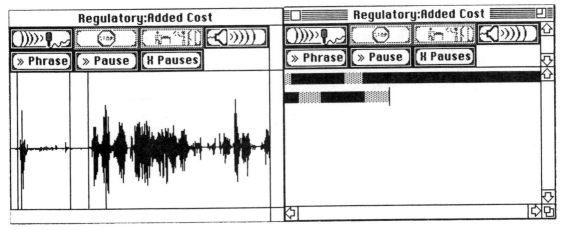

**Figure 4.13.** The PX sound editor showing two sound representations. The left view is a waveform envelope, while the right view shows speech and silence intervals. (©1990. Reprinted by permission of BNR.)

representations of sound. Figure 4.13 shows the same sound displayed in two windows: one using a waveform envelope and the other showing speech and silence intervals much like the Tioga Voice editor. This simple editor was meant to be a common tool used in a variety of applications such as creating a voice mail greeting and annotating text. In addition to the playback and recording functions described previously in this chapter, the PX editor allowed the user to skip to the next phrase during rapid playback.

PX utilized small segments of sound file storage called "voice clips," which were stored and accessed much like Xerox's voice ropes. Unlike Etherphone, however, the PX editor was implemented entirely on a single computer; there was no server process involved. Voice clips described a series of portions of a file to play in sequence, and every edit operation could produce multiple new voice clips. A sound file held a number of voice clips followed by the reference audio data, which was played as indicated by the clips. In contrast to Xerox's voice ropes, the voice clip database was stored in the same file as the raw audio so it could refer only to data in that file. If a new sound was to be made by merging two other sounds, these would have to be copied into the data area of the new sound file.

### Sedit, Olivetti Research Center, and M.I.T. Media Laboratory

A similar audio editor, sedit, was originally written at Olivetti Research Center as part of the VOX audio server project [Arons *et al.* 1989].[4] It was subsequently extended substantially at the Media Laboratory where it is in use today. Sedit uses the X Window System for its graphical user interface and employs a sound editor widget.[5] The sound editor widget (see Figure 4.14) uses black and white bars to display periods of speech and silence; this display is similar to that used by Tioga Voice. A scroll bar beneath indicates how much of the entire sound file is visible and allows the user to choose a portion of the sound to view in detail. As the sound plays, a cursor (a vertical bar) moves across the display synchronously with playback; if necessary, the scroll bar also moves to keep the current location in view.

Sedit can edit multiple sounds simultaneously allowing data to be cut and pasted between sound files; Figure 4.14 shows several sounds active within the editor. The horizontal lines in the figure indicate the portion of a buffer selected for the next operation. Selection is performed by dragging the cursor across the sound with the mouse. Once a region is selected, the edit operation is indicated by clicking on the appropriate button.

---

[4]VOX is described in detail in Chapter 12; discussion here is limited to support for editing.

[5]In X Windows a "widget" is a basic user interaction object such as a button or scroll bar that can be instantiated multiple times in multiple applications.

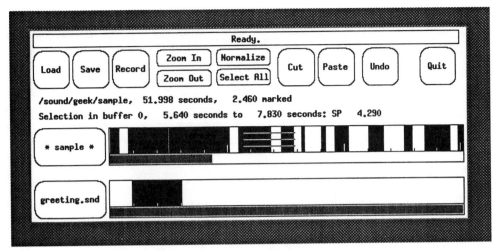

**Figure 4.14.** The *sedit* audio editor.

A year after the demise of the VOX project, sedit was revived at the MIT Media Lab. Capabilities that formerly had been implemented in the server were included in the editor and new functionality was added. One new function normalizes audio level among all buffer segments; this is useful when editing together source material recorded with different microphone gain levels. Other functions allow changing the time scale of the sound display widget and interaction with a selection mechanism allowing sound to be moved between applications (see Chapter 12). This is the version of sedit shown in Figure 4.14.

### Pitchtool, M.I.T. Media Laboratory

Pitchtool was a special-purpose editor written at the Media Laboratory to aid in the study of intonation. It is mentioned here as an example of an editor interface designed specifically for a particular application. Pitchtool was used as much to analyze recordings as to change them and so included such capabilities as variable playback speed, textual annotations, and spatial scaling of the sound to show extended portions of dialog or detailed views of individual phrases.

Pitchtool, shown in Figure 4.15, displayed pitch, energy, and segment duration of a digitized speech file. In the figure, the solid line represents pitch, while the broken line represents energy. Pitchtool also provided for modification of these parameters to allow hand-editing of the pitch and energy for experiments in the synthesis of intonation. The mouse could be used to "paint" a new pitch track or two points could be selected with pitch interpolated linearly between them.

Because it was designed to manipulate the pitch of sounds, Pitchtool used Linear Predictive Coding (see Chapter 3) for its speech storage. LPC encoding was

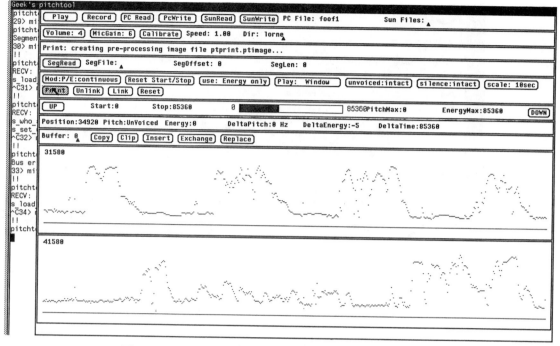

**Figure 4.15.** Pitchtool allowed editing of pitch and energy.

performed by a server, which included a signal processing card and small computer with local storage, communicating to the host workstation via a serial interface (this server is described in more detail in Chapter 12). As with the original sedit editor, all manipulation of sound data was implemented in the server; Pitchtool merely provided the user interface.

## SUMMARY

This chapter described classes of applications for stored speech with emphasis on the underlying system and coder requirements for each. For some of these classes, speech is played only while others require recording as well. Recordings can be casual as in voice mail messages or more formal for presentations or audio memoranda. Recording for dictation may be short lived before it is converted to text. Each class of operation places different requirements on audio storage in terms of the quality required for data compression algorithms, speed to access voice data, and the synchronization of playback with a graphical user interface or other presentation media.

Particular emphasis was placed on interactive audio documents because they highlight requirements for screen-based user interfaces and sound editors. The range of example systems and editors has revealed a variety of graphical user interfaces and representations of sounds. Editors generally employ in-memory buffers to describe sound file segments during editing, but this capability may be included in the set of primitives provided by the sound file management system. Similar storage issues arise with file formats and editors for all multimedia data that require very large files that may become fragmented as a result of editing operations.

# 5

# Speech Synthesis

The previous two chapters discussed techniques for digital encoding of speech and how different classes of applications utilize this recorded speech. In some instances, such as a voice mail system, the computer treats recording as opaque data; it captures what one person says and relays it to another without knowledge of its lexical content. In other applications, such as telephone-based access to flight schedules or announcements of the approaching station on a subway, the application knows the content of prerecorded snippets of speech and pieces them together to generate spoken output. But although the computer "talks" in such applications, its repertoire is limited to a few prerecorded phrases. Speech synthesis is the process of generating speech from text; for any string of words a speech synthesizer can approximate the way a human would read these same words.

Although synthesized speech cannot be expected to achieve the quality of the human speech that it mimics, the flexibility of synthesis makes it extremely useful for a variety of applications. Synthesis allows voice output in discourse systems in which the computer has a wide variety of things to say, and it can easily be driven by language generating programs that produce text. Synthesis is helpful for voice access to databases because databases may have a very large number of entries to pronounce (such as names of people, streets, or businesses). Finally for some applications the computer may need to speak human-authored text such as an electronic mail message or a text file.

Transforming text into speech is done by a process called **text-to-speech synthesis** or **synthesis-by-rule.** These terms are chosen to contrast some speech coding methods such as Linear Predictive Coding (see Chapter 3), which are sometimes called **analysis-synthesis** algorithms. Such coders first analyze the speech in terms of parameters to control an underlying vocal tract model, and then "resynthesize" it for playback through a digital system that implements this model. Speech coders can only store spoken speech; speech synthesizers accept arbitrary text as input and generate speech. Throughout this book, the term "speech synthesis" is used to refer exclusively to text-to-speech generation.

To begin to appreciate the difficulty of synthesizing speech, let us consider an apparently simple approach to synthesis that is actually impractical although quite suitable as a substitute to synthesis in certain limited situations. Suppose we simply record a person speaking every possible word and then string these audio segments together for speech output? This approach is impractical for several reasons.

First, there are simply too many words. Not only do we need to digitize the root forms of nouns and verbs, we also need their forms in combinations. For "play," for example, we might want "plays," "playful," "playing," "played," etc. or compounds such as "horseplay."[1] Even if we somehow coped with storing all these word forms, it would be even less practical to store all the proper nouns that might be required to speak from some databases [Spiegel 1985]. Finally, languages change and new words and acronyms ("DRAM," "ISDN," "downsize") keep appearing in English or any language, necessitating recurring updates of the recorded speech.

Second, even if we *could* store every word which might be spoken, they would sound very awkward when strung together. Words change pronunciation in a spoken context. Sentences have a melody and rhythm that changes the pitch and duration of syllables. Phonemes at the beginnings and endings of words are spoken with variations that harmonize with surrounding words. A word spoken in isolation is said to be in **citation form,** but this is not how we speak in normal conversation. Consider the word "the"; when asked to say this word by itself, many people instinctively pronounce it as "thee," but we actually speak it this way only when the following word begins with a vowel. Many words exhibit this phenomenon. "To" is usually spoken more like "ta," and the vowel in "for" practically disappears in fluent speech.

Although these observations are meant to argue that conversion of text to speech is more difficult than patching together digitized words, in some situations it may suffice to record a number of short phrases and concatenate them; this technique is used in many telephone-based applications. For example, the caller speaks with a human directory assistance operator, but then a computer voice recites the number. What actually transpires is that a number of short recorded segments are played starting with "The number is . . ." followed by a separate recording of each digit.

Although the phone number is spoken by concatenating recordings of each digit, some sophistication is required to make the number sound natural. All dig-

---

[1]Note that we know not to pronounce the "e" in such a compound word.

its in a telephone number are not pronounced the same; intonation is used to group them. North American numbers consist of three digits (area code), three digits (exchange), and four more digits. Each group is pronounced separately, with a falling pitch indicating phrasing (see Figure 5.1). The last digit in each of the first two groups has a rising pitch, which serves as a continuation marker or cue that more information will follow the pause. For each digit, three (or sometimes four) recordings are made, and the appropriate one is chosen depending on whether the digit is in the initial, medial, or terminal position in the number.

## SYNTHESIZING SPEECH FROM TEXT

How can text be transformed into speech? As just discussed, it is impractical to simply record each word because of pronunciation problems as well as the amount of storage required for the lexicon. We cannot go directly from text to sound by pasting words together; instead, some smaller unit of representation is required for sound generation. For efficient synthesis, this unit should be significant either from the perspective of the written language (words or letters) or from the spoken language (syllables or phonemes).

English is a difficult language to synthesize largely because its orthography (the written version of the language) is highly irregular; more specifically, the mapping from letters to sounds is not one to one. The same sound may be produced from various letters (e.g., the initial phoneme in "kid" and "cat"). Worse still, the same letters can be pronounced in different ways (e.g., the final four letters in "tough" or "through").

In some languages, the stronger relationship among letters and sounds would suggest that letters be used as a unit of synthesis. An example is the Turkish language; the Turks replaced their former Arabic script with a Roman alphabet earlier this century as part of the "modernization" of the country. The new alphabet was created specifically for the language from symbols used in other languages,

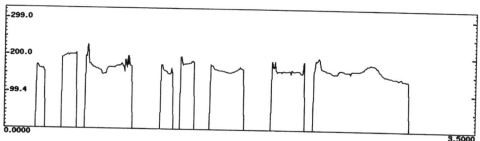

**Figure 5.1.** Pitch track of a telephone number including area code. Note the phrasing of the three groups of numbers. The first two number groups show a small terminal rise, which is a cue to the listener that there is more to come. There is no such rise in the final number group. The vertical axis is pitch in Hertz, the horizontal axis shows time in seconds.

and it is conveniently phonetic. Equally important, spoken languages continually change but only slowly. So spoken Turkish has not yet diverged from its recently specified written form. In the new Turkish alphabet, not all the letter symbols are recognizable in any single European language; for example, both "o" and "u" exist in an umlaut and nonumlaut form as in the German "u" and "ü," but "i" also has a dotted and undotted form ("ı" and "i"), which German does not. However, once the single pronunciation of each letter is learned, it is easy for someone who does not speak Turkish to read it aloud. This is exactly the task of a speech synthesizer.

Since English is not this simple, it is necessary to first convert the letters to a less ambiguous representation and then apply sound realization rules to that representation. The most common alternative form to the letter is the phoneme as there are a fairly small number of phonemes in any language, simplifying the sound generation rules.[2] Synthesis is composed of two steps; the first converts the text to a string of phonemes (with intonational markers), and the second realizes the output of the first as a speech waveform. This is depicted in Figure 5.2. Note that in the Turkish example, since each letter maps to exactly one phoneme, we can simply skip the first step in this model except that intonational markers must still be added to each syllable.

## FROM TEXT TO PHONEMES

So how can text, an ordered series of letters, be converted to the equivalent string of phonemes? Two general approaches may be identified: a **pronunciation lexicon** (dictionary) or a set of **rules** similar to what we learn in elementary school. Both are useful and a hybrid approach is optimal.

The dictionary approach is simple. A string of phonemes is stored for each word, and conversion of text to phonemes is accomplished by lookup. Several problems prevent a lexicon-only solution, however. First, the dictionary grows rapidly as a result of the sizable vocabularies required for many applications. Second, the dictionary must be stored in nonvolatile memory in a stand-alone synthesizer. Third, at some point in the dictionary lookup a "morphological decomposition" analysis of the text must occur, if only to identify simple forms such as plurals and past tense; if both "cat" and "cats" are to exist as distinct

---

[2]The number of phonemes in a language varies from a low of 13 (Hawaiian) to a high of about 75. English is in the middle with approximately 40 phonemes.

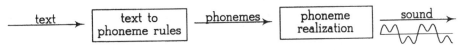

**Figure 5.2.** A basic model of speech synthesis.

entries, the dictionary must be much larger. Fourth, sometimes correct pronunciation cannot be gained from looking at a word in isolation, but rather, sentence context must be employed ("read" has two pronunciations depending on tense; some other examples are discussed below on the topic of lexical stress). Finally, no matter how large the dictionary is, there will always be words it does not contain such as proper nouns, jargon, and new words.

The rule-based approach, in contrast, uses knowledge of spelling rules to derive pronunciation from the text. There are several advantages to such techniques. First, the set of rules is much more concise than a lexicon of pronunciations for each word. Second, it is more flexible; effective rules can generate a plausible pronunciation for almost any word including names. Third, rules represent succinct knowledge about a language. Rules may be portable across languages, and the rules for a language can generate pronunciations for names from that nationality even while synthesizing a different language.

Although a completely rule-based synthesizer is attractive, this is quite difficult and not the easiest path to the goal of accurate synthesis of commonly used words. Since a dictionary may more easily embody correct pronunciation than some of the more general spelling rules, the usual approach is to store common words in the lexicon and apply rules to the remaining words. It is best to put in the lexicon only those common words that are known *not* to be pronounced well by the rules. If lookup fails, a rule is invoked which is either correct (or else the word would be in the lexicon) or at least a reasonable guess for an unlisted and probably unusual word (which would not be in the lexicon under any circumstances).

Even for a completely rule-based synthesizer, it is quite useful to include a user-definable phonetic exceptions dictionary to deal with important words that are not pronounced correctly such as names or acronyms common in a particular organization. Although these words may be uncommon in the language as a whole, local use may be frequent; if they are mispronounced, the result will be greater listener dissatisfaction.

The process of text-to-phoneme translation is performed in several steps. The first step is text preprocessing or **normalization** to convert symbols and abbreviations into their full-text spellings such as converting the symbol "$" to "dollar." Normalization is not quite as simple as it may first appear; the best full-text spelling of "$4.35" is "four dollars and thirty-five cents," but "$2.00" is simply "two dollars." Similarly, some abbreviations, such as "Dr." and "St.," can represent one of several possible words. "Dr." is usually "doctor" when the word following is a proper noun ("Dr. Jones"); it is pronounced "drive" when a proper noun precedes it ("Jones Dr.").

The next step is **morphological analysis,** which copes with words composed of several root parts (morphemes) including plurals and compound words such as "baseball" and "backpack." Many words in English are built by combining root forms with **affixes.** An affix may be a prefix such as "un" in "unusual," or a suffix such as the "ing" in "buying." A word may have multiple affixes at either end, such as "usability," from "use" + "able" + "y." This last example also shows how spelling may change as affixes are added; these regular spelling changes must be included in the morphological decomposition.

Since words are built from morphemes, there will be far fewer morphemes than words, making storage in a lexicon more practical. Text is broken down into morphological units, pronunciation is looked up for each, and rules are applied to those units for which lookup fails. This process of producing phonemes from text is summarized in Figure 5.3.

## Additional Factors for Pronunciation

Unfortunately, simply converting text to a stream of phonemes is inadequate for the next stage of synthesis: generating sound. Several confounding factors complicate the model shown in Figure 5.2; additional information, such as **lexical stress, coarticulation,** and **intonation** must accompany the phonemes. Lexical stress is the pattern of syllabic emphasis within a word. Coarticulation is the change in pronunciation of phonemes as a function of their phonemic environment, i.e., the sounds preceding and succeeding them. And overall sentence intonation, or **prosody,** requires adjustments to the output of the text-to-phoneme processing.

### Lexical Stress

In English, as in many languages, not all syllables are created equal. We learned in elementary school that every word has one syllable carrying primary stress and possibly others carrying secondary stress. How do we generate stress acoustically? Although the intuitive answer is the volume (amplitude) of the speech, this is only a secondary factor. As Fry demonstrated in some key experiments [Fry 1958], stress is carried primarily as variations in pitch and duration of the appropriate syllables. A stressed syllable is somewhat longer than an unstressed syllable and will also carry higher (or lower) pitch than it would otherwise as shown in Figure 5.4.

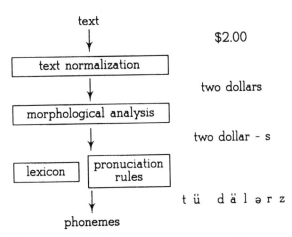

**Figure 5.3.** Steps in converting text to phonemes.

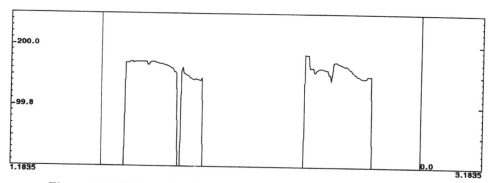

**Figure 5.4.** Pitch tracks showing lexical stress. The word on the left is CON-duct. The word on the right is con-DUCT. Note that the stressed syllable is longer and higher pitched.

Lexical stress is part of a complex interplay between the intonation and rhythm of a whole sentence. Discussion of lexical stress is limited to that which can be detected in a word spoken in isolation, in its citation form. Stress covers many phenomena, all realized as variations in rhythm and meter; lexical stress is what differentiates syllabic "accent" as opposed to emphasizing one word over another in a sentence. Lexical stress is important for understanding spoken language; incorrectly assigned stress may make a word unintelligible. For some English words the assignment of stress differentiates noun and verb forms, e.g., "convert" and "conflict" (see Figure 5.4). Determining which syllable to stress requires a reliable syntactic analysis of the sentence.

Stress confounds text-to-phoneme conversion because stress is not directly phonemic. In addition to producing the proper phonemes, the syllables containing those phonemes also must be marked for stress. This is done by assigning pitch and duration for each voiced phoneme during the conversion to phonemes.

### Coarticulation

Coarticulation is the process whereby the pronunciation of a phoneme changes as a function of its surrounding phonemes. This change may be an allophonic variation, that is, substitution of an acoustically distinct version of the same phoneme. An example of this is the "t" sound in "but" versus "butler"; terminal stop consonants tend to be released. Alternatively, the substitution may result in an entirely different phoneme from the citation form. Consider the second "d" in "Did you . . . ," which can be pronounced much closer to a "j" without loss of intelligibility.

Coarticulation occurs because the vocal tract is a physical system. The articulators (tongue, lips, etc.) have mass and make continuous motions that are not instantaneous, due to inertia and the physical processes controlling the various muscle groups. Although for each phoneme there is a desired target configuration for the articulators (such as tongue touching the palate), in practice the articulators may never fully realize that configuration. Instead, they simply make a gesture in its direction, which is sufficient to change the sound emanating from the vocal tract just enough to cue the listener to the identity of the intended phoneme. Pronunciation is sloppy. This is not a defect in speech; rather it is an accommodation to the speech production process that results in an ability to communicate faster than we could otherwise.

In some cases these coarticulation effects are localized within a word. The consonant "r" is a good example; the sound of "r" is realized largely through modification of the preceding vowel. In other cases these effects occur across word boundaries. Consider the fricatives in "the cats went" and "the cats sat"; the pause required to distinguish the plural form of cats in the latter introduces more aspiration on the first "s." Speech synthesized without considering these coarticulation effects will be stilted and perhaps less intelligible. Fortunately, many coarticulatory effects can be predicted as they follow rules [Oshika *et al.* 1975], although a complete set of such rules has not yet been compiled for English.

There is also interaction between coarticulation and lexical stress; in general, the unstressed syllables are much more subject to change. An example is **vowel reduction,** in which the vowel of an unstressed syllable is shortened and turned into a schwa.[3] In the extreme, the reduced vowel may simply vanish; consider how many syllables are pronounced in "chocolate" (two or three?). Note what happens to the "e" between "manager" and "managerial"; in "managerial" the "e" is stressed and hence not reduced.

### Intonation

A final consideration, before phonemes can be realized as sounds, is the overall melody or intonation of the sentence. Intonation refers to the pitch contour of the sentence, both in terms of which words receive greater emphasis as well as the general slope (rising or falling) of the pitch contour. Intonation differentiates questions from statements even when the words themselves may be identical, and it also reveals which words in a sentence are particularly emphasized.

Consider the intonation of the sentences "She went to Paris." (simple statement of fact) and "She went to Paris?" (expression of disbelief, or request for clarification). The first sentence (see Figure 5.5) has overall falling pitch typical of simple declaratives. The second sentence (see Figure 5.6) has pitch that rises on the last word (more precisely, on the last stressed syllable) because it is a question. But a so-called "Wh-question"[4] has its stress on the "wh-" word (see Figure 5.7).

The sentences just used as examples are deceptively simple since it is easy to deduce correct intonation from the words and punctuation. Intonation is much

---

[3]The *schwa,* often represented as an upside-down "e" in dictionary pronunciation guides, is approximately the unstressed initial vowel in "abut" and is the "generic" vowel in English.

[4]"Wh-"questions begin with "Who," "What," "Where," "When," etc. They are in contrast to the questions that expect a yes-or-no answer.

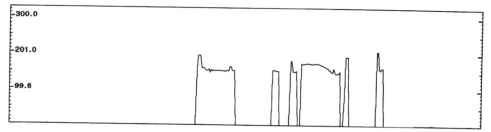

**Figure 5.5.** Pitch track of *"She went to Paris."*

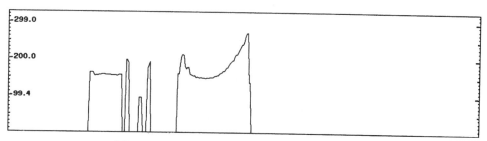

**Figure 5.6.** Pitch track of *"She went to Paris?"*

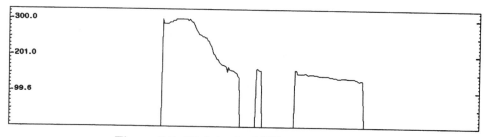

**Figure 5.7.** Pitch track of *"Who went to Paris?"*

harder to predict for longer sentences that are syntactically more complex; each phrase contributes its own intonation. Questions may be embedded in statements, and we cannot determine from orthography alone whether *"She went to Paris?"* is asking about the traveler (Who went to Paris?), the destination (Paris or Rome?), or verb tense (Has she gone there already?). In short, intonation is difficult.

### Consequences for Synthesis

The factors just considered, namely lexical stress, coarticulation, and intonation reveal the limitations of the simplistic model of text-to-phoneme interpretation described earlier. To determine lexical stress, one must examine the underlying morphological composition of the word. The realization of particular phonemes may change during the composition; for example, consider the "s" in "use" and "useful" as contrasted with "usability," in which the fricative is voiced. Further, identification of the stressed syllable is a prerequisite to application of coarticulation rules as unstressed syllables are more amenable to change.

Text-to-phoneme rules and lexical lookup generate a string of phonemes. Coarticulation may then substitute or remove phonemes or may call for allophonic variations; this suggests that allophones are a better intermediate representation than phonemes. Stress must then be realized as pitch and duration applied to these phonemes. Finally, sentence-level intonation adds an overall pitch contour above and beyond the syllable stress. To convey all this information, the string of phonemes or allophones must be marked with pitch and duration information.[5] Figure 5.8 summarizes the interaction of the components of more complete text-to-phoneme generation.

## FROM PHONEMES TO SOUND

After text has been converted to a string of phonemes accompanied by prosodic information, the phonemes must be realized acoustically. Two approaches are used to generate the appropriate sounds to produce speech. The first method controls a digital vocal tract model by modifying internal parameters over time, while the second method pieces together small segments of digitized speech.

### Parametric Synthesis

**Parametric synthesis,** which is also called **terminal analog** or **formant** synthesis, generates speech by varying the parameters that control a software vocal tract model; changing these parameters over time generates speech-like sounds. Vocal tract models for phoneme synthesis are similar to those outlined in the dis-

---

[5]This process is consistent with the discussion in Chapter 1 about how prosody does not fit cleanly into the layered model of speech communication.

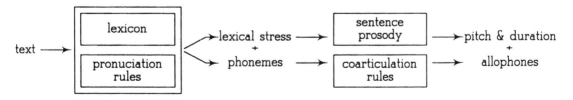

**Figure 5.8.** A refined diagram of text-to-phoneme reduction with output marked for pitch and duration.

cussion of Linear Predictive Coding in Chapter 3. This model includes a source and a number of filters to implement the transfer function (resonances) of the vocal tract. The source may be voiced (periodic) or unvoiced (noise); if voiced, the pitch (period) must be specified. This signal is then modified by a number of filters that produce the formants in the speech signal. Although the details of such a model are beyond the scope of this book (see the general references, especially [Klatt 1980, Klatt 1987a]), Figure 5.9 shows a partial list of the parameters used to control one of the early experimental synthesizers.

The vocal tract model produces a steady sound for a particular set of control parameters. It produces this sound by taking an input (a periodic or aperiodic pulse train) and filtering it to produce an output value; the parameters control the source and filtering functions. A new output value is produced 8000 or 10,000 times per second. The vocal tract model alone is not enough; its control parameters must be changed over time to mimic speech. The phoneme-to-sound portion of the synthesizer must model the dynamic character of phonemes by updating the parameters frequently (every 5 milliseconds is typical). The phoneme realization model takes account of how the vocal tract is configured to produce the spectra typical of the various speech sounds.

In many commercial synthesizers, the text-to-phoneme rules run in a general purpose microprocessor, and the vocal tract model runs as a continuous process on a digital signal processor. The control parameters are passed across a hardware interface between these two components. Considering the relatively small bandwidth of the control parameters, this is an effective task distribution in the hardware. However, general purpose processors have now achieved speeds where it is practical to implement the entire speech synthesis process on a workstation

```
Amplitude of voicing (dB)
Amplitude of frication (dB)
Amplitude of aspiration (dB)
Fundamental frequency of voicing (Hz)
First formant frequency (Hz)
First formant bandwidth (Hz)
First formant amplitude (dB)
Nasal zero frequency (Hz)
Nasal zero amplitude (Hz)
Nasal pole frequency (Hz)
Nasal pole amplitude (Hz)
Nasal formant amplitude (Hz)
Glottal resonator frequency (Hz)
Glottal resonator bandwidth (Hz)
```

**Figure 5.9.** Some of the control parameters for the synthesizer described in Klatt [1980]. These parameters control filters in the vocal tract model, e.g., the center frequencies and bandwidth of the various formants.

without any additional signal processor. This will lead soon to a new generation of all-software speech synthesis products.

## Concatenative Synthesis

Consonants are generally more difficult to synthesize than vowels because of their short duration and dynamic behavior. Therefore, it should come as no surprise that the intelligibility of synthesized consonants, especially consonant clusters ("str," "sp," "bl," etc.), is lower than that of vowels [Spiegel 1988]. This problem has spurred an alternate form of phoneme realization called **concatenative synthesis** because it is accomplished by putting together short segments of recorded speech.

A concatenative synthesizer speaks by "gluing" together small units of digitized speech. What segments of speech should be used as the basic units? As stated at the beginning of this chapter, storage of each word in the language is impractical simply because there are too many of them. The next smallest unit is the syllable, but this too is impractical as there are over 10,000 syllables in English.

At the opposite extreme lies the phoneme. Any language uses a limited set of phonemes so storage would be minimal. But there are several problems with the use of phonemes as the base unit of concatenation. First, some of the voiceless consonants cannot be spoken independent of the associated vowel, rendering pure phoneme concatenation impossible. Second, it is exactly the dynamic nature of phonemes that motivates concatenative synthesis.

Since the dynamic and coarticulatory aspects of phonemes are most prevalent at their boundaries, this suggests a compromise consisting of a unit going from midway in one phoneme to midway into the next. This unit is called a **diphone** [Peterson *et al.* 1958]. Related units of speech for synthesis are the **dyad,** or vowel-consonant-vowel segments [Sivertsen 1961], and the **demi-syllable** [Fujimura and Lovins 1978], which is as the name implies half a syllable. Since there are about 40 phonemes in English, there are 1600 possible diphones as a diphone is simply a pair of phonemes. But not all these possible diphones exist in the language; for example, "sl" does occur in English, but "sr" does not. In practice, some extra diphones must be included to allow for allophonic variations and perhaps for differences between stressed and unstressed syllables.

In whatever form these units are encoded, it is important that their boundaries match closely. For example, if "bad" is to be synthesized by concatenating "ba" and "ad," the formants in the vowel portions of each must match or the discontinuity will be audible. Furthermore, it is necessary to be able to modify the pitch and duration of the stored diphones in order to support stress and prosody. LPC speech has often been used for concatenative synthesis because its pitch can be changed by modifying a single coder parameter, and segments can be lengthened by adding frames. Several successful diphone synthesizers have been built, perhaps the most notable (for English) by AT&T Bell Laboratories [Olive 1977]. At Bellcore (Bell Communications Research), Orator is a demi-syllable synthesizer that has been optimized to pronounce names [Spiegel et al. 1991, Spiegel and Macchi 1990].

## QUALITY OF SYNTHETIC SPEECH

From the application developer's point of view, recorded and synthesized speech are very different because the latter allows an application to speak arbitrary text instead of a few prerecorded responses. However, from the end user's perspective, the two are functionally similar and share many problems relevant to user interface design; they will be treated jointly in the next chapter. In the user's experience there is one difference, however, that is difficult to disguise—intelligibility. Although some studies have compared synthesized speech favorably with very low bit-rate digital speech, few users are likely to encounter such degraded recorded speech except perhaps in children's toys. Although intelligibility is always a potential issue with speech output, it is especially pernicious with synthesized speech.

There are a number of possible sources of mispronunciation. The text-to-phoneme rules may be inadequate, or the morphological decomposition may break down resulting in an incorrect phoneme string. Lexical stress may be incorrectly assigned to confuse the noun and verb forms of a word or adjective and verb forms (e.g., "elaborate" and "live"). Coarticulation may be omitted or applied incorrectly, or prosody may be inappropriate. Incorrect intonation or duration rules can result in poorer listener comprehension than no prosody at all (monotone) [McPeters and Tharp 1984].

Even if the phoneme string is correct and marked with accurate pitch and duration, the phoneme-to-sound rules may not produce correct output. The consonant clusters are especially difficult to synthesize because of their dynamic aspects. Nasal consonants also pose problems because of the inability of simple vocal tract models to mimic the effect of the nasal cavity's absorption of some frequencies.[6]

Synthetic speech is sometimes likened to noisy recorded speech in terms of intelligibility. But as Nusbaum *et al.* discovered, the listeners make different mistakes when listening to synthetic speech [Nusbaum *et al.* 1984]. Different sets of phonemes are confused for synthetic or noisy human speech. Pisoni attributes the difference to the paucity of distinguishing cues in synthesized phonemes versus the rich set of cues in human speech [Pisoni *et al.* 1985].

Proper names are particularly difficult for text-to-phoneme analysis; this is due in large part to the broad ethnic diversity of names in English (at least in North America). Yet names are one of the more likely types of data found in text databases. Storing names in a lexicon is difficult simply because there are so many of them. Although a small number of common names covers a significant portion of the population, there are a tremendous number of names remaining; Spiegel [Spiegel 1985] estimates that although the top 5% of the names covers

---

[6]An all-pole model cannot cope with the zeros present when the nasal cavity is connected to the vocal tract.

90% of the population, there is probably a total of 1.5 million names in the United States. In addition, the names popular in one region of the country may be uncommon in another; German names are common in Milwaukee, Chinese and Hispanic names in Los Angeles, and Irish names in Boston.

How can rules be used to pronounce surnames? English pronunciation rules fail for many other languages, resulting in incorrect pronunciation of names derived from those languages. A better strategy is to identify the ethnic origin of a name based on spelling and then apply rules specific to that language. Even this may not be adequate as many foreign names have been Anglicized, and there are often several variants of the Anglicized form. Perhaps a suitable performance criterion is whether the synthesizer chooses a pronunciation of the name that may be plausible if spoken by a person. Vitale details a name pronouncing algorithm similar to that described here in [Vitale 1991].

### Measuring Intelligibility

How can intelligibility be measured? There are a variety of methods, none of which reveals the entire picture (a good description plus some experimental results for all methods discussed here is found in [Pisoni *et al.* 1985]). A common test is the Modified Rhyme Test (MRT) [Fairbanks 1958], in which the listener is presented with a synthesized monosyllabic word (Consonant-Vowel-Consonant), and a set of six alternatives from which to choose the word that was spoken. Half of the stimuli vary the initial consonant (e.g., "hit," "wit," "mitt"), and the other half vary the final consonant. Thus, the MRT provides insight into the intelligibility of individual phonemes. With an "open form" of the same test, subjects are *not* given a list of choices, but instead simply indicate which word they heard. Not surprisingly, scores on the open response form are significantly lower than for the closed form. It should be noted, as pointed out by Spiegel [Spiegel 1988], that the MRT does not test intelligibility of consonant clusters, which we would expect would be particularly difficult to synthesize. More recent synthesizers score higher on the MRT than the older and less-developed ones, yet still do not approach natural speech.

However, we rarely listen to single words spoken in isolation; words are parts of a sentence or dialog, and we can often guess the next word even before it is spoken. By comparing listener transcription accuracy for semantically meaningful sentences (the Harvard psychoacoustic sentences [Egan 1948]) and nonsense sentences (e.g., the Haskins syntactic sentences [Nye and Gaitenby 1974]), we can see the contribution of meaning to intelligibility. As would be expected, semantically meaningful sentences are more intelligible than meaningless ones, but the difference is much greater for synthetic speech than for human speech [Pisoni *et al.* 1985]. This suggests that the semantic constraints on word possibilities play a stronger role in decoding the less intelligible synthetic speech.

The tests just mentioned measure the intelligibility of isolated words or single sentences based on the correctness and speed of a listener's response. For many applications, a synthesizer does not speak in isolation, but rather in the context of a dialog or while reciting a longer passage of text. Listening comprehension tests have been used to quantify performance in such circumstances. Passages are either read by a human or synthesized, and subjects answer standard reading comprehension questions. Such tests have indicated that comprehension scores for synthesized passages may be as high or higher than for natural speech [Pisoni and Hunnicutt 1980], which suggests that general linguistic knowledge is a significant factor in comprehension.

## Listener Satisfaction

Intelligibility metrics do not tell the whole story; other indications of listener satisfaction are more subjective and generally negative. Even if intelligible, synthetic speech is generally less pleasant to hear. This implies that it should be used sparingly, and in applications for which it will provide some clearly recognized added value to the user. Speech synthesis is still reserved for limited situations in which its poor sound quality is offset by the specific advantage of speaking from text.

It is important to note the difference between intelligibility and naturalness. Naturalness may be a particularly elusive goal, and, reassuringly, its achievement may not be required for many computer interaction tasks. On the other hand, unnatural speech may be tiring or boring to pay attention to. Poor prosody interferes with word intelligibility and, equally important, makes it difficult to attend to sentence breaks and the introduction of new material in a conversation. These are certainly important aspects of naturalness that impact listener satisfaction.

## Performance Factors

Intelligibility and listener satisfaction cannot be summarized in single numbers. Although perhaps useful for comparison, ranking of synthesizers by intelligibility does not tell the entire story. Additional factors may contribute to the judgment on the viability of speech synthesis for a particular application.

One issue in user performance is the increased **cognitive load** associated with listening to synthetic speech. Because it is more difficult to decode the phonemes in synthetic speech, more demand is placed on the listener's short-term memory. If listening to synthetic speech takes short-term memory, this may interfere with whatever else the listener may be doing, such as keeping track of position in a menu hierarchy or remembering the information being spoken. In a series of experiments requiring subjects to memorize a string of numbers while listening to synthetic and then natural speech, Luce, Feustel, and Pisoni [Luce, Feustel and Pisoni 1983] found that subjects were able to recall the natural speech significantly better than the synthetic.

Another, possibly related, issue is **response time.** Because more processing is required to understand synthetic speech it takes longer. Measurements of subjects' response times in a task in which they were required to identify which word had been spoken showed significantly increased time for synthetic speech [Pisoni

1981]. This can also be detected using a method known as "gating," in which subjects are presented with short initial pieces of a previously recorded word (either natural or synthetic) and asked to identify it. A longer portion of a word is required for correct identification of synthetic versus natural speech.

On the positive side, there is strong evidence that understanding synthetic speech is a skill which can be learned and retained once learned. One experiment [Schwab *et al.* 1985] demonstrated that comprehension soared after a half-hour of daily exposure to synthesized speech over a 10 day period; this skill was retained 6 months later. If prospective users have sufficient reason to begin using synthetic speech, they quickly become proficient at its use.

## APPLICATIONS OF SYNTHETIC SPEECH

For the reasons discussed in the previous section, synthetic speech is inferior to digitized natural speech as a computer output medium. Even when explicitly "mechanical" speech is desired,[7] digitized speech passed through various signal processing algorithms may be preferred to synthetic speech. For what purposes, then, is synthetic speech useful?

An obvious application is a reading machine for the blind. This concept started much of the original speech synthesis work in the 1970s and was the focus of several early commercial ventures. Such a reading machine relies on optical character recognition for input and synthetic speech for output. Even without a scanner, synthetic speech can be used by the blind and visually impaired to provide computer access. With their experience and increased dependence on the auditory senses, blind users learn to use synthesizers set at a very rapid speaking rate. Blind programmers are capable of writing and maintaining large programs with such an interface. Despite its importance and tremendous potential for the individuals involved, aid for the disabled is a rather small application niche.

Synthetic speech is valuable for prototyping an application using speech output, even though the final product will employ recorded speech. During interactive design, phrasings are liable to change significantly as the designer experiments not only with selecting the most appropriate words but also with how the system should articulate these words. Prototyping these systems with synthetic speech may save much time in the long run, as the speech output can be changed in the program source code with a text editor instead of recording a whole new set of prompts. Recording speech can be a difficult and time-consum-

---

[7]At the Atlanta airport, an automatic subway system moves passengers between terminals. When someone holds the door open, a voice announces that the train will depart the station when the doors are released. A monotone recorded voice was chosen for this recording to emphasize that no conductor was on board the train to intervene. The desired effect is that the passengers already on board the train glower at the offender and this intimidation generally frees the doors. From personal observation, the theory seems to be effective.

ing task typically requiring multiple attempts before resulting in a recording of agreeable quality.

For larger scale uses of synthetic speech, the indicators of a suitable application should be the size and complexity of the output vocabulary. The first class of appropriate applications for synthetic speech are those where the system has a relatively small repertoire of phrases it can say, but the words that make up these phrases come from a very large vocabulary. An example is an automated system to report an address for a given telephone number; the street name database could be huge. Automatic telephone directory assistance is a related problem due to the size of the name database and its diversity from city to city.

For applications such as these, the primary reason to choose synthetic over recorded speech is the logistics of building and maintaining the required database of voice recordings. Because the set of possible computer utterances is small, a number of whole phrases could be recorded with a few appropriate words substituted such as "The address is" "fifteen" "martin road." But it would be tedious to build the database, and both street and surname databases change over time. By the time the new recording is needed, the person who originally spoke the recordings may no longer be available, and switching voices in the middle of a sentence sounds confusing. With synthesized speech there is no need to record new words in the database, although a phonetic-exception dictionary may be required for those that are not pronounced correctly.

A second class of applications are those which generate natural language to describe some data in response to a query. Examples might include an electronic training manual describing how to diagnose and repair heavy machinery or a context-sensitive computer help system [Nakatani *et al.* 1986]. Such applications might be capable of generating a wide variety of utterances, and it would be difficult to exhaustively list and record them all. Synthesis of such material is sometimes referred to as **synthesis-from-concept** [Witten and Madams 1977].

The two types of applications just described are likely to be very different in terms of underlying software sophistication. The first is typified by simple queries into a very large database. The second type exhibits a much broader range of conversational ability arising in situations where the system is trying to convey in English some derived reasoning about the database. It is ironic that a sophisticated language-generation program may have a well-developed notion of syntax and the salience of particular words. This would be invaluable for synthesis of proper intonation but is lost when the utterance is reduced to a character string to be synthesized.

Finally, a third major area for use of synthesized speech is recitation of human-authored text. Since the text is created by a human, it is hardly predictable and cannot be limited to a small number of prerecorded words or phrases. One use of synthesis in this context is proofreading; it may be easier to hear errors than to see them especially for the author of a document. More widespread applications will come from telephone-based access to electronic mail or such common databases as a calendar or personal address book. Recently consumer products have appeared that use synthesis to speak traffic alerts, which are broadcast as text over pager frequencies.

## SUMMARY

This chapter has served as an introduction to the technically difficult subject of synthesis of speech from text. The difficulty is due to the broad scope of the problem, ranging from linguistic analysis (parsing to find syntactic structure and prosody) to digital signal processing (vocal tract models and control parameters). It should be clear to the reader that speech synthesis is far from trivial and many factors influence the effectiveness of synthetic speech for the listener. There is much left to be learned about the fundamentals of speech production and the acoustic characteristics of natural speech. Speech synthesis will continue to improve, although progress may be slow and take place across a number of research areas.

There are some applications for which speech synthesis is superior to recorded speech, or where the latter simply is not adequate. Because of the steep learning curve encountered with synthetic speech, the prospective user must be enticed into initial use. The initial negative reaction to the speech quality can be overcome by an appropriate application with a well-designed user interface. The next chapter discusses in detail some guidelines for the development of such applications and offer examples of working systems as a means of exploring these issues.

## FURTHER READING

Much of the pioneering work in speech synthesis in the United States was done by Dennis Klatt and Jonathan Allen at MIT's Research Laboratory in Electronics. In Allen *et al.* they describe along with coauthors the algorithms of MITalk, one of the early complete synthesis schemes. Klatt provides an excellent although slightly dated survey of international speech synthesis research in Klatt [1987b]. A section of Furui and Sondhi 1992 is devoted to speech synthesis with an especially strong overview by Allen. Witten [1982] provides a valuable perspective on speech synthesis in Witten, which is also a bit dated.

# 6

# Interactive Voice Response

This chapter is about building *interactive* computer systems that use speech, either recorded or synthesized, as their sole form of output. The focus will be on the advantages and liabilities of speech as an output medium and on interaction techniques for applications to employ speech output most effectively. It is essential to understand the limitations of voice output, both when deciding whether speech output is appropriate to an application as well as when designing details of the interface.

Chapter 3 discussed techniques for digitally encoding and compressing stored voice, and Chapter 5 described the process of converting text to speech. This chapter considers attributes of both digitized and synthesized speech as components of interactive systems. Although most of the growing number of commercial voice response systems employ recorded speech, this chapter also includes applications of synthesized speech, which are emphasized in the case studies.

Chapter 4 discussed the role of stored voice as a data type, primarily in the context of its role as a component of an electronic document. For most of the examples in that chapter, a visual user interface was employed because most documents contain visual material. In this chapter we consider applications with no visual interface by focusing on telephone-based interactive voice response systems. Such systems are interactive because the caller employs touch tones, or occasionally speech recognition, to make selections, and the application responds appropriately using speech output.

For the purposes of this chapter it is assumed that user input is accomplished with touch tones as the basics of speech recognition are not discussed until Chapter 7. Touch tones provide an abstract user input, that has no innate meaning except in the context of an application. In contrast to speech recognition, touch tones are unlikely to be detected incorrectly by application hardware; this allows some simplification in discussions of user interaction techniques. This chapter ignores the technical details of the operation of telephones and transmission of touch tones except as they impact interaction techniques; details of the operation of telephones and telephone networks is included in Chapter 10.

This chapter also contrasts the assets and liabilities of speech as an output medium. After this, the focus shifts to details of interaction techniques for voice output and then to issues in menu selection or data entry for telephone-based voice systems. The final section offers three case studies as sample applications illustrating the techniques described in this chapter.

## LIMITATIONS OF SPEECH OUTPUT

Chapter 3 raised the issue of intelligibility of recorded speech, mostly as an issue of speech coder design or selection. In the discussion of speech synthesis in Chapter 5, intelligibility was again highlighted as a major item of concern. Because synthetic speech is generally of poorer quality than encoded human speech, sources of pronunciation error and effects of listener learning are important when using speech synthesis.

Although intelligibility is certainly one factor in determining the appropriateness of using voice output in a particular environment, there are a number of other issues that also need to be considered in designing a user interface that uses any form of speech output. Speech is both slow and serial as well as "bulky," requiring listener attention to scan the contents of recorded voice files. Speech broadcasts within an acoustic environment, which raises issues of personal privacy and possibly disturbs one's neighbors. These characteristics are not limited to synthetic speech although they may be exacerbated by its decreased intelligibility and the suspected increase in cognitive load on the listener. These issues, as much as intelligibility, place constraints on whatever interaction techniques might be employed by an application.

### Speed

Speech is slow; listening is much slower than reading. Typical speaking rates are in the range of 175 to 225 words per minute. People can easily read 350 to 500 words per minute. A 9600 baud computer terminal can receive nearly 10,000 words per minute, while a 1200 baud modem (nearly obsolete in current communications technology) transmits more than 1000 words per minute. Both recorded and synthesized speech can be sped up, but time-scaling to more than 1.5 to 2.0 times the original speed reaches an upper limit and requires considerable attention by the listener. Reading rates can be increased with practice as well.

As a consequence of its slow speed, using voice to access information can become quite tedious. A few paragraphs of text may take a minute or more to speak. The information to be spoken, either by synthesis or digital playback, needs to be concise and direct. One of the banes of voice mail systems are loquacious users who leave long, rambling messages. Because of speed considerations some text-based interactive computer activities such as browsing through network news may be unsuitable for speech output.

In comparing the speed of speech to conventional screen and keyboard interaction, it is important to note that the speed difference is not symmetrical with respect to input and output. Although listening is slower than reading, speaking is faster than writing or typing in many situations. For example, the author of a recorded voice message has a speed advantage over the listener; this may likely influence the circumstances under which voice may be chosen over text if both media are available.

## Temporal Nature

Speech is an acoustic phenomenon consisting of variations in air pressure over time. By definition, once spoken the speech is gone. If the listener was inattentive or absent when a message was spoken the information is lost. This is the antithesis of graphical user interfaces with dialog boxes that persist until the user clicks on a mouse button. The temporal nature of speech requires a means of focusing the listener's attention to attend to sporadic auditory events; many international airports play a distinctive chime before speaking a boarding announcement over the public address system.

## Serial Nature

A stream of voice conveys only one word at a time;[1] we must wait for the first word to be spoken before we can hear the second. If a menu is displayed on a terminal, all the items appear very quickly and the user then visually scans them until a choice is made. With speech each item must be recited in turn; once spoken it is gone unless the user remembers it. If the user misses a portion of the message, it must be repeated in its entirety. Because this serial nature of speech places additional memory requirements on the user, menu items and other application responses must be short and precise.

A consequence of the temporal nature of speech and the serial presentation of menu items is the interaction between presentation sequence and the timing of user input. As shown in Figure 6.1, it may be difficult to detect which choice a user responds to if expected to make a selection immediately after hearing the desired choice.

## Bulkiness

The storage space required for recorded voice was of much greater concern five or ten years ago than today. As the costs of computer memory and magnetic disks

---

[1]This is not quite true. Speech is not just a string of disjoint phonemes; there is a certain amount of parallel transmission of phonemes in that the allophonic and acoustic realization of a phoneme is influenced by its neighbors.

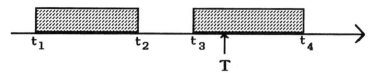

**Figure 6.1.** Difficulties synchronizing user input with speech output. Two utterances are spoken spanning $t_1$ to $t_2$ and $t_3$ to $t_4$. At time $T$ the user responds. Is this response a delayed reaction to the first utterance or a very quick response to interrupt the second?

have dropped, storage has become a less important issue. However, managing stored voice and providing the user with sufficient access to it remains a difficult problem for other reasons.

If we wish to hear information recorded in a sound file, how can we determine which file to play, or what part of the file to play if it is many seconds or minutes long? Retrieval can be facilitated if a text-based description accompanies the sound; this can be stored as "header" information in the sound file itself. Situational cues, such as when the recording was made, the identity of the speaker, and which computer application created the recording may also help limit the number of files that must be searched. But such information is of marginal additional value and in no way approaches the power of keyword searching among text files.

Finding a small number of words in a large quantity of speech is known as keyword spotting; unfortunately, this is one of the most difficult forms of speech recognition and currently not widely available. Instead, a person must listen to the recorded speech to find a particular piece of information. Listening requires *attention*. Although the user can perform other tasks while executing a long text-based keyword search, this is not possible while listening.[2] Although both synthesized and digitized speech may be sped up during presentation, this demands still more attention from the listener.

**Privacy**

Voice announcements, messages, or warnings are much more public than visual notification. A message displayed in a small font on a computer screen may be visible only to the typist or someone sitting nearby, but voice messages may be heard across a room. In addition, if a visitor to an office tries to read the screen, this is apparent to others by their gaze; eyes are more directional than ears. Excessive use of voice output can lead to a distracting and tiring work environment, and sensitive messages should never be voiced without a guarantee of privacy. But this characteristic of speech can also be advantageous in some classes of applications; speech is useful in public address systems precisely because

---

[2]We *can* perform other visual or manual tasks while listening but still must devote significant attention to the auditory channel.

everyone can hear the announcements regardless of the focus of their visual attention. Voice can be similarly used to alert the computer user in an office when the user requires mobility or is not paying attention to the screen.

## ADVANTAGES OF VOICE

Given these significant liabilities of voice, what advantages could possibly justify its use? Chapter 4 suggested several roles of voice in conjunction with text in the context of document-oriented applications. Voice is richer than text and more expressive of information that may be tentative or subject to multiple interpretations. Voice is useful for annotation because it acts as an added dimension for placing comments on an otherwise two-dimensional view of a document page. The rest of this section describes assets of voice beyond document-oriented uses.

For many styles of application discussed in this chapter, the main advantage of speech is its **accessibility** via telephone-based interfaces. Telephone-based applications can be used from nearly any telephone. Most public telephones in the U.S. and Canada are equipped with touch tone keypads, but this is not true in some other parts of the world, notably some European countries. When touch tones are not available, speech recognition must be employed; unfortunately, speech recognition over the telephone is much more error prone than touch tone decoding.

The accessibility advantage of voice also applies to the authoring or creation of information. The ability to capture speech as a recording for subsequent playback allows data to be entered into a system when no other means of input is available, such as recording notes on a pocket tape recorder, dictation, or leaving messages to oneself on one's answering machine. Telephones allow callers to record information at a distance; for example, Resnick describes a community bulletin board enabling callers to browse as well as enter events in a public events database by recording them [Resnick 1992a]. Voice mail allows subscribers to record messages, and Chapter 12 describes telephone access to desktop computer applications that allow a user to record voice entries in a personal calendar. Telephone-based recording also can be used for functions such as order entry by filling out an audio "form" for later transcription.

Although the previous section describes the **broadcast nature** of speech as a liability, in other circumstances it is an asset. The ability to reach a number of listeners simultaneously over a broad area, such as airport flight departure announcements, simply could not be provided by visual displays.[3] Because our ears are much less directional than our eyes, auditory cues can be delivered with more confidence that the intended audience will be more able to be attentive at the moment of presentation. Voice output is effective when the user is mobile or

---

[3]It should be noted that displays clearly are of value. Imagine having to locate your departure gate by listening to a continuous recitation of all flights departing within the next hour!

less likely to be focusing on a display. The user may be staring out the window, reading a book, or walking around the office and not notice a new message on the computer screen.

Voice can also be useful even when the intended recipient is in a more restrained physical environment such as sitting in an office using a workstation or in an airplane cockpit, because it provides an alternate channel of interaction when the user's **hands and eyes are busy** elsewhere. If appropriate and informative words are spoken such as "System shutdown in ten minutes" or "New mail from Kaya," then users would not need to shift their gaze to the screen.[4]

Spoken messages offer a performance improvement in addition to providing the ability to audibly distinguish the message content. Experimental evidence (see [Allport *et al.* 1972, Wickens 1981, Treisman and Davies 1973]) indicates that if a user is performing multiple tasks, performance improves if those tasks can be managed over independent input/output channels, or modalities. For example, although we cannot listen to two conversations simultaneously, subjects were able to sight read piano music while repeating what they heard with no decrease in proficiency [Allport *et al.* 1972]. How do such experimental results apply to voice in an office environment? Voice notification to indicate the status of a task to which the user is not paying immediate attention or for which the associated window is not visible could effectively deliver a message with minimal disruption of the visual attention a user is simultaneously applying to other tasks.

Speech synthesis affords systems the capability of **media translation** to turn text documents into voice. Although this seems to be a trivial continuation of the earlier discussion about remote access, it should not be dismissed quite so quickly. Much of the current work in multimedia computing uses different media for distinct purposes to present disjoint, although related, information. For example, a voice narration accompanying the display of a simulation program is meant to comment on the program's graphics rather than act as a substitute output medium. Speech synthesis lets text data be converted into voice for any purpose. Some blind users make remarkable use of it. Voice output is a first step towards employing multimedia technologies to make computers accessible to a variety of users under many different circumstances.

## DESIGN CONSIDERATIONS

An understanding of the limitations of speech as an output channel enables us to design better voice interfaces. Speech can be used effectively for computer output, but care must be taken to avoid allowing the liabilities of the medium to overcome the usefulness of the application. The next two sections of this chapter

---

[4]Displaying the text message *in addition* to speaking it is necessary for several of these applications. If I am out of the office when an important notice arrives, I will miss the speech output but may look at the screen when I return.

outline a number of design considerations and discuss some interactive techniques in this light.

Most of the limitations of voice output described earlier can be summarized by the broader observation that speech takes place *over a period of time.* The amount of time required to listen to a voice recording, the necessity of reciting menu items in sequence, and much of the difficulty associated with the bulky nature of voice are all a direct consequence of the temporal nature of speech.

Speed is thus one of the primary factors distinguishing voice from other interface media; for example, most graphics applications can be written with the assumption that display operations such as drawing lines or text are performed nearly instantaneously. Much of the time the application is idle while the user reads text, picks a menu item, etc.; this is punctuated by sporadic user input and display update. For telephone-based interfaces, the exact opposite is true; presentation accounts for most of the total time the user interacts with the application.

Voice response systems must therefore strive to minimize the amount of time required to retrieve information: they must be brief, selective about content, and interruptible. Applications must plan what to say so as to avoid utterances that are irrelevant by the time they are spoken. A real-time speech output system may have to formulate conflicting goals and choose among them if there is not sufficient time to say everything, which requires estimating how long it will take to speak an utterance. The awareness that speech takes time (and acceptance that time is a commodity of which we never have enough) should permeate the design process for building any speech application. This argues in favor of shortening spoken menus and precludes many applications that may be quite feasible in text such as browsing through a newspaper. Time motivates strategies to filter an application's output requiring careful judgment as to the relevance of a specific system comment. The remainder of this section explores these design considerations in more detail.

### Application Appropriateness

Because speech is so difficult to employ effectively, discretion is essential in determining effective voice applications and in choosing the appropriate speech output device. Poor quality speech, whether synthesized or recorded, quickly becomes annoying unless it serves a clear purpose. For example, speech output has been employed effectively as a warning medium in airplane cockpits. On the contrary, few car drivers appreciate a tinny voice reminding them to close the doors of their automobile. The cockpit is a busier place, and the consequences of an error may be more severe. A more effective use of speech in the car may be traffic information (drivers already tune to commuter traffic reports on their radios) or as part of a navigation system (as described later in this chapter).

In retrospect, another example of a misguided speech interface is the recitation of a customer's purchases at a cash register. As each item is scanned by the bar code reader, its description and price are announced. The original motivation for these systems was a concern over customer skepticism at the accuracy of the bar code readers. However, public acceptance of this technology came rapidly, and as a result the voice output soon was considered annoying, both to the cashier who had to listen to this drivel all day as well as to the customer who perhaps was not interested in having his or her purchases announced to the surrounding patrons. A text version of this information, both on a register display as well as on a detailed receipt, adequately satisfies customer doubts.

Speech offers more opportunities in telephone-based interfaces because it offers a means of remote access to important information. Such systems are the focus of much of the remainder of this chapter. However, for such applications to be useful, access to the information being requested over the phone must be a priority to the user. Under most circumstances, few sighted computer users would choose to hear their electronic mail synthesized when they could read it. But timely access to certain messages may be important enough to recipients to make telephone access to messages a valuable application.

Speech quality interacts with the perceived utility of an application. If both can be used equally effectively, it is rarely the case that synthetic speech is more appropriate to an application than recorded speech. If only a few spoken messages are needed, prerecorded speech generally is adequate, less expensive, and likely to be better understood. For some data, however, synthesis is essential.

## Data Appropriateness

Since speech is slow, only essential data should be spoken. For example, while speaking electronic mail, such information as dates, times, and many other extraneous fields detailing message routing should be discarded. The point is less "Is this data useful or interesting?" than "Is this data *really* necessary?" Removing extraneous information can save the listener a substantial amount of time and increase the likelihood of acceptance of the application. Information that is spoken should be presented in a simple and accommodating form. Computer time stamps often include the date and time in seconds or even milliseconds, but a person likely prefers to hear "this morning at 10:30" or "yesterday evening" instead of "Wednesday October two 1991 at seven twenty-one and twenty-three seconds."

The wording of recorded speech output is also critical. Prompts should be as brief as is practical; excessively friendly or chatty systems wear thin. Some voice mail systems offer their users the option to choose between normal and abbreviated prompts that allow experienced users a more streamlined interaction. Whether a system is oriented towards novice or experienced users should depend on the expected user population. A service such as national weather information may have a broad base of occasional users, but a service to report the availability of a particular computer system may experience frequent use by a small number of individuals who benefit from terse phrasing.

If the data can be spoken as many variations in a sequence of information elements such as the set of 10 digits spoken as components of a telephone number, recorded speech is superior to synthesized voice. An example of such an application is telephone presentation of weather information; a forecast could be composed from small units such as "The weather in . . . Boston . . . is partly cloudy . . . with a temperature of . . . seventy-eight degrees."

Because listener comprehension of synthetic speech improves rapidly with exposure, frequent users of specialized applications may find it acceptable regardless of the data. If the data is human-authored, e.g., electronic mail or entries in one's calendar, synthetic speech is the only practical means of speaking. The data may be difficult to synthesize well, however. Surnames are particularly hard to pronounce correctly as they are derived from many languages. Complete sentences such as those found in electronic mail are more easily comprehended than isolated words or phrases that might be found in a meeting agenda announcement.

For all these reasons, the data must drive presentation strategies. Filtering, terseness, and use of an appropriate form of voice output are all essential.

## Responsiveness

User input should trigger some voice response, either an acknowledgment of the input or actually speaking the information the user just requested. But because speech is slow, explicitly echoing every keystroke is not appropriate. If an application offers frequent feedback, then the user can be confident that input was detected; application silence might cause the user to press a key repeatedly and lead to errors.

If a system employs multiple menus, feedback can be a form of navigational cue by which each menu identifies itself ("top level," "main menu," "configuration menu") before presenting its choices. Such a cue would also be appropriate if the user enters ill-formed input; the system can remind the user what it thinks he or she is supposed to be doing. ("You are entering a telephone number. Please enter the number terminated by a pound sign.") Similar vocal prods can also be made during the invocation of time-outs such as when the user does not make a selection after hearing an entire menu of choices.

## Speech Rate

One method of increasing an application's apparent responsiveness and minimizing message retrieval time is to speed up voice output. Most speech synthesizers support commands to vary speech rate, expressed as words per minute. Informal observations of experienced users accessing electronic mail over the telephone at the Media Lab indicate acceptable comprehension at 300 to 350 words per minute with a synthesizer with a default speech rate of 180 words per minute. Blind computer users can understand significantly faster synthesized speech. Recorded speech can be sped up for playback as well as described in Chapter 3.

Time compression of speech output is most effective for experienced users who are already familiar with the application, especially its menus and interaction structure. The more predictable the output, the faster it can be spoken.

## Interruption

A voice interface should almost always be interruptible. This is a direct consequence of the slow transmission time for a message. A passage may be irrelevant, unintelligible or redundant, and the user should be able to skip over it. If the system can detect input while speaking by allowing "type ahead" control (most commonly controlled by touch tones), an experienced user need not endure a long-winded introduction or menu repetition. This allows a clean compromise between abbreviated instructions for expert users and lengthier tutorials for novices. Unfortunately, users tend to be more hesitant to interrupt than system designers might expect or desire. It may be that users lack confidence in their ability to recollect the proper keystrokes or simply cannot be bothered to learn them, so it is helpful to keep explanations short.

One problem with supporting interruption is that it may be difficult for the system to determine exactly where the interruption is intended; this was alluded to earlier in this chapter. There is a time delay of at least several hundred milliseconds between the transmission of text to the synthesizer and the onset of speech output, and an additional delay while the user makes a decision; this is a challenge when building an interface that presents choices as "When you hear the item in which you are interested, press any key." Even the slightest of delays due to the user's processing of the information may result in an erroneous interpretation as the next prompt begins to play.

Another problem with interruption is that it may not be possible in a telephone-based system utilizing voice recognition for user input. Analog telephones are two-wire systems; the voice from each party is mixed in the circuit. This implies that the speech recognizer hears the system's transmitted speech as well the user's voice, and this prevents reliable recognition because the recognizer is not able to discriminate between speech sources. Touch tone recognition is not as difficult as it is acoustically dissimilar from speech.

A solution to this mixed channel problem is available to allow the user to "talk over" the system's speech output to the speech recognizer. Since we know which signal corresponds to the spoken speech output, we can "look through" the signal by using it as a reference and sampling the telephone line during short silent periods in the system's speech. These silent periods may correspond to some of the longer stop consonants or pauses that occur between phrases. If a significant signal is detected by the computer at these times, it must be the user trying to interrupt; speech output can be stopped so recognition processing can be begun. Such a configuration, shown in Figure 6.2, was built and proved successful in limited testing in the author's laboratory.

## Repetition

A means must be provided for the system to repeat itself. This applies both to reciting menus several times as well as to repeating sentences of human-authored text or computer-generated discourse. Repetition will likely be combined with an interruption strategy if long messages are being recited.

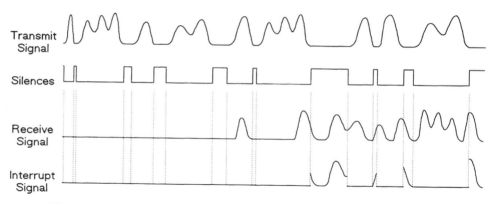

**Figure 6.2.** A configuration to "look through" transmitted speech to detect user interruptions.

How should a repetition be spoken? In the case of a menu, it suffices to repeat the menu items with identical wording as the items are often short and the listener most likely was just having trouble recalling them all. If output consists of recorded speech, the application can only replay the recording, possibly doing so at a slower speed. If the text is a passage of computer-generated discourse, it may be effective to generate an alternate phrasing of the text in the hopes that this would help with any pronunciation errors. However, this is also problematic as the user may be expecting a word-for-word repetition and thus be put off balance. There is little empirical evidence one way or the other.

In the case of synthesizing human-authored text, however, the problem could be either a spelling or typographical error, failure of the synthesizer's text-to-phoneme rules, or lack of user attention. One repetition strategy is to speak the same text again at a slower rate in the hope that this enhances intelligibility. The system to read electronic mail over the telephone, which will be described as a case study, chose to repeat more slowly and then to switch to "spell mode" and pronounce the text letter by letter. Spelling a mail message or almost any other data is tedious. An alternative strategy involved passing the text passage through a spelling checker program and during repetition combining a slower speech rate with letter-by-letter spelling of any words not found in the dictionary. This technique helps catch text-to-phoneme errors as proper names are likely to be pronounced poorly but would not be found in the dictionary. Most typographical errors would also fail the spelling check and thus would be spelled out.

### Exception Pronunciation

Words may be pronounced incorrectly. Ideally, the programmer should be able to add to the morpheme dictionary in the synthesizer, but no synthesizer product currently provides this capability. Some synthesizers allow for alternative pronunciations of a small set of words to be downloaded into the synthesizer, but if the synthesizer only uses this list with simple string substitution, it is not a very powerful capability. For example, if "Schmandt" is in the dictionary, will "Schmandt's" be pronounced correctly?

Because of their limited capacity and literal string translation (instead of direct application access to the morpheme pronunciation tables), synthesizer-based exception dictionaries are not very powerful. Improved functionality can be provided in more capable workstations that might employ speech synthesizers. In fact, many workstations are now able to perform real-time speech synthesis entirely with software.

Instead of using simple exception lexicons, applications can better benefit from domain-specific text-to-phoneme rules. Consider several examples. My phone number, spelled 253-5156, should not be pronounced "two hundred fifty three hyphen five thousand one hundred fifty six." If the string "253-5156" is known to be a telephone number, it can be pronounced properly as three digits, a pause, and four digits. Postal Zip Codes are similarly pronounced digit by digit but street addresses are pronounced as ordinary numbers. My email host, "media-lab.mit.edu," is pronounced "media hyphen lab dot  m  i  t  dot  e  d  u" by those familiar with Unix and Internet addressing.

While it is difficult to employ this knowledge to speak free-form human-authored text, much of the data to be synthesized is highly structured. Electronic mail headers, name and address databases, telephone lists, and appointment calendars each contain much structured data, which can benefit highly from string processing before synthesis. In this way, applications can employ much more intelligible synthetic speech.

## Multiple Voices

Many synthesizers have the ability to use one of several vocal tract models or "voices." Switching voices may be invoked by software that offers a selection between male, female, deep, or raspy speech. The use of several different voices *may* make it easier for the user to discern various separate system functions, such as a command from data or a narrative mode from a multiple-choice mode. Realistically, however, even though a synthesizer may support multiple voices, a primary voice generally emerges as being significantly more intelligible than the auxiliary voices. Rosson studied users' responses to synthetic voices while varying a number of characteristics of the vocal tract model; she discovered that users preferred different speech qualities for different tasks, which she categorized as information providing, entertainment, and feedback [Rosson and Cecala 1986].

Little work has been done to determine how effective such a technique is in practice although frequent users of synthetic speech often modify pronunciation. For example, a telephone pager at the Media Lab uses speech synthesis to announce calls. Each user of the system is able to configure his or her own personal announcement message, and some users have included in their message the necessary escape sequences to change the synthesizer's voice to better differentiate their call announcement from others. Other users achieve a similar effect by modifying the prosody of their message or the duration of some of its syllables.

## USER INPUT WITH TOUCHTONES

This chapter emphasizes telephone-based applications of speech output. These applications use touch tones for user input; when the user presses a button on the telephone keypad, a tone is generated that is decoded into one of 12 symbols at the application end, usually using special but inexpensive hardware. This section discusses a variety of user interaction techniques employing touch tone input.

User input can be divided into two classes: making a selection and entering data. Menus are a selection mechanism, and the response to a yes-or-no question can be thought of as a menu limited to two choices. Data entry may be numeric using the obvious numbers on the telephone keys or may involve the spelling of words by making use of the letters that also appear on most keys. As already noted, telephones outside of North America may not have letters in addition to numbers.

When presenting menus, how should keys be described? Although most references are straightforward, a few are confusing. The "0" key is likely to be called "oh," both because that is how the digit is usually pronounced in phone numbers as well as because it is used to reach the operator. The "#" key is alternately called "pound" (as in weight), "sharp" (from music notation), or "number sign"; in the telecommunications industry it is very rarely referred to as the "octothorpe." The key labeled "*" may be called "star" or "asterisk."

### Menus

Menus may be either **temporal** or, more commonly, **enumerated.** In an enumerated menu each choice is presented accompanied by a number: "Press one to hear your messages, press two to send a message, press star if you are finished." A temporal menu asks the user to press a key when he or she hears the choice desired and pauses between each choice: "Hit any key when you hear the city you want. Somerville . . . Cambridge . . . Boston. . . ." A binary menu (i.e., yes or no) is simply a degenerate case and may be implemented in either way. If a default is to be assumed, then a short form can be used such as "If you want to send a reply, press any key now."

Each style has both advantages and disadvantages. Timing is more critical with the temporal menu style because the application must know when the prompt was spoken and measure a consistent amount of time before presenting the next choice. In the event of a user entering input just at the beginning of the speaking of a choice, it may be unclear as to whether the user's response was an early acceptance in anticipation of the next choice or a delayed response to the previous choice. The enumerated menu also needs a timer to handle circumstances in which the user makes no response to the enumerated list; the usual approach is to repeat the menu after the predetermined time-out period elapses.

An advantage of the enumerated over the temporal menu is that the experienced user need not listen to the entire list but can interrupt its recitation by entering a choice. The temporal menu necessitates waiting until the desired choice is presented.[5] But if the list of choices changes (perhaps it is a list of voice mail users and a new employee joins the organization), then the associated numbering may change and the experienced user who types ahead may make an incorrect selection. The enumerated menu also requires the user to keep track of both the choice and the number associated with the choice; with a temporal menu one can concentrate exclusively on the list items themselves.

An issue with all menus is their size. Human factors folklore suggests that four items is the comfortable number. In a system implementing voice mail for athletes at the 1984 Olympics, Gould *et al.* found four items to be too many based on evaluations of a prototype system [Gould *et al.* 1987]. In a somewhat more contrived test task based on a laboratory experimental setup, Englebeck and Roberts [Englebeck and Roberts 1989] confirmed the proposal of four items, but note that a larger number of items may be more effective for experienced users. In their study, two important factors influenced the choice of an acceptable menu size: interruptions and user confidence. Although users are normally hesitant to interrupt the system, as menu items increase users appear more likely to interrupt when their choice is heard. This interruption generally results in faster selection time, although it could indicate frustration at the long menu. Confidence in the choice about to be made is also key and suggests that the phrasing of menus is very important. When the user hears a choice that is clearly the desired selection, interruption is more likely.

With an enumerated menu another issue is whether it should be presented in the order of action ... key ("Reply press one") or key ... action ("Press one to reply"). According to the Englebeck and Roberts study, users were more likely to interrupt with the action/key presentation. Additionally, this order was preferred in the subjective evaluations of tests using the two options.

## Data Entry

Under some circumstances user input is required and a list of menu choices is impractical simply because there are too many possible selections (such as looking a name up in a company telephone book). In this case, to gather user input the system must speak a prompt, receive the responding keypresses, and detect the termination of the input. User input may be **numeric** or **alphabetic.**

Numeric input has many uses and is relatively easy to explain to the user as we are all quite used to dialing numbers to place calls. As part of an interactive service, a user may be required to enter a credit card number, telephone number, or the digits of an address. Services offering weather reports for locations around the country may ask for the telephone area code for the location. Interactive banking services prompt for an account number or a dollar amount.

Alphabetic input is somewhat more awkward. Fortunately, in North America the telephone keypad has letters inscribed on the keys remaining from the days

---

[5]A temporal menu can eliminate the wait by allowing the user to press a special key to skip to the next item [Resnick and Virzi 1992].

when telephone exchanges were referred to by a name instead of number.[6] This alphabetic labeling tends to get carried over into other public keypad style devices such as automated bank teller machines. But there are two problems with this arrangement: each key maps into three letters (see Figure 6.3), and the letters "Q" and "Z" do not appear on any key of the telephone.

For the two missing letters several options are in use. Both letters may be mapped to the otherwise vacant 1 key; this seems the most common alternative. They are also sometimes mapped to the 0 key. For the implicit key-to-letter decoding, described below, they can be assumed to occupy the keys on which they would appear if they had been left in the alphabet. In this scheme, Q appears invisibly on the 7 (PRS) key and similarly Z appears on the 9 key.

Alphabetic input techniques may decode the three-to-one letter-to-key mapping either explicitly or implicitly. Explicit mapping requires the user to type two keys for each letter; the first key chooses a group of three letters and the second selects one from this set. The second key may be constrained to one of the set 1, 2, or 3 or better could be any key with the column position of the key selecting the first, second, or third letter. For example, the letter H might be selected by entering 4 5; 4 selects the GHI set, and 5 from the middle column selects the middle letter from the triplet.

The implicit letter mapping technique accepts the confusability of the user's input and attempts to decode the input by matching it against the set of valid inputs. For example, while selecting a name from a menu (see Figure 6.4), the user is really picking one of a set of names, each of which may have a distinct touch tone "spelling" uniquely specifying that each letter is not necessary. In fact, in the illustrated example, four of the names would be uniquely specified after the first touch tone. (One might, however, wish to gather all five digits to confirm that the user was not trying to select a name not on the list.)

Explicit spelling requires twice as many keystrokes but is required for some tasks, e.g., if a new subscriber to a service is asked to spell his or her last name to create a new account. In the case of spelling to make a selection from a list, implicit character mapping may be quite adequate, faster, and easier to explain to the user; examples include looking up a last name in an electronic database, spelling a street name, or logging in to a computer account.

A problem with implicit spelling is the degree of overlap between the items being selected and their keypad equivalent. For example, the login names "Leo" and "Ken" are both spelled "536." In such a case, the collision must be detected by the system and an alternate selection mechanism invoked, e.g., "If you mean Leo, press one; if you mean Ken, press two." (Note that this is a menu and could be either enumerated or temporal).

Clearly the degree of overlap between the items is a function of the particular set of items, and therefore the confusability of implicit spelling will vary from

---

[6]Where I grew up in Chicago we were in the **ED**gewater exchange, although this convention is no longer followed.

**Figure 6.3.** The labels on a telephone keypad.

database to database. But even explicit spelling can encounter collisions between choices. Although the login IDs mentioned above may be unique on a particular computer system, for other kinds of databases uniqueness is less likely. There may be many "Smiths" in a large company, and there are quite a few "Cambridge" streets in the Greater Boston area, for example. Whenever this occurs, an alternative selection will have to be provided regardless of the data input method.

Implicit spelling may be very effective. For many databases, confusability due to letter-to-key mapping is less significant than collisions due to duplicated spellings. For example, Davis [Davis 1991] reported on two databases of names of job applicants and students at a university. In one list of approximately 9,000 individuals, 40% of them shared a last name with at least one other individual, but only 8% of all names collided with another name using implicit spelling. A second list of 25,000 individuals exhibited 38% shared names with 21% of the names colliding.

| Choices | Touch tone spelling |
|---------|---------------------|
| Brown | 27696 |
| Davis | 32847 |
| Green | 47336 |
| Jones | 56637 |
| Smith | 76484 |
| South | 76884 |

**Figure 6.4.** A menu of last names and the associated touch tone spelling.

For either numeric or alphabetic input, termination of the input sequence may also be implicit or explicit. If the input is of a fixed length, e.g., the three digits of an area code, no terminator is necessary. If the input is of variable length, input may be terminated by a specific key, the system may detect that the user is finished by a pause, or the system may automatically complete the input as soon as a unique choice is identifiable.

**Implicit termination** requires a timer. The system asks a user for input and gathers digits until the user has paused for a predetermined period of time. The time-out may be longer during the period before the user has entered any digits to provide for thinking time. In the event of a time-out without any input, a help mechanism should be triggered. **Explicit termination** requires the use of a key that cannot be confused with user input. The "#" key is often used for this purpose.

Explicit termination requires more explanation to the user than does implicit termination and also requires that one remembers what to do at the end of input. Explicit termination also requires a timer as it must cope with the user who inputs the requested data but then forgets the terminator. Explicit termination is faster if the user does remember the terminator as the time-out period is not necessary. Explicit termination can also accept multiple, sequential fields of input more easily than implicit termination, such as the house number and street name of an address as the user can type each in sequence indicating segmentation of the items with the terminator key. For example, I could enter "E 1 5 * 3 2 7" as my building and room number without waiting to hear a prompt to enter my room number. To be more general, explicit termination allows type ahead; if the user knows what the system will ask next he or she can start to enter it without waiting for the time-out.

Because the input is of variable length, both input techniques should perform range checking on the input if possible (for example, the number of digits in a valid house number) and warn the user when errors are detected. It may be that the user forgot the delimiter and started to enter the next field.

Hybrid termination schemes are possible. One example is **optional termination;** if the user enters the termination key, then the input is complete; otherwise input is ended by a time-out. This approach allows the experienced user to save time, while not confusing the novice about the use of a terminator. Such a scheme is used for dialing the number for an international telephone call, since there is considerable variation in the length of international telephone numbers. The local telephone switch does not know how many digits to collect before connecting to the destination country and therefore must wait for the caller stop dialing, using a time-out. The caller can terminate the dialed digits with a "#" to indicate the end of input, avoiding the delay caused by the time-out.

Another hybrid approach allows automatic completion of user input when a unique choice is made; this saves keystrokes for the user. In the simplistic database illustrated in Figure 6.4, for example, the first digit will uniquely select one of the first four names but "Smith" and "South" require three digits for a unique choice. With automatic completion the system responds by echoing the selected choice as soon as it can be determined. But the user may be in the process of entering the next digit(s) anyway so the system must quickly determine whether the additional input is a continuation of the spelling or the next step in the user interaction. One technique reported in [Gould *et al.* 1987] is to "absorb" this further input as long as it conforms to the remaining digits in the selected item.

Another shortcut for selecting alphabetic choices by spelling is user-initiated completion. A special key is used to jump from spelling input to a menu style selection. For example, to continue with the name database example, the user could type "3*" and get "Davis," which is unique. But entering "7*" or even "76*" would invoke a menu to select between "Smith" and "South." With user-initiated completion, the user gets to choose between pressing more digits in trade for a shorter menu, but with a large database it may not be intuitive how many names will match a sequence of a few digits.

## CASE STUDIES

This section describes three voice response applications that illustrate application of the design considerations and interaction techniques just mentioned. Three different systems all employing speech synthesis for output are discussed. Both the first and third examples are telephone-based information retrieval systems, one for receiving driving directions and the other for reading electronic mail. The remaining system also gives driving directions but operates in real time in an automobile.

### Direction Assistance

Direction Assistance [Davis and Trobaugh 1987] is a program that gives driving directions over the telephone.[7] It is an example of the usefulness of speech synthesis in situations where recorded speech would be much more difficult to employ for two reasons. First, Direction Assistance generates fairly complicated textual descriptions of an abstracted data structure, i.e., a route traversing links in a street database. Second, the database of street names is large enough that preparing a recording of each would be tedious. The database does accommodate phonetic spellings for those street names that the synthesizer mispronounces.

To use Direction Assistance, a user calls and enters both source and destination addresses with touch tones. The system then determines a route between these two points and translates the route into a textual description to be read by the speech synthesizer. The motivation for a telephone-based interface is to make this service available while driving around a city and, in particular, when one is

---

[7]Direction Assistance was written by Jim Davis and Thomas Trobaugh initially at Thinking Machines, Inc., and later at the MIT Media Lab. Davis also used it as a basis for work in intonation at AT&T Bell Laboratories [Davis and Hirschberg 1988].

lost. At such times, access to a computer terminal is unlikely.[8] Spoken directions can be sufficiently effective; a study by Streeter [Streeter *et al.* 1985] found recorded spoken directions to be more easily followed than either written directions or annotated maps.

Direction Assistance includes a street database covering 45 square miles of the Greater Boston area roughly centered on M.I.T. (see Figure 6.5). This map includes portions of a number of the municipalities surrounding Boston. (In Boston several common street names occur in multiple towns on different streets, which is a source of trouble.) This street database has been augmented with information such as street quality, locations of traffic lights and stop signs, and selected major landmarks. The database also notes some other geographic entries, including the locations of traffic circles, railroad tracks, and bridges.

The software components to satisfy these design goals are quite distinct and operate serially. Figure 6.6 shows these program segments. The first part of a user interaction is with the Location Finder, which has the job of eliciting from the caller his or her present location and desired destination. The Route Finder then consults the database to find a path to the destination; this path consists of a series of street segments found in the database. The Describer generates a textual description of the route describing it in terms of the actions a driver must take to follow the path. This text is then read to the user with appropriate pauses by the Narrator.

### User Input

The Location Finder handles all user input. It describes the use of the touch tone keys on the telephone and explains that the "*" key is always available for help. It then asks the user for his or her location. All of the prompts are interruptible and type ahead is enabled for all except the yes-or-no questions. The input buffer is cleared whenever the system detects an error, and the error message is *not* interruptible; this is so the error message will not be lost due to type ahead.

In some versions of Direction Assistance, the Location Finder had access to a database linking telephone numbers to street addresses; such databases are commercially available. This access would be particularly useful if the caller were lost and calling from a pay phone, since in most states pay phones are required to display the phone number and address. As street signs are often missing in Boston, it is easy to get into a situation where a driver has no idea which street he or she is on. In telephone number gathering mode, the Location Finder waited until seven digits were entered, looked them up, and pinpointed the location of the caller.

More relevant to our discussion of user input is address mode, in which a house number and street name must be entered. The system uses explicit termination

---

[8]A company in the San Francisco area installed direction giving machines in public places such as convenience stores, much like video games. These systems used visual menus for selecting a destination and printed detailed driving directions.

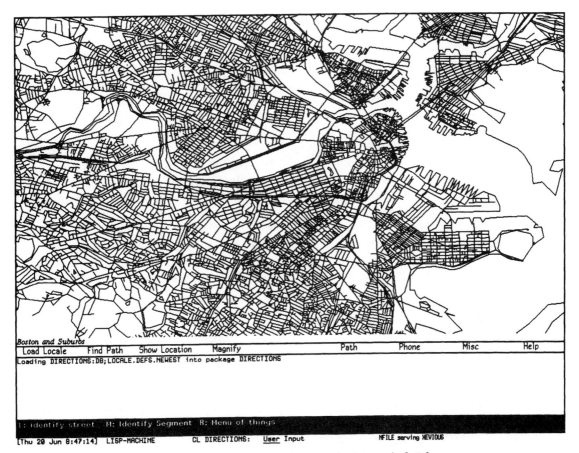

**Figure 6.5.** The streets in Direction Assistance's database.

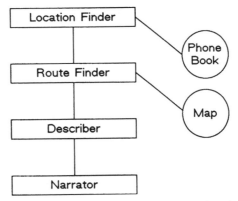

**Figure 6.6.** Major software modules in Direction Assistance.

for both house number and street name and informs the user to use the "#" key after entering the house number. Of course, explicit termination can fail if the user neglects to use the termination key. If the user pauses, waiting for a response, the program indicates that it thinks the caller is still entering an address and notes that a terminator key is required. If the user forgets the terminator and simply continues, next entering the street name, the system may detect this. When the number of digits entered exceeds the highest known house number in the database, the system indicates that this is an unknown address, reminds the caller to terminate address entry with a pound sign, and starts over.

Entering a street name is more challenging due to multiple instances of the same street name in the database. The caller is prompted to spell the name of the street using one telephone key per character. Again explicit termination is requested. In the case of multiple streets having identical touch tone "spellings," Direction Assistance resorts to a temporal menu of the possible choices. However, much more common than spelling confusion is that the same street may be found in multiple municipalities, or the same name can apply to multiple streets even in one municipality (e.g., Hancock Street, Hancock Place, and Hancock Park in Cambridge). In these circumstances, Direction Assistance again resorts to a temporal menu to finish the selection. To help explain the selection process, the system first indicates why it is confused, e.g., "I don't know whether you mean Hancock Street, Place, or Park. Hit any key when you hear the one you want."

### Route Description

Once the origin and destination are known, the Route Finder determines a route. The route consists of a path traversing a number of street segments (each segment being approximately one block long). The route is optimized on the basis of distance, quality of the streets, ease of driving (e.g., a penalty is imposed for left turns), and ease of explanation (a zig-zag route may be shorter but may be more complicated and difficult to follow).

The next step is the most challenging language-generation task of this application. The Describer must take the series of segments from the database and turn it into a coherent description of how to drive to the destination. A list of what to do at each intersection is hardly useful to the driver and interferes with the goal of speaking succinctly. Instead the Describer generates instructions comparable to those a person gives. A passenger assumes the driver takes the "obvious" route (e.g., stays on the main street) until told otherwise. This allows the Describer to compress many sequential segments into a single driving act, e.g., "Stay on Main Street until it merges with Massachusetts Avenue."

The Describer employs a taxonomy of intersection types including such classes as **continue, forced-turn, turn, fork, onto-rotary,** and **exit-rotary.** A software module associated with each is consulted in order at each intersection. The appropriate module chooses to describe the driving act to perform at this intersection. Succinctness is achieved by having the **continue** expert usually choose to say nothing unless a street name changes or a significant landmark is encountered.

The output of the Describer is the text description of a "tour," an example of which follows.

"If your car is parked on the same side of the street as 20 Ames Street, turn around and start driving. Drive all the way to the end and take a left onto Memorial Drive. After about one quarter of a mile, take the easy left and merge onto Main Street. It becomes the Longfellow Bridge. After you cross the bridge you will come to a rotary. Go about three quarters of the way around it, and turn onto Charles Street. Merge with Storrow Drive."

The text of the tour must be recited by a speech synthesizer; this is done by the Narrator. It is the Narrator's responsibility to recite the tour at a rate that allows the user to write down the directions. Unfortunately people write directions at greatly varying rates; some have elaborate shorthand notations and can record the directions quickly, while others write them word-by-word. The Narrator's only recourse is to pause between each part of the route and wait for touch tone input from the user as a flow-control mechanism, but this does not make for a very comfortable interface. More graceful flow control requires spoken feedback from the direction recipient; an attempt at this is described in Chapter 9.

## Back Seat Driver

Back Seat Driver is a subsequent Media Lab project that also employs speech synthesis for direction giving but in the very different context of operating in a car in real time while the user is driving. Although much of the software from Direction Assistance proved useful to this project, Back Seat Driver is different in two respects. First is the motivation to use voice because a driver's eyes are busy watching the road, whereas Direction Assistance focused on remote telephone access. This raises the issue of how to instill user confidence in a system that cannot be seen and speaks only when necessary. Second is the real-time nature of Back Seat Driver; it must know when to speak, how long it will take to say an utterance, and detect when the driver has made a mistake.

Back Seat Driver utilizes a vehicle navigation system to report the automobile's position, speed, and, direction to the route planner.[9] This navigation system uses an inertial guidance system in combination with the constraints provided by the map database (which is stored on CD-ROM) to determine position; for more discussion of the various location determining technologies, see [Davis 1989]. Route planning and discourse generation are done by software running on a computer in the trunk speaking via a speech synthesizer connected to one of the serial ports of the computer (see Figure 6.7).

The initial task of the Back Seat Driver is identical to that of Direction Assistance, namely, to elicit the destination from the driver (the current position of the

---

[9]The vehicle navigation system was built by the project's sponsor, Nippon Electric Company.

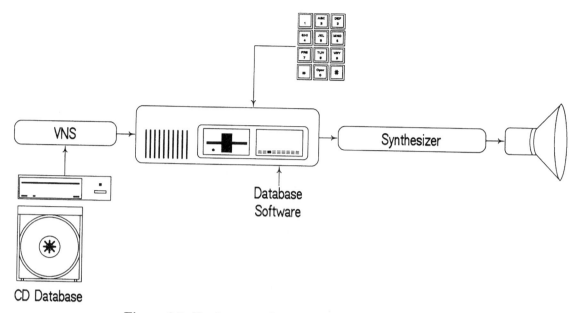

**Figure 6.7.** Hardware configuration of the Back Seat Driver.

car is known to the system) and plan a route. In various implementations, the destination has been entered by means of a telephone keypad (an interface identical to that used by Direction Assistance) or a computer keyboard. Having obtained the destination, Back Seat Driver plans a route, speaks the initial instruction (e.g., "Turn around and start driving"), and waits for the driver to proceed. From this point on, its task is to provide spoken directions, as they are needed, for each segment of the trip.

The goal of Back Seat Driver is to get the user to the destination; this is facilitated by the secondary task of keeping the driver confident that the system is working and correct. These tasks are closely related, both requiring a richer discourse capability than Direction Assistance as well as an improved method of time management.

Getting the user to a destination requires careful phrasing of the directions. A major problem with the use of synthetic speech for this task is that some street names may not be pronounced correctly. Names are also less useful than other cues in Boston due to the lack of proper street labeling. In an early version, Back Seat Driver would say "Take a left at Fulkerson Street"; this was changed to "Take the next left; it's Fulkerson Street." The driving action is described in a simple sentence for ease of intelligibility [Davis and Schmandt 1989]. The street name becomes a secondary cue, and the drive can still follow the directions even if the name is badly mispronounced or the street sign is missing.

Back Seat Driver also offers advice and warnings to make the drive safer and increase the probability of the driver completing the requested turn. For example, it may say "Get into the left-hand lane because you are going to take a left at the next set of lights" or warn when a one-way street becomes two way. To provide adequate warning, each step of the directions is repeated twice: once about 30 seconds before the intersection in question and another just before the decision point.

Precise timing of detailed utterances such as "Take a left at these lights" just as the vehicle approaches the intersection, along with the use of deictic pronouns[10] help instill confidence in the driver. Because there is no display and Back Seat Driver does not speak more often than is necessary, it is easy to doubt that it is actually "alive." Utterances of this type affirm that the system is tracking the vehicle's location correctly and will speak when necessary.

To speak at the right time Back Seat Driver needs to manage time in concert with the real world of a vehicle in motion. Time management is achieved by maintaining a series of goals with an estimated time to speak each goal. The time at which an utterance must commence changes relative to the vehicle's speed, and there may not be adequate time to speak all goals. The goals are prioritized so that the most important are spoken first. A goal that would be interrupted by a higher-priority goal (given an anticipated moment to speak the goal) will instead choose not to start as it would be confusing for the system to interrupt itself as well as waste valuable time. Knowing how long it will take to speak a goal enables advance planning and allows some goals to be merged if there is not enough time for each in isolation [Davis and Schmandt 1990]. For example, just before a short jog in the road, Back Seat Driver might say "Take the left at the end of the road, and then you're going to take the very next right."

Goals are dynamic and can change during the course of the trip because the driver does not always follow the directions correctly. Back Seat Driver must cope with these driver errors. It indicates the mistake ("Oops, I meant for you to take a right . . .") but then adapts to the error by computing a new route after telling the driver (". . . but that's OK, I'll figure out a new way to get there"). The Route Finder can operate incrementally while the vehicle is in motion although the driver is told "Slow down while I think about it." All the utterances were carefully chosen during a long iterative design cycle; it is inappropriate to speak in a manner that encourages the driver to simply slam on the brakes possibly causing an accident.

The primary focus of Back Seat Driver has been to experiment with discourse generation in real time so as to determine the appropriateness of speech output for a computer driving assistant. The project was based on the belief that voice could be employed effectively in a real-time application by implementing a goal-oriented discourse model. Although it was never rigorously tested against a display-based system, many users who test-drove the car found it effective and even reassuring. This was achieved in large part by the careful wording and timing of each utterance to match the car's position and speed.

---

[10]Deictics are pronouns that refer to objects identified by their position relative to the speaker. "This" and "these" refer to nearby objects, "that" and "those" to distant objects.

## Voiced Mail

Most telephone-based systems employing speech output involve a process of explicit user selection followed by a system response often repeated step-by-step while the user performs several operations. These systems spend a substantial portion of their time reciting menus. The menus may be hierarchical requiring the user to traverse several submenus and enter multiple key presses to achieve the desired action. While it is likely that a hierarchical structure may be well suited for the novice or occasional user, the experienced user learns the sequences and, provided the menus are interruptible, never hears much of them; callers are still often annoyed to key-press their way through the thick layering of commands to get to the information being sought.

This section presents as a case study a system that took a rather different view of user interaction. Voiced Mail [Schmandt 1984] was a program developed at M.I.T. to allow telephone access to electronic mail using speech synthesis. Voiced Mail provided a streamlined user interface oriented towards experienced users. It tried to minimize the time and attention required to navigate the user interface by avoiding automatic recitation of menus. Instead, the application followed a default sequence of presenting information about each message, then the message itself. The small number of commands were always active, and the application was always interruptible.

Voiced Mail applied extensive filtering to messages to remove extraneous information, made presentation decisions based on the length of each message, and rearranged message order to simplify presentation. These tasks were performed to minimize the time and attention required to use the application. Voiced Mail also employed a repetition strategy to help cope with the vagaries of synthesizing free-form, human-authored text.

Voiced Mail illustrates some advantages of incorporating multiple speech technologies into a single application. In Voiced Mail's later stages, recorded voice was used for generating replies to text messages as the keypad was inadequate to select between a limited repertoire of precomposed text messages. The synergy from employing multiple channels for computer interaction and supporting multimedia databases is a theme to which we will return in Chapter 12.

### Flow of Control

To access Voiced Mail, a user dialed in and logged onto the system using his or her computer login ID and a password. The application would scan the user's new mail messages and decide how to present them. A default path was then taken through the messages; with no additional user input, the system would read each message in order to the caller. At no point was the user confronted with an explicit "If you want me to do . . . (some action), press a key"; rather, an active presentation was started, which could be interrupted at any time. There were places where the system would pause a moment to encourage possible user input, but if none was detected it would continue reading messages. This was all part of the strategy of avoiding menus.

Instead of using an explicit menu, Voiced Mail used an implicit set of commands that were always active and interruptible. These commands allowed forward or backward movement among messages or senders and invoked a few other functions. Since there were no explicit menus, each digit on the keypad was assigned to one command (the keypad mapping is shown in Figure 6.8.) This was a principled and deliberate choice because ease of use was more important than the number of functions supported by the application.

Voiced Mail sorted messages according to the sender and then presented all messages from the same sender sequentially, beginning with the sender who had sent the most messages.[11] Most mail systems present messages in the order in which they are received, but time-sequential messages bear little relationship to each other. Sequential messages from the same sender are often related; this ordering tried to preserve such context. A more thorough strategy would have been to identify a "thread" of messages with the same subject line (generated automatically by the "reply" command found with most text-based electronic mail systems) but from various senders.

After Voiced Mail determined presentation order, messages would be played one by one. If the message was brief, it was played immediately. If it was long (as measured by number of words), the system would warn "It's a long message, about . . ." and recite the subject line. The system would then pause to invite user input (for example, to skip the long message). In the absence of any input, the message body would be played.

---

[11]It would have been useful to have included an optional user profile that identified important message senders by name and played their messages first. This is an aspect of the filtering approach mentioned later and was implemented in a later email reading program.

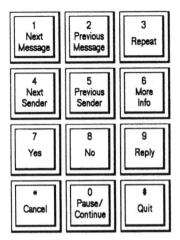

**Figure 6.8.** The command set for Voiced Mail.

This design was based on the observation that it would take more time to ask the user "Do you want to hear this message?" and wait for a response than to just play the message. The subject was not recited for the very short messages, as it was often redundant to the message body. This, however, was a mistake for some messages, e.g., that shown in Figure 6.9. A sample user interaction is shown in Figure 6.10.

### Text Presentation Strategies

Because it avoided menus Voiced Mail spent most of its time actually reading messages. Recitation of a message required some careful filtering and an effective presentation strategy. There is much useless header information in a mail message. There may be punctuation or spacing conventions that should be preserved if possible, e.g., a double space between paragraphs is "spoken" as a short pause. Since there may also be typographic errors or words in the message that the synthesizer mispronounces or the user may need to hear a sentence again, a single linear pass through the message may be insufficient: the presentation must be interactive.

Figure 6.11 shows the full text of an electronic mail message including the rather voluminous header. Many fields, such as the message ID and the chain of hosts through which the message passed during transmission, are pointless to synthesize so they must be removed. Voiced Mail went further and decided that the only fields in the header that were vital were the sender and possibly the subject. A "more info" key offered more information, such as the full name of the sender and when the message was received. The time data was processed to produce text such as "Yesterday morning at 10" instead of "Wednesday 25 August 1993 9:57:32 EDT," which both takes longer to speak and is more difficult to follow.

For the sake of its repetition strategy (see below), Voiced Mail parsed the message into sentences. To aid clarity, a pause was introduced between each sentence; this pause was about twice as long as would ordinarily be produced by the synthesizer. A pause twice as long again was used at each paragraph in the message body as the paragraph structure is also important for understanding the message's content.

```
Message 141:
From derek Thu Mar 15 18:05:25 1990
To: geek
Subject: Metal-Oxide Varistor
Date: Thu, 15 Mar 90 18:05:21 EST


It's here . . . I'll leave it in the sound room on the middle shelf . . .
```

**Figure 6.9.** A mail message for which the subject is required to understand the message.

"Welcome to Voiced Mail. Please log in."

*user presses 4-3-3-5* (sequence for "geek", the user's login).

"Hello Chris Schmandt. You have twelve new messages. <pause>
Four from Walter Bender. <pause>
Message one. This is a very long message; it's about window system
subroutines . . ."

*user presses 1* (next message).

"Message two. It's about the new conference room. <pause>
Can we get together tomorrow afternoon to decide about chairs?"

*user presses 7* (affirmative reply).

"Message sent. Message three. It's about Monday's demo . . ."

*user presses 4* (next sender).

"Two messages from Ben Stoltz. <pause>
Message one. It's about the driver bug . . ."

**Figure 6.10.** A sample Voiced Mail session.

Voiced Mail compromised intelligibility for speed by playing text somewhat faster than the default synthesis rate specified by the synthesizer hardware. At any moment, the user could invoke the **repeat** command. This command would cause the sentence currently being spoken (or which had just been spoken) to be repeated at 75% speed. If **repeat** was invoked again on the sentence, the sentence was spelled letter by letter.

Spell mode is so slow as to be nearly useless, however, and it is also quite difficult to follow. An alternate strategy, developed shortly after Voiced Mail, passes the message body through the local spelling checker dictionary. Those words not found in the dictionary are spelled. This will catch most typos as well as many of the proper nouns that might be particularly challenging to synthesize. For example, the phrase, "Schmandt debugged the sotfware yesterday morning" would be pronounced "S-c-h-m-a-n-d-t debugged the s-o-t-f-w-a-r-e yesterday morning."

### Advantages of Multiple Media

One of the advantages of electronic mail is the ease of posting a reply to the sender of a message. While reading mail, one is usually positioned at a screen and keyboard, which also provide the user interface for typing a reply. A single

```
From dcj@Sun.COM Tue Sept 22 15:53:21 1991
Received: by media-lab (5.57/4.8)   id AA11928; Tue, 22 Sept 91
15:53:15 EDT
Received: from snail.Sun.COM (snail.Corp.Sun.COM) by Sun.COM (4.1/SMI-
4.1)
id AA24516; Tue, 22 Sept 91 12:53:51 PDT
Received: from jacksun.sun.com by snail.Sun.COM (4.1/SMI-4.1)
id AB18658; Tue, 22 Sept 91 12:51:56 PDT
Message-Id: <9109221953.AA06751@jacksun.sun.com>
To: Chris Schmandt <geek@media-lab.media.mit.edu>
Subject: possible bug in fax.c
In-Reply-To: Your message of Tue, 15 Sept 91 12:43:41 -0400.
            <9109151643.AA27528@media-lab>
Date: Tue, 22 Sept 91 12:53:13 PDT
From: dcj@Sun.COM
Status: RO


I received your sound attachment email just fine.
This is a nice addition to Phoneshell!
```

**Figure 6.11.** An electronic mail message including its full header.

keystroke to the mail reader ("R" for "Reply") initiates a reply with the return address generated automatically. Since the Email medium is asynchronous, the sender need not worry whether the recipient is awake to receive the message in whatever time zone the destination lies.

It was important for Voiced Mail to support a reply mechanism as well, so three of the twelve telephone keys were devoted to reply commands. One key would generate a message of the form "I read your message about . . . My answer is yes" and another generated a similar negative reply. A third key prompted the user for a phone number and sent a "please call me at . . ." message. Unfortunately, replies are rarely so unconditional as a simple yes or no. Also, when traveling one's location and hence phone number are often transient, so the reply mechanism was enhanced to include the ability to record a voice message. The party who sent the original message would receive a computer-generated text mail message containing instructions on how to access the reply, which would involve calling the Voiced Mail telephone number and entering a special code at the login prompt. Upon hearing the message, the caller could then leave another voice recording in reply.

Of course, the recipient of the recorded message might be another subscriber to Voiced Mail. In this case, while reading mail from a terminal the recipient would see the same text message as delivered to the non-subscriber, i.e., he or she would have to call in to hear the voice message. If the subscriber were reading mail with Voiced Mail, the text message would never be seen as the system would simply play the recording. Such a unified interface to both voice and text messages was extended and incorporated into the Phone Slave conversational answering machine described in Chapter 11.

An important advantage of merging voice and text messages is the elimination of the need to consult multiple devices (telephone for voice mail, computer terminal for text mail) to find out whether any new messages have arrived. In the case of Voiced Mail, the initial motivation for including voice messages was the new reply capability required by telephonic access; text messages could be turned to voice, but voice replies could not be converted to text. This, therefore, is a case in which a new user interface medium results in the need to support multiple media in the underlying database being accessed.

### Voiced Mail Today

Voiced Mail addressed universal access to electronic mail messages. At the time it was built (1983) modems were still 300 baud and computer terminals at home uncommon even at a research institution like M.I.T. But even under these circumstances, synthesis was too tedious to use for longer messages. Instead, users would scan messages to see if they had anything important to deal with (such as scheduling lunch) before coming into work. The exception was when users were traveling and had no other access to their mail.

Modem speeds have increased and terminals or personal computers at home are now commonplace; this decreased the need to use speech synthesis to access mail messages at home (although we do like to joke about hearing mail while in the shower). An interface such as Voiced Mail is more valuable to mobile users who may want to call in from airport lobbies or roadside phones. Voice is also particularly useful when used while doing other activities. One example is using a cellular telephone to scan mail while driving to work (the morning commute otherwise being wasted time.) A safer version of this scenario would involve uploading email as text into a laptop computer over telephone lines in the morning and then synthesizing it in the car while using speech recognition (instead of touch tones) to navigate among messages.

Speech synthesis access to Email over the telephone remains in surprisingly high demand at the Media Lab, and it has been included in a more integrated messaging environment. Phoneshell, which as described in Chapter 12, brings increased functionality to Email access including the ability to record a voice reply, to type a text reply using the telephone keypad, to send copies of replies to multiple parties chosen from an address listing, and to send a message to a third party as a fax. Another feature of the newer version is the ability to *filter* messages into broad categories (e.g., "urgent," "important," "personal," or "junk") based on pattern matching against email header fields (such as sender and subject) and the message body. Email filtering was first introduced by Malone in the Information Lens and has been shown to be an effective means of managing mail [Malone *et al.* 1987, Mackay *et al.* 1989]. For Phoneshell users, filtering makes it possible to attend to the most important messages first, which is essential when dealing with a slow communication channel.

Although the ability to reply and sort messages is crucial for the current success of speech access to email, the primary reason Email is popular is simply the ease of dialing in. Although most of Phoneshell's present users possess computers and modems at home, telephone access allows casual and low-overhead message retrieval from locations such as stores, pay phones in airports, other offices on campus, or even the kitchen when one merely wishes to check on message status. Even if email is automatically sent to alphanumeric pagers (this is done at the Media Lab and many other locations), each page is limited to several hundred characters; this asynchronous notification provides even greater motivation to immediately call in from the nearest telephone to hear the entire body of an urgent message and possibly send a timely reply.

## SUMMARY

This chapter has discussed the advantages and disadvantages of voice from the perspective of interactive systems employing voice response. Speech output may be difficult to employ effectively for information providing because it is slow, temporal, serial, "bulky," and may not be private enough for some office situations. At the same time speech is advantageous over other media because it can be used at a distance over the telephone or heard across a room or when a user's hands and eyes are otherwise occupied.

A number of design considerations were suggested based on comparing the advantages to the disadvantages of speech output and how it should be employed in an application. Some applications may simply be inappropriate for speech output. For appropriate applications, speech may be sped up to increase performance, but a means of repeating an utterance may be needed to clarify messages when a user fails to understand them. There may be a role for multiple voice styles in a single speech-output application.

Because many interactive voice response systems are telephone based, we paid particular attention to the issue of user input with the telephone keypad. Touch tones can be used to select an item from a list, to answer yes-or-no questions, or to make a selection from a menu. Implicit or explicit termination of input may be more suitable to different tasks being performed over the telephone.

Three case studies were presented to illustrate the points being made in this chapter. Direction Assistance employs a variety of input techniques to trigger discourse generation from a complicated computer database of street segments. Back Seat Driver, using the same database, must generate directions in real time and instill confidence in the user that it remains on target despite periods of silence—a need not present in graphical interfaces. Finally, Voiced Mail illustrated how text filtering and organizational issues can minimize the amount of information that must be attended to while reading electronic mail with speech synthesis; it also eschewed prompts and menus in favor of a default flow of control during a session with a caller.

# 7

# Speech Recognition

This chapter is about the technologies used to allow computers to recognize the words in human speech. It describes the basic components of all speech recognition systems and illustrates these with an example of a simple recognizer typical of several inexpensive commercial products. After this discussion of basic recognition, the chapter details a larger range of features that can be used to differentiate various recognizers according to the styles of speech interactions they support. Several more advanced recognition techniques are then introduced followed by brief descriptions of selected research projects in large vocabulary and speaker independent word recognition.

## BASIC RECOGNIZER COMPONENTS

There are three basic components of any speech recognizer.

1. A speech **representation** that is computationally efficient for pattern matching. The representation is the form into which the recognizer converts the speech signal before it begins analysis to identify words. Typical representations include the output of a bank of filters (similar to a spectrogram), Linear Predictive Coding (LPC) coefficients,[1] and zero crossings of the speech waveform. Recognizers of

---

[1]See Chapter 3.

increased sophistication incorporate more abstract representations of speech such as phonemes or distinctive spectral features. Hidden Markov Models, described later in this chapter, are a statistical representation based on the various ways words or phonemes may be pronounced.

2. A set of **templates** or **models,** which are descriptions of each word to be recognized, in the representation of speech used by the recognizer. The templates describe the words in the recognizer's vocabulary, i.e., those words that the recognizer can identify. They are reference models against which an input can be compared to determine what was spoken.

3. A **pattern matching** algorithm to determine which template is most similar to a specimen of speech input. This element of the speech recognizer must determine word boundaries, locate the most similar template, and decide whether the difference between the input and the selected template is minor enough to accept the word. In very large vocabulary recognizers, the pattern matching technique usually includes access to more advanced knowledge of language such as syntax and semantics, which constrain how words can be combined into sentences.

To identify a word the recognizer must capture incoming speech and convert it to the chosen internal representation (see Figure 7.1). The pattern matcher then selects the template that most closely matches the input or rejects the utterance if no template is a close enough match.

## SIMPLE RECOGNIZER

This section describes a simple recognizer typical of many inexpensive, commercially available devices. This recognizer is designed to identify a small number of

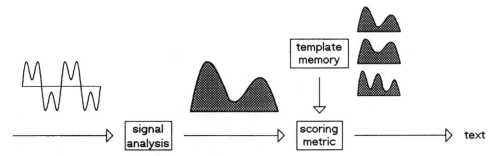

**Figure 7.1.** The functional elements of a speech recognizer. The user's speech is digitized and converted to the recognizer's internal representation. The captured speech is then compared with the words stored in the recognizer's template memory. The pattern matching algorithm then determines which template, if any, is the closest match.

words spoken in isolation by a specific individual. The purpose of the description that follows is not to provide details of a particular product but rather to offer a sample implementation of the basic components described previously.

### Representation

A simple recognizer digitizes incoming audio by means of a codec[2] and then uses a digital signal processing algorithm to extract frames of Linear Predictive Coding (LPC) coefficients every 20 milliseconds. The LPC coefficients are a concise representation of the articulatory characteristics of speech as they capture both the resonances of the vocal tract as well as its voicing characteristics. The 20 millisecond sampling interval results in 50 LPC frames per second, providing significant data reduction to simplify later pattern-matching.

### Templates

Templates are gathered by prompting the user from a word list and then saving a set of LPC frames for each word generated as just described. To build a template, the recognizer must determine when the user begins and finishes speaking to know which LPC frames to include in the template. Since each LPC frame or set of coefficients in one 20 millisecond sampling period includes an energy value, this task can be accomplished easily. As shown in Figure 7.2, once the audio exceeds the threshold of background noise, LPC frames are saved until the audio drops below the threshold. It is necessary to wait until the signal has dropped below the threshold for a short period of time as silence or low energy can occur within a word, such as at stop consonants.

In the case of this simple recognizer, templates are trained by a user saying each word once. More sophisticated recognizers may take multiple specimens of a

---

[2]See Chapter 3.

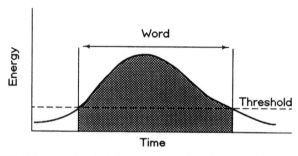

**Figure 7.2.** Energy thresholds can be used to find word boundaries if the words are spoken in isolation.

word to build a more robust template. Once templates are trained successfully, the user can save them as a disk file on the host computer and reload them before each session, to avoid template training each time the recognizer is used.

This recognizer also allows retraining of a single template, in which case the new LPC frames replace the old. Retraining is useful if the vocabulary changes, if the original training was poor, or if the user decides that a different pronunciation of the word is more comfortable. Retraining may also be necessary when the user has a cold, due to an obstructed nasal cavity.

## Pattern Matching

Word recognition requires the detection and classification of speech input. Just as with template creation, a word is captured by detecting that the audio input exceeds the background noise threshold and then converting the input to LPC frames until the input again drops to the background level. The input word is then compared with each template; each frame or set of LPC parameters of the input is compared to the corresponding frame of the template. The frame-by-frame error is the sum of the differences between each of the dozen or so LPC parameters; the error for the word is the sum of the errors for each frame. The template with the smallest word error most closely matches the audio input. If the error exceeds a rejection threshold, a failed recognition attempt is reported. Otherwise the recognizer reports the word corresponding to the closest template.

Both the templates and the captured audio input are multidimensional vectors, with one degree-of-freedom per LPC parameter and one for time. But to illustrate pattern matching let us assume that the templates consist of only a pair of values that display on two axes. One parameter is assigned to the X-axis and the other parameter maps to the Y-axis so that each template occupies a point whose coordinates are the two parameters (see Figure 7.3). Speech input is converted into this representation, i.e., a pair of parameters specifying a point in the same parameter space as the templates. The closest template is the nearest neighbor template to the point representing the input. The four templates divide the space into four regions; any pair of parameters in each region most closely matches the template in that region.

Even the simplest of speech recognizers can improve its accuracy by employing a better pattern matching algorithm. Two additional refinements, illustrated in Figure 7.4, contribute to this recognition improvement. The first refinement is that the input cannot exceed a threshold distance ($r$ in the figure) from the nearest template. When the audio input is further from the nearest template than this distance, a rejection error is reported. This is necessary to avoid inadvertently accepting noise, breath sounds, or a mistaken utterance as one of the acceptable words in the recognizer's vocabulary.

The second refinement is a requirement that the input word maps significantly closer to the best match template than any other. If a point is very nearly the same distance from two or more templates, the recognizer is confident that one of these was spoken but uncertain which particular word was spoken. This is depicted in Figure 7.4 as the shaded regions around the lines partitioning the

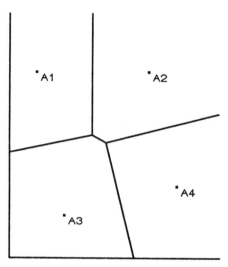

**Figure 7.3.** To illustrate pattern matching decisions, assume that each template represents two degrees of freedom defining a Cartesian coordinate space. Four templates occupy four points in this space.

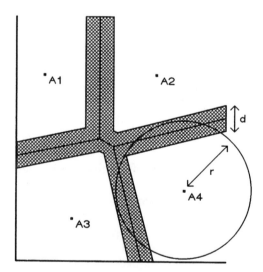

**Figure 7.4.** A more refined classifier has upper bounds **r** on the distance between an input specimen and a chosen template. It will also reject values which are closer to one template but also close to another, i.e., within distance **d.**

space between neighbors; the distance **d** defines the minimal difference required to differentiate candidate choices. Points within the shaded region are nearly the same distance from each of the two closest templates and will also cause a rejection error.

This section described an extremely simple recognizer that identifies only isolated words. The speech recognizer's simplicity is due in part to its unsophisticated processing of acoustical information: It does not extract significant features but merely considers LPC frames in isolation. Because each template may contain many frames, the pattern matcher has to make a large number of frame-by-frame difference calculations, making it computationally difficult to recognize a large number of words. More sophisticated recognizers detect and classify key acoustic features of an utterance and use this for the internal representation.

Additionally, the pattern matcher just described makes no provision for templates of different lengths and, more importantly, assumes that the input utterance will be of the same length as the correct template. If acoustic boundary detection operates slightly differently from word to word or if the words are spoken at different speeds, this pattern matcher will likely fail. A technique known as **dynamic time warping** or **dynamic programming** (discussed later in this chapter) is often used to compensate for time differences.

## CLASSES OF RECOGNIZERS

Recognizers vary widely in their functionality. In addition to performance, other distinctions between recognition techniques are important in selecting a recognizer for a particular application. These distinctions are summarized in Figure 7.5, which displays a three-dimensional space representing the range of possible recognizer configurations. Some of these recognizers are commercially available and have been in use for some time, whereas others are the subject of ongoing research and are just beginning to emerge from research laboratories.

### Who Can Use the Recognizer?

A **speaker-independent** recognizer is designed to recognize anyone, while a **speaker-dependent** recognizer can be expected to understand only a single particular speaker. A **speaker-adaptive** recognizer functions to an extent as a combination of the two; it accommodates a new user without requiring that the user train every word in the vocabulary.

Speaker-independent recognition is more difficult than speaker-dependent recognition because we all speak the same words slightly differently. Although we usually understand each other, this variability in pronunciation and voice quality among talkers plays havoc with the pattern matching algorithms of simple recognizers. Speaker-independent recognition requires more elaborate template generation and a clustering technique to identify various ways a particular word may be pronounced.

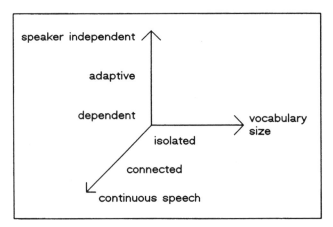

**Figure 7.5.** A three-dimensional space defined by the different function-alities provided by a recognizer.

This process of classifying the acceptable variations in word pronunciations is the equivalent of the training method just described for the simple illustrative recognizer. Since speaker-independent recognition is such a difficult task, most speaker-independent recognizers are limited to small vocabularies (10 to 20 words) and recognize only single words spoken in isolation. Several commercially available speaker-independent recognizers accept the digits "0" through "9" plus "yes" and "no." Speaker-independent recognition for a larger vocabulary or with words spoken together must rely on additional constraints such as a heavily restricted grammar to achieve adequate recognition performance.

An individual pronounces a single word in a much more consistent fashion than that of a number of different people; this is why speaker-dependent recognition is less difficult. Most speaker-dependent recognizers use a training method similar to the one described for the simple recognizer in the previous section. Multiple templates may be trained and merged together to give an average pronunciation for each word in the vocabulary.

A speaker-adaptive recognizer learns to adapt to a particular speaker either by calibrating itself to a known sample of that person's speech or by incorporating user feedback when it recognizes a word correctly or incorrectly. Such a recognizer has a basic acoustic model for each word that it refines to fit a particular speaker. One common technique is to have the user read a passage of training data; the recognizer can then determine how this particular person speaks.

If a large vocabulary size is needed, a recognizer must be either speaker-adaptive or independent because training many templates is tedious and time consuming. Some adaptive recognizers require many hours of computer time to derive the user model from the training data, but once the data has been acquired the user is freed from the task. The resulting user model can be saved in a host computer and downloaded later, similar to the set of word templates for the speaker-dependent recognizer.

### Speaking Style: Connected or Isolated Words?

A **discrete speech** recognizer requires pauses between each word to identify word boundaries. A **connected speech** recognizer is designed to recognize a short series of words spoken together as a phrase. A **continuous speech** recognizer is capable of identifying words in a long string of ordinary speech without the talker pausing between groups of words. A **keyword spotting** recognizer can locate a few words in the midst of any amount of speech.

"Connected speech" for recognition purposes is not natural speech. Users of a connected speech recognizer can speak a few words or perhaps a whole sentence at a time but then must pause to let the recognizer catch up. Users must also speak distinctly. Pausing after each sentence provides reliable boundary points for the first and last word, which facilitates recognition of the entire phrase. But we do not pause between sentences in fluent speech. Human listeners can keep up, and this is the goal of continuous speech recognition, which may become a reality as computer speeds increase.

Keyword spotting searches for a small number of words in a stream of continuous speech. For example, a keyword recognizer might be designed to recognize the digits from an utterance such as "The number is three five seven . . . um . . . four one, please." Successful keyword spotting is comparatively new [Wilpon *et al.* 1990] and more difficult than simply separating speech from non-speech background noise.

Most currently-available commercial products recognize isolated or connected speech. Connected speech is much faster to use because it eliminates the need for unnatural pauses and requires less attention to speaking style on the part of the user. But because connected recognition is more difficult, it may manifest higher error rates, which could outweigh the speed advantage. It can also be argued that speaking discretely is more effective because it requires the user to keep in mind the need to speak clearly from a limited vocabulary while using speech recognition [Biermann *et al.* 1985].

Connected word recognition is much more difficult than isolated word recognition for several reasons.

- Coarticulation changes the pronunciation of a word as a function of its neighbors. Initial and final syllables are particularly subject to modification. Words spoken in isolation do not suffer from coarticulation effects between words.
- It is difficult to find word boundaries reliably from within fluent speech. There is no pause between words, nor is there a significant decrease in speech energy at word boundaries; low energy syllables containing stop consonants are often more discernible than word boundaries.
- The probability of error increases with the number of words in an utterance. If the first word is incorrectly matched against a template which is either too long or too short, then the data to be analyzed for the second word will be incorrect, making the error propagate to subsequent words.

Because of these factors many current applications of speech recognition are based on isolated word recognizers.

## Vocabulary Size

Another criterion by which to differentiate recognizers is vocabulary size, which can be grossly categorized as small, medium, or large. Small vocabulary recognizers with less than 200 words have been available for some time. Medium size recognizers (200 to 5000 words) are being developed, usually based on the same algorithms used for smaller vocabulary systems but running on faster hardware. Large vocabulary recognizers aim for the 5000 to 10,000 word level. Much ordinary office language could be handled with a vocabulary of this breadth, which marks the range being aimed for in "listening typewriters" designed to accommodate dictation of business correspondence.

Several issues conspire to complicate the recognition of large vocabularies. One factor is the computational power required for the pattern matching algorithm. The input must be compared with each template, so classification time is a function of the number of templates, i.e., vocabulary size. The requirement of an acceptable response time therefore puts an upper limit on vocabulary size. As microprocessor speeds increase, this computational limit will become less of an issue. Some search-pruning techniques can also be employed to quickly remove candidate templates from the search if they are obviously poor choices, such as if they are much too long or short. If the recognizer employs a grammar, it can use this knowledge of how words can be combined to eliminate syntactically incorrect candidates at each point in the search.

A more serious limitation to vocabulary size is simply that as the number of words increases, it is more likely that the recognizer will find some of them similar. To return to the two parameter template model discussed earlier, compare Figure 7.3 with Figure 7.6. As the number of templates increases, the average distance between them decreases, allowing for a smaller margin of difference in pronunciation between the input sample and its associated template.

Decreased distance between templates is confounded by the fact that as templates or words are added to the recognizer's vocabulary, they are not uniformly distributed throughout the recognizer's representation space. In fact, some words in the vocabulary are likely to sound so similar that to distinguish among them on acoustic evidence alone is extremely difficult. For example, if a vocabulary consisted of the words, "sun," "moon," and "stars," we might expect that distinguishing which word was spoken to be easy. But if we add "Venus," "Earth," and "Mars" to the vocabulary, we might anticipate confusion between "stars" and "Mars."[3]

---

[3]This is a simplistic example. The strong fricative and stop at the beginning of "stars" should be easily differentiated from the nasal of "Mars" if suitable acoustic features are used for the recognizer's representation. It is hard to predict which words will sound similar without intimate knowledge of the recognizer's internal speech representation.

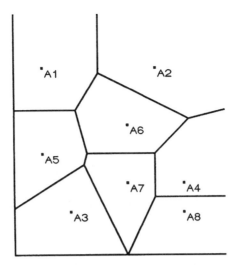

**Figure 7.6.** As the number of words increases, the mean distance between templates decreases.

## ADVANCED RECOGNITION TECHNIQUES

This section explores several techniques to enhance speech recognition. The simplest recognizers, supporting a very small speaker-dependent vocabulary of isolated words, occupy the region near the origin of the three-dimensional model depicted earlier in Figure 7.5. In moving away from the origin in any direction, recognition errors are more likely as the process becomes more complicated. But a large vocabulary, continuous speech, and speaker independence are precisely those attributes that make recognition more widely useful.

Unless users can be convinced to change their habits to speak more clearly and consistently, recognizers must be improved. More advanced recognizers generally employ one of two techniques to make pattern matching more powerful for dealing with variations in speech patterns. These techniques, **Dynamic Time Warping** and **Hidden Markov Models,** are the topics of the next two sections. The descriptions that follow provide an overview of the two techniques; the curious reader is encouraged to consult the references for a more rigorous description of the algorithms. A third approach to managing speech pattern variation uses **neural networks** for speech recognition; this approach is far less developed than the previous two and still speculative.

Data reduction can facilitate pattern matching by minimizing its computational requirements. **Vector Quantization** is a technique employed by many recognizers to capture important variations in speech parameters without overloading the classifier—so it will be described in this section as well. Finally, the last part of this section considers how nonspeech evidence could be used to improve large vocabulary speech recognition.

## Dynamic Time Warping

Dynamic Time Warping is a technique that compensates for variability in the rate at which words are spoken. Dynamic Time Warping (DTW) was developed primarily as a mechanism to compensate for variable word duration in connected speech recognition [Sakoe and Chiba 1978]. This method can also help determine word boundaries when an unknown number of words are spoken together. DTW is based on a more general computational technique known as **dynamic programming.**

The duration of spoken words is quite variable, especially if we compare connected speech with the isolated words that may have been used for training a recognizer. Coarticulation may shorten words by combining their boundary syllables with the preceding or subsequent words. Words spoken in isolation (citation form) are longer and often more clearly enunciated. The stress pattern of the sentence lengthens some syllables, as stressed syllables are longer than unstressed syllables. Such changes in length are not linear; every phoneme is not lengthened by the same scale factor. DTW compensates for such nonlinear phenomena.

Consider the simple recognizer discussed earlier in this chapter. It computes an error between the input speech and a template by computing the frame-by-frame difference between the two. But if the talker speaks at a different rate, successive frames of input may not align with the same phoneme in the template, giving a deceptively large error. For example, if the word "fast" is trained but the talker lengthens the vowel ("faaast") during recognition, some frames of the lengthened vowel would be scored against the frames corresponding to the unvoiced "s" in the template. DTW detects that successive "a" frames of the input match the fewer "a" frames of the template better than the "s" frames that follow, and it computes an error based on the selected matchup.

DTW operates by selecting which frames of the reference template best match each frame of the input such that the resulting error between them is minimized. By allowing multiple frames of one to be matched against a single repeated frame of the other, DTW can compress or expand relative time. Because this decision is made on a frame-by-frame basis, the time-scaling is local; DTW may compress one portion of the input and expand another if necessary.

DTW provides a mapping between the sample and a reference template such that the error when the two are compared is minimized. This mapping defines a path between sample and reference frames; for each frame of the sample it specifies the template frame best matched to the next sample frame. In Figure 7.7, the *nth* sample frame is compared to the *mth* reference frame. If the sample is spoken more quickly, then multiple reference frames correspond to a single template frame; this case is indicated by the vertical path, which allows the *nth* sample frame to also match the *m + 1st* reference frame. If the reference and sample are proceeding at the same rate, the *m + 1st* reference frame will match the *n + 1st* sample frame forming a path at a 45-degree angle (slope = 1). Finally, if the sample is spoken more slowly than the reference, multiple sample frames must be compared to a single reference frame as indicated by the horizontal line.

Figure 7.8 shows how these frame-by-frame decisions combine to produce a path for comparing the sample to the reference. The DTW algorithm computes

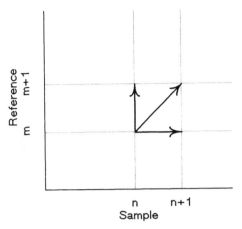

**Figure 7.7.** Dynamic Time Warping defines a path between frames of a sample utterance and a template such that the frame-by-frame error between the two is minimized. If sample point **m** matches reference point **m,** then reference point **m** + **1** may match either sample point **n** or **n** + **1**.

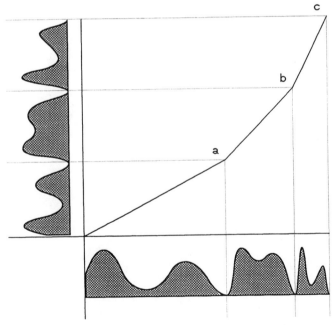

**Figure 7.8.** Dynamic Time Warping provides nonlinear time-scaling between a sample (horizontal-axis) and reference (vertical-axis) utterances. In region **a** the sample is spoken more slowly; in region **b** they are spoken at the same rate; and in region **c** the template is spoken more slowly.

the minimal error path between the input and template frames; relative speaking rate can be inferred from the slope of this path. A slope of 1 (45-degree line) is optimal when both are spoken at the identical rate.

It is necessary to place limits on the degree of time-scaling allowed by DTW. It would be senseless to compare 50 milliseconds of the sample to 1200 milliseconds of reference; normal speech does not exhibit such wide variability. Constraints on the maximum time-warping ratio are imposed by placing upper and lower bounds on the slope of the DTW path. The typical range of slopes is one-half to two, which accommodates a sample being spoken either half or twice as fast as the reference.

"Two-level" dynamic programming can be used to find word boundaries in a connected utterance containing an unknown number of words. At the lower level, DTW allows time-scaling of each word by computing the minimal error path matching the input to each template. At the higher level, these word-by-word error values are used to compute the best path through the set of all possible word combinations that could comprise a sentence. The two levels operate in concert to apportion the duration of the utterance among the set of selected templates. Figure 7.9 shows how a number of words of different lengths could consist of similar phones, or speech sounds.[4] It may be that the first three phones most closely match the short word "her," which would suggest that the utterance contained three words. But a better *overall* score might be obtained by matching these three phones against the beginning of "heartfelt" and selecting the utterance with only two words.

Dynamic programming is most beneficial for connected speech recognition. Word durations show greater temporal variation in connected speech than in isolated speech. Additionally, word boundaries must be found by considering how the continuous stream of phones can best be segmented into words in the absence of interword pauses. Dynamic programming is used in a number of commercial connected speech recognition systems, but its popularity for research purposes has faded in favor of Hidden Markov Models.

## Hidden Markov Models

A **Hidden Markov Model (HMM)** is a two-stage probabilistic process that can be used as a powerful representation for speech. A Hidden Markov Model is a well-behaved mathematical construct, and a number of detailed algorithms exist for solving problems associated with HMMs; introductions to these can be found in [Rabiner and Juang 1986a]. This section first explains HMMs in the abstract and then demonstrates how they can be applied to speech recognition.

An HMM consists of a number of internal states; the model passes from an initial state to the final state as a step-by-step process generating an observable output at each step (state transition). For example, the states may correspond to phonemes contained in a word with the observable output corresponding to the

---

[4]Such a representation is called a **word lattice.**

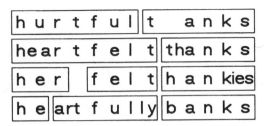

**Figure 7.9.** Different sequences of words could match an utterance; each sequence implies different word boundaries in the input utterance.

presence or absence of a number of acoustic features. At each step, the model can either move to a new state or stay in the current one. The model is "hidden" in that we cannot observe the state directly but only its output. From the series of observable outputs, we can attempt to guess when the model was in each state. Alternatively, we can say whether some series of outputs was likely to have been generated by a particular HMM.

For example, consider the arrangement shown in Figure 7.10, in which a box and a bowl are each full of black balls and white balls. The box has many more black balls than white while white balls dominate the bowl. Starting with the box, we remove one ball from it at random and pass it to an observer in another room who cannot see what is being done. Then a normal six-sided die is tossed. If the result is less than four, then the source of the next ball is the bowl. If the die is greater than three, then the next ball will be selected from the box. The cycle is then repeated.[5] Whenever we select from the box, a die throw of less than four shifts attention to the bowl. Once we start selecting from the bowl, we continue selecting from it unless the die shows a one, at which point we are finished. This model is likely to spend a majority of its cycles selecting from the bowl since a state transition from the box has a probability ½ of shifting to the bowl, but a bowl transition has a probability of only ⅙ of terminating and ⅚ of continuing with the bowl.[6] We should expect this arrangement to initially present more black balls than white to the observer (while it is in the box state) and then to produce more white balls. We should also expect more white balls overall. But keep in mind that this is a probabilistic process: Not all black balls come from the box and not all selections come from the bowl.

The box-and-bowl setup is a Hidden Markov Model; it is characterized by a number of *states* and associated probabilities for each *transition* from any state. The box and bowl are each a state; the rules about throwing the die define the

---

[5]This pedagogic example was inspired by Rabiner and Juang [Rabiner and Juang 1986b].

[6]Probability is expressed as a number between zero and one. If an event occurs with probability ½, we would expect it to happen once in two trials. A probability of ⅙ implies that we can expect the event once out of six trials. A smaller probability indicates that an event is less likely to occur.

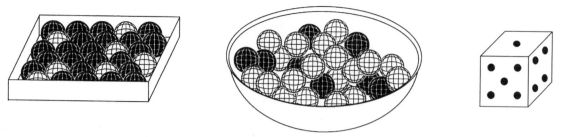

**Figure 7.10.** A box and a bowl full of colored balls illustrate a Hidden Markov Model.

transition properties. Figure 7.11 shows a more general HMM; in each state **S(n)** there is some probability **P(n,n)** of remaining in that state and some probability **P(n, n + 1)** of transitioning to the next state. In some models, it may be possible to bypass a state or a series of states as indicated by the dashed arc labeled $P_{13}$ in the figure. The sum of the probabilities of all the arcs leaving a state is one; the model accounts for every possible path through its states.

How does this apply to speech recognition? An HMM can be used to represent a word with internal states representing characteristic acoustic segments, possibly phonemes or allophones. The output of a state is a frame or vector of acoustic parameters or features; this output is probabilistic to allow for variability in pronunciation and hence differences in the acoustic representation. The duration of an acoustic segment is a function of the number of steps in which the model is in the state corresponding to the segment. Staying in the same state, i.e. lengthening a phone, depends on the probability associated with the transition from that state to itself ($P_{11}$ in Figure 7.11). Arcs such as $P_{13}$ may be included to indicate that an intermediate state **S2** is optional during pronunciation, such as the second syllable in "chocolate."

In terms of the basic recognizer components, the "templates" consist of a set of HMMs with one HMM associated with every word. The acoustic representation of an input specimen of speech is *not* a collection of states but rather a set of acous-

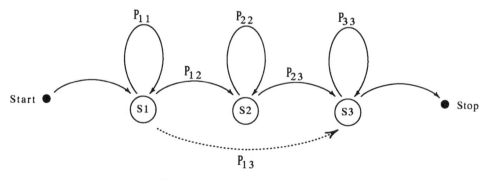

**Figure 7.11.** A Markov Model.

tic parameters corresponding to the possible observed sequences from the template HMMs. For the HMM-based recognizer, classification consists of determining which HMM has the highest probability of producing the observed acoustic sequence. The Viterbi algorithm is a commonly used method of solving this classification problem; a more detailed description is beyond the scope of this book but see [Lee and Alleva 1992] for an overview of its theory.

There are two related HMM problems which can also be solved mathematically. One is training the statistically defined HMMs that the recognizer requires as templates. Given some number of observation sequences (i.e., repetitions of the word), an HMM must be derived to represent that particular word. The second problem, not directly relevant during recognition, is to determine for some HMM and a set of observed outputs the internal states of the model that were most likely at each step.

Hidden Markov Models are a powerful representation of speech and consequently are used in many speech recognition systems currently under development. Although this section has described isolated word recognition, HMMs can also be used with connected speech to represent not only the phones of each word but also the probabilities of transitioning from one word to another. For connected speech recognition, the observed sequence would be generated by passing through a sequence of states in a sequence of HMMs with one HMM for each word spoken. The combination of words is also described statistically as another layer of HMMs in which each state corresponds to an entire word thereby encoding syntactic and semantic information.

## Vector Quantization

**Vector Quantization (VQ)** is a technique employed for data reduction in speech coding and speech recognition. VQ is used to reduce a widely ranging input value into a smaller set of numbers representing typical values of the input. Because the input is classified as one of a small number of values instead of the value itself, less storage space is required. More importantly, the input is usually multidimensional (e.g., a set of LPC coefficients), and it is reduced to the single dimension identifying the nearest vector-quantized value.

In order to perform Vector Quantization, it is first necessary to decide how to efficiently cluster all possible input values. The analysis of sample data, which must be typical of the data to be encoded, determines how to cluster similar input values. The cluster's "center of gravity," or average value, then represents the entire set of data in the group. Each cluster is represented as one entry in a **codebook,** which lists the average value of each group. Having created a robust VQ codebook from specimen data, new data can be classified by selecting the codebook entry nearest in value to that data. The original value of the input data is lost; it is now represented by the single value associated with the codebook entry.

Building the codebook divides the space of possible values into regions and *typical* values. This is much like the process of selecting word templates for recognition as shown in Figure 7.6. The number of entries required for the codebook depends on how well the data clusters into groups and the accuracy with which the data must be represented. If the data points are widely scattered, it is difficult to cluster them efficiently. The range of values subsumed by each cluster determines the accuracy with which vector quantized data can be represented since the codebook entry is used to look up a value for the data and only one value is stored per cluster.

Representing an input as a codebook entry having a similar value significantly reduces both storage and computation during pattern matching. To vector quantize an input value based on a codebook of $N$ entries, the input must be compared with at most $N$ possible values. The error between each of the codebook values can be computed in advance and stored in a two-dimensional array. During pattern matching the error between an input value and a corresponding template value can be found by table lookup instead of direct computation. The sum of the errors for each frame is the error between the input and that template.

As a simple example, vector quantization can be used to represent the number of hours per day that light bulbs are left burning in a home. If daily use is represented as an integral number of hours from zero to twenty-four, five bits of storage are required for each bulb. Higher resolution, such as minutes in addition to hours, requires even more bits of storage per bulb. However, by observing the individual bulbs we discover some interesting patterns of usage. Many bulbs are rarely turned on. Some bulbs are always left on all night like an outdoor lamp or a child's night light. Other bulbs, in the living room and kitchen, may typically be on from dusk until the occupants go to sleep. Still other bulbs such as in a closet may be turned on occasionally for brief periods of a few minutes each day.

This situation can be described by a vector quantization scheme employing a codebook with four entries to cover the four typical cases described in the previous paragraph.[7] Each entry in the codebook (see Figure 7.12) corresponds to one case of light bulb use, and the value stored for that entry indicates how long such a bulb is likely to be used. Using this codebook, light bulb use is encoded in two bits at a savings of three bits per bulb.

Vector quantization is usually employed to represent multidimensional quantities so the compression to a single-dimensioned codebook offers further data compression. To continue with the light bulb example, we might observe that many of the lamps used rarely or left on all night are low wattage, e.g., 60 or 75 watts. The living room and kitchen lights are more likely to be 100 or 150 watts to illuminate work areas. So we might vector quantize this information as well as shown in Figure 7.13. This new codebook indicates that a bulb assigned value two is typically 120 watts and on for five hours a day. Note that a 150 watt bulb used seven hours a day and a 75 watt bulb used four hours a day will both be represented by codebook value 2 as well. It may be that there is actually no single bulb of 120 watts; this is an average that represents the least error when compared to all the bulbs in the sample set with this codebook value.

---

[7]Such a codebook is said to be "of size four."

| codebook entry | codebook value |
|:---:|:---:|
| 0 | 0 hours |
| 1 | 15 minutes |
| 2 | 5 hours |
| 3 | 10 hours |

**Figure 7.12.** A simple VQ codebook representing light bulb use.

Once quantized, detailed information about a particular light bulb is lost, but we still have a general idea of how much each is used. This would be useful for identifying which bulbs should be replaced by more expensive energy-efficient models. While the memory savings are small in this example, vector quantization can be used for much greater data reduction in speech coding applications where it represents complex acoustical information about an utterance.

How is vector quantization used in speech representation? Consider the output of an LPC coder; it includes precise indications of the locations of each of the formants, or resonances, in the vocal tract as conveyed by filter parameters. But for gross categorization of the position of the vocal tract, e.g., to differentiate the vowels by their F1/F2 ratio, such precision is not necessary. Furthermore, not all combinations of F1 and F2 are possible since they are constrained by the physical characteristics of the vocal tract. Vector quantizing these filter coefficients can capture the overall vocal tract configuration in a very concise form when great precision of each parameter is not necessary.

### Employing Constraints

A recognizer's task becomes increasingly difficult as the number of words to be recognized increases. To improve recognition large vocabulary systems apply constraints to the set of all possible words that can make up an input utterance.

| codebook entry | codebook value | |
|:---:|:---:|:---:|
| | time | wattage |
| 0 | 0 hours | 65 |
| 1 | 15 minutes | 75 |
| 2 | 5 hours | 120 |
| 3 | 10 hours | 70 |

**Figure 7.13.** Vector quantization is usually used to represent multidimensional quantities. Here it encodes both the average duration of illumination as well as the wattage of bulbs.

Constraints limit the search space during word classification by ruling out improper combinations of words. Although we readily employ general syntactic and semantic constraints to rule out many ill-formed or nonsense sentences while trying to understand a talker, it is difficult to express the knowledge that underlies such decisions in computationally tractable terms. Current recognition systems incorporate limited constraints specific to a given task.

Some of these constraints are specific to the the input; for example, North American telephone numbers have seven digits (ten if the area code is included). Other sets of constraints can be derived from a specification of all the legal utterances for a set of words and a task. For example, simple rules of syntax tell us that every sentence must have a verb, and common sense dictates that an application for ordering pizza should expect to encounter the word "large" adjacent to "pepperoni." To define these constraints the application designer must specify every legal sentence to be recognized. This is facilitated by lumping groups of words into classes which have meaning in a particular task context, such as "digit," "size," or "topping." Sentences can then be described as series of words combined from particular classes instead of listing every possible word sequence.

Because they are derived by observing people perform a task and computing the likelihood of particular sequences of words, constraints can also be probabilistic. This requires a large body of data from which to derive the probabilities as there may be many possible sentences and statistical representations that require a large quantity of training data. Some language models have been based on analysis of a large corpus of text documents. Although spoken and written language differ, the advantage of this approach is that the text is both readily available and easily analyzed by a computer.

The effectiveness of constraints is related to the degree to which they limit the possible input utterances; this can be stated as the predictive ability of a string of $n$ words on the $n + 1st$ word. Alternatively, the constraints may be quantized as the **branching factor** associated with any node in a string of input words; this number indicates how many different words can follow one or more previous words. A question requiring a yes-or-no answer has a branching factor of two, for example, while one requiring a single digit has a branching factor of ten. **Perplexity** is a measure of the branching factor averaged across all possible word junctures in the set of legal utterances. The lower the perplexity, the more effectively lexical constraints can improve recognition.

Recognizers based on either *ad hoc* or statistical models of language and the task at hand may be subject to limited portability. The words a talker uses change as a function of the topic of discourse, and a recognizer may not be able to make such a shift. For example, a carefully constructed grammar for a task that allows the user to make inquiries into the state of ships in a navy's fleet will be rather different from one used in general business correspondence. Recognizers do not yet make use of language representations general enough to make specification of the task a simple problem. A more general discussion of methods of specifying both syntactic and semantic constraints is found in Chapter 9.

## ADVANCED RECOGNITION SYSTEMS

This section briefly describes details of three advanced speech recognizers that are considerably more sophisticated than the simplistic example presented early in this chapter. These recognizers are research projects, not yet commercial products. This is hardly an exhaustive list of speech recognition research, but it is intended to be representative of the approaches being used in modern, large vocabulary recognition systems. These descriptions will almost certainly be out of date by the time this book is actually published so they should be taken as little more than a snapshot of a rapidly evolving field.

### IBM's Tangora

IBM's Tangora speech recognizer is designed to recognize 5000 to 20,000 words of isolated speech [Jelinek 1985]. A real-time version of this research project was implemented on a single-slot personal computer board. The Tangora recognizer is speaker adaptive with training based on the user's reading a few paragraphs of text to calibrate its acoustic model.

The Tangora recognizer uses a vector quantization front end to classify acoustic input, which is then matched to words using discrete Hidden Markov Models of phoneme realization. A linguistic decoder then classifies the output of the acoustic front end producing a word for output. Tangora is targetted at automatic transcription of speech to text in a dictation context.

The linguistic constraints employed by the second stage of this recognizer are based on the probabilities of groups of two or three words occurring in sequence. This statistical model, called a **bigram** or **trigram grammar,** was derived through analysis of a large quantity of text from business correspondence. It should be readily apparent that such a representation of the language includes both syntactic and semantic information as well as indirectly encoded world knowledge. Not only is "late I slept" an unusual sequence due to constraints, but similarly "I slept furiously" is improbable due to its ill-formed semantics; "the green cat" is unlikely due to world knowledge that cats do not have green fur. But this model cannot distinguish the source of knowledge; it merely represents the end result of all factors that contribute to likely word sequences.

### CMU's Sphinx

Carnegie-Mellon University's Sphinx recognizer is designed for speaker-independent connected speech recognition [Lee and Hon 1988, Lee 1988]. At the time of this writing, it operates in nearly real time using hardware multi-processor peripherals to aid in the search process. Sphinx operates with a 1000 word vocabulary and achieves a recognition accuracy percentage in the mid-nineties when provided with a bigram language model; however, accuracy drops to the mid-fifties without the grammar model.

Sphinx makes extensive use of Hidden Markov Models: each phone is represented by an HMM, each word is a network of phones, and the language is a network of words. Phones in function words are modeled separately from other phones because of the higher degree of coarticulation and distortion in function words. Because function words are common to all vocabularies, they can be modeled using more thoroughly trained HMMs.

Sphinx uses multiple codebook vector quantization as its acoustic front end. Separate codebooks are used to encode energy, cepstral, and differential cepstral parameters. The cepstrum is a signal analysis construct gaining popularity with speech recognition because it differentiates voicing and vocal tract aspects of the speech signal. Differential cepstrum measurements indicate how the cepstrum changes from one sampling period to the next; this measure is particularly useful for analysis of the most dynamic aspects of speech such as many of the consonants.

## MIT's SUMMIT

The SUMMIT [Zue *et al.* 1989a] system is a phoneme-based connected speech recognizer being developed by the Spoken Language Systems Group at M.I.T. In recognizing speech, SUMMIT first transforms the speech signal into a representation modeled after the auditory processing that occurs in our ears. This is a nonlinear transformation based on Seneff's auditory model [Seneff 1988]; it enhances acoustic information crucial for recognizing speech and suppresses irrelevant detail. Part of this analysis models the transduction between the hairs in the cochlea and their associated nerve cells to enhance temporal variation in the input emphasizing onsets and offsets crucial to detecting consonants. Another portion, which models the nerve cell firing rate related to the characteristic frequency of the cell, emphasizes spectral peaks; this is useful for vowel identification.

The next stage of recognition segments the transformed speech by finding acoustic landmarks in the signal. Regions between the landmarks are grouped into segments on the basis of similarity. A set of phonetic classifiers assigns probabilistic phonetic labels to each of these portions of the speech signal. Different classifiers may be invoked for differentiating among distinct classes of phonemes. Words are represented by a network of phonemes; several networks may be used to encode alternate pronunciations. A pattern matching algorithm similar to dynamic programming matches the phoneme labels of the input against the word networks, deducing word boundaries in the process. Coarticulation rules compensate for some phonemic aspects of connected speech.

## SUMMARY

This chapter has detailed the process of recognizing speech by computers. It began with an overview of the recognition process as a set of three basic components: an acoustical representation, a vocabulary or set of templates, and a pattern matching process to measure the similarity of an input utterance with each of the set of templates. This process was illustrated by considering a simplistic, hypothetical recognizer. The chapter then discussed a full range of possible recognizer configurations differentiated by the specificity of the talker, the style of speaking, and the size of the vocabulary to be recognized. Several techniques important for connected and large vocabulary recognition were then introduced; these included Dynamic Time Warping, Hidden Markov Models, Vector Quantization, and language constraints. The chapter concluded with a descriptive overview of three well-known research projects on large vocabulary speaker independent recognizers.

This chapter was intended to introduce the technology of speech recognition and some of the difficulties it must overcome to be effective. Speech recognition algorithms are under continual development and are useful for an ever-expanding range of applications. Even more important for its deployment, the steady increases in microprocessor speeds enable even the more sophisticated algorithms to be implemented entirely as software thus encouraging the more widespread distribution of applications that make use of recognition.

The next chapter explores the utility of speech recognition, the classes of applications for which it may be well suited, and interaction techniques to make effective use of recognition. Of central concern is the issue of speech recognition errors; error rates remain the primary deterrent to the successful application of speech recognition. But in some specialized application niches speech recognition is already being used to improve personal productivity.

## FURTHER READING

O'Shaughnessy covers many topics in speech recognition thoroughly. Furui and Sondhi is a collection of particularly current papers about all aspects of speech processing with particular emphasis on recognition. Although rather technical, it has chapters describing most of the concepts and some of the speech-recognition research projects discussed in this chapter. Waibel and Lee present a collection of previously published research papers about speech recognition. Dixon and Martin is a similar collection of key papers from the 1970s. Another good source of very good working papers are conference proceedings of the DARPA Speech and Natural Language Workshops.

# 8

# Using Speech Recognition

The previous chapter offered an overview of speech recognition techniques and the difficulty of identifying the words in a speech signal. This chapter discusses how speech recognition can be used in applications. It examines the merits as well as the constraints of using voice input, which limit the classes of applications for which it is suitable. Because the dominant difficulty with using speech recognition devices is usually their poor performance, this chapter emphasizes interaction techniques to manage recognition errors. Finally, several case studies in applications of voice input are detailed.

## USES OF VOICE INPUT

Voice input can be suitable to an application for one of several reasons. In some circumstances, no other input channel may be available due to the lack of an interface device such as a keyboard or mouse. Even when alternative input devices are available, speech recognition may be more efficient; we can speak faster than we write or type. Voice can also be employed effectively when the user's hands and eyes are occupied with another task.

### Sole Input Channel

Regardless of its limitations, voice input is useful when no other input mode is available or when alternative modes present only limited functionality. For this reason, speech recognition currently attracts wide interest from the manually-

154

disabled population for whom conventional keyboards and mice are extremely demanding.

For many telephone-based voice applications such as those described in Chapter 6, the 12 button keypad is sufficient. Speech recognition can be employed instead of or in addition to touch tones to provide access to a greater number of commands, to make it easier for the caller to remember them, and to enable users to phone in from rotary-dial telephones. Although speech recognition provides a more flexible interface, it is also significantly limited in this context. Because of the limited bandwidth of the telephone audio channel, both high and low frequency sound is lost, removing some cues useful to acoustic classification. Although the quality of telephone networks is improving, some calls, such as from cellular phones, contain significant noise. Even when the telephone circuit itself introduces no noise, users of telephone-based services are often travelers calling from public telephones in noisy locations. Also, as discussed in Chapter 6, because the telephone circuit mixes both the transmitted and received speech it is difficult for the user to interrupt and be correctly recognized.

Speech recognition has been used in a number of telephone-based services usually employing small vocabulary speaker-independent recognition because the identity of the caller is not known. An alternative approach uses speaker-independent recognition or touchtones for the caller to "login" and then loads that caller's personal vocabulary into the recognizer for the remainder of the call. Some examples of telephone-based recognition are listed here.

- Telephone-based financial services. A caller enters an account number by voice and is told the current trading level of stocks in his or her portfolio or speaks code numbers for a specific stock to hear its price. Because speaker-independent recognition is often limited to the digits zero through nine plus "yes" and "no," it has not been possible until recently to use a more convenient interface that allows the user to speak stock names.
- Automatic directory assistance for pay-per-use telephone services. Voice menus list the types of services one can call, and the user selects one by speaking choices while traversing the menu. The application then gives a telephone number for access to the chosen service.
- Automated collect call completion. The calling party is prompted to record his or her name. A computer phones the called party, announces the requested collect call, plays the recording of the caller identifying herself, and then asks whether the charges will be accepted. The words "yes" and "no" are recognized; failed recognition results in transfer to a human operator for confirmation.

Speech recognition has enormous potential as the primary means of interacting with new generations of very small hand-held computers. Improvements to laptop computers are mostly in performance; a full keyboard suitable for touch typing places limits on further size reductions. A number of "palm top" computers provide applications such as a calendar and telephone directory but are limited in the amount of data input allowed by their tiny keys. An all-voice computer, perhaps including a small touch-sensitive display, could be built in a package similar to a miniature tape recorder. At the time this book is being written several manufacturers have introduced families of integrated circuits for digital consumer answering machines; these inexpensive parts are also suitable for a pocket computer.

### Auxiliary Input Channel

Speech recognition is useful as an input channel even when a keyboard is available, i.e., when speech is not the only possible means of interacting with a computer.[1]

Limited vocabulary speech recognition has been used for a variety of applications in which it essentially substitutes for the keyboard; for a survey of such comparisons see [Martin 1989]. In many traditional screen and keyboard applications such as authoring computer programs, speech recognition has not yet offered a great advantage over keyboard input. However, speech has proven effective in applications in which the user's hands and eyes are otherwise busy, such as baggage sorting, examining printed circuit boards for defects, and entering the results of visual analysis of specimens under a microscope. Speech input is attractive in such situations because of the inconvenience of putting down the object of one's attention for the sake of using the hands on a keyboard.

A particularly strong motivation for voice input is our ability to perform multiple tasks simultaneously if we can employ multiple input modalities. As discussed in some detail in Chapter 6, dividing tasks between verbal and manual channels can result in increased effectiveness and speed by a user. Voice input has particular importance for computer workstations because users are already using a keyboard and often a mouse for a variety of tasks. Computer users are usually occupied manually by typing or using the mouse and visually by the computer display. Although a good typist does not watch his or her hands, most computer tasks involve interacting with data, text, or an operating system for which visual feedback is essential. Because the mouse is used for *relative* positioning, it cannot be operated without attention to the screen. Computer users also often perform multiple tasks in parallel, especially if multiple phases of the same application, such as using a menu and typing data, are considered to be separate tasks.

Computer users, then, can take advantage of voice input for both reasons: being otherwise occupied manually and visually and performing multiple tasks in parallel. In Chapter 6 the same arguments were made to justify potential advantages of voice output. Martin [Martin 1989] demonstrated that for a computer-aided design task involving extensive use of display, keyboard, and mouse, experienced users were able to get more of their tasks done while spending less time looking at the screen when voice input was added. These results motivated

---

[1]The "listening typewriter" is a special case of keyboard replacement which will be discussed in the next section.

Xspeak, a Media Lab interface using speech recognition for navigation in a window system, which is described as a case study later in this chapter.

Another potential use of voice as an auxiliary channel of user input is interacting with a computer at a small distance. A user might wish to start issuing commands such as logging in or initiating a time-consuming task such as sorting electronic mail while walking into the office and hanging up his or her coat. Unfortunately, few recognizers can perform adequately under the highly variable acoustic conditions occurring while the talker moves about in an office, but it may be feasible to electronically "point" an array of microphones at the mobile sound source.

Voice input can also be found in commercial products to speed-dial telephone numbers. The user trains templates and enters the associated digits using the telephone keypad. The user later places a call by picking up the handset and speaking the name to call. Since the caller is about to speak into the telephone during the call, voice-dialing is an intuitive extension of the voice modality. For speech recognition, the telephone handset microphone is well positioned with respect to the mouth; picking it up provides the cue to begin recognizing.

## Keyboard Replacement

The previous section argued that there are situations in which speech recognition may be a useful supplement to the keyboard because of other activities a user needs to perform manually. This section considers the potential of speech recognition as a direct keyboard replacement for the purpose of text entry. Although dictation is in many aspects the antithesis of conversational interactive systems, such a "listening typewriter" is the subject of much speech recognition research and the focus of several attempts to develop recognition products.

A listening typewriter may offer several advantages over a keyboard. We can speak significantly faster than we can write or type; we usually speak at several hundred words per minute; an excellent typist can produce 80 or 100 words per minute, and we handwrite at less than half that rate. Of course many of us are not efficient typists, and some professionals are quite adverse to using a keyboard. Even efficient typists may suffer from physical disabilities that interfere with productivity.

At first glance, speech recognition seems to be a superb keyboard replacement. We could imagine such a device useful in any number of large vocabulary computer applications, but we must consider a number of factors in assessing the utility of the listening typewriter. Can speech recognition devices take full advantage of the faster rates of speaking over writing? What portion of the time needed to create a document is consumed by the text input stage? How difficult is it to learn to dictate, and are dictated documents of comparable quality to written ones? Finally, just how extensible is the listening typewriter?

Large vocabulary speech recognition by machine is extremely difficult. As the number of words stored in memory increases, there is an increased likelihood that words will be confused, and pattern matching to select which word was spoken will take correspondingly longer as well. Because a large number of words may be spoken at any time, word boundary detection is also confounded: As a result many very large vocabulary systems are being developed using isolated word recognition.

Although there are several products and a number of research projects offering some degree of large vocabulary recognition, this work is not yet mature enough to allow an assessment of speech effectiveness for text entry using these devices. The number of similar sounding words confounds recognition in large vocabularies. As a result, current recognizers operate either in less than real time or are constrained to isolated word recognition. But insights into the utility of speech for text input can be gained both from simulations in which a hidden human performs the voice-to-text transcription in real time and by studying how people dictate. Much of the research in this area was done in a series of experiments by John Gould at IBM, who studied dictation as well as simulated listening typewriters.

In one study focusing on the difference between speaking and writing letters, Gould found that speaking required 35% to 75% of the time required for writing and that across both media about two-thirds of the time was spent in planning [Gould 82]. In another study, Gould determined that although people thought their written letters were of better quality, independent judgments did not show this to be true [Gould and Boies 1978]. This work and a similar study [Gould 1978] suggested that dictation is not a difficult skill to acquire.

Gould then provided a simulated listening typewriter to subjects who used it to dictate letters [Gould et al. 1983]. He wished to evaluate the importance of vocabulary size as well as the constraints of discrete versus connected speech input. A human transcriber behind the scenes played the role of the speech recognizer and enforced interword pauses for discrete input mode. Depending on the selected vocabulary size, the transcription software determined whether each word should be "recognized." The subject was required to spell an unrecognized word letter by letter. The subjects included both expert as well as naive dictators.

Gould measured the composition time and evaluated the quality of the letters produced by his subjects who used the simulated recognizer. He found that by both criteria speaking letters was comparable to hand writing them. The fact that expert subjects (experienced with dictation) were not significantly faster than novices suggests that the experimental setup was not as efficient as simple dictation; using any of the simulated technologies, someone talking to a computer was slower than speaking into a tape recorder.

Although Gould's subjects preferred connected over discrete speech, the difference was not as large as one might expect given the requirement to pause between each word. This may be due in part to the nature of the experiment. In one task, subjects were required to write a final draft version of a letter. If the recognizer made an error, the user's only recourse was to back up and delete each intervening word, replace the misrecognized word and then repeat all the deleted words. This may have encouraged subjects to pause between words until each recognition result was displayed on the screen, even while using the connected speech mode. This may also partially explain why expert dictators did not perform as well as might have been expected, given their experience.

What do Gould's studies indicate as to the suitability of speech as a keyboard replacement? It seems easy to learn to input text by voice, and the resulting documents are of equal quality to those written or typed. Although isolated word recognition is significantly slower than connected recognition, it does appear to have utility and may be acceptable in an office environment. But there is more to writing a passage than entering words. Although speaking may be five times faster than handwriting and two to three times faster than an experienced typist, *composing* a letter takes a significant portion of the time spent creating a document, thus diminishing some of the speed improvement afforded by voice input. After initial authoring, documents may require editing, which Gould noted is easier with handwriting. Some editing functions such as moving a cursor to select a region of text may be awkward to perform by voice, and it is a challenge for the recognizer to detect when the user wants to switch between text input and editing.[2] Finally, it must be noted that although Gould's studies compared voice to handwriting, typing is becoming an increasingly common skill and is much faster than handwriting (although still much slower than fluent speech).

Despite these objections, the listening typewriter would still undoubtedly be useful for some users and in some work environments. Research in this direction hastens the arrival of large vocabulary general purpose recognizers as well. However, specific assumptions about the structure of written language used to constrain the recognition task may render the recognizer less useful for other potential applications. For example, the language, or sequences of words, that a user would speak to a computer operating system would possess its own unique syntax very different from the business correspondence used to seed the trigram probability tables. In addition, operations such as selecting a file name or entering the name of a new file to be created much less constrain the choice of the next word than natural languages and therefore are harder to recognize. The terseness of text-based computer interfaces is efficient for the skilled user, but by removing redundancy they comprise a more difficult language for recognition.

This section has considered the production of text documents by voice in contrast to keyboard or handwritten input. Voice as a document type was considered in depth in Chapter 4. Although dictation and using a speech recognizer instead of a keyboard are similar tasks, both involve quite different authoring styles than recording short voice memos that are never converted to text. Comparisons of creation time with quality across voice and text documents may not be very meaningful as the document types are most likely to be used for rather different styles of messages.

---

[2]To achieve acceptable rates of recognition with such large vocabularies, recognizers must take advantage of the context in which the word occurs. The requirements imposed by assumptions of context, both preceding and following the word just spoken, interfere with providing immediate editing commands. For example, the Tangora recognizer described in the previous chapter does not report a word as recognized until at least one additional word has been spoken to afford adequate context for effective recognition.

## SPEECH RECOGNITION ERRORS

The primary limitation of speech recognition is the accuracy of current recognizers. As a result, coping with errors dominates user interaction techniques. The difficulty of recognizing speech further limits the range of applications for which it is suitable. Accuracy is so impaired by noise that speech recognition can be used only with great difficulty in even moderately noisy environments or over impaired communication channels such as cellular telephone connections. Speech recognition applications must operate with smaller vocabularies, making it difficult to support broad functionality, in order to attain acceptable recognition rates. Even the most simple application must deal with recognition errors; for complex applications error detection and correction may require more programming than the portion of the application that actually performs the user's suggested action.

### Classes of Recognition Errors

Speech recognition errors may be grouped into three classes.

1. *Rejection:* The talker speaks a word from the recognizer's vocabulary but it is not recognized.
2. *Substitution:* A word spoken from the vocabulary is recognized as some other word.
3. *Insertion:* Extraneous words are recognized in response to stimuli such as the talker's breathing or lip smacking or perhaps environmental noise such as a door slam or keyboard clicks.

Different strategies are required for coping with each type of error. All errors are more likely to occur when using connected recognition, large vocabularies, and speaker-independent devices. Because of rejection and insertion errors, a connected recognizer may even report incorrectly the *number* of words spoken in addition to making a substitution error on any particular word.

Users want the best recognizer they can buy; however, it is very difficult to measure error rates of a particular device. Error rates will be a function of the background noise level, the vocabulary set, the speaker's cooperation, attitude, and experience. Most manufacturers claim recognition accuracy in the high 90% range, but these rates are unrealistic and rarely realized in practice. Accuracy measurements across recognition devices are a meaningless basis for comparison unless the same test conditions are reproduced for each measurement. This requires using a standardized test, with both test and training data taken from the same audio source, e.g., a test tape or CD.

Real users rarely achieve the rates claimed for a device by the vendor. Reducing accuracy to a single metric can be misguided because rejection, substitution, and insertion errors may have different impacts on the underlying application. The difference between 95% accurate recognition and 98% may be very significant in terms of the difficulty in improving the recognition algorithm (to halve the error rate), but this reduction is much less significant for user interface design; in both cases, the recognizer is correct most of the time but makes occasional errors. The speech input interface still has to cope with errors or it will have little utility.

## Factors Influencing the Error Rate

Recognition errors are caused by many factors; some are more obvious than others. Techniques can be employed to minimize errors, so it is important to recognize early in a design what factors are likely to contribute to an increased error rate. Understanding the causes of errors also helps us appreciate why some applications are more amenable to speech input than others. The necessity of detecting and correcting errors precludes the use of recognition from some applications where it may seem ideal at first glance.

### Word Similarity

Words which sound similar, such as "bat" and "bad," are difficult for humans to distinguish, so it should not be surprising that they are also frequently confused by a speech recognizer. Without a thorough understanding of the acoustic representation used by the recognizer, it is difficult to know which words sound similar, but a good first approximation is that words containing similar phoneme sequences are likely to be a source of recognition errors.

As previously mentioned, as the number of words to be recognized increases it becomes increasingly difficult to distinguish between them. Longer words contain more phonemes and hence are more likely to contain cues allowing them to be distinguished from other words. For example, the words "impossible" and "improbable" contain nearly identical sequences of phonemes, but the fricative "s" is a robust cue for differentiation. Errors can be minimized by careful selection of the vocabulary set to be used in an application, avoiding short and similar sounding words. When using a discrete word recognizer, it is helpful to string together short words such as "to the right of" into phrases which are trained and spoken as if they were single words.

But modifying one's vocabulary to optimize recognition performance may not be possible or may detract from the advantages of speech input. "Five" and "nine" could be confusing words for recognition because of their common vowel, but if the application requires the user to enter a telephone or credit card number, the use of these words cannot be avoided. Although "affirmative" and "negative" are more easily distinguished than "yes" and "no," they take longer to pronounce and more importantly are not part of most of our daily vocabularies. In situations in which speech recognition is essential, users may be amenable to using specialized vocabularies; however, this is at cross purposes to the claims of naturalness and ease of use for voice input.

### Acoustic Environment

Noise interferes with recognition—although some recognizers are more sensitive to noise than others. Environmental noise varies widely; there are vast differences in the amplitude and spectral characteristics of the acoustical ambiance in an office, on a factory floor, or inside an automobile. In a noisy environment, special noise-canceling microphones may assist recognition (see Figure 8.1). These microphones attempt to remove background noise from the speech signal and are usually worn on the head or held near the mouth. This position is a hindrance in many circumstances.

Impairments in the acoustic channel may be constant or vary with time; constant characteristics are easier to model and hence are easier to compensate for. Speech recognition over the telephone provides an example of each. As discussed in Chapter 10, a telephone circuit transmits only the portion of the speech spectrum below approximately 3500 Hertz,[3] so a recognizer designed for telephone use must not rely on acoustic cues based on frequencies above this. This limited bandwidth is a predictable characteristic of the telephone channel. In addition, if a call is placed from a public telephone, there may be highly variable background noise such as traffic sounds, flight announcements, or the caller at an adjacent telephone. Because it is difficult to model such noise, it is also difficult to compensate for it.

---

[3]A manifestation of limited bandwidth is the increased difficulty we have in identifying a person by voice over the telephone.

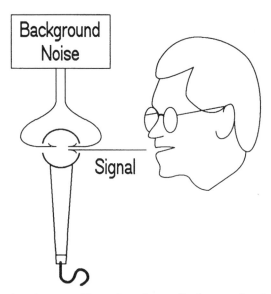

**Figure 8.1.** A noise-canceling microphone. Background noise enters the microphone in both the front and rear openings, but the user's speech is detected primarily at the nearer opening. This allows the microphone to subtract the background noise from the combined input of speech and background noise signal.

### *Talkers' Characteristics*

Recognition simply works better for some people than others; this is what is sometimes referred to as the "sheep-and-goat" problem. Some users, the "sheep," can achieve high recognition accuracy. They are more cooperative and adaptive with their speech habits or perhaps simply more consistent in how they speak. Others, the "goats," have considerable difficulty with recognition. They may experience "microphone fright" or be resentful of the implications of a computer assisting them on the job. Many people compensate for errors during recognition by speaking louder, which may cause distortion by overloading the audio circuits, or by trying to speak more distinctly, which may make their speech less similar to the templates that they trained while relaxed. A user with a cold and congested nasal passages may need to train a new set of templates to achieve acceptable recognition due to the changed spectrum of the vocal tract transfer function.

## INTERACTION TECHNIQUES

It is impossible to build an effective speech recognition application without taking care to minimize errors if possible and incorporating a means of coping with recognition errors. The previous section catalogued factors influencing the error rate; some of these may be at least somewhat under control of the application, such as utilizing a recognition vocabulary that avoids words that sound similar. This section also discusses other activity that can be incorporated into the user interface to diminish error probabilities. But errors will happen. This section emphasizes interaction techniques that can be employed by the user interface to allow applications to utilize recognition despite the errors.

Because recognition errors may be due to different causes (insertion, rejection, and substitution errors were just described) multiple error recovery techniques may be needed in a single application. There are two aspects of coping with errors. **Error detection** identifies that an error has occurred. Detection can be triggered by the user's apparently requesting an improper or meaningless action by the system or by the recognizer's reporting that a rejection error has occurred. **Error correction** techniques can then be employed to rectify the error and allow the application to determine what the user actually requested. Recognition errors may not be readily detectable by an application. If the user says "Call Barry" but the recognizer reports "Call Harry," this semantically correct substitution error might easily pass unnoticed, so the application must provide for user-initiated error correction as well.

This section focuses on techniques, largely conversational, for understanding the user's spoken input. If an error is detected, what should a user interface do about it? If the user detects the error, what corrective action does the application provide? This section discusses techniques to minimize recognition errors based largely on the observations made above on factors contributing to errors. It then examines confirmation strategies whereby the user is informed of what the application is about to do and has an opportunity to veto any command triggered by erroneous recognition. The final part of this section presents methods whereby either the application or the user may invoke iterative techniques to detect and correct recognition errors from input command sequences already in progress.

## Minimizing Errors

Recognition errors result in impaired application performance and increased user frustration. Whenever a recognition error occurs, a repair strategy must be invoked by either the user or the application. Repair inevitably necessitates the user speaking more words, which may in turn be misrecognized in addition to the error that the dialogue is meant to correct. As the error rate increases, it takes correspondingly longer to complete whatever task is supported by the application, and user satisfaction with speech recognition plummets. Error rates can be diminished by compensating for the factors resulting in errors; several factors were discussed in the previous section:

- Careful selection of the recognition vocabulary.
- Control of environmental acoustics and the use of a head-mounted noise-canceling microphone.
- Training users to speak clearly and consistently.

Several additional techniques can be used to further minimize recognition errors.

### Vocabulary Subsetting

Many recognizers allow the application to specify that only a subset of the full vocabulary should be available for recognition at a particular moment. This dynamic modification of vocabulary size can result in significant performance improvements if the structure of the task permits. Many speech recognition applications use speech input much like filling out a multiple choice form; at any juncture in the user interaction there are a small number of choices of what to say next. For example, if the user is asked to speak a telephone number, recognition can be restricted to the digits plus a few key words, such as "area code" and "quit." If the application asks a yes-or-no question, the active vocabulary can be reduced to just the two possible responses.

### Language Model Subsetting

Most current large vocabulary speech recognizers employ language models to improve accuracy by specifying all possible input sentences prior to recognition. This is similar in concept to vocabulary subsetting where the subsetting is done on a word-by-word basis while attempting to recognize a sequence of words. The application can facilitate this process by activating and deactivating portions of the language model (sometimes called "contexts") during the course of interaction. For example, at the stage of a transaction where the user is expected to speak a dollar amount, the recognizer can be told to use only the small portion of its language model dealing with dollars, cents, digits, etc.

### Explicit Indication of Attention

In many acoustic environments background noise is highly variable, which results in spurious insertion errors when short, loud sounds are picked up by the microphone. Insertion errors also occur if the user speaks with another person such as a telephone caller or a visitor. Such errors can be minimized by disabling recognition when it is not in active use.

One simple means of disabling recognition is the addition of a mechanical switch on the microphone cable. A hand-held device employing speech recognition may require a push-to-talk button in a noisy environment. If the user is at a computer, a mouse button may be used the same way. But any mechanical switch detracts from the benefit of being able to use recognition while one's hands are otherwise occupied.

Another alternative is to use voice commands such as "stop listening" and "pay attention." After the user says the first of these commands, recognition results are discarded until the second is spoken. Note that it is important to use phrases for this software switch that are unlikely to be spuriously recognized themselves. Another disadvantage of the stop listening approach is that the user is likely to forget that recognition is disabled until speaking several times with no apparent results.

Some versions of CMU's Sphinx recognizer used a key word to indicate attention and trigger recognition: "Computer, when is my meeting?" "Computer, cancel the meeting." Recognition control can also be implemented using the keyboard or mouse if the user works at a computer console. Finally, it is possible to use the direction in which the user speaks as the focus mechanism. The Media Lab's Conversational Desktop project [Schmandt et al. 1985] used such an approach; the user turned toward the screen when he or she wished to be heard, and an array of microphones detected this change of attention.

## Confirmation Strategies

The need to cope with the high likelihood of errors must play a lead role in the choice of interaction techniques. The interface designer must consider the consequences of the application performing an incorrect action on the basis of misunderstood input and how to improve the chance that the user will notice the error before doing further damage. By setting a high rejection threshold, an interface designer can decrease the number of misrecognized words but at the cost of an increase in rejection errors. The user can be more confident that the application will not err, but it will likely take longer to perform the correct action.

Whether it is faster to reject many possibly correct utterances or accept errors and allow the user to correct them depends on the nature of the task, the complexity of the input, and the time required for recognition. Depending on the probabilities of making errors with particular vocabulary sets, different correction or confirmation techniques can be modeled as Markov processes and their behavior predicted [Rudnicky and Hauptmann 1991]. But for some applications an error cannot be repaired. This is the case when the computer is going to perform some action with dangerous or irrevocable side effects (launching a missile or deleting a file). Such performance errors can be avoided by offering the user a chance to cancel a misrecognized request before the application has acted on it. At the cost of requiring greater participation from the user, several different confirmation strategies can be invoked to avoid making a mistake.

### Explicit Confirmation

When misrecognition would cause an irrevocable performance error, explicit confirmation may be required from the user, elicited by echoing the request as recognized: "Please confirm that you wish to delete the file named 'book'." If the user's response is then limited to "yes" or "no," vocabulary subsetting can be employed to decrease the chance of misrecognition. In addition, the rejection threshold can be increased for the reply for added confidence that the user really wishes to proceed with a dangerous action.

Explicit confirmation is slow and awkward, requiring responses and user feedback with each interaction. As described here, it offers the user little recourse for misrecognition except the opportunity to try again without causing damage. Hence, it should be used sparingly. If the consequences of system action and recognizer accuracy together suggest use of explicit confirmation on every user request, the task is likely to be ill suited to speech recognition.

A more flexible variation is to use explicit confirmation only when the user's choice is implausible or the recognition score for a word is low. In such circumstances an effective technique is to ask "Did you say . . . ?" and temporarily switch to explicit confirmation mode.

### Implicit Confirmation

An alternative to explicit confirmation is *implicit confirmation,* in which the application tells the user what it is about to do, pauses, and then proceeds to perform the requested action. The application listens during the pause, thus giving the user the opportunity to cancel the request before any action occurs. If the request takes significant time to perform, such as dialing a number from a cellular phone, the application may be able to begin performing the task during the pause; if the user cancels, the call attempt is abandoned before the call has had time to go through.

Implicit confirmation allows the system to perform more effectively as recognition accuracy improves. The user is required to intervene only in the case of an error; otherwise the request and resulting action proceed smoothly. Implicit confirmation could be slightly slower than explicit confirmation as the application must pause long enough to provide ample time for the user to respond. The user can be allowed to terminate the pause by saying "OK"; this is similar to the optional termination techniques discussed in Chapter 6. If the user always responds, this is identical to explicit termination. Although the application is idle during this pause, the user can be performing other tasks and thinking about what to do next. Because the application has confirmed what it is about to do, the user need not devote additional attention to the task.

## Error Correction

The previous section described confirmation techniques to ensure that erroneous recognition did not occur or was canceled by the user. This was based on a binary judgment by the user as to whether recognition was correct; rejection caused the entire input to be discarded. While this may be necessary in error-critical situations, a more effective strategy is to attempt to detect recognition errors and invoke repair dialogue to resolve misrecognized words.

An error may be noticed by the application or it may escape detection only to be noticed by the user. The application may detect that an error occurred because the resulting sentence is syntactically ill formed or semantically meaningless; techniques for such analysis are discussed in Chapter 9. Or it may be that an apparently well-formed request is meaningless in the current state of the application and its associated data. For example, consider a spreadsheet in which the rows are numbered and the columns are lettered. "Add row five and row B" is a syntactically well-formed sentence in and of itself but does not describe an operation that can be performed on this spreadsheet. "Add row five and row twelve" could be a valid operation, but if row twelve has not yet had values assigned to it, the operation still cannot be performed. An application supports a more limited set of operations than can be described with the associated vocabulary, and the current state of the application further constrains acceptable user input.

Depending on the class of recognition error (rejection, insertion, or substitution), the application may be faced with an incomplete utterance, a meaningless utterance, or a valid request that is unfortunately not what the user asked. If the application detects the error, how can it determine what the user wants? If the user detects the error, how can the application allow the user to make repairs?

### Additional Recognition Information

In addition to identifying which word was detected, some recognizers supply additional information that can be used during error recovery. One such piece of useful information is the word that is the **next best match** to the spoken input. The similarity scores for each word indicate how reliable that choice is and how plausible the second choice is if the first is deemed to be in error. If the first choice is not meaningful in a particular context, the second choice may prove to be an acceptable alternative.

Some recognizers are capable of reporting the **confusability** of the words in its vocabulary. Confusability is a measure of how similar each word is to every other word in the vocabulary and gives an indication of the probability that any other word will be substituted. If the recognized word is inappropriate in the current context but another word that is highly similar is appropriate, the application could use the alternate instead of the recognized word.

In the spreadsheet example, the phrase "row B" was suspect. Either second choice or confusability information could be used to indicate whether the user actually spoke "row three" or "column B," for example.

### Alternate Input Modalities

In addition to speech, other input channels may be used to point or select the data represented by an application. Hauptman found that users were able to make effective use of pointing in combination with limited vocabulary speech recognizers to describe graphical manipulations [Hauptmann 1989]. Pointing devices may be two dimensional (mouse, stylus, touch screen, joystick) or three dimensional (gesture input using a variety of magnetic or ultrasonic techniques). Eye trackers report the angle of the user's gaze and can be used to manipulate an object by looking at it [Jacob 1991].

The selection gesture may be redundant to some words in a spoken command; this is especially true of deictic pronouns ("this," "that," "these," "those"). If the gesture can be correctly synchronized with the reporting of speech recognition results, the gestures can be used in place of any pronouns not recognized. This technique was first used in Put That There, a project described later in this chapter. Carnegie-Mellon University's Office Manager (OM) system used mouse-based pointing as a means of explicit error recovery [Rudnicky et al. 1991]; after recognition, a text display of the user's request was presented, and the user could click with the mouse on a word to be changed. Voice has been combined with gesture in a three-dimensional model building task [Weimer and Ganapathy 1992, Weimer and Ganapathy 1989]. Starker and Bolt combined speech *synthesis* and eye tracking into a system that discussed what a user was looking at [Starker and Bolt 1990]; and more recently the same research group has incorporated speech recognition as well [Koons et al. 1993].

### Dialog With the User

The errors that an application detects result in a meaningless or incomplete request. The application must then employ techniques to elicit additional information from the user. The simplest but not very effective technique is to ask the user to repeat the request. If the user repeats the request word for word, it is quite possible that the same recognition error will occur again. If the user instead rephrases the request, different recognition errors may occur, and it is challenging to merge the two requests to decide what the user really wanted.

It is better for the application to ask the user one or more specific questions to resolve any input ambiguity. The phrasing of the questions is critical as the form in which a question is asked strongly influences the manner in which it is answered. The goal of efficiency suggests that the questions be brief and very direct. The goal of minimizing user frustration would also suggest asking questions that can easily be answered by a single word because words spoken in isolation are more easily recognized than connected speech. Consider a schedule application as an example. The user requests "Schedule a meeting with Rebecca tomorrow at three o'clock"; however, the word "three" is rejected. Because the application requires that a time be specified to complete a schedule request, the error can be detected. In return, the application could ask "At what time?"

### Echoing

Asking a terse question is fast but conveys little information about the words that the application assumes to be correct. In the above example, if the application responded "What city?" the user would realize the application had probably completely misunderstood. But if instead of "Rebecca" the speech recognizer had detected "Erica," the query "At what time?" could not convey the occurrence of this error to the user.

Echoing is a technique to offer extensive feedback to the user. For example, the application might have asked "At what time do you wish to meet with Erica tomorrow?" so an alert user could notice the error. Even when the application receives an apparently correct command sequence, echoing it to the user provides an opportunity for the user to take further action. The major drawback of echoing is that it takes time and makes the application much more verbose.

### Backtracking

When recognition errors result in a well-formed and plausible command, an application cannot detect the error and will perform the wrong action in the absence of a confirmation strategy. The user may recover from such an error by backtracking, in which the user simply cancels a request or asks the application to "undo" the action. This is appropriate only when the command can, in fact, be canceled with little or no penalty. To implement backtracking, the application must remember its state before each round of user input; the complexity of this memory is task dependent. Backtracking is a corrective behavior invoked entirely by the user but assisted by the application's ability to track its state.

## CASE STUDIES

What do these factors lead us to conclude as to the suitability of speech recognition to real world work situations? Speech is fast and can be effective for text entry provided the recognizer performs adequately. Performance is enhanced by constraining the recognition choices at each word boundary, i.e., by minimizing the perplexity of the recognition task. This implies that recognition for free-form dictation is more difficult than for application-specific tasks.

Recognition is often suitable for tasks in which one's hands and eyes are busy, providing a valuable auxiliary channel for tasks such as computer-aided design. But note that recognition in this context is more suited to selection of one of a small number of items from a list (e.g., a menu) or selecting an object from some number on display than for continuous tasks such as positioning a cursor.

Recognition is particularly difficult in noisy situations, such as in an automobile or on a factory floor; under these circumstances users may be forced to wear head-mounted microphones. Recognition may be possible in a relatively quiet office environment, but privacy concerns and social conventions make it unlikely we will talk to our computers if we share our office.

This chapter has discussed both the characteristics of applications that may make them successful candidates for speech recognition as well as interactive techniques required to allow users to cope with recognition errors. This section considers two case studies to illustrate these themes. The first case study examines Xspeak, which used rudimentary isolated word recognition to manage windows on a workstation display. Xspeak illustrated how commercially-available recognition may already perform adequately for deployment into normal office environments[4] and discusses experiences of real users incorporating recognition into their jobs.

The second case study, Put That There, demonstrates an early application of multiple error management techniques. Put That There employed connected speech recognition, and the nature of the application required very different error management than Xspeak. Put That There was one of the first speech user interfaces to merge both recognition and synthesis into a conversational system.

### Xspeak: Window Management by Voice

This chapter has contrasted the large vocabulary listening typewriter with smaller vocabulary application-specific recognition. But few workstation-based applications use recognition, and the discussion of error handling techniques should make it clear that incorporating recognition into an application requires considerably more programming than simply reading from an additional device for input in addition to the mouse and keyboard. Furthermore, most desktop computers are now running window systems, allowing users to employ multiple applications during the same work session. If several applications use speech recognition, will they compete for the microphone? Recognition results must be distributed to the correct application process using some indication of the user's intention, such as knowledge about the vocabulary employed by each application, or which window is currently active.

Window systems are ubiquitous on computer workstations. The window system divides the screen into multiple regions ("windows"), each of which can be devoted to a single application. An operating system may allow multiple programs to execute simultaneously; the window system allows each of them to display output without disturbing the others. A typical workstation user is likely to run many

---

[4]Since this project was completed, a number of products to control windows by voice have appeared on the market.

applications as a matter of course, each utilizing one or more windows (see Figure 8.2). These might include a clock, calendar, mail reader, text editor, and perhaps a debugger with a graphical user interface.

The window system may allow windows to overlap or may tile them such that all are visible simultaneously. Overlapped windows are currently more popular; the added load on the user to keep track of partially "buried" windows allows more applications to make effective use of the screen simultaneously [Bly and Rosenberg 1986]. A **window manager** controls which window receives keyboard input or **focus.** A **real-estate-driven** window manager assigns input to the window on which the mouse cursor appears; **click to focus** requires the user to click a mouse button on a window to shift the focus there. The mouse is also used to hide and expose windows and to specify their size and location. A third use of the mouse is user input for applications supporting direct manipulation interfaces with buttons, scroll bars, sliders, and toggle switches.

Xspeak was a Media Lab project that explored an alternative use for voice in the multiple-application workstation environment [Schmandt, Ackerman, and Hindus 1990]. Instead of focusing on the applications themselves and rewriting them to support speech recognition, Xspeak instead used voice input to supplement the mouse for switching *among* applications under X windows. Xspeak provided an extension to window systems by matching limited recognition capabilities to a well-defined set of window operations. Xspeak is an example of an application for which small vocabulary speaker-dependent isolated word recognition is adequate. Although Xspeak was implemented using external recognition

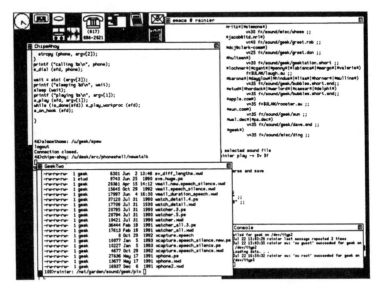

**Figure 8.2.** Many windows may be displayed simultaneously on a single screen.

hardware, suitable software-based recognition requiring no additional hardware is already becoming commercially available.[5]

### Xspeak Functionality

Xspeak provided for the use of voice for the first two mouse functions previously mentioned: focus management and navigation among windows that may be obscured by other windows. Xspeak worked with real-estate-driven window managers supporting overlapped windows. Each window had a name; speaking its name exposed the window. Xspeak then moved the cursor into the window so the window manager assigned it the keyboard focus. Thus the user could move among applications sending keystrokes to each in turn without removing his or her hands from the keyboard. Additional commands allowed the user to raise or lower the window in which the cursor currently appeared.

Xspeak employed a small window to provide both textual feedback to the user and recognition control capabilities (see Figure 8.3). As each word was recognized, it was displayed in this window. In ordinary use this window was ignored as the window reconfiguration provided adequate feedback, but the display panel was useful when recognition results were particularly poor and the user needed to confirm operation of the recognizer. Through the control panel the user could name a new window; this involved clicking on the window and speaking a name that was then trained into a recognition template. The control panel also provided a software "switch" to temporarily disable recognition when the user wished to speak with a visitor or on the telephone. Another button brought up a configuration window, which allowed the user to retrain the recognizer's vocabulary, configure the audio gain of the speech recognizer, and transfer the recognition templates to disk.

Xspeak was an application not a window manager (see Figure 8.4). It worked by capturing recognition results and sending X protocol requests to the server. As with any client application, these requests could be redirected through the window manager, and the window manager received notification of the changes in window configuration or cursor location. Because Xspeak did not replace the window manager, it could be used across a wide range of workstation window system environments.

### Why Speech?

Xspeak was motivated by the belief that window system navigation is a task suitable to voice and well matched to the capabilities of current speech input devices. Using speech recognition to replace the workstation keyboard would be very difficult; it would require large vocabulary speech recognition devices capable of dealing with the syntaxes of both English text as well as program text and oper-

---

[5]Xspeak has recently been revived using all-software recognition. This greatly facilitates deployment of the application.

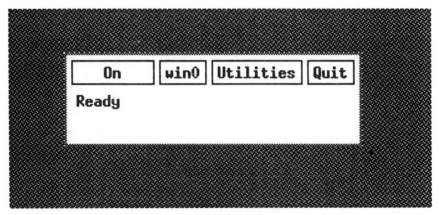

**Figure 8.3.** Xspeak control panel.

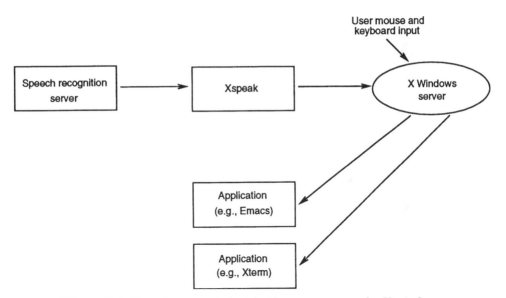

**Figure 8.4.** Xspeak cooperated with other processes under X windows.

ating system commands. In contrast, a typical user employs a relatively small number of windows, and because the user need speak only the name of the window, isolated word speech recognition suffices for the task. Using speech recognition to replace the mouse takes advantage of the fact that the user's hands and eyes are busy on the keyboard and screen. Using voice input saves the trouble of finding the mouse manually, performing an action, and then repositioning the hand on the keyboard.

Voice input also overcomes the dimension mismatch between windows and the mouse. The mouse is a two-dimensional input device, but windows are two-and-a-half dimensional; windows are planar but the plane of any window can be in front of or behind the planes of other windows. Once a window gets buried, the mouse must be used to move other windows out of the way until some part of the buried window is exposed, so mouse actions increase with the number of windows. But speech input bypasses the dimension problem and exposing windows is no more (or less) difficult than recalling an element from a list of names.

Finally, it was hypothesized that the divided attention theories previously mentioned would support improved performance by allocating multiple input channels to the task of working under a window system. To the extent that navigation and focus management are distinct tasks from the operations being performed inside the selected windows, dividing these tasks across modalities should enhance user performance.

### Xspeak in Use

A small number of student programmers used Xspeak during their normal workday for several months and were observed by interviewing, videotaping, and logging of window system events [Schmandt *et al.* 1990]. These observations support the hypotheses about the utility of voice in this task only weakly, yet clarify some of the difficulties of speech recognition.

The dominant factor in user interactions and acceptance of Xspeak was errors. Even in this simple task, recognition rates were abysmal (often less than 80% correct), in large part due to the microphones selected. Because it seemed doubtful that programmers (or the real users toward whom an interface such as Xspeak would eventually be targeted) would wear head-mounted microphones, high quality directional microphones were positioned on stands next to the computer monitors. These microphones admitted much nonspeech noise, and the recognizer responded with a propensity for insertion errors due to sounds such as the keyboard, doors closing, and conversations in the hall. An insertion error would result in the user's keystrokes going into the wrong window; unless noticed immediately this could cause serious damage. To eliminate insertion errors, rejection thresholds were set rather high, resulting in the tendency towards rejection errors reflected in the recorded error rates.

Despite these errors, several users expressed a preference for the recognition-equipped workstations. Those realizing the most advantages from Xspeak were the very active users who kept themselves busy with tasks running in many windows. One such user had already developed techniques using an "icon manager"[6] to control windows and found no added value to speech input. One user employed very few windows and spent much of his time at the workstation during this study thinking and never made much use of recognition. All users abandoned the

---

[6]An icon manager displays a control panel listing the names of all windows. The user can make windows appear and disappear by clicking on this icon manager menu.

microphone-equipped consoles when significantly faster workstations became available elsewhere in the laboratory. Nonetheless, a majority of the users were able to use Xspeak effectively and incorporated it into their daily work routines. Some were extremely enthusiastic and competed for access to Xspeak.

Users did make frequent use of the control panel to test the recognizer and retrain words when recognition was especially poor. Users needed help selecting a vocabulary set appropriate for recognition; one user tried to train nonspeech sounds such as a sigh and a hiss as window names with no success. Summarizing the observed usage and opinions garnered from interviews, Xspeak was certainly intriguing and was perceived positively despite the high error rates, but it simply did not work reliably enough to change work habits. Most users thought that Xspeak was much faster than using a mouse (when recognition succeeded), despite measurements showing that for the most common very simple window actions (switch focus between two exposed windows) the mouse was actually somewhat faster.

The last observation might lend some credence to the divided attention theory, as performance would have to be measured by software production quantity or quality and the perceived speed of recognition might indicate that it interfered less with the programmers' cognitive processes. But the users' strongest complaint (after poor recognition accuracy) was that they wanted to use speech to interact with applications, not just select between them. The clean division of mouse functionality presented above did not dominate the users' perceptions, which suggests that using recognition for window management is just one aspect of multimodal input at the workstation. Although an interaction language to integrate speech recognition into application commands by simulating X input events and distributing them to application windows was designed, it was not implemented.

## Put That There

An early example of an application employing several of the techniques described in this chapter was Put That There, done at an MIT Media Lab predecessor, the Architecture Machine Group, in 1980 [Schmandt and Hulteen 1982, Bolt 1980]. Put That There was an exploration into the use of multimodal input and conversational techniques to resolve recognition errors. While using this application, the user sat in front of a large-screen video projector and used voice and gesture to manipulate ships on a display of a map. Gesture was tracked via a magnetic six-degree-of-freedom sensor worn on the user's hand. The application responded with visual as well as aural feedback using synthesized or digitized speech.

Put That There was a command-and-control application that, depending on the selected database, let the user either create, move, modify, name, or destroy a fleet of ships in the Carribean or build towns, forts, and churches around colonial Boston. The work described here was based on an earlier prototype allowing for manipulation of abstract shapes on a blank screen. Although the prototype presented an impressive demonstration of the technology, the lack of voice response made for an interface only marginally usable: If a single word of an utterance was not recognized, the mute application offered no feedback, and the user's only recourse was to repeat the utterance until something was recognized.

Speech was the primary input to Put That There, via a connected-speech recognizer with a vocabulary size of about a hundred words. The version described here accepted such utterances as these.

- Create a large red sailboat north of Haiti.
- Delete the cruise ship.
- Move the yellow oil tanker east of the Bahamas.
- Copy that (pointing to a ship) . . . north of that (pointing to another ship or a feature on the map).
- Where is Havana?
- Move the yellow oil tanker south of the large green sailboat.

The application's main input loop waited for recognition results while tracking the hand and recording gestures as they were detected. When speech was recognized, the first stage of the application's parser analyzed the input word by word. Each word was classified as an instance of a small class of semantic types from a grammar very specific to this application. Examples of these classes include the following.

- *Command:* the requested action.
- *Movable-object:* a type of ship, e.g. freighter, oil tanker.
- *Color.*
- *Size.*
- *Destination:* either a map location or another ship.
- *Destination-relative:* prepositional phrases such as "north of" or "below."

The parser generated a frame, i.e., a data structure describing a request in progress, which contained slots for the various semantic classes filled in with the specific instances of the words heard. The input loop then dispatched to command-specific procedures for semantic analysis. These procedures were hard-coded program segments that analyzed the frame to determine whether it adequately specified the requested action; for example, a "move" command requires an object to be acted upon as well as a destination. At this point, pronouns such as "that" or "there" were associated with screen coordinates by mapping gestures to objects identified by the bounding boxes of the various targets on the screen. Even if the pronoun were missing due to a rejection error, a recent gesture could satisfy the target specification requirement if it uniquely identified an object or position.

Database routines were invoked to associate descriptions with objects. If the user spoke "the red freighter" and this uniquely matched a ship, parsing could continue. If no ships matched the description, Put That There would ask "Which object?" In the case of multiple matches it would ask "Which one?" These terse responses were barely adequate for guiding the user to an unambiguous request; they would have benefitted from echoing or other explanatory behavior to help understand the nature of the misrecognition.

If an utterance was complete, then these command-specific analysis routines invoked action routines to update the ship database and modify the display accordingly. Most often, however, one or more words would have been misrecognized, resulting in an apparently incomplete request. Each semantic analysis routine included code to generate a query to the user; these queries were designed to elicit single-word responses because the recognizer exhibited much better performance on isolated word input. The queries such as "Where?", "Which one?", and "Relative to what?" were spoken to the user by a primitive speech synthesizer. Since there was a limited set of queries, the synthesizer was later replaced with higher quality digitized speech stored on magnetic disk.

Parsing and semantic analysis were **re-entrant;** after a query was spoken to the user, additional input was gathered from the main input loop and inserted into the utterance frame exactly as before. Since the frame was not initialized after the query, any new information was merged with the old and the semantic analysis routines could then examine the frame again. This query–response–parse cycle continued until an action could be executed or the user reinitialized the process by saying "restart." The net effect was that as recognition accuracy deteriorated, more time and user interaction were required to complete a request but breakdown was rarely catastrophic.

Several error correction strategies were available to the user if misrecognition resulted in a semantically meaningful sentence and a corresponding erroneous action. Put That There maintained a short history of location and attributes for each ship, allowing the user to invoke the *undo* command. If a ship was created with the wrong attributes such as being green instead of the requested yellow, the *change* command allowed for repairs without the need to start the transaction over, e.g., "Change that to yellow."

Another feature of Put That There was dynamic vocabulary management. The *name* command allowed the user to name a ship and thenceforth refer to that ship by name. Naming was accomplished by putting the recognizer into a selective training mode to create a new template when the user spoke the name and associating this template with the ship in the object database. Dynamic training was facilitated by the fact that the recognizer built vocabulary templates from a single training pass; otherwise, the user might have been required to speak the name several times.

The speaker-dependent aspect of the speech recognizer was used to advantage when a multi-user version of the application was desired. The outputs of two microphones were mixed, the vocabulary size was trimmed to occupy only half of the available template memory, and each user trained his own version of each word. As long as the two operators did not speak simultaneously, recognition proceeded as normal. Since the application knew which user had created an object, this information was added to the database to prevent unauthorized modification of one user's ships by the other user.

Put That There is noteworthy as one of the earliest user interfaces employing either multimodal input or conversational techniques using voice input and output. Although the application itself was only marginally relevant to real command and control systems, the user interaction techniques are applicable to a variety of voice interfaces. Subsequent projects, most notably Conversational Desktop (described in Chapter 12), focused on the parsing and error management techniques initiated with Put That There.

## SUMMARY

This chapter discussed incorporating speech recognition into interactive applications. There are many approaches to recognition, and different classes of speech recognizers are amenable to varying styles of applications. Recognition may be employed when no other input channel is available, as an adjunct to existing input channels (keyboard and mouse), or as a direct substitute for the keyboard for text entry. Each of these application areas has different recognition requirements and derives unique benefits from the use of voice input.

Poor recognition accuracy is the dominant concern in designing interaction techniques to employ speech input. Insertion, rejection, and substitution errors all degrade performance but in different ways. Errors can be minimized by careful choice of vocabulary and microphone placement and by chosing cooperative subjects, but these factors may not apply to real-world deployment of recognition technology. As recognition accuracy improves, errors inevitably occur and can be managed through user participation in a variety of confirmation and repair strategies; however, it must be stressed that some interaction techniques will always be required to ensure accurate communication. This chapter discussed the use of language and task constraints in the automatic detection of recognition errors; we will return to the topics of language understanding and dialogue structure in Chapter 9.

This chapter's discussion of error recovery implies that developing recognition-based applications is much more demanding than simply adding a new input device to existing applications. Xspeak was offered as an example of a meta-application, controlling the window system, and thereby selecting an application to receive keyboard events rather than modifying the applications themselves. Put That There was described as an example of simple parsing techniques and spoken dialogue with the user to resolve ambiguities. Although Xspeak illustrates an attempt to closely match the specific assets of speech recognition to the range of tasks performed at the workstation, the experience of its users also demonstrate the frustrations associated with using recognition in daily work.

# 9

# Higher Levels of Linguistic Knowledge

Chapter 1 presented an analysis of human voice communication as a hierarchical stack of linguistic layers. In this schema (depicted in Figure 1.1), each layer of the stack is progressively more removed from the acoustical events associated with speech. The higher layers pertain to the meaning and intention of an utterance rather than to the actual sounds used to convey individual words. As proposed in Chapter 1, analyzing conversation into layers is useful for computational purposes because each layer is likely to necessitate its own representation.

The discussion of speech recognition and synthesis technologies emphasized the lower linguistic layers of communication, i.e., speaking or recognizing words. Syntactic and semantic constraints were introduced as aids to connected speech recognition and influences on intonation and stress. The previous chapter focused on interactive techniques to recover from speech recognition errors with the goal of properly decoding the words in an input utterance. From the user's perspective, speech recognition is not about identifying words; rather, it is a means whereby a computer system understands and acts upon the user's desires. Performance and utility of speech systems are ultimately judged against the highest layers of speech understanding. To this end, this chapter presents representations of syntactic, semantic, pragmatic, and discourse structure that serve the reader as an introduction to topics in natural language processing. The chapter includes several case studies to illustrate the wide range of conversational interactions made possible by models of discourse.

## SYNTAX

Syntax is structure in language imposed by the limited number of ways in which words may be combined in various linguistic roles. Words have different characteristics in a language. Nouns refer to persons, places, concepts, and sensations, while verbs describe actions performed by or on nouns. Adjectives modify nouns, qualifying or quantifying them, and adverbs similarly modify verbs by further specifying the action.

Syntactic structure groups words into phrases and phrases into sentences and describes the relationships between components at each level of structure. At a low level, syntax constrains the gender and number of adjectives and pronouns to agree with the noun to which they refer. The pronoun in "Jane ate his candy bar" is ill-formed if the candy bar belongs to Jane. In many languages the gender of nouns is more significant than in English, and adjectives exhibit different forms for each. For example, in Spanish "el rey blanco" (the white king) and "la reina blanca" (the white queen) illustrate the change in form of the adjective ("blanco") as well as the determiner ("el"/"la") depending on whether they modify a masculine or a feminine noun.

Conversational systems may utilize knowledge of syntax while trying to understand a user's request using speech recognition; because syntax limits the possible combinations of words, perplexity can be minimized. Syntax must also be incorporated into language generation or else the system's replies may be incoherent or less intelligible due to grammatical errors. For a conversational system to make computational use of syntax, two components are required: a grammar and a parser.[1] A **grammar** is a formal specification of language structure; it defines how words can be combined into syntactic units and how these units can be used to build sentences. A **parser** analyzes a sentence to determine its underlying structure as defined by the grammar. The following sections describe several grammatical representations and then present some basic parsing techniques.

### Syntactic Structure and Grammars

Syntax provides structure in a language by constraining the manner in which words can be combined according to a regular set of rules. In this section we consider representations of syntactic structure and formalisms for expressing the rules that comprise a grammar. We can represent the layers of syntactic structure as a **tree,** starting by representing the complete sentence as the root node; this is similar to the technique of diagramming sentences, which many of us learned in elementary school. For example, the most simple sentences contain only a noun

---

[1]Language structure can also be represented probabilistically, e.g., using Hidden Markov Models. Although such an approach is adequate for encoding constraints to aid speech recognition, it is less well suited for representing the grouping of words into syntactic components.

(the subject) and a verb and can be represented as in Figure 9.1, e.g., "Cats purr." Trees capture the order and grouping of words and also indicate the unique label (noun, verb, etc.) associated with each word.

To generalize to more complex sentences we must introduce the concepts of **noun phrase** and **verb phrase.** A noun phrase is a group of one or more words that act as a noun in a sentence. A verb phrase similarly allows multiple words to act as the verb. Because they can contain multiple component words, these phrases introduce another level of structure to our tree representation. A sentence such as "Orange cats purr loudly." is represented as in Figure 9.2. The branching of this tree structure indicates that the adjective "orange" modifies the noun "cats," while the adverb "loudly" is likewise related to the verb "purr."

While trees such as these examples convey the structure of particular sentences or classes of sentences, they do not tell us how to derive the structure for a

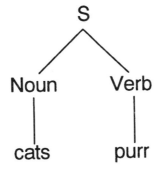

**Figure 9.1.** The figure shows the root node representing the entire sentence above two leaf nodes: one for the noun and one for the verb.

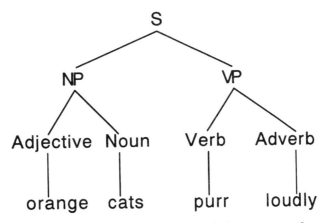

**Figure 9.2.** The tree representation expanded to account for a noun phrase and a verb phrase.

given sentence. Such analysis requires a set of rules that can describe all sentences of a language. A formal set of rules is a **grammar;** a complete grammar specifies the rules for all syntactic structures in a language. Grammars can be specified in several ways.

A **context-free grammar** describes syntactic structures as a series of **rewrite rules.** Each rule defines how a single symbol (on the left side of the rule) can be decomposed into one or more components (the right side of the rule). The grammar is "context free" because the symbol on the left appears in isolation, i.e., removed from the context of the other symbols. Although this constraint limits the range of sentences that can be expressed by a context-free grammar, it is nonetheless quite powerful and frequently used.

Using a context-free grammar, a sentence is broken down step by step into its constituent components through successive invocation of the rewrite rules. The symbols on the left are **nonterminal,** while those on the right may be either nonterminal or **terminal;** terminal symbols are individual words. Successive application of rules reduces all nonterminal symbols to terminals.

A grammar specifying the two sentences previously shown in tree form might resemble that shown in Figure 9.3. The first of these rules (S ← NP VP) specifies that a sentence "S" consists of a noun phrase and a verb phrase. The second rule defines a noun phrase as a single noun ("cats") or an adjective and a noun ("orange cats"); the vertical bar symbol means "or." Although this grammar describes both "Orange cats purr loudly" and "Cats purr," it excludes many other sentence structures such as "Purr!" (no explicit NP), and "Large orange cats purr loudly" (multiple adjectives). Note that each rule breaks the sentence into the same component parts as appear on the branches of the tree representation.

We can include the first of these exceptions by modifying the first rule to read.

S ← NP VP | VP

The new version of the rule specifies that a sentence can consist of a noun phrase followed by a verb phrase or just a verb phrase in isolation. A minor modification of the second rule allows an arbitrary number of adjectives to precede the noun.

NP ← N | Adj NP

```
S  ←  NP  VP

NP  ←  N  |     Adj  N

VP  ←  V  |     Adverb  V
```

**Figure 9.3.** A simple context-free grammar. The symbols S, NP, and VP are nonterminal, whereas the rest are terminal and correspond to individual words.

Context-free grammars can describe many sentences in a natural language such as English; they also specify most programming languages in their entirety. Note that the abbreviated discussion of context-free grammars presented here has avoided some of the issues of gender, number, and case agreement mentioned earlier. For example, the modified verb phrase rule just described allows "Purr!" which is a valid imperative sentence, as well as "Purrs," which is incomplete.

A second powerful representation for grammars is the **transition network** or a slightly more general variation, the **recursive transition network, RTN.** A simple transition network consists of nodes and arcs as shown in Figure 9.4. Each arc is labelled with a word category, and each node is a state in the syntactic analysis of a sentence. Starting at the beginning of the sentence, each word is compared with the label on the arc from the initial state, **S.** If the word and label match, analysis transitions to the next node and word and label comparison continue as before. The last arc is labelled **pop** and always succeeds, indicating completion of the network.

This linear network does not convey the syntactic relationships between the adjective-noun and adverb-verb pairs as well as do the equivalent tree or context-free grammar representations. The network can be enhanced by allowing arcs to be labelled with the names of other networks as well as individual words; with this ability, the network has become recursive. For example, Figure 9.5 illustrates a transition network describing a noun phrase as an arbitrary number of adjectives followed by a single noun. Figure 9.6 shows how the noun phrase net-

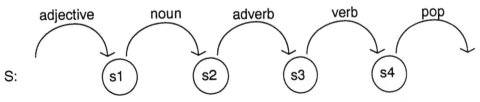

**Figure 9.4.** A simple transition network for sentences consisting of a single adjective, a noun, a single adverb, and a verb. The states, s1 through s4, are connected by arcs labelled with the classes of words required at each transition.

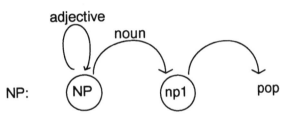

**Figure 9.5.** A transition network for a noun phrase allowing an arbitrary number of adjectives.

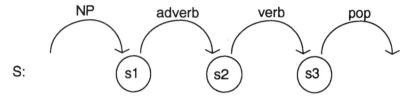

**Figure 9.6.** The transition network shown in Figure 9.3 modified to use the noun phrase network in Figure 9.4. This network is now recursive.

work can be incorporated as a subnetwork by modifying the simple network shown in Figure 9.4.

Let us return to the issue of agreement of gender, number, case, tense, etc. mentioned as an open issue in the discussion of context-free grammars. RTNs can manage some of the agreement issues but in a rather tedious manner. For example, we can define subnetworks for a singular noun phrase as well as for a plural noun phrase, restricting the number of the constituents of each, and then pair these with verb phrases of the appropriate number as shown in Figure 9.7. But a more succinct method is to return to Figure 9.6 and apply a condition to the arc labelled "verb" from state **s2** to state **s3**. This condition stipulates that the number (singular or plural) of the verb satisfying this arc must equal the number of NP satisfying the arc from **S** to **s1**. Although we cannot use conditional transitions within the constraints of the RTN formalism, we can extend the RTN to an **augmented transition network,** or **ATN.** Two features of ATNs are the conditional transition just mentioned and the ability to save information during transitions.

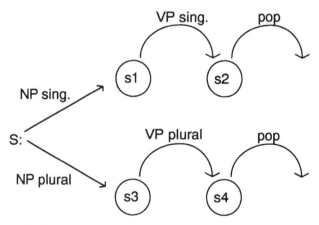

**Figure 9.7.** One way of representing number agreement between subject and verb using RTNs.

**Parsers**

We have just described the various means of representing or specifying the syntactic structure of sentences in a language. It is the task of a **parser** to determine the actual structure of a specific sentence. In its most simple form, a parser takes a sequence of words as input and given the constraints of grammar determines whether the sequence is a valid sentence. By itself this tells us little: only whether the sentence is well-formed. A more complete parser also produces a representation of valid input, which can be employed in higher layers of sentence meaning analysis.

A parser can operate in a **top-down** or **bottom-up** manner to relate the set grammatical rules to the actual structure of the given input. A top-down parser that uses rewrite rules starts with the most general rule describing sentences, i.e., that rule for which the whole sentence "S" is the symbol on the left side of the rule. Applying rules breaks the sentence into smaller components, that eventually become terminal symbols, i.e., specific words in the rewrite rules. For example, using a context-free grammar, a top-down parse of the sentence "Orange cats purr loudly" would first identify the sentence as containing a noun phrase and a verb phrase. Then the noun phrase rule, specifying a NP as some number of adjectives followed by a noun, would be selected, and as a result the parser would identify "orange" as an adjective and "cats" as the noun. At this point, the parser would analyze the remainder of the sentence by identifying the verb phrase, i.e., the right side of the tree from Figure 9.2.

The RTN version of this parse is nearly identical because the top-down parser operates from left to right within a level of syntactic structure. The first constituent of the highest RTN from Figure 9.6 is the NP; this causes the parser to invoke the NP RTN (see Figure 9.5), which allows a NP to begin with either an adjective or a noun. After traversing the adjective arc (for "orange") the parser is still in the initial state. The next word, "cats," is a noun leading to state **np1,** which is followed by the pop arc that returns to the RTN describing the main sentence. At this point the VP RTN can be applied.

Top-down parsing starts with the constituent units such as NP and VP and attempts to match them against incrementally smaller units and eventually words. By contrast, bottom-up parsing begins with the individual words of a sentence and tries to match each word against the grammar's smallest constituent units. These units are, in turn, matched against higher units until the structure constitutes an entire sentence. The bottom-up parser consults a lexicon to identify the syntactic sense of each word. To continue with the example sentence, the first word "orange", is taken to be an adjective from the lexicon. The second word is a noun. These can be matched to a NP. Similarly, "purr loudly" can be matched to a VP in the form of a verb followed by an adverb. A NP followed by a VP makes a complete sentence and the parse is finished.

In the course of parsing, **backtracking** may be required due to ambiguous sentence structure. "Orange" could be taken as a noun (a fruit) instead of an adjective in which case the bottom-up parse would hypothesize that the NP consisted of the single word "orange" (the simplest NP consists of a single noun). But then "cats" would have to be taken as a NP too since "cat" is also a noun. At this point the parse would fail since there is no sentence structure containing two adjacent NPs in this grammar. A bottom-up parser keeps track of each decision in a data structure called a **chart** and uses this to backtrack to a previous state. For the example we have been pursuing, the parse would return to the decision to classify "orange" as a noun, classify it instead as an adjective, and proceed smoothly to complete the sentence.

Both top-down and bottom-up parsers have advantages and disadvantages. Because a top-down parser starts from a syntactic constituent and maps it to individual words, it never considers word categories in grammatically incorrect sentence positions. On the other hand, the top-down parser may process many rules before it ever considers an actual word, and it may repeatedly parse the same segment by backtracking further than necessary. A bottom-up parser avoids repetition; once words are successfully matched to a higher syntactic category they are never reconsidered. But as previously discussed, the bottom-up parser may need to consider multiple senses of each word in the process of matching it to constituent structures. These considerations have led to hybrid parsers, which are top-down in part and bottom-up in part as well.

The parsing process just described either succeeds or fails in its attempt to analyze a sentence. Success indicates that the series of words presented to the parser is a valid English sentence, and failure implies the opposite. But this conclusion alone is of little use to a language understanding system; a practical parser must also produce a computational representation of the syntactic structure and its composition from individual words. For example, if the user says "Delete all files," a language understanding system needs to know which command the user uttered as well as its object; this specific information is more valuable than knowing the NP and VP structure of the sentence. This information is conveyed by recording the actual word that triggers each rule in a context-free grammar or each transition in an ATN. The parse then produces not only the success or failure indication, but more importantly a representation of the sentence structure and how the words of the sentence satisfy this structure.

The discussion so far has assumed that either a sentence was valid in which case the representation is desired, or the input did not form a valid sentence. But for voice interactions additional flexibility is desirable. If the user speaks a 10 word sentence and one of the words is not recognized, it is appropriate to detect this and employ some of the error correction techniques described in Chapter 8. Even if a recognition error does not occur, we often speak utterances that are only partial sentences. A **robust** parser should be able to cope with such fragmentary or ill-formed input, but most natural language processing work to date avoids this issue.

## SEMANTICS

Semantics is the realm of **meaning,** in particular the meaning of a sentence considered in isolation from other sentences. A sentence has meaning in terms of how it relates to the world and objects in it; the sentence stands for some concept or real entity. Meaning is what differentiates nonsense utterances of arbitrary words from rational sentences, and much of the study of semantics is devoted to representations of knowledge about the world.

Semantics begins with meaning at the lexical level; we cannot understand a sentence unless we know the meaning of each word in the sentence. Further, most words have multiple meanings or **senses,** and we must choose among these senses to understand the sentence as a whole. For example, "green" when used as an adjective usually denotes color ("green leaves") but also has another sense in which it means novice or naive ("a green first baseman"). These two senses may be differentiated by considering the noun that "green" modifies. Experience is a concept applied to sentient beings not plants so the sense of "novice" is appropriate only when green modifies a noun that corresponds to a person. One word in a sentence may constrain the interpretation of other words in the sentence. Note the interplay between syntax and semantics: syntax reveals that "green" is used as an adjective and indicates which noun "green" modifies, from which we can then determine the sense in which "green" is being used.

The intended senses of words in a phrase or sentence are mutually constrained; this is called **selectional restriction.** Our knowledge of the attributes of objects in the world helps us identify the sense in which a word is being used to describe an object as we did in the example in the previous paragraph. In addition to objects, i.e., noun phrases, we also apply knowledge about how objects interact, i.e., verb phrases, while selecting word sense.

**Case grammar** attempts to enumerate the cases, or roles, a noun phrase can take with respect to a verb. One case is AGENT; the agent is the instigator of an action and is usually the subject of a sentence. The object acted upon, often identified as the object of the sentence, is a case called THEME. In the sentence "John smashed up the car," John is the agent and the car is the theme. Cases such as AT, TO, and FROM indicate location. An animate object for which an action is performed is the BENEFICIARY, while an animate object in a mental state is the EXPERIENCER. The number of cases is extensive because noun phrases can be used in many different relationships to verbs. Just as real-world knowledge helps establish the meaning of noun phrases, case grammar provides a representation of meaning derived from the roles of noun phrases in an action or state of being.

From this very brief discussion it should be apparent that we obtain cues for the cases of noun phrases from their position in a sentence. For example, subjects, or AGENTS, precede objects, or THEMES, in an active voice sentence, but this order is reversed for passive voice. Prepositions are particularly strong cues for the location cases (AT, TO, and FROM). Selection of cases is controlled by verbs in other ways as well. The verb "move," for example, has a strong requirement for a TO location case to complete its usual meaning as in "we moved to Wyoming." For other sentences a different case is appropriate; an EXPERIENCER completes the sentence "Her singing moved the audience." The concept of case conveys some aspects of the meaning of noun phrases in a sentence, but in the case of a noun phrase it also depends on the meaning of the verb with which it is associated. The presence or absence of a particular case is, in turn, a cue towards selecting the sense in which the verb is being used.

Earlier in this section we discussed how the noun selects between various senses for the adjective "green." The "green first baseman" refers to the lack of experience by a person. How can we represent the knowledge that a "first baseman" is a kind of person to provide the selectional restriction on "green"?

**Semantic networks** are a powerful representation for such relationships. A semantic network is a directed graph where nodes represent an individual word or a class of words, and the links represent relationships between child nodes and their parents. A very simple form of semantic network is the **type hierarchy** in which every arc represents the "is-a-kind-of" relationship. Figure 9.8 shows a partial type hierarchy indicating that a first baseman is a baseball player, baseball players are athletes, athletes are people, people are mammals, and mammals are animate objects. The type hierarchy also indicates that reptiles are animate objects and that rattlesnakes are a particular kind of snake.

The hierarchical nature of this representation indicates that all members of a lower node possess all the characteristics of their parent node, or superclass; this concept is called **inheritance.** Inheritance is useful to express generalizations concisely. With any taxonomy of this sort it is important to select the levels of classification with care; ideally, each step down the hierarchy represents a consistent increase in specificity across the breadth of the network.

A significant limitation of this form of type hierarchy is that any node can be a child of exactly one parent node, representing a subclassing of the parent along a

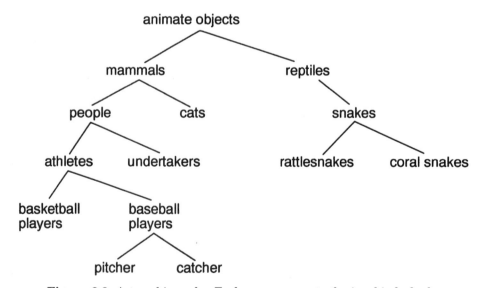

**Figure 9.8.** A type hierarchy. Each arc represents the is-a-kind-of relationship.

particular set of criteria. However, many conflicting subclassifications may be possible. For example, Figure 9.8 subclassed people on the basis of their profession. Figure 9.9 shows other ways of subclassing people based on sex or age. All these subclassification schemes are valid and express a set of differences among people. But these simple two-dimensional type hierarchies break down when attempting to depict multidimensional classification parameters, e.g., differentiating male basketball players from female first basemen.

Semantic networks can be used to convey concepts more general than type hierarchies and are used to represent more complex knowledge relationships. Figure 9.10 shows a sentence displayed on a semantic network in which both the type hierarchy relationships (ovals) as well as case grammar roles (squares) are drawn. Networks can be partitioned into subnetworks to keep close, specific relationships distinct from more general background knowledge or situational context, much of which may be irrelevant to the meaning of a particular sentence. Identifying the meaning of a sentence with semantic networks involves matching the sentence to a particular path or grouping within the network, so that the specific words in the sentence are mapped to their own specific meanings and the case relationship between the words becomes manifest.

## PRAGMATICS

Pragmatics refers to the meaning or purpose of an utterance in a context broader than the semantic meaning just discussed. Pragmatics is about how language is used both in terms of the forms in which speech is invoked as well as in terms of its effects on the conversants. This chapter includes in the scope of pragmatics the role of the utterance in the world and among conversants (To which specific objects in the world does the utterance refer? What does the talker seek to accomplish in speaking it?); to this end it covers knowledge representation as well.

This section introduces three topics in pragmatics, beginning with knowledge representation and plan recognition, which are particularly computational views. The second topic is speech act theory, which views utterances as actions in and of themselves. Finally, a set of guidelines that regulates how much or how little we say and when we say it is introduced; this is formulated from the perspective that an utterance often contains much more meaning than is obvious from the words themselves (the semantic meaning).

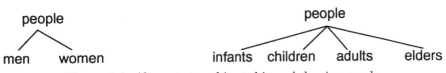

**Figure 9.9.** Alternate type hierarchies subclassing people.

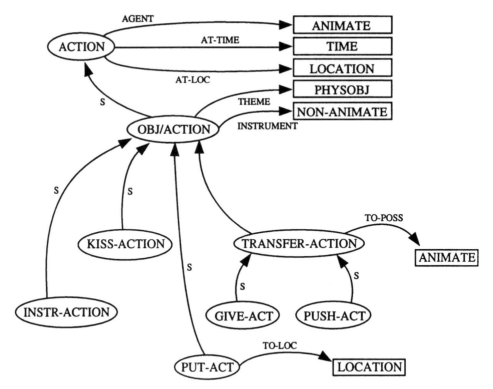

**Figure 9.10.** A semantic network including both a type hierarchy (ovals) and case grammar (squares) categories. After [Allen], p. 209.

### Knowledge Representation

To understand what a person intends by an utterance we need to employ knowledge about the world and the objects in it being referred to by the sentence. For example, to interpret "It's a bit too breezy in here" as a request to close the window of a car, we need to know that a breeze is motion of air, that solid objects block the flow of air, and that windows are solid objects that can be closed by some mechanism such as a crank or motor. A **knowledge representation** provides a means to store and computationally access information about the world, which may be general facts (although windows are clear, they can close an opening) or details of a specific current situation (the car window is open, and the crank will close it).

Knowledge representation systems contain two components, a knowledge base and the inference engine. A **knowledge base** is a database containing facts about the world or information about a situation, and the **inference engine** operates on the knowledge base according to a set of rules. Inference may be primarily **declarative** or **procedural,** depending on whether it stresses the knowledge database or the inference operations to draw conclusions. This section touches upon several aspects of applying world knowledge to language understanding; this is meant to be just an introduction to a complex topic.

**Frames** are a very general representation used by many procedural language understanding systems. A frame is a loose collection of facts about a situation, some of which may be relevant to understanding a specific utterance [Minsky 1975]. Inferences are made by comparing relationships described by the frame with the semantic representation of the utterance. The important objects contained by a frame are called **roles.** For example, a frame for an airplane would likely have roles such as wings, tail, and engines; for a particular aircraft, the role of the engines might be associated with details such as the number of engines, their configuration, and manufacturer. Frames are often implemented in concert with a type hierarchy and likewise may incorporate inheritance.

**Planning** systems focus on the roles of actions and their grouping as a sequence to effect a change of state, or **goal.** Actions are described in terms of preconditions, the set of situations that must be true for the action to occur, and effects, or changes in the world situation as a result of execution of the action. For example, preconditions to sending a letter are writing materials and an addressee, while the effect is for the addressee to receive a written message. **Linear** plan reasoning analyzes goals in terms of sequential subgoals; the satisfaction of each subgoal yields the preconditions for the next. **Nonlinear** planning merges all subgoals into a global set of actions worrying about order of the actions only when necessary. Planning systems seek to understand utterances by recognizing the talker's plan, i.e., a sequence of actions to achieve a goal state. As a plan is likely to evolve over multiple utterances, planning systems are equally salient to discourse analysis as to semantics.

Another representation for commonly performed actions is **scripts,** which specify all the actions ordinarily required as steps toward completion of a "typical" activity [Schank and Abelson 1977]. For example, commercial air travel usually involves consulting schedules, choosing flights, making reservations, purchasing tickets, arriving at the airport, checking baggage, flying, retrieving baggage, and leaving the airport. These actions can be represented as part of a general script for traveling by public transportation (traveling by private car, bicycle, or foot must be described by a different script). Note that some steps, such as checking baggage, may be optional. Plan reasoning can be applied to scripts as well by considering each step in a script to be a precondition for the next step.

Scripts can be used to recognize the real-world activity to which an utterance refers. "I bought my ticket" could refer to any of an extensive class of activities for which admission is required (flights, plays, movies, baseball games). "I bought the ticket for my flight" can invoke the travel script, including the related concepts of departure time and destination city. Once the travel script has been recognized, other components of the script provide a framework for reasoning about the talker's activity. Once we know the ticket is for air travel, for example, we might ask "Where are you going?" or "When will you arrive?"

**Speech act theory** considers utterances as actions in and of themselves. Much of modern speech act theory began with the work of Austin [Austin 1962]. Austin started by considering **performative** utterances, for which the act of speaking itself constitutes the action, such as:

> I now pronounce you man and wife.
> I hereby declare war on Germany.
> I apologize for your inconvenience.

As the first two utterances indicate, these performative utterances are often of a legal or religious nature in which the talker has been granted a higher authority to speak for a society rather than merely speaking as an individual. Austin extended the notion of performative utterances with the concept that many utterances manifest a **force,** or ability to change the state of the world by their very existence, due to their impacts on the beliefs or intentions of the conversants. He identified three senses in which action is performed through an utterance.

1. The **locutionary act** is the actual utterance of a meaningful sentence.
2. The **illocutionary act** is the sense in which the utterance itself contains force to effect a change in state among conversants, e.g., the utterance may act as a promise, offer, decree, statement of commitment, or admission of guilt.
3. The **perlocutionary act** is the manner in which the utterance changes the audience by changing their beliefs or causing them to perform some action.

There have been some attempts to associate force with sentence form; some obvious examples include commanding, using the imperative form, and questioning via the interrogative form. But the mapping from force to form becomes problematic for **indirect speech acts** in which the force depends on speaking conventions. "Can you pass the salt?" is usually meant as a request not a question about the other's ability to pick up the salt shaker. In a similar vein, "It's pretty noisy in here" might be uttered as a request to turn down the radio volume.

[Searle 1976] offered a more detailed taxonomy of five classes of illocutionary action conveyed by an utterance.

1. **Representatives** are sentences by which the speaker asserts or commits to the truth of the utterance.
2. **Directives** are requests to the listener to do something. Questions are directives in that they attempt to evoke a response.
3. **Commissives,** or promises, commit the talker to future actions. Threats are also examples of commissives.
4. **Expressives** create a psychological state rather than causing a physical action. They include welcoming, apologizing, thanking, etc.
5. **Declarations** are the performative statements mentioned earlier such as declaring war or firing an employee.

The notion of speech acts is a very insightful explanation of the purpose of utterances, and much of our speech can be effectively analyzed according to Searle's taxonomy. But speech act concepts have practical limits. Speech is very social in nature, and many utterances are oriented less towards causing an action than towards establishing or maintaining a social relationship. The Coordinator, a software product that utilizes speech act theory for tracking work team assignments by requiring users to assign speech act classifications to electronic mail messages, has met with mixed acceptance in actual use [Winograd 1988, Medina-Mora *et al.* 1992]. Although utterances may be successfully classified by speech act theorists, in the actual interplay of office communication correspondents may not wish to be so direct with each other.

## Conversational Implicature and Speech Acts

**Conversational implicature** is the principle that an utterance often contains much more meaning than the words themselves indicate directly. Imagine that two people meet on the street and the following conversation ensues.

A: Did you do it?
B: Not again.

This conversation is largely meaningless to us; the conversants make extensive use of shared knowledge and history, and we cannot know to what action they refer. We can, however, make certain inferences about the dialogue: A and B have discussed "it" before, "it" is dominant enough in their relationship not to be ambiguous, and A assumes "it" is unlikely to be ambiguous. Another inference from the conversation is that B has done this "it" in the past and likewise understands that A knows about this prior occurrence (or most recent of several prior occurrences of "it").

To make these inferences with any degree of confidence, we resort to some implicit assumptions about the use of language. We assume that the utterances have a purpose, e.g., A and B are not total strangers but in fact have a common history. We make assumptions about shared belief, e.g., that A does expect B to know the referent for "it" and is not simply teasing B to see whether he or she can guess what is being talked about. In short, we assume an order or regularity to these utterances.

Grice's theory of conversational implicature [Grice 1975] is based on the concept that there is a set of guiding assumptions molding how a conversation is organized. Such guidelines allow us to make the inferences described above, and any deviation from the guidelines must itself have implications beyond the actual words used. Grice's **maxims of conversation** can be summarized as follows.

- **The cooperative principle:** Speak to support the accepted purpose or direction of the conversation as it is at the moment of the utterance. This is the underlying theme of all the maxims.

- **The maxim of quality:**   Speak the truth; do not speak what you know to be false nor that for which you do not have adequate evidence of truth.
- **The maxim of quantity:** Be direct. Say as much as is required at the current point of the interchange, but do not say more than is required.
- **The maxim of relevance:** Make your utterances relevant and to the point.
- **The maxim of manner:** Be brief and orderly; avoid ambiguity and obscurity.

The cooperative principal defines conversation as an organized, purposeful, and efficient series of spoken exchanges, and the remaining maxims are specific techniques to support this principle. In this framework, conversants work together in a conversation, their utterances are mutually relevant, and they do not speak nonsense or seek to confuse each other.

In reality, language often is not nearly as orderly as these underlying principles seem to imply. However, in many cases when Grice's principles appear to be violated, they unify otherwise disjoint or seemingly purposeless utterances. Consider the following exchanges.

A:   Did you feed the cat?
B:   There's a pile of feathers at the doorstep.

B appears to violate the maxim of relevance; A wishes to know whether B has fed the cat, yet B talks about a pile of feathers. By assuming that B's reply must be relevant, we can infer that B suspects that the cat has caught a bird, and perhaps that this should substitute for the cat's dinner or that the cat should not be fed as punishment.

## DISCOURSE

Discourse refers to multiple utterances over time often by different talkers. Discourse is a broad term covering several distinct areas of language understanding. The utterances in a discourse are not disjointed but rather related or connected. Discourse deals with understanding the purpose of these multiple utterances, including issues such as plans that extend across several utterances, references in one utterance to objects or concepts specified in a prior utterance, and the use of multiple utterances to comprise a single speech act. Discourse issues in conversations include the use of language to regulate the conversation's flow, the temporal distribution of contributions among its participants, and the coordination of the effective exchange of information among the participants such that all arrive at the same understanding of what was said.

Discourse issues have formed a theme of conversational interaction and feedback throughout this book. This section emphasizes how conversation is broken into turns. The flow of turn-taking provides a collaborative environment for each talker's contributions to the conversation. Conversants maintain a common focus across turns; without this, pronouns could not refer to ideas and objects mentioned in an earlier sentence. Feedback techniques to ensure mutual understanding are discussed in the subsequent section.

## Regulation of Conversation

We all know from personal experience that in a conversation the various talkers take **turns** speaking. After each turn, remarkably little time transpires before the next turn begins. Occasionally turns overlap, as one participant begins before the previous has completely finished, but it is remarkable that conversations can be as dynamic and fast paced as they are without more "stepping on each other's toes." Equally remarkable are the conversational processes for selecting a mutually agreeable topic, moving on to new topics, and returning to a previous topic.

Conversation is rich in social conventions that invite discourse and most utterances occur in a discourse context [Goffman 1981]. Turns in conversations are regulated and ordered to allow a chain of utterances to refer to a single topic; often subsequent utterances can be understood only in the context of the earlier portions of the discourse. The most simple example of this dependency is the **adjacency pair** [Sacks *et al.* 1974], in which something is presented or proposed in the first utterance and responded to, accepted, or rejected in the rejoinder. For example:

A:  I brought in the mail.
B:  Thank you.

A:  How much does this cost?
B:  Two dollars.

Note that the second utterance in the pair, which brings the pair to some form of closure, has little clarity of its own outside of the adjacency pair.

Where applicable, adjacency pairing simplifies the question of how the listener knows when the talker's turn is over as the listener must clearly wait for the proposition to be presented in the first member of the pair. Although it may be suggested that all conversations can be reduced to sets of adjacency pairs possibly with inserted sequences of other adjacency pairs between the first and second member of a pair, most conversations are more complex and resist this analysis.

In the absence of simple pairs, it is harder to specify when one turn has ended and another talker may begin a new turn. What constitutes a turn? How does the talker signal this to the listener? Turns are often composed of one or more syntactically or semantically meaningful units. These units may correspond to sentences, but they are equally likely to be smaller phrase-like units; fluent conversation often contains incomplete sentences. One appropriate unit is the **breath group,** or the string of words between catching one's breath, which usually expresses one or more coherent thoughts.

For detecting turn boundaries, the problem lies with the "one or more" of the preceding paragraph. If one talker spoke and the second always picked up when the first stopped for breath, turn taking would be more predictable. But the talker may continue to "hold the floor" for multiple utterances or the listener may interrupt before the talker has even finished or otherwise signal so that the talker modifies the utterance even as it is being produced.

The time between turns is too short (often shorter than pauses within a turn) to believe that the listener simply waits to hear if the talker has more to say. [Duncan 1974, Duncan 1972] analyzed a number of conversations and suggested the following indicators in addition to the completion of a syntactic unit of subject and predicate by which the talker can signal the end of a turn.

- **Intonation:**  A level or falling pitch at the end of a sentence indicates termination of the thought being expressed.
- **Syllable lengthening:**  The final syllable, or more correctly the final stressed syllable at the end of a turn, is longer than it would be otherwise. Duncan refers to this as "drawl."
- **Gesture:**  Termination of a hand gesture while speaking acts as a cue that the accompanying turn is drawing to a close.
- **Key phrases:**  Certain phrases such as "you know . . ." at the end of a syntactic unit are often spoken at turn termination.
- **Visual attention:**  Talkers often avert their gaze from the listener during an utterance so looking back to the listener could cue the end of a turn.

The completion of each syntactic unit or phrase is a possible end of the turn. If the talker indicates termination by cues such as those just listed, this invites the listener to take a turn. If the current talker desires to continue the turn, i.e., to present a subsequent phrase, the end-of-turn cues can be avoided or more strongly, the opposite behavior can be invoked such as using a rising intonation or beginning a hand gesture.

Conversation does not always break into turns cleanly. Sometimes, either deliberately or accidently, the listener may **interrupt,** i.e., begin speaking before the other has finished. Interruption is usually dealt with effectively in conversation: Often one party will back off and quickly cease speaking, in which case whichever party is then the talker tends to repeat or summarize what was said during the period of overlap to insure that it was heard correctly. During overlap, the conversants have not yet resolved who should have a turn; one party may attempt to assert control by emphasis such as speaking more loudly or with increased pitch range or lengthened syllables.

Speech may be used by the listener in a manner that initially seems to be a short turn or an interruption but does not really take a turn away from the talker. **Back channels** refer to a number of behaviors whereby the listeners give feedback to the talker [Yngve 1970]. They include paraverbal utterances ("Hmmm," "Uh-huh"), completing the other's sentence or offering a paraphrase of it, short interjections ("Of course," "You don't say?"), head nods, and various facial expressions.

Back channels are a cooperative mechanism; listener feedback indicates what is known or accepted so that the talker can continue the exposition with confidence. Back channels make for more productive conversation. For example, in an experiment by [Kraut *et al.* 1982, Kraut and Lewis 1984], subjects described scenes from a film to a listener who attempted to identify the film. If the listener who was out of sight could not speak back, it took longer for the talker to adequately describe the scene. Even an eavesdropper who could never be heard benefited from the listener's back channel utterances but not as much as the listener did. This suggests that some aspects of back channel cooperation produce generally "better" utterances from the talker, while other aspects of performance improvement are specific to the participation of the back channel provider.

## Discourse Focus

Back channels are just one aspect of collaborative behavior in conversation. In the course of speaking conversants change or agree upon the topic of conversation, refer back to previous topics, and reaffirm their basis of mutual belief upon which they can build successful references to world knowledge, either generic or specific and situational. The discussion of turn taking emphasized pairs or short sequences of talk. We now turn our attention to longer conversations with perhaps quite a few turns.

At any moment in coherent discourse the conversants usually agree on what is being discussed. From time to time, the topic of conversation changes. The group of sequential utterances that refers to the same topic is a **discourse segment.** Transitions between discourse segments are often indicated by **cue phrases** such as "By the way . . . ," "Yes, but . . . ," and "Well. . . ." Throughout a discourse segment, all utterances refer to the same topic or noun phrase; this is the **focus** or **center** of the discourse segment.

Identification of the focus of a discourse segment is required to resolve **reference,** which arises from several sources. **Deixis** is the reference of certain pronouns, such as "this" and "those" that point at something either physically or conceptually. **Anaphora** is the reference implied by pronouns such as "he" or "their." The entity referred to by deixis or anaphora is the **referent.** The referent corresponds to the focus of the discourse segment; changing the referent introduces a new discourse segment.

A discourse segment can be interrupted by the introduction of a new discourse segment, and the original discourse segment can be returned to. For example, consider the discourse fragment.

A:   California gets so green in the winter, I love it!
B:   Seattle gets a lot of rain in the winter too, but not much sun.
A:   It's a nice city, but you should check out Hawaii if you want wonderful winter weather.
B:   Last winter we went hiking there.
A:   Sometimes it gets a spell of rain in February.
B:   But it's not as bad as back there! It's so dreary all winter.

In the first sentence, speaker A references "California." Speaker B then introduces a new reference "Seattle." Speaker A refers back to Seattle at the beginning of the next utterance but then introduces a third focus "Hawaii" using the cue phrase "but." The next two utterances then refer to Hawaii as well. In the last utterance, speaker B jumps back to the focus of "Seattle" without needing to further specify the pronoun. How is this accomplished without further negotiation?

[Grosz and Sidner 1986] proposed a discourse model differentiating the **attentional structure** that specifies the target of reference from the **intentional structure** that is roughly the pragmatic purpose of the discourse segment. They suggested a **stack** model for the attentional structure. A stack is a data representation in which items are put on ("pushed") and removed ("popped") from the top so that the most recently pushed item is always the one that gets popped. Figure 9.11 shows the stack progressing during the course of the example discourse. In the last snapshot, the top focus "Hawaii" has been popped, leaving "Seattle" exposed as the prime candidate for reference.

This model suggests that once popped, an object cannot be referred to again by a pronoun without being specifically introduced as a new focus so that it appears on the top of the stack again. But this is not entirely true, revealing that the model although powerful is incomplete. Speaker B might say, after a pause and somewhat longingly, "It was so nice there, what a great place to walk" referring back to Hawaii. Somehow the conversants would shift back to this focus, aided by the tense shift in B's utterances.

How do we know when a new discourse segment is introduced? In addition to the cue phrases mentioned above, the way reference is used signals a new discourse segment. Grosz, Joshi, and Weinstein use the term **backward-looking center** to refer to the entity in the current utterance that refers to the previous utterance [Grosz *et al.* 1983]. They suggested that as long as the center of the current utterance is the same as that of the preceding utterance, a pronoun should be used. If a pronoun is not used, this might suggest that a new discourse segment is being introduced. As the focus of conversation changes, the new topic may be introduced explicitly as the theme of a sentence, or it may be selected by reference from a series of things that have already been talked about (i.e., past backward-looking centers). Which of the possible backward-looking centers is selected depends on their ordering, which is dominated by recency.

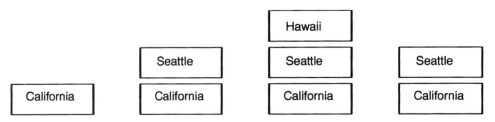

**Figure 9.11.** A series of snapshots of a stack model of the shift in focus of the weather discourse. Two new topics are introduced. The last utterance pops the top topic Hawaii to refer back to Seattle.

Intonation is a strong cue to shifts in focus. New information, i.e., potential new centers, are usually stressed more than old information. Intonational cues can also be used to override the default ordering of centers.

1:  John hit Bill and then he called the police.
2:  John hit Bill and then HE called the police.

In sentence one John calls the police; in sentence two Bill does. Ordinarily we would expect that "he" refers back to John, but if this word is emphasized as in sentence two it indicates to choose an alternate center, i.e., Bill.

Focus management requires the agreement of all participants in a conversation—if one party introduces a new topic without the appropriate cues, then other conversants do not receive the intended message. Conversation is a cooperative process. Another aspect of collaborative conversational behavior relates to synchronizing mutual beliefs. Clark *et al.* identify a number of conversational moves to make sure that both conversants agree to the identity of the current focus [Clark and Marshall 1981, Clark and Schaefer 1989, Clark and Wilkes-Gibbs 1986]. Clark and Brennan [Clark and Brennan 1990] introduce the concept of **grounding** to describe the process whereby we ensure that the listener understands our utterances as we intend them to be understood and that we agree that they stand for the same entities in the world.

Although much of conversation is purposeful and can be categorized as an attempt at communicating a concept or performing an action, conversation also serves a social nature. Part of the feedback provided by back channels, for example, informs the talker "I am paying attention to you. I am listening. I value your contribution." Sometimes talk exists as much to fill a communication space between people who feel awkward in silence as it does to change the other conversant's opinion or affect changes in the physical world [Goffman 1981].

## CASE STUDIES

This section presents case studies of several projects that attempted to maintain interactive conversations utilizing the aspects of higher-level linguistic knowledge described in this chapter. Although only fragmentary use was made of the formalisms just described, these case studies offer some evidence of the potential of the topics in this chapter for enabling more sophisticated conversational interaction. Syntactic and semantic knowledge can be used to detect speech recognition errors and to determine the meaning of an utterance. Pragmatics relates an utterance to the larger world situation, and discourse structure helps cue appropriate responses.

### Grunt

**Grunt** was an experiment that explored the utility of a discourse model in isolation from other linguistic knowledge [Schmandt 1988]. Grunt attempted to maintain a conversation by listening to the user, but without the use of word recognition. Without word recognition, the ability to negotiate conversational roles or topics was limited, so Grunt was engineered around the predefined, specific task of giving driving directions between two known points. The goal of the system was to employ acoustic feedback (or lack of it) from the user to improve his or her ability to understand and transcribe the directions. Grunt was complementary to its contemporary, Direction Assistance (described in Chapter 6), which allowed its user to choose a source and destination but did not offer any conversational flow control while reciting driving directions.

Grunt's discourse model was developed after recording and analyzing conversations between two people who could not observe one another, in which one was assigned the role of writing down the directions spoken by the other. Grunt's task was to present segments of the route as a series of turns, and the user was encouraged to engage in natural discourse behavior for conversational flow control. Subjects spoke to Grunt over the telephone without having been given any hints about its capabilities before the interaction; they had been told that they would hear driving directions to a bakery on the other side of town and that they were requested to write down the route.

Initially Grunt employed a very simple discourse model which was then elaborated over the duration of the project. Grunt would speak a sentence and then listen for a reply, relying on back channel utterances from the listener to speed up the conversation. Since there is great variability in how fast people transcribe directions, if Grunt waited after speaking sufficient time for the slowest writers to finish most others would become frustrated. Hence the need for flow control. A user's spoken response was detected by the change in audio level; at the end of the reply, Grunt would proceed to the next step of the bakery directions. If the user said nothing, Grunt would wait a rather long time and then proceed with the directions. To encourage back channel behavior by the user, Grunt would occasionally query a mute listener "Are you there?" (subjects always responded to the question) and offer hints such as "I'm listening to you too."[2] Such exchanges, called **channel checking** in [Hayes and Reddy 1983], are not uncommon during telephone conversations in which one conversant speaks much more than the other.

This model might have worked if the listener consistently and completely understood the directions when they were first spoken but this was not the case. People sometimes misunderstand each other, and successful communication was further hampered because the listener had to cope with Grunt's text-to-speech synthesis. When we cannot comprehend each other's directions, we ask for clarification; how could Grunt differentiate these requests from back-channel utterances? Based on the observation that back channel acknowledgment responses tended to be very short ("uh-huh," "OK," "hmm . . ."), Grunt measured the dura-

---

[2]As further encouragement of listener participation, subjects were asked "What is your name?" and "Are you ready?" by Grunt before any directions were given to help them realize that their speech could be heard by the computer.

tion of each utterance, and if the response was longer than 800 milliseconds, it assumed that the listener was confused and had asked either a question or for repetition. In response to this "clarification" reply, Grunt said "I'll repeat" and repeated the directions verbatim but at a slightly slower rate. Because Grunt's assumption that the listener was confused was based on skimpy evidence, it was important to explain "I'll repeat" so as to not risk misleading the user. For example, in the following dialog the user might insert an extra mile-long leg followed by a left turn into the directions.

> Grunt:    Go about one mile and take a left at the first stop sign.
> Listener: I think I know where that is.
> Grunt:    Go about one mile and take a left at the first stop sign.

Although extremely simple, the discourse model described so far (see Figure 9.12) was surprisingly effective and robust. In the constrained context in which subjects were exposed to Grunt, it behaved flawlessly for about one out of five users. Observations of failure modes in which the conversation digressed from Grunt's discourse model and its responses were therefore inappropriate resulted in several improvements.

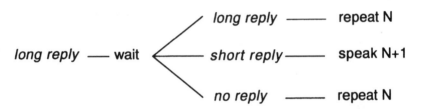

**Figure 9.12.** The states in Grunt's discourse model.

The first improvement extended the discourse model to cope with synchronization responses by the listener. If the listener was having difficulty keeping pace while writing, he or she might utter "Just a minute, please" or "Hold on a second." In normal human interactions, utterances such as these suspend the conversation, giving the requestor the floor until explicitly yielded.[3] This final return of the floor is often accomplished by exactly the same short back channel style utterances that Grunt already used as a cue, e.g., "OK". This timing cue was utilized as shown in Figure 9.13. When a long utterance was heard, Grunt no longer immediately repeated the current direction segment. Instead, it waited in anticipation of further speech to differentiate synchronization from clarification requests. If the next utterance was short, Grunt assumed that a synchronization

---

[3]Resumption of conversation after the granting of the synchronization request need not be explicitly triggered if it becomes obvious to the conversants that talk may continue. For example, if the note-taker were visible to the person speaking directions, the direction-giver could watch for the note-taker to finish writing or to look up.

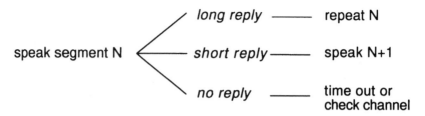

**Figure 9.13.** Modified Grunt behavior to detect synchronization requests.

cycle had just been completed and moved on. If the subsequent utterance was long, Grunt repeated the current segment assuming that the listener had previously asked for clarification, grown tired of waiting, and was now reiterating the request. This model thus provided for a correct response to a synchronization request and a delayed, but still correct, response to a clarification request.

The second improvement to Grunt's discourse model involved recognizing intonation to detect questions among the short utterances. Initially, Grunt erroneously treated short questions like "What?", "Where?", and "Left?" as acknowledgments. When this occurred, listeners became both annoyed and more confused since Grunt would apparently ignore their question and proceed with the next segment. With the improved model short utterances were analyzed for pitch, and those with clearly rising intonation were treated as clarification requests instead of acknowledgments (see Figure 9.14).

Toward the end of the project Grunt's discourse model was extended to include interruptions by the listener. When interrupted, Grunt would cease speaking, thus yielding the floor. The problem then was how to resume the dialog. Grunt could not know why the listener interrupted so it attempted to respond properly to any back channel acknowledgments. If an interruption was short and not a question, Grunt would repeat a few words and continue the utterance. If an interruption was longer, Grunt would wait for further input after it ceased speaking. After the listener spoke again, the current direction sequence would be repeated from the beginning as Grunt could not ascertain how much the listener had heard the first time.

Figure 9.15 depicts Grunt's final discourse model minus the interruption branches. Each of the advancements over Grunt's original, simple discourse model improved the probability that Grunt would do what the human listener expected;

**Figure 9.14.** Grunt analyzed short utterances to detect whether they might be questions and reacted accordingly.

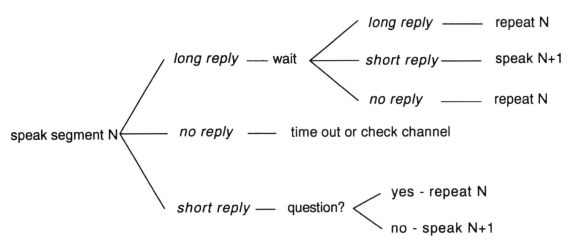

**Figure 9.15.** Discourse states for the final modified version of Grunt. Interruption is not shown.

this was based on observing breakdowns during its use. However, at its best, Grunt had considerable limitations and exhibited several distinct failure modes.

Summarizing or completing the talker's sentence is a back channel behavior that ordinarily moves a conversation along, and while transcribing directions many listeners invoked such very explicit flow control, but Grunt misinterpreted these as clarification requests. A related behavior is to recite word by word what one is writing as timing feedback to the direction-giver. Grunt interpreted these as a series of short acknowledgement utterances and became confused. Grunt tried to minimize the confusion resulting from false conversational moves by stating very explicitly that it was repeating or paraphrasing, which unfortunately sometimes led to wordy exchanges.

Other failure modes were caused by listeners changing their conversational behavior due to misconceptions of the discourse capabilities of computers. Almost one quarter of the participants said nothing while listening to the directions except when asked directly "Are you there?" Even when the period of time that Grunt waited during the silence between utterances was increased to the extent that interaction became exceedingly slow in the absence of acknowledgments, a significant number of listeners were simply mute, either not realizing that the computer could listen or feeling uncomfortable speaking to it. Some knowledgeable subjects believed that the computer was listening via speech recognition; based on the essentially correct understanding of recognition technology, they spoke in single word utterances, e.g., "Repeat," in order to be understood. But Grunt was not using word recognition, and these misguided attempts to cooperate broke the discourse model.

As a research project, it was intriguing to see how well Grunt could manage a discourse model in the absence of speech recognition. In a way, it was refreshing simply because so much work with recognition gets bogged down in syntactic and semantic analysis and requires corrective discourse which, in turn, detracts from the naturalness of smooth conversation. The extent to which Grunt succeeded greatly surprised its designers, even though this success was heavily dependent upon having chosen a very limited and focused task with well-defined roles for the conversants. Nonetheless Grunt did demonstrate the power of even a minimal discourse model.

## Conversational Desktop

Conversational Desktop, another Media Lab project (1984), provided an integrated voice interface to an integrated office telecommunications and message-handling environment [Schmandt et al. 1985, Schmandt and Arons 1986]. Conversational Desktop could place telephone calls, take voice messages, schedule meetings, and answer queries about airline itineraries; its functionality and telecommunications aspects are detailed in Chapter 12. The case study here discusses its language understanding and dialog-generation components, which utilized connected speech recognition for input and text-to-speech synthesis for output.

Conversational Desktop's conversation model provided a context in which to interpret spoken commands and also engage the user in a dialogue to correct recognition errors. Conversational Desktop's language understanding approach illustrates how syntactic, semantic, pragmatic, and discourse knowledge all contribute to conversation management. Although the contributions of this project at each layer were small and informal, their combination shows the richness of a conversational user interface.

The discourse system of the Conversational Desktop project can be thought of as a simple frame-based system. An empty frame was a data structure with fields for the different semantic classes of words in a small vocabulary. Some of these fields were filled in with specific words detected while parsing the user's input. Various procedures were then invoked to determine if sufficient information had been gathered to perform the requested action; these procedures could look to other sources of knowledge (databases) to support inferences.

In Conversational Desktop, the syntactic and semantic portions of language understanding were combined into a context-free grammar-based parser. Semantic knowledge was incorporated into the parsing process by basing the grammar on word categories more specific than the usual syntactic classes of noun phrase, verb phrase, preposition, etc. For example, Figure 9.16 illustrates a fragment of the grammar describing sentences such as "Schedule a meeting with Walter tomorrow at 10:00" or "Phone Chris and Barry." During execution, the parser recorded two categories of information when each grammar rule was applied. First, when any terminal symbols were encountered, both the word and its semantic role were stored in a frame-like structure describing the utterance. The frame had positions (roles) for the various "cases"[4] that might be found in a sen-

---

[4] The cases used were ad hoc and specific to the task as opposed to the more general cases described earlier in this chapter.

```
sentence := CMD | CMD_N NAME | CMD_NT N_AND_T

CMD_N := phone | where is

CMD_NT := schedule a meeting

N_AND_T := PERSON_NAME TIME  | TIME PERSON_NAME

NAME := PERSON_NAME | PERSON_NAME and PERSON_NAME

PERSON_NAME := Chris | Barry | Walter

TIME := DAY HOUR | HOUR DAY

Day  := today | tomorrow | Monday | Tuesday ...
```

**Figure 9.16.** Conversational Desktop's parser used a context-free grammar based on semantically meaningful word categories.

tence; as the parser recognized a word fitting into a case, that word was saved in the frame as an instance for its case.

The second result of the parser's analysis was a list of additional information that would be required to complete the sentence. For example, when the parser noticed the SCHEDULE-MEETING action, it would note that a PERSON, a DAY, and a TIME were required and add these word classes to the list. Similarly, when encountering AT used in the temporal sense, Conversational Desktop would note that a DAY and a TIME were required to complete the sentence. As each of these missing classes was located later in the parsing process it was removed from the list. If this list was not empty after further pragmatic and discourse analysis, Conversational Desktop had an incomplete understanding of the user's request and engaged in dialogue to identify each item in the list.

A unique attribute of Conversational Desktop's parser was the underlying assumption that the input from connected speech recognition would be error-prone. With the use of connected recognition, not only can any individual word be misrecognized, but the possibility of insertion and rejection errors also implies that even the number of words sent to the parser can be incorrect. The goal of the parsing process was to extract whatever useful information was contained in the recognized words. In other words, it was to identify the most likely utterance spoken given the words reported by the recognizer, the syntactic and semantic constraints of the context-free grammar, and knowledge of error probabilities.

```
input words:  ABCD      parser candidates:  ABCD

                                           ABC  ACD  BCD  . . .

                                           AB   AC   AD   BC  . . .

                                           A    B    C    D
```

**Figure 9.17** The Conversational Desktop attempted to parse all substrings of the input utterance. Each substring was evaluated, and those which could be parsed were candidates for selection.

Because any word reported by a speech recognizer might be a spurious insertion error, all substrings of the input words were parsed as shown in Figure 9.17. If *any* words were recognized correctly, one of the substrings would contain exactly all these words without the insertions. All of the substrings were submitted to the parser, which had to reject those strings containing grammatically correct insertions, but accept the substring that represented the original sentence minus the insertion.

Rejection errors caused incomplete sentences and resulted in fragments of syntactically correct tokens. To cope with such errors, the grammar was modified to describe sentence fragments as well as complete sentences, e.g., the word sequence "Barry Friday at two o'clock" is a well-formed fragment from a sentence about scheduling a meeting. This parsing strategy also handled those substitution errors resulting in semantically incongruous sentences; if one of the substrings contained exactly the correct words, then the resulting sentence fragment would be accepted by the parser's rules for fragments.

These parsing strategies had to be combined because any type of error could occur in each sentence. Because of the fragment rules, multiple substrings from each input sequence would usually be accepted by the parser; the next stage of analysis selected the best of these. Evaluation of "best" was based on empirically derived weightings of the following.

- **Completeness:** Assuming that the user spoke well-formed sentences, a successfully parsed complete sentence was more likely spoken than was a sentence fragment.
- **Number of words:** A greater number of words in an input string was preferred because recognition results were more likely to be correct than erroneous. This judgment was also based on the assumption that the user spoke sentences based only on words in the recognizer's vocabulary. If both "ABC" and "AB" could be parsed, "ABC" would receive preference from this metric.
- **Sequences of words:** Because of the difficulty of word endpoint detection, connected recognizers tend to produce runs of correct or erroneous results. If the endpoint of one word is incorrectly identified, not only is that word likely to be misrecognized but also the following word. The scoring metric favored substrings that included

consecutive tokens matching the input. Substring "AB" was favored over "AC" from input "ABC."

Once all candidate substrings had been evaluated and the best guess selected, further processing could be invoked if the user's request was not adequately specified by the recognized utterance. Pragmatic analysis consisted of resolving situational references in the context of the user's current or planned activity. For example, if the user said "Schedule both of us a meeting . . ." while on the telephone, Conversational Desktop assumed that the person at the other end of the connection should be included. Similarly, "When's my flight?" was evaluated with reference to the situational context; if asked while a call was in progress, flights to the caller's location were checked before the default, i.e., next scheduled flight. Pragmatic processing associated descriptions of events ("my flight") with known entities in databases (Boston to San Francisco flight on August 12th at 5:37 PM) so that action could be taken on behalf of the user.

At the final stage of language understanding, discourse analysis was invoked to resolve remaining ambiguities. This was a weak model of focus based on tracking the current task frame; there was no stack or other history mechanism in the model, so previous topics could not be recalled. The model of the current task allowed limited resolution of anaphora, thus supporting transactions spanning multiple sentences. For example, the user might inquire about someone's availability for a meeting: Conversational Desktop would consult schedules and suggest a time, which the user could accept by saying "Confirm it." Or having requested information about a scheduled activity, the user might command "Delete it."

Conversational Desktop also initiated dialogue. Despite the various stages of language analysis just described, errors in speech recognition often prevented complete identification of the user's request. When this happened, the list of missing roles for the sentence would not be empty, but instead it would specify missing information required to complete the request. Conversational Desktop phrased a question around the needed information but also echoed much of the request as understood so far: "At what time tomorrow do you wish to meet with Barry?" Echoing provided feedback and reassurance that the transaction was proceeding, and it could alert the user quickly when the recognizer had been severely mistaken. More importantly, revealing to the user what had been recognized allowed human detection of semantically correct recognition errors that Conversational Desktop could never detect. If, for example, the user had requested a meeting with "Harry," but this was recognized as "Barry," user intervention ("Change that to 'Harry'.") was the only recourse. Without echoing, this semantically correct error would go undetected.

Much like the research project Put That There (see Chapter 8), Conversational Desktop awaited further input after speaking a query. Except for a few special commands ("Change that" and "Cancel"), this additional input was merged with what had previously been recognized and the parsing cycle was repeated. This process continued until an action could be taken. As recognition accuracy decreased, it took longer for the user to complete a transaction, but the interaction rarely broke down completely.

## SUMMARY

This chapter considered computational aspects of the higher-layer aspects of speech communication whereby words are combined into sentences and sentences into conversation and how these structures imply intentions and actions in the real world. Syntax and semantics embody the constraints whereby words are combined in certain sequences to form rational utterances. Pragmatics allows these utterances to carry force, while discourse provides a framework that structures a sequence of utterances into a coherent whole. To employ such concepts in interactive computer systems, underlying representations of each layer must be specified, and then procedures must be developed to operate on these representations.

The syntactic structure of a sentence may be represented as a tree, but a grammar is better defined by a set of context-free rules or an augmented transition network. Parsers analyze sentences in a top-down or bottom-up order as they apply these grammar rules. Semantic analysis requires representation of word meaning, and in particular it must differentiate the various senses in which a word may be used in a sentence. Case grammars represent the roles or functions a word plays in the action of a sentence, while semantic networks and type hierarchies describe the meaning of a word in terms of the other entities of which it is an instance.

Pragmatics relates the sentence both to the talker and to the situation in which the sentence is spoken; it links words to objects in the real world. This aspect of meaning, either general or specific to the current situation, requires a knowledge representation of which scripts and frames are examples. Pragmatics also considers the implicature of speech, i.e., the meaning beyond the words in a sentence such as "Do you have the time?" Speech act theory considers the utterances themselves to be actions in the world.

A number of aspects of conversation come together at the discourse layer. Discourse describes the methods and possible rules for determining who holds the floor, how talk is divided into turns, and the duration of a turn. Discourse also encompasses maintaining a focus across multiple utterances so that all conversants speak about the same topic and mutually agree on the referents for anaphora. Lastly, discourse provides a context in which conversants collaborate to discover or construct a common ground of experience and understanding so that the pragmatic implications of an utterance can be shared by all.

A case study description of Grunt illustrated that discourse models may be surprisingly useful in very constrained contexts even without word recognition. By building on accepted expectations of the flow of discourse, this simple mechanism added surprising vigor to the interface. A description of Conversational Desktop highlighted the interplay between language understanding components operating at all the communication layers described in this chapter. In this project, information gathered during parsing and further analysis was used to direct dialogue with the intent of resolving ambiguities which arose during conversational interaction.

## FURTHER READING

Allen [1987] is an excellent textbook covering all aspects of the material discussed in this chapter. Winograd [1983] focuses on syntax, covering this topic in great detail. Levinson provides an excellent textbook on material included as both pragmatics and discourse in this chapter. Grosz *et al.* 1986 is a collection of readings on computational linguistics and includes many of the classic papers on plans and discourse models. Cohen *et al.* is another excellent collection of readings relevant to this chapter.

# 10

# Basics of Telephones

This and the following chapters explain the technology and computer applications of telephones, much as earlier pairs of chapters explored speech coding, synthesis, and recognition. The juxtaposition of telephony with voice processing in a single volume is unusual; what is their relationship? First, the telephone is an ideal means to access interactive voice response services such as those described in Chapter 6. Second, computer-based voice mail will give a strong boost to other uses of stored voice such as those already described in Chapter 4 and to be explored again in Chapter 12. Finally, focusing on *communication*, i.e., the task rather than the technology, leads to a better appreciation of the broad intersection of speech, computers, and our everyday work lives.

This chapter describes the basic telephone operations that transport voice across a network to a remote location. Telephony is changing rapidly in ways that radically modify how we think about and use telephones now and in the future. Conventional telephones are already ubiquitous for the business traveler in industrialized countries, but the rise in personal, portable, wireless telephones is spawning entirely new ways of thinking about universal voice connectivity. The pervasiveness of telephone and computer technologies combined with the critical need to communicate in our professional lives suggest that it would be foolish to ignore the role of the telephone as a speech processing peripheral just like a speaker or microphone.

Although the telephone network was designed for voice communication, it is being increasingly used to carry data either by modem to computer or by facsimile. Technology at either end of the phone call has revealed new roles for voice connections over the telephone network: answering machines and voice mail allow asynchronous "conversations"; echo cancellation and speakerphones enable multiparty conferences; increasingly flexible call routing services allow more freedom in associating a telephone set with a number; and the telephone accesses a growing number of information retrieval services such as those described in Chapter 6.

It is useful to abstract the major features of a telephone system into the functions of signaling and transport as these concepts transcend the implementation details of any particular network. After many years of relative stability, telephone systems are now changing rapidly with increased use of digital components and radio links to mobile telephones. While network implementation details affect the capabilities of many telephone services provided by computer systems, many of the underlying functional aspects of the network remain unchanged. Analog and digital telephone networks require unique interface hardware and consequently each may present different characteristics of the voice channel. For these reasons, this chapter describes implementations of analog and digital telephone networks in the broader context of the major functional units of any telephone system.

## FUNCTIONAL OVERVIEW

This chapter considers telephones from the perspective of their role in providing transport of voice in a system that employs computers for storage, databases, applications, and user interfaces. This view is based on the minimal requirements that make effective use of voice, or any medium as an information type on a computer.

- *Transport:* The ability to move the data from one location to another. Telephones, computer networks, and package delivery services all provide a form of transport.
- *Storage:* The means to save the data for later access. Computer disks hold files, videotapes store images, and answering machines store voice messages.
- *User interface:* A means of allowing a person to retrieve and manipulate the stored information through tools such as editors. The user interface of an answering machine consists of buttons, knobs, and lights.

The telephone network provides the most commonly utilized means of transporting voice, although computer networks have also been used in some experimental systems. Since the telephone network is expansive and eventually will be uniformly digital (i.e., able to transmit speech reliably and with higher quality), researchers choose to use it in many computer scenarios.

We can separate the telephone functions for moving voice between locations into two phases. An **addressing** or **signaling** activity both specifies and establishes a connection to the desired recipient with the help of routing and signaling via the telephone network. Call setup refers to the procedures invoked from the time the caller begins the call (usually by picking up a handset) until the time the called party answers (again usually by picking up the handset). If a connection is established (i.e., the other party answers), the **transmission** phase begins during which voice is carried over the network. Either party can terminate the call (usually by hanging up), which initiates a final signaling phase of call teardown. Note that if the called party does not answer, a call can proceed directly from the setup to teardown stages. Signaling and transmission phases exist in all telephone systems, but they are implemented differently in analog and digital telephone networks.

## ANALOG TELEPHONES

Many of the telephones we use every day including almost all home and public phones are **analog.** As discussed in Chapter 3, analog devices use a continuously varying signal to convey information. Analog phones may be for a single line[1] or for multiple lines with buttons to select between lines and put a call on hold (a **key set**). These phones may have rotary dial or push buttons, which usually generate tones. The analog phone has a ringer (bell) that indicates incoming calls. The telephone is connected to the central office (CO) by wires that run along aboveground poles or in underground cables (see Figure 10.1).

The central office contains the telephone switch, which is connected to the wires from all the telephones in the neighborhood as well as to lines that connect with the remainder of the telephone network. Older telephone switches consist of various types of relays and electromechanical steppers that count the digits as they are dialed, switch lines, and ultimately complete a call. Such switches are rapidly being replaced by modern switches that are digital computers performing essentially the same job as their mechanical predecessors. For each call, the central office connects the telephone to the rest of the network by helping to complete a **circuit** that carries the voice signal between two telephones. A **circuit switch** constructs a path between two points; the circuit is dedicated to this particular path and information on the circuit automatically flows directly to the destination. By contrast, most digital computer networks are **packet switched,** allowing multiple packets of data, each with an embedded address, to share the same physical circuit or wire. The switch characteristics are invisible to the users of the telephone system, however. It is likely that someday all voice telephony will be packet switched although now it is circuit switched.

Analog telephones are connected by a pair of wires to the central office, which is where the first level of telephone switching occurs. Although telephone cable often has four wires, colored red, green, yellow, and black, only the first two are in use in most telephones. The other pair is reserved for special functions such as lighting for illuminated dials, coin collection in a pay phone, or installation of a

---

[1]The classic American telephone from the Western Electric design is called a "2500 set."

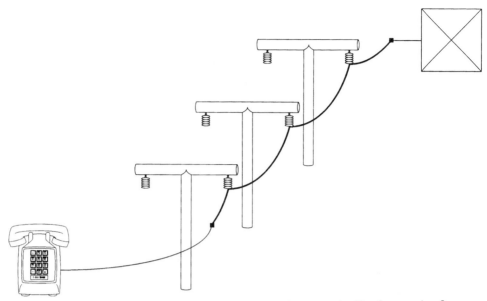

**Figure 10.1.** A telephone is connected to the central office by a pair of wires.

second line.[2] The two primary wires, called the **local loop,** are connected to a battery at the CO, which supplies a 48 volt DC voltage. The green wire is connected to the positive side of the battery and is called **tip,** while the red wire, called **ring,** is negative.[3] Using a battery to power the loop allows the local telephones to continue operation in the event of a power failure and provides a constant voltage source.

**Signaling**

Signaling encompasses sending the dialed digits as well as alerting the destination party to an incoming call. Signaling is the transmission of control information for call management, which includes both **call setup** to establish a voice connection with another party and **call teardown** to free the resources associated with the call at its termination. With analog telephones, signaling is accomplished through a combination of varying the current in the loop and sending audible waveforms over it.

---

[2] The specifications discussed in this chapter such as color coding, voltages, frequencies, and durations of audible signals are specific to the United States and may vary in other countries. The discussion of digital telephony is based on international standards.

[3] These terms date back to the portions of the jacks used to complete connections via patch cords on old manual switchboards.

The wire gauge (thickness) of the wire pair, or loop, at the central office is standardized, and the entire circuit is typically balanced to provide a specified current (20 milliamps) at the telephone. These characteristics provide a uniform operating environment allowing telephones to be attached easily to different circuits. When **on hook,** the telephone presents a high impedance (10 MegaOhms) to the loop and little current flows.

When the handset is picked up, it goes **off hook** and the impedance drops to about 600 Ohms causing a larger amount of current to flow in the loop, which, in turn, signals the switch in the central office that the line seeks attention, and the switch puts a dial tone on the line. The dial tone consists of voltage variations at audible frequencies superimposed on the 48 volt battery; it is transmitted in the same manner as voice. The dial tone notifies the caller that the switch is ready to receive the digits specifying the destination address. The spectral characteristics (i.e., what frequencies are combined in what ratios) of the dial tone allow us to distinguish it from other phone sounds; this is a feedback mechanism designed for human ears.

If the dial tone is heard, the caller may then dial. The verb *dial* refers to the operation of the older style rotary switch telephone (which, incidentally, remains more prevalent in other parts of the world than in the U.S. or Canada). Each digit is entered by rotating the dial a set distance delimited by holes in the dial and a finger stop bar. As the dial is released, it is driven by a spring at a constant angular velocity, and a small switch and cam inside the dial mechanism alternately connect and disconnect the loop wires. The total of such *make/break* cycles specifies a digit. The CO switch detects these pulses as alternate presence and absence of current flowing through the loop. Both the rate of the pulses and the ratio of time during which the loop is open or closed are standardized. The necessity of waiting for the dial to return to its original position before positioning the finger for the next digit enforces a pause between digits.

The switch in the central office counts the digits and makes certain routing decisions locally. In old mechanical switches, the digit pulses actually physically moved relays to close electrical contacts; modern equipment samples the signal on the line and stores the number digitally while deciding how to route it. If the call is local and the first three digits are the same as those of the originating telephone, the call is in the same exchange and the routing of the resulting connection is entirely through the local switch.[4] If the destination is in the same local area, the local switch may find a free trunk line to the CO switch that serves the dialed exchange. A trunk is a wire pair that may be used to carry calls associated with different numbers for different calls over time as opposed to the wires of a particular telephone, which are dedicated to that telephone exclusively. The local switch will then send the remaining four digits to the remote switch, which is

---

[4]Again note that this assumes the North American numbering plan, which allows three digits for an area code and seven digits for a number, of which the first three digits specify the exchange. In other parts of the world, different numbers of digits may be allocated to each of these functions.

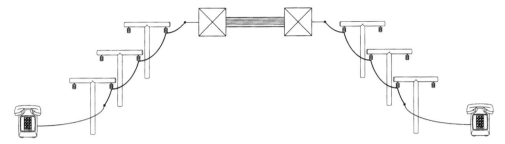

**Figure 10.2.** Telephones connected through trunk lines between two central offices.

responsible for the next stage of switching, i.e., connecting the trunk to the local loop of the destination telephone, as shown in Figure 10.2.

Switching becomes more complicated in long-distance dialing. In the United States long-distance numbers are usually preceded by a "1" to signal that a 10 digit number follows instead of a 7 digit local number.[5] *Long-distance* is somewhat of a misnomer these days as the regional operating companies are no longer part of the long-distance company. If two area codes cover adjacent areas, calls may be handled by the same regional company and the service charge may or may not appear as a separate itemized billing item at the end of the month. If the destination is more distant, the call travels through the network of one of the long-distance carriers.

Of course, the call may not be completed. The called party may not answer the phone or the called line may be busy; this information is signaled to the caller by audible tones. These tones, **ringback** and **busy** signals, are distinguishable by the caller because they sound different. Each of the audible signaling tones contains a mix of particular sine waves that compose its spectrum and is presented as an identifiable tone followed by silence. Tones are further differentiated by cadence (the rate at which the tone-silence cycle repeats) and duty cycle (the fraction of each cycle in which sound is present). For example, ringback occurs in six second intervals in the United States with two seconds of sound followed by four seconds of silence.

Other signaling tones convey different information. The **reorder** (or **fast busy**) sound indicates that the network, not the called number, is busy. In the case of a caller error such as dialing an unassigned number or a number that has been changed or not dialing the required "1" for a toll call, a series of three tones in a rise-fall pattern, known as **intercept** (or "special information tones") is heard, usually followed by a digitized voice explaining the error. All these sounds are indications of **call progress**, i.e., the various steps a call may take towards completion. Call progress tones may be distinguished by differing periods and

---

[5] "1" is also the United States' country code for international dialing so the same number can be used to call across the country or from another country.

duty cycles, and they are designed to be recognized easily by human listeners.[6] For a computer to recognize the tones it must sample the audio signal from the telephone line to detect cadence, and additionally it may need to analyze the signal's spectrum, which is a more computationally intensive process.

Dialing can also be accomplished by touch tones. When a phone is taken off hook and current flows, depressing a key on the keypad generates a sound, technically called a **DTMF (dual tone multifrequency)** signal. This tone is the sum of two sine waves, one specifying each row and one specifying each column of the keypad. The frequencies were chosen to allow maximal distinction between their harmonics. A decoder in the central office detects the two frequencies and determines which digit was dialed. In addition to the 10 digits, touch tone phones include two extra keys: "*" (asterisk, star) and "#" (sharp, pound sign, number sign, or octothorpe).[7] Telephone services rely on these keys to differentiate the digits directed to the service from dialed digits specifying a destination number. For example, to cancel variable call forwarding on my telephone I may enter "*73" when I hear the dial tone.[8]

The fact that a telephone has buttons instead of a dial does not necessarily mean it uses DTMF tones to transmit digits. Many less expensive phones have buttons (they are much cheaper to build than dials) but actually use a series of timed make/break pulses like a rotary dial to send the digit. Some of these telephone sets have an option switch between tone and pulse, which is especially useful if a subscriber is not configured for touchtone service at the central office (the local operating company often charges a monthly fee for it) but still wishes to interact with tone-driven interactive telephone services.

The frequencies and amplitude of touch tone signals were chosen to transmit well over the telephone network. When you push a button on your touch tone phone, your phone mutes since the tone generator is quite loud, as someone on another extension will testify. The amplitude makes touch tone detection easy and reliable even over a long-distance connection, which is beneficial for interactive services. It may be difficult to detect DTMF tones while the parties are talking as speech contains energy at a variety of frequencies that interferes with tone detection. Speech may contain frequencies close enough to the touch tone components to trigger false tone detection, especially in less expensive tone detector integrated circuits. This is not a significant issue at the central office, however, as the switch listens only to set up the call, i.e., before any conversation has begun.

---

[6]There is some variation in the spectrum and cadence of call progress tones. Technical recommendations describe these tones, but network operating companies are not forced to comply. The sounds are consistent enough in the United States that we can usually recognize them but they may be very different abroad.

[7]Actually, the DTMF signaling system supports 16 keys. The extra column, labeled "A" through "D," does not appear on most telephones, however. The extra keys are intended to select a call priority on military telephones.

[8]Of course, I must remember that "73" cancels call forwarding. We will return to the topic of user interfaces to telephone services in the next chapter.

The signaling sounds contain information about the state of the call because they are passed over the same circuit path as the voice signal; they are called **in-band** signaling. Various forms of **out-of-band** signaling may also be provided (e.g., on a key set a light for a particular line will turn on when another extension of that line goes off hook), but out-of-band signaling is mostly limited to digital telephone systems.

When the destination is specified fully by the proper number of dialed digits and the destination line and network are not busy, the destination telephone must audibly alert the called party to the incoming call. This is done by the local switch at the receiving end, which periodically sends a ringing voltage of roughly 100 volts AC down the loop, superimposed on the 48 volts DC. In a traditional phone, this voltage is applied to the windings of an electromagnet; a doorbell-like mechanism then causes a small hammer to vibrate between two bells, producing the classic telephone ringing sound. In more modern phones this signal is detected by a circuit, which makes a sound to imitate the ring using a small transducer. Telephone devices for the deaf detect the ring signal and flash lights for a visible alert. Although this signal as well as the sound of distant ring back that the caller hears are generated in the switch to which the destination phone is connected, the two sounds are often out of phase. This leads to situations where the called party may answer on the first ring, but the calling party has not yet heard any ringback indication.

During the connected portion of the call, the voices of the two parties are transmitted as explained in the next section. Any touch tones generated during this phase of the call are ignored by the switch.[9] When finished, the parties terminate the call by hanging up their telephones. Going on hook brings the loop back into the high impedance initial state and allows the network to free any resources that may have been associated with the call, i.e., the voice circuit. This termination process is referred to as **tearing down** the call.

Additional in-band signaling may occur during the conversation. For example, a click or special tone indicates an incoming call during a conversation if one party has **call waiting** service. In response, the called party may briefly depress the hook switch (known as a **hook flash**); the switch detects this brief change of line state and puts the first call on hold while completing the second. While on hold, the first call remains connected through the network to the central office associated with the called party, and the circuit resources associated with the call are not freed (nor is billing suspended).

Another new form of signaling information on analog lines is **calling number identification** currently being introduced by regional telephone operating companies. The calling telephone number is transmitted as analog audio in the silent interval after the first ring, using modem-style encoding of digits. Special equipment on the called line can display this number or send it to a local computer.

[9]A few pay phones disable tone generation during the call often to deny callers the option of selecting a long-distance carrier of their choice.

Calling line identification is not yet available on a widespread basis, so the caller's number is generally available only for local calls. Calling number identification is part of a range of new signaling services currently being deployed. These new services include **call blocking** (automatically rejecting calls from a particular number), **distinctive ringing** for calls from a particular number, **call back** (placing a return call to the number that most recently called without the caller knowing what that number was), and **call trace** (which stores the calling number in the switch to be disclosed to law enforcement agencies acting on charges of telephone harassment).

Yet another form of in-band signaling is the **stutter dial tone,** which is associated with voice mail when a message-waiting light is not available. In this situation, the dial tone is not a continuous tone but instead is interrupted, i.e., it stutters, which indicates the presence of new messages in one's voice mailbox. Stutter tone may also be used to indicate an alternate call appearance. For example, an exchange may allow a call to be put on hold by a hook flash. A stutter dial tone then indicates that a new call may be dialed and reminds the caller that there is already a call in progress. After the second call is dialed, the two calls may be conferenced together if desired.

There are many external devices that connect to analog telephone lines, such as answering machines, computer modems, and facsimile machines. These devices employ the same kind of signaling techniques characteristic of analog systems even though some devices transmit data instead of voice. These consumer devices tend to be taken for granted and may be sorely missed in a digital telephone system, which, as described below, uses very different signaling methods.

### Transmission

Voice communication can commence once call setup completes. In the simplest case in which both lines are on the same local mechanical switch, the two loops are electrically joined through switching relays and current flows through the completed circuit. Voice is transmitted as current variations in the circuit. The battery from the central office is connected through the local loop to the handset microphone. This microphone typically is full of carbon granules behind a diaphragm located just inside the "mouthpiece." Since sound is composed of variations in air pressure over time, the talker's speech will move the diaphragm, changing the resistance inside the microphone. The loop current changes in proportion to the change in resistance. At the receiving end, the varying loop current flows through a coil around a magnet, which is connected to another diaphragm similar to a conventional loudspeaker. As the diaphragm moves in and out, sound pressure variations are reproduced corresponding to those that impacted the microphone. As a result, we hear the calling party.

The task of the switch and telephone network is to construct a path or circuit for the call. The circuit may actually be a single electrical circuit involving physical connection of the loop coming from the originating phone with the loop terminating in the destination phone. Originally all calls were carried on individual circuits with patch cords in the central office switchboards completing the circuits. Now it is most likely that once the circuit leaves the local central office, the voice is digitized. The digitized voice is then combined with several other digitized conversations, transmitted some distance by wire, fiber-optic cable, microwaves, or radio transmission to a satellite, eventually demultiplexed from the stream of many conversations, turned back into an analog signal at a distant central office, and sent down the final loop. This entire procedure is virtually transparent to the user except possibly for the delays associated with transmission time on satellite links; we may think of the network as switching virtual analog circuits.

Recall that the loop is a two-wire system. Both parties may talk at the same time and consequently one transmit signal (what one party says) and one receive signal (what the other party says) become mixed on the line. A **hybrid** circuit in the telephone attempts to separate these signals; this is a difficult task in that each connection has a different phase and amplitude response. In other words, the acoustic response of a line varies as a function of frequency, which, in turn, varies from call to call. Some of the signal from the talker's microphone comes back to the talker's earpiece: this is called **sidetone** and provides useful feedback to the caller as a cue to the line quality and a hint as to when to speak up.

But there are several drawbacks to the mix between transmit and receive signals. With telephone-based speech recognition, it is difficult to build an application in which the caller can interrupt ("barge in") while the computer is talking because the computer's speech will be feeding back into the recognizer. Speaker phones encounter feedback problems when the transmitted signal comes out through the speaker and back into the microphone.[10]

Consequently, speaker phones are **half duplex,** meaning that at any moment they are either transmitting or receiving but not both concurrently. Whichever party speaks louder will monopolize the channel ("get the floor"). This makes it much harder to interrupt or offer back channel responses (See chapter 9) and as a result conversation becomes awkward. Several companies (Shure, NEC, VideoTelecom, to name a few) sell full duplex echo-cancellation systems that can be used in a telephone environment. These more sophisticated systems determine the impulse response of the system, i.e., the correspondence between the transmitted and received signal to properly subtract the transmitted element from the received element of the conversation. These devices are still relatively expensive ($1000 and higher in 1993) pieces of equipment intended for conference rooms, but lower priced consumer models for the desktop are just around the corner.

Telephone audio is band limited to lie between approximately 300 and 3100 Hz. The lower bound is established by blocking capacitors that separate the audio

---

[10]This is not a problem with handsets since the signal coming out of the earpiece is not strong enough to make its way into the mouthpiece. A piece of cotton may often be found inside the handset to prevent acoustic coupling through the hollow body of the handset.

signal from the battery current. The higher frequency is set in part by character-istics of the carbon microphone and in part by the constraints of the digital por-tions of the network. It is important to limit the upper frequency. The digital segment of the network carries the signal sampled at 8 kHz with 8 bits of μ-law encoded data per sample. As discussed in Chapter 3, μ-law encoding is a loga-rithmic pulse code modulation scheme, and these 8 bits allow about 12 bits of real dynamic range. The 8 kHz sampling rate cannot represent a signal with fre-quency components exceeding 4kHz without introducing aliasing distortion; this translates to a little higher than 3kHz for real-world audio filters.

Because of the limited bandwidth some acoustic information is lost during a telephone conversation. A significant amount of low frequency information is lost, generally including the fundamental frequency of voicing, although this does not prevent us from perceiving the pitch of the speech. The higher frequency limit interferes most significantly with the intelligibility of fricatives. These particular frequency limits were chosen with care to allow adequate intelligibility at mini-mum cost (in terms of bandwidth). Much of the trouble that consumers experi-ence with understanding telephone conversations stems from noisy lines or inadequate amplitude rather than with the bandwidth limitations. Still it is often more difficult to identify a caller over the telephone than in person. On a positive note, users may find synthetic speech less objectionable over the telephone as they are already accustomed to its band-limited characteristics.

**Conference calls** allow more than two parties to be connected simultaneously. Such a call may be established by a single subscriber with conference service, which allows two calls to be merged by one line; the calls are actually merged in the switch at the request of the common telephone. Local conferencing usually can merge three callers, i.e., two incoming calls; for a larger group a conference service must be involved to establish a **bridge** across the circuits. With a limited number of lines, conferencing can be accomplished by simply adding the signals and perhaps decreasing their amplitude first to prevent clipping speech when multiple parties speak simultaneously. For more than two or three parties, sim-ply adding all the signals is undesirable since the background noise accumulated from each line results in a poor signal-to-noise ratio for the single person speak-ing. It is better to add together the signals from the one or two lines producing the loudest signals, presumably those conferees who are talking at a given time, and mute the remaining lines to keep their noise out of the conference. This technique interferes with interruption; if many parties speak at once, some will not be heard. Communication is also horribly confounded if inexpensive half-duplex speaker phones are used.

Conference calls are often used as the audio paths for teleconferences in which multiple sites share voice as well as video. Teleconferencing usually requires spe-cially equipped conference rooms. There is growing research interest in less for-mal conferences in which low cost video equipment is located in ordinary offices, connected together for "video calls," and possibly sharing windows of workstation screens among conferees.

Devices such as modems and facsimile (fax) machines transmit digital data over analog voice circuits. They do so by generating different sounds for "1" bits and for "0" bits.[11] The sounds for various bit patterns are transmitted with differing frequency and/or phase, and the receiver decodes these sounds back into digital data.

## DIGITAL TELEPHONES

A digital telephone is one connected to the local switch via a digital connection for both signaling and transmission. Most modern telephone switches are internally digital because digital technologies are often less expensive than analog, digital signaling techniques allow for easier extensions to support new services, and a digital audio signal can be more easily transmitted without degradation.

Unfortunately, all early digital switches used vendor-proprietary signaling techniques, which allowed use of telephones produced by that vendor alone and frustrated attempts to build telephone interfaces for computers. But an international digital standard, ISDN (Integrated Services Digital Network), has been emerging over the past decade, and is the focus of this section. The chief advantage of ISDN over other digital protocols is that it is a standard that ultimately will allow interoperability of equipment across vendors and among countries, making hardware and applications development much more attractive. Unfortunately, true portability across vendors and among countries has not yet been achieved even under ISDN.

With ISDN the connection to each telephone is digital and supports three simultaneous channels called "2B + D."[12] In such a configuration (Basic Rate ISDN), the 2B, or "bearer," channels can each carry 64,000 bits of data per second in each direction, which corresponds to the familiar 8 kHz 8 bit μ-law encoding of speech. Speech is usually carried on the B1 channel with the B2 channel reserved for a data call such as the connection of a terminal to a host computer. The 16,000 bits per second D or "data" channel is used for signaling between the phone and the switch. Thus, ISDN signaling is entirely out of band; signaling occurs over a channel entirely different from that which transmits voice.

There are two, three, or four pairs of wires between the switch and the digital telephone depending on how power is supplied to the telephone, but unlike analog phones a pair is not dedicated to each channel. Rather, one pair of wires is for transmit, one is for receive, and the third pair supplies power to the telephone. The bits associated with both B channels and the single D channel are merged together into small data packets (see Figure 10.3), and electrically encoded in a scheme that maintains a balance of "0" and "1" bits on the line.

---

[11]Actually most current modem schemes encode pairs of bits, i.e., "00" will be encoded one way and "01" another.

[12]Other configurations are supported. Primary rate ISDN (PRI) supports 23 B channels and a single D channel. Broadband ISDN provides even greater data rates.

**Figure 10.3.** The bits of two B channels and one D channel are combined in a single packet.

## Signaling

All signaling takes place over the D channel. As with most data communication schemes, ISDN call control may be broken down into a number of layers. The lowest layer, Layer 1, specifies the physical characteristics of the signal including the encoding schemes to balance the bit levels on the wire. Layer 2 defines the addressing scheme, data verification, and retransmission requirements. Layer 3 defines a protocol, Q.931 (ANSI T1.607 in the U.S.), for signaling between the telephone and the switch. Layer 3 is our primary concern for signaling purposes. ISDN currently defines no services above Layer 3. Signaling under ISDN uses data communication schemes similar to those used in computer communication. Although attractive for its power, implementing the ISDN protocol is not trivial, and ISDN telephones (or "terminals" as they are called) or computer interface cards ("network adapters") are much more expensive than current analog equipment and usually incorporate microprocessors to track the state of each call in progress.

The Layer 2 ISDN D channel protocol is LAP-D (LAP stands for "Link Access Protocol"), or Q.921. LAP-D defines the format of data packets and provides for error checking, retransmission, and flow control. LAP-D also supports a two-tiered addressing scheme to allow multiple data link connections simultaneously over a single D channel. The SAPI (Service Access Point Identifier) portion of the address specifies a service, e.g., a SAPI of 0 identifies the call control service that manages calls on the B channels. Another service, which would use a different SAPI, could be an electronic meter reading service. Digital utility meters could be attached to the ISDN telephone line and accessed from a remote location over the D channel. The second address field is the TEI (Terminal Endpoint Identifier), which corresponds to a particular device being served. Multiple telephone extensions each have a unique TEI so that each can send and receive independent call control messages to the central office switch. For the example meter-reading service, the gas, electric, and water meters might each have its own TEI.

Contained within the LAP-D packets are Layer 3 messages. Layer 3 includes the Q.931 protocol, which implements basic call control. Another portion of Layer 3, Q.932, is designed to implement supplemental services, although the definition of these is still evolving.[13] Q.931 provides a protocol to set up and tear down voice connections on the B channel as well as data connections on the B or D channels.

---

[13]Supplementary services include conferencing, call transfer, hold, and drop, as well as managing multiple directory numbers on a single key-set telephone. Most supplementary signaling is at this date switch specific. National ISDN One is an attempt to standardize a core of supplementary services in the U.S.

When a telephone is first plugged in, it brings up its Q.921 layer and establishes a Q.931 link with the switch after negotiating a TEI. When a calling party picks up the handset, a SETUP message is sent to the switch to establish basic parameters such as the type of call; the switch responds with a SETUP ACKnowledgment (see Figure 10.4). Individually dialed digits are then sent as a series of INFO messages to the switch. If all the digits are known in advance, they can be sent within the SETUP message. When enough digits are dialed, the switch returns a CALL PROCEEDING message. Most current ISDN telephones generate audible touch tone frequency sounds during dialing: these tones provide both feedback to the caller and once the call is established in-band signaling support for nonISDN interactive services. During dialing, there may be no B channel established to the switch and the switch does not listen to these tones.

The telephone of the called party then receives its own SETUP message, which may contain INFOrmation fields identifying the number of the calling line as well as other information. The telephone set may use this information to post a message in its display if it has one. The phone itself then generates a ringing sound; this is produced locally not by the central office (although the central office may specify *which* of several different ring patterns to use in support of services requiring distinctive ring sounds). The phone sends back an ALERTing message

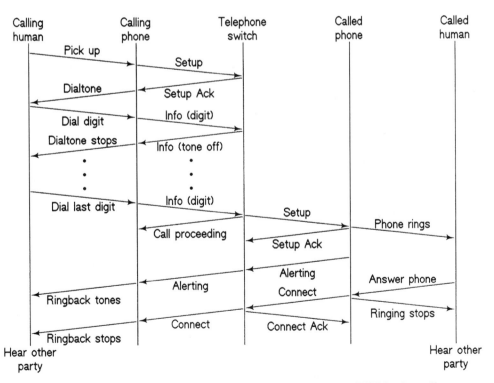

**Figure 10.4.** The exchange of messages in setting up an ISDN voice call.

to the switch, which passes an ALERTing message back to the calling telephone, which can then generate a ringback indication. If the called party answers the phone, a CONNECT message is sent back to the switch. The switch acknowledges this CONNECT message to the answering party and passes it on to the calling party. At this time, the B channels for each phone are connected and digitized audio is exchanged. At the end of the call, one party hangs up the telephone, which generates a DISCONNECT message, and the switch passes on a RELEASE message to the other phone. Thus, all parties (calling phone, called phone, and both switches) know that the call has been torn down.

Each Layer 3 message is a packet containing a number of fields called information elements. Some information elements are mandatory, some are optional, and, at this point in time, many are specific to a particular switch vendor; these elements are implemented using special "code sets" for each switch. Figure 10.5 shows a sample message and its contents.

## Transmission

Digitized voice is carried easily on a B channel. A codec in the telephone digitizes the signal from the microphone as 8 bit μ-law encoded samples at 8 kHz and transmits the samples on the appropriate B channel. At the receiving end, another codec turns the digitally encoded speech into an analog signal, which then drives the earpiece. Applications such as digital answering machines can capture the digital voice data directly from the network to store in a file. An ISDN network is all digital, which allows end-to-end transmission of the digital signal. The main advantage to the consumer is higher quality telephone connections with no difference in audio quality between local and long-distance calls as no additional acoustic information is lost after the initial digitization. Another feature of ISDN voice transmission is that the two sides of a call are carried independently without the mixing that occurs in the analog local loop circuit.

If appropriate equipment is available at each end of the connection, enhanced audio encoding can be carried over the 64,000 bit-per-second B channel. A technique to apply ADPCM coding to several audio frequency sub-bands gives an effective bandwidth of over 7kHz [Mermelstein 1988].[14] The higher bandwidth is especially beneficial for audio conference calls as it facilitates identifying the person talking.

During call setup under ISDN, pressing keypad buttons on the telephone sends digital messages to the switch; any acoustic feedback of standard touch tone sounds is for the convenience of the person dialing. But during the transmission phase of the call, pressing buttons does *not* send messages to the remote switch or telephone. To allow users of interactive voice response services access to those services over ISDN telephones, audible touch tones must be sent in-band over the voice channel. Some digital telephone systems generate the appropriate touch

---

[14]CCITT standard G.722.

```
C SAPI=  0 (CCP) TEI=127
PD=08 UCC  Ref=O 10


M 05 SETUP
I 04 Bearer Capability              Len=3
  80 Coding standard                CCITT
     Transfer capability            Speech
  90 Transfer mode                 Circuit
     Transfer rate             64 kbits/s
  A2 Layer 1 protocol         G.711 u-law
I 18 Channel Identification         Len=1
  88 Interface identifier explicit    No
     Interface type               Basic
     Indicated channel exclusive     Yes
     Channel is D-channel             No
     Channel selection              None
I 1E Progress indicator             Len=2
  82 Location               Local public
  83 Progress description   Orig non-ISDN
I 34 Signal                         Len=1
  4F Alerting off


              C SAPI=  0 (CCP) TEI= 64
                PD=08 UCC  Ref=D 10
                M 01 ALERTing
                I 18 Channel Identification       Len=1
                  81 Interface identifier explicit    No
                     Interface type             Basic
                     Indicated channel exclusive    No
                     Channel is D-channel           No
                     Channel selection              B1
```

**Figure 10.5.** The information elements contained in a SETUP message and the ALERTing message sent in response.

tone sounds in the local switch instead of the telephone when the caller uses the keypad, but this provides less effective auditory feedback to the user.

## PBXS

Not all telephones are connected directly to the central office. In business environments with a large number of telephone lines, it is more common that the phone in an office is connected to a switch owned by the business called a PBX (Private Branch eXchange). The PBX provides an initial level of switching internal to the organization. As illustrated in Figure 10.6, a PBX can either connect two internal phones to each other (without incurring a charge from the telephone operating company as none of its resources are used) or connect an internal telephone to an external number through trunks to the central office. In an alternative arrangement sold under the trademark Centrex, each telephone is connected to the central office, but software in the central office switch emulates the internal number dialing and other features of an independent PBX.

PBXs provided many calling features, such as conference, transfer, and hold long before these were available to single line customers.[15] Because PBXs usually serve many fewer lines than a central office, they represent a much smaller capital investment and are marketed by many vendors. Because their interconnection with the public switched telephone network is limited and well specified, the PBX is free to implement its own internal call management protocol. Presently PBX vendors offer a variety of incompatible and proprietary digital protocols to support services such as display of calling party and call routing information such as "forwarded from" that can be used by a receptionist answering many lines.

PBXs also offer the flexibility of providing their own numbering plan. For example, in the sample PBX in Figure 10.6 all the internal extensions consist of two digits beginning with "2." This numbering plan interferes with dialing the outside number 232-1234 as the internal call to extension "23" would be initiated when the second digit of that number was dialed. Although the PBX could delay after the second digit waiting to see if the caller dials any additional digits, this would slow down all internal calls. Instead, most PBXs employ a numbering plan specifying that the prefix "9" precede all outside calls.

PBXs are often used to form private telephone networks within large companies that are geographically dispersed. For example, the PBX we have been using as an example might provide calling to a remote office when the first dialed digit is "8"; to reach telephone "25" at the remote site, the caller would dial "825." The PBX would route this call to a trunk (see Figure 10.7) leased from one of the long-distance operating companies tied to the distant PBX. The distant PBX would then complete the circuit to the local telephone line numbered "25." This archi-

---

[15]A set of central office services called CLASS (Custom Local Area Signaling Services) provide these as well as many of the other features discussed in this chapter, but CLASS is only now becoming widely available in the U.S.

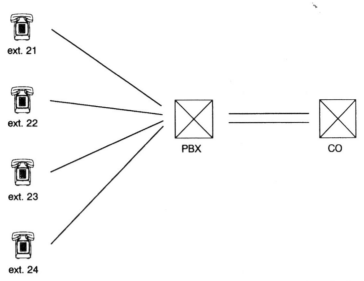

**Figure 10.6** A PBX provides an internal telephone network. Telephones served directly by the PBX can be connected without using the public telephone network. The PBX can connect an internal telephone to the central office switch through trunk lines.

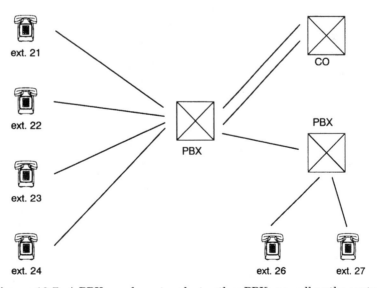

**Figure 10.7.** A PBX may have trunks to other PBXs as well as the central office, providing private telephone networks.

tecture mirrors the arrangement of central offices and connections to remote central offices through the public telephone network; the only difference is who owns the equipment.

In practice it is more common that each telephone number is unique. The PBX would know from its routing tables that telephone numbers in the range of "25" to "30" are at the remote site and route these calls to the distant switch. In any case, the digits "25" must be transmitted to the remote switch so that it can route the call to the appropriate remote telephone.

## SUMMARY

The telephone plays an important role in many aspects of using computers for communication. Telephone-based interactive voice services provide remote access to a variety of databases. The next chapter discusses computers as mediators of telephone conversations between people. Chapter 12 describes stored voice as a computer data type; at the moment, most such data arrives over the telephone, e.g., voice mail messages. This chapter has discussed operational characteristics of telephone networks so that the reader appreciates both the underlying issues in using computers to control calls and how properties of the telephone voice channel require particular interaction techniques for voice services.

Telephone management can be broken down into a signaling phase that sets up and tears down calls and a transmission phase during which two or more parties converse. Signaling and transmission are handled very differently in analog and digital networks, although most *functionality* can be had using either. Analog signaling is in-band, i.e., carried as audible sounds. A computer interfaced to the analog network must listen in and analyze the acoustic properties of sounds on the local loop to track the progress of a call or use hardware that does essentially the same thing. Digital signaling uses protocols similar to those used in existing computer networks and hence can be more easily integrated with other workstation operating system activity than analog signaling. Digital signaling is also faster and allows more readily for management of multiple calls simultaneously.

Analog and basic digital voice transmission support similar audio coding quality and bandwidth; the data rate of the ISDN B channel was chosen so as to model the characteristics of analog telephone circuits. But the digital network offers several additional advantages. Foremost in an all-digital network there are no further reductions in audio quality after digitization no matter how many miles the circuit spans; analog circuits exhibit signal degradation at each stage of amplification, which can be numerous over a very long distance. An end-to-end ISDN circuit keeps both partys' voices separate, making it easier to use speech recognition to interrupt an interactive service while it is speaking. The digital network can be used to carry speech based on improved coders offering higher audio bandwidth over existing channel capacity. As ISDN offers multiple B channels on a single telephone line, voice and data call or multiple voice calls may be in progress simultaneously over a single connection to the network.

Although ISDN is attractive for many reasons, it will be slow to penetrate the consumer market because digital telephone equipment is more expensive than analog, and few residential customers require telecommunication services that can benefit from ISDN's capabilities. At least in North America, the first wave of ISDN deployment has been limited generally to select business environments. Although the economics of wide-area networking or the need to merge voice and data services dominate deployment decisions, business environments also have the most to gain from integration of computers and telephones for call management—which brings us to the topic of the next chapter.

## FURTHER READING

There are a limited number of references that explain telecommunications technologies to a broad audience. Chorafas presents a survey of of network technologies and weaves them into their roles in an evolving global network Stallings presents ISDN in a very readable manner. Briley focuses on details of switching in the telephone network, while Talley concentrates on data communication protocols; both books are readable by a general audience but more focused than was this chapter.

# 11

# Telephones and Computers

The previous chapter discussed interactions between people, telephones, the central office switch, and the remainder of the telephone network. In this chapter we consider the benefits computers offer for call management through the enhanced services and flexible call routing they can provide. Computers can provide a user interface more powerful than the keypad or low-power display of conventional telephones. Computers can personalize telecommunications and change the way we think about using telephones.

The signaling and transmission functions of the telephone were explained in the previous chapter. Extending signaling capabilities to computers allows the computer to place calls, employ a variety of means to alert the user to an incoming call, and automatically route calls on the basis of who is calling, the time of day, and the current activity of the called party. Interfacing computers to the transmission phase of the telephone network allows the user to place calls by name or from other personal information management applications. Computers can be sophisticated answering machines providing store-and-forward capabilities so that we can "converse" asynchronously; the telephone may prove to be the primary source of voice as data to the office workstation.

Current digital telephone switches and voice mail systems are in fact computers, some running operating systems similar to those on our workstations. But the programs and run-time environments of these switches are specialized for telephone tasks, such as switching voice circuits in real time, maintaining billing records, and periodically running diagnostic checks on the integrity of the network and its constituent circuits. Telephone switches are designed to execute a specific task quickly and reliably; they are not designed to run user applications.

This chapter examines telephony applications that run on the same workstations we use to edit documents, develop software, or read our electronic mail.

This chapter begins by exploring the benefits of involving a workstation in the call management process and then offers examples of the kinds of services it can provide. The hardware requirements and underlying architectures that allow workstations to participate in call setup are then discussed. Finally, several case studies are presented for a more detailed description of the services that can be offered by interfacing computers to telephones.

## MOTIVATION

In many contemporary office environments it is common to find a workstation or personal computer and a telephone in each office, a communal fax machine, and a voice mail system housed in a telecommunications closet. The voice mail system interacts with the telephone via a message-waiting light but otherwise these devices each function in isolation. This chapter proposes linking the functionality of these various devices with particular emphasis on including telephony functions in the computer, from which a number of benefits may be realized.

### Access to Multiple Communication Channels

Providing *ease of access* to communication facilities over different media motivates computer-mediated telephony. Facsimile use has exploded, fostering boards that allow personal computers to send and receive faxes as well as display bit-mapped images on the screen. Many users keep their phone number databases on computers and consult them when placing a call, or dial by holding the handset next to their palm-top computer. Electronic mail use is taking off and is now widely available; its existence relies on the computer network, but messages are also being forwarded to pagers and cellular telephone-equipped mobile computers.

Making all these communication media available from a single desktop computer allows the user to easily cross media boundaries during a single communications session. For example, receipt of an email message might imply that the difficult-to-reach sender is in the office and hence available by phone for a more interactive discussion. Then during the course of discussion, conversants could exchange pertinent documents by email or fax. A caller may prefer to send a message by email instead of leaving one with a receptionist if the called party is unavailable.

Integrating disparate communication media at the workstation affords immediacy and convenience to employing multiple media simultaneously or sequentially. Bringing incoming messages into a single computing entity simplifies the task of discovering whether any new messages have arrived and enables a variety of alerting, filtering, or message forwarding policies under control of the recipient.

**Improved User Interfaces**

A second reason to integrate telephony into the workstation is the potential for significantly more powerful user interfaces than can be provided with telephone equipment alone. Most sophisticated telephones provide a touchtone keypad and perhaps a few dedicated function buttons such as *hold, conference,* and *transfer.* User interfaces to all telephony services must be implemented using these buttons, and feedback to the user is limited to a small repertoire of sounds such as the busy or dial tone signals. Without a display, it is difficult for the user to determine the current state of any features that may have been activated. For example, my telephone has speed dialing but it cannot tell me the contents of my speed-dialing list; instead, I have to place the call and see who answers or tape a piece of paper with my speed-dialing list to the phone. Likewise, I can touch a *redial* key to dial the most recently called number but cannot find out what that number is without trying it. I can key "*73" to cancel my call forwarding, but I cannot find out the number to which my calls are currently being forwarded.

Each year a greater number of sophisticated telephone services are offered: call waiting, call back the number that last phoned, block calls from certain calling numbers, assign distinctive ring to some calling numbers, identify multiple incoming lines with a distinctive ring, speed dialing, calling line identification, and voice mail, to name just a few. But the telephone keypad provides a sparse user interface, making it difficult to use even the existing services much less new ones. A few users may read the manual to safely reconfigure their phone, but many avoid or underutilize the new services.

One approach to providing improved user interfaces has been to build more complex telephones, with displays, soft keys, menus, and even voice prompts. However, workstations are already suited for this task. Computer displays are typically high-resolution CRT screens, whereas telephone displays if available are small and difficult to read due to hardware cost and electric power limitations. Workstations offer additional and more elaborate input devices including full keyboards and mice. Even more beneficial is the fact that powerful window systems provide rich and flexible user interfaces and allow several concurrent applications to share the screen. Workstation operating systems allow resources such as memory or digital signal processors to be shared among a number of applications; the hardware in a "smart telephone" is wasted when the telephone is idle.

There is limited experimental evidence on the value of screen-based interfaces to telephony. [Roberts and Engelbeck 1989] compared the computer and advanced telephone user interface media using standard touchtone telephones, display-based telephone terminals, and telephones augmented with speech synthesis for voice menus. They found the display-based interface both faster and most well received by subjects who routed calls, screened calls, and retrieved messages. But long-term studies based on MICE users (Bellcore's telephony development environment, described shortly) were somewhat less convincing. [Root and Koster 1986] substituted mnemonic key codes for the conventional numeric ones (e.g., "CF" instead of "72" for call forwarding). They found that subjects recalled more system functions with the mnemonic codes but did not increase their use of the services. Similarly, [Root and Chow 1987] found that users readily employed a screen-based interface to manipulate and edit their speed-dialing lists, but this did not increase the number of entries they kept in the lists. Although subjects could speed-dial by the screen in addition to the keypad, they did not do so. Interestingly, speed-dial usage increased somewhat during the course of the study.

It is difficult to draw strong conclusions from this evidence. The evidence does indicate, however, that while some advantage can be rightfully claimed for improved interface technology, the underlying service offerings may themselves lead to stable usage patterns. These experiments tested limited computer telephony services, and although the "improved" interfaces employed new technology, the new services offered small improvements over those to which they were compared. More sophisticated services can be built from the interactions between multiple functions, e.g., returning the call of a voice mail message with a single mouse click or automatically rerouting calls when the user's calendar indicates that the user is out of town. But it is much easier to measure the effects of a small, constrained change to a user-interface than it is to compare the utility of one set of features with another very different set over an extended period of use. Of the research projects described later in this chapter only MICE included an evaluation component.

## Enhanced Functionality

A workstation can offer enhanced functionality by personalizing call setup for both outgoing and incoming calls. Placing a call can be facilitated by allowing the user to spell the name of the desired party with the computer keyboard, speak the name to a speech recognizer, or use another application such as a personal address book to specify the number. Or using interactive cut-and-paste or drag-and-drop paradigms, a user may be able to deposit an email message into a telephone icon to place a call to the mail sender. For incoming calls, the computer may route the call to a different phone according to a predetermined set of conditions or play a caller-specific outgoing voice mail message.

Call routing is the most sophisticated of these functions. Factors influencing how a call might be handled include the identity of the calling party, the time of day, the location and activity of the called party, and whether a receptionist is available to take an unanswered call. For example, an "important" call could invoke a distinctive ring sound or be forwarded to the nearest telephone if the recipient of the call is in another office. A call may be classified as "important" by virtue of having originated from a recently dialed phone number so as to help prevent "phone tag" in which repeated calls back and forth go unanswered. A variety of technologies can be used to determine the location of the called party or deliver notification of an incoming call while absent from the office.

Much of this potential routing information is dynamic and relies on knowledge about the user. When two parties play "phone tag" they alternate calling each other and leaving messages. If outgoing calls are placed using the same workstation that screens incoming calls, phone tag can be detected, which might initiate a more thorough search, or page, by the workstation in response to an additional incoming call. Similarly, if a meeting with someone is scheduled for tomorrow morning and that person calls today, it is likely to be relevant to the meeting and hence a more important call than otherwise, but this can be known only by accessing the called party's calendar and telephone directory to make the association.

It would be difficult to implement this degree of personalization and style of experimentation with the standard services in the telephone switch.[1] Telephone switches are designed to establish calls according to relatively static routing tables, which are modified by very limited touchtone based user interfaces. They do not have access to personal information such as a user's calendar. An entirely new dimension of flexible call establishment requires more varied per-call conditional routing factors as well as a more sophisticated user interface to manage the more complex routing rules.

### Voice and Computer Access

Another motive for connecting telephones and computers is the potential for *remote voice access* to personal databases. Although a personal workstation is capable of storing many megabytes of information, its utility is limited if the data is inaccessible when the user is away from the office. Databases, such as calendars, electronic mail, and telephone numbers can be made available through interactive telephone interfaces using the techniques described in Chapter 6. Once connected to an application by voice, it is useful to be able to add to a database, e.g., to put an entry in one's calendar by speaking. Such voice interfaces may make the telephone the primary source of voice as a data type on multimedia workstations; examples will be offered later in this chapter as well as in Chapter 12.

## PROJECTS IN INTEGRATED TELEPHONY

Several research projects have attempted to integrate computers and telephones in different ways. This section describes the set of telephone features of each and the system architectures upon which they were implemented. These descriptions highlight the many benefits of flexible call management by computers.

### Etherphone

One of the seminal attempts to merge computers and telephones was the Etherphone project at the Xerox Palo Alto Research Center (PARC). Etherphone

---

[1] It should be noted that in some ways MICE, described later in this chapter, developed an architecture allowing a greater degree of user access to the configuration tables in the telephone switch. This certainly facilitates call setup services, but such tables alone cannot deal with dynamic call routing depending in real time on user input or situational information.

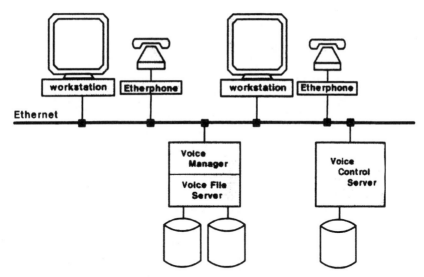

**Figure 11.1.** Etherphone architecture. (From Terry and Swinehart, "Managing Stored Voice in the Etherphone System." Reprinted with permission from *Transactions on Computer Systems* ©1988, ACM.)

included hardware to digitize voice and control analog telephone lines, both under the control of a workstation in concert with various networked servers. The project included call control applications, integration of audio with the local computing environment and its associated user interfaces, and voice-oriented applications such as audio editing, voice annotation of text, and scripted documents.[2]

The Etherphone itself was a hardware device, capable of digitizing and playing back speech over an Ethernet. Its physical components included a speaker, microphone, and a telephone handset, as well as a standard analog telephone line interface, which enabled calls to be placed over the external telephone network. Internal "calls" were transmitted over the Ethernet. During call setup, a centralized call control server negotiated with the user's workstation and then sent commands to an Etherphone agent, which dealt with the physical devices in the Etherphone and the stream of audio data packets. Voice was transmitted over the Ethernet either between Etherphones or between an Etherphone and a variety of servers as shown in Figure 11.1. The servers included a storage server to save or retrieve sound from disk, and a text-to-speech server that received text and transmitted the synthesized speech over the network.

Internal and external call processing proceeded differently within the Etherphone environment. In the case of an internal call between Etherphones, the entire conversation was transmitted over the Ethernet and local distributed pro-

---

[2]See previous discussion of scripted documents in Chapter 4.

cesses coordinated the setup and tear down of the call. For external calls, the Etherphone provided ring detection for incoming calls and touchtone generation to place a call, but switching occurred outside Etherphone in the ordinary telephone network.

For basic telephony, Etherphone provided several methods of dialing a number including a personal directory and dialing by name. A log was kept of all call activity. Tools, primarily text-based (see Figure 11.2), provided user interfaces to the dialing functions. For incoming calls, each Etherphone user had a distinctive ring "tune" to distinguish whose phone was ringing when within earshot of several offices. If the caller was also an Etherphone user, his or her ring tune alternated with that of the called party, giving an audible form of calling party identification. A telephone icon on the screen also indicated the incoming call and visually displayed the caller's identity.

With local call routing and voice distribution over the Ethernet, a number of new services were possible. The tight binding between a name and a telephone number could be broken; while the called party was logged in on any workstation, Etherphone calls could be forwarded to the nearest Etherphone. While in another office, an Etherphone user could enable "call visiting" from any workstation, causing one's calls to forward to that office. Because incoming calls were indicated with the distinctive ring tune, the host and visitor knew who should answer the telephone. A meeting service allowed multiple listeners to tune in to a meeting

---

Finch

| Phone | Answer | Disconnect | SpeakText | StopSpeech | Directory | Drop Out |
| --- | --- | --- | --- | --- | --- | --- |

| Called Party: | Aquarius Theater info | Calling Party: | wyatt.pa |
| --- | --- | --- | --- |

40: Speaking text: "Suppose Alexander Graham Bell had waited..."
November 12, 1986 11:45:52 am PST
    52: Placing call to Aquarius Theater info (327-3240)

Call to swinehart.pa at November 12, 1986 11:24:18 am PST is completed, duration = 00:01:08
Call to Recording service at November 12, 1986 11:26:46 am PST is completed, duration = 00:00:55
Call from outside line at November 12, 1986 11:33:17 am PST was abandoned, duration = 00:00:06
Call from wyatt.pa at November 12, 1986 11:35:08 am PST is completed, duration = 00:01:04
Call to Text-to-Speech service at November 12, 1986 11:42:40 am PST is completed, duration = 00:00:39
Call to Aquarius Theater info (327-3240) at November 12, 1986 11:45:53 am PST is in progress

Telephone Directory [] pellet dirty

| Clear | Reset | Get | GetImpl | PrevFile | Store | Save | Time | Split | Places | Levels | (C) | Log |
| --- | --- | --- | --- | --- | --- | --- | --- | --- | --- | --- | --- | --- |

| Name | Office | | Home | Details |
| --- | --- | --- | --- | --- |
| Services | | | | |
| AAA Emergency Service | 595-3411 | | 408/246-5811 | Palo Alto, Mtn View |
| Time Announcement | 767-2676 | | 767-2676 | |
| Aquarius Theater info | 327-3240 | | | |
| PA Square Theater info | 493-1160 | | | |
| Enrico's Foreign Car | 961-4848 | | * | Fiat repairs, 2145 O. Mdfd MV |
| Dr. Kanemoto, Benson | 326-6319 | | * | Dentist |
| Dr. Stegman, Deidre physician | 321-4121 | | * | TakeCare Primary Care |
| Menlo-Atherton Insurance | 329-1150 | | * | renter's insurance: Eleanor |
| A Time For You | 941-7034 | | 967-9180 | haircuts |

**Figure 11.2.** Etherphone telephone tools. (From Zellweger, Terry and Swinehart, "An Overview of the Etherphone System and its Applications." Reprinted with permission from *Proceedings of 2nd IEEE Conference on Computer Workstations* ©1988, IEEE.)

or lecture from their separate offices; remote participants could speak to the meeting as well as listen in. The meeting service was implemented by multicasting the voice packets from the meeting room Etherphone to those of the parties listening in.[3]

Etherphone implemented fully-distributed call control by allowing workstations to place calls through requests to the connection server, i.e., a "software PBX." Both voice and call control data passed through the local area computer network. Calls originating outside the Etherphone service area were also handled in a distributed manner as each workstation's Etherphone interfaced directly to the outside analog lines.

Through its layered architecture, Etherphone brought a greater degree of sophistication to call management. The flexibility of its hardware and network implementation enabled broadened concepts of a telephone "connection." As a highly integrated environment, Etherphone made major contributions for voice applications development in the context of a larger operating system; such styles of integration are the focus of Chapter 12. It was known for its variety of applications for voice in documents as discussed in Chapter 4. Finally, Etherphone helped extend the concept of *services* by partially bridging the gap between the services offered by the telephone industry such as call forwarding and those offered by the computer industry, such as file storage.

## MICE

MICE (Modular Integrated Communications Environment) at Bellcore (Bell Communications Research) was built as a testbed for prototyping enhanced services and evaluating their use over time. The subjects of these evaluations were local laboratory members, who used MICE on a daily basis from 1985 to 1988. Although many of the trial services implemented under MICE were fairly simple, MICE provided a foundation for forging closer links between the workstations and telephones in each person's office. The trial services included "memory dialing," a mnemonic form of speed dialing, and MICEmail, an integrated voice and text message system. MICEmail provided both local and remote (using speech synthesis) access to both types of messages.

MICE explored several issues from the point of view of a local telephone operating company by defining the services and resources to be accessed over a future telephone network. MICE placed emphasis on *personalization;* messages were sent to users instead of terminals with the network turning the name into an address and determining a suitable delivery mode. These services were designed to be *customizable;* the user-configured services by changing a profile table within the MICE system. Finally, MICE worked with *integration* of voice and text message types.

---

[3]Broadcast sends the same packet to every host on the network. Multicast also sends a single packet, but only selected hosts read it.

The MICE architecture was based on a centralized server, which provided basic telephony functions as well as voice storage, speech recognition, and text-to-speech synthesis. Telephony functions were provided by a small PBX closely controlled by a workstation, which acted as a server to other computers on the local area network. A central control process on the server controlled the telephone switch by executing a finite state machine defined by a call control table, which was accessible to other workstations on the network. The call control tables could be programmed to implement the new server by means of a graphical "service editor," but making changes to the tables was a complicated procedure. Some work was done to explore screen-based interfaces to such simple service definitions such as time-of-day dependent call forwarding.

MICE was considered to be a prototype open-architecture central office telephone switch in which switching is performed entirely within the switch but outside entities can program how switching occurs. Although its primary purpose was to provide a flexible service development environment for its creators, MICE

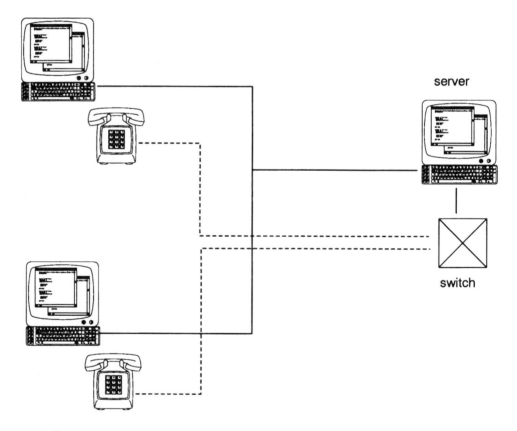

clients

**Figure 11.3.** MICE architecture. Desktop computers interface to telephones via a server computer controlling a telephone switch.

also allowed computer access to the call control tables that described how calls were handled. Client workstations did not handle each call as it came in; rather, they could update the tables which the server used to route subsequent calls.

Being centralized, MICE transmitted audio to users' offices for services such as voice mail over the telephone network. Even when using a screen-based interface to access voice messages, a user was required to pick up the telephone to hear a message. Using telephone wiring to transmit audio from a specialized server was advantageous at a time when each workstation could not play audio locally. However, the inconvenience limited voice to a few applications instead of allowing it to become a widely available data type to multiple applications.

## BerBell

BerBell,[4] also from Bellcore, was used for telephone and voice services for a real user population, and it offered increased flexibility for the creation of new services under control of the users' workstations. The Berbell project was initiated in 1985, became operable in 1986, and continues in use today. Some of the more well-known services provided by Berbell include speech synthesis for a national weather forecast, a music synthesis demonstration, and local voice paging using speech synthesis over a public address system.

Berbell utilized three servers: one for the telephone switch, one for speech synthesis, and another for digitization and playback of audio. The system included a number of basic services and features that could be invoked by the user with touch tones; in this sense, it was not very different from many PBXs. But since the Berbell servers were also on the local computer network, the same features could be activated from the user's workstation. Additionally, a programmatic interface allowed users to program new services. Over its lifetime, Berbell evolved in the direction of providing complete control over telephone calls at the workstation; in this sense, it allowed much more dynamic call control than MICE.

## Personal eXchange

The Personal eXchange (PX) project at the Computer Research Laboratory of Bell Northern Research took a distributed approach to the integration of voice and telephony with computer workstations [Kamel, Emami and Eckert 1990, Bowles *et al.* 1991]. PX also employed a central digital switching facility (a Northern Telecom Norstar PBX); however, this was an "open" PBX, and all routing commands were delivered by computers and telephones distributed around an office. As shown in Figure 11.4, located on each desk were the following.

- A telephone used for its microphone, speaker, and to serve as backup equipment if the computer failed.

---

[4]Named after the login ID of its creator, Brian E. Redman.

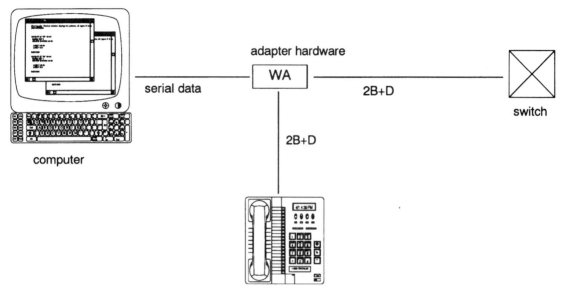

**Figure 11.4.** Architecture of the PX project. A workstation adapter, WA, allows a computer to interface to both the telephone instrument and the telephone switch by converting digital signalling protocols.

- A "workstation adapter" that brought both speech and signaling information to the computer via a digital telephone line.
- A computer, that controlled the telephone set in addition to call processing.

The wiring of the digital telephone system was used for both voice transmission and exchange of messages between call management applications and the telephone switch. Protocols similar to ISDN allowed simultaneous transmission of voice and signaling messages. When a call arrived, the switch broadcast a call setup message to all workstations with access to the dialed number. Multiple recipients could respond; for example, a screen-based telephone (such as that shown in Figure 11.5) or the telephone set next to the workstation could try to claim the call. Whichever recipient responded to the call sent an acceptance message to the switch and a voice connection was established.

A wide range of applications were implemented around this architecture; the telephone dialing interface of Figure 11.5 is but one example. In another PX application, a conversational answering machine took an interactive message by playing prompts and recording answers, and a graphical user interface allowed message retrieval (see Figure 11.6). Towards the end of the project, speech recognition and speaker verification were being incorporated into the workstation as part of the set of local services available to applications. Although much of PX focused on providing mechanisms for distributed call management, it was also concerned with the larger issues associated with the management of voice in the workstation (such as the voice editor described in Chapter 4) along with software toolkits to support audio and telephony in applications.

Richard W. Snapper
Outside Line :
Inside Line :
Bob Eckert
Inside Line :
Voice Call :
1 2 3
4 5 6
7 8 9
* 0 #
HFree ON
Hold
Feature
Page
Release
Calling BOB E

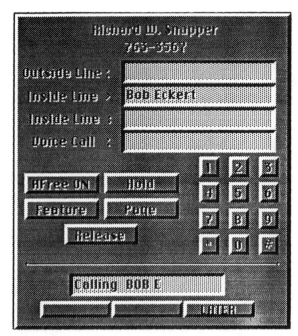

**Figure 11.5.** A PX screen-based telephone application. (Printed by permission of BNR.)

Messages
Message From
Length
Arrived
New
Ian Bowles
5.62
9:21 am
Today
Kamyar Emami
5.5
9:13 am
Today
Larry Brunet
10.6
10:42 am
Yesterday
No call info.
24.62
2:21 pm
Wed, Mar 7
Integrated Playback
Call Back
Stop Playing

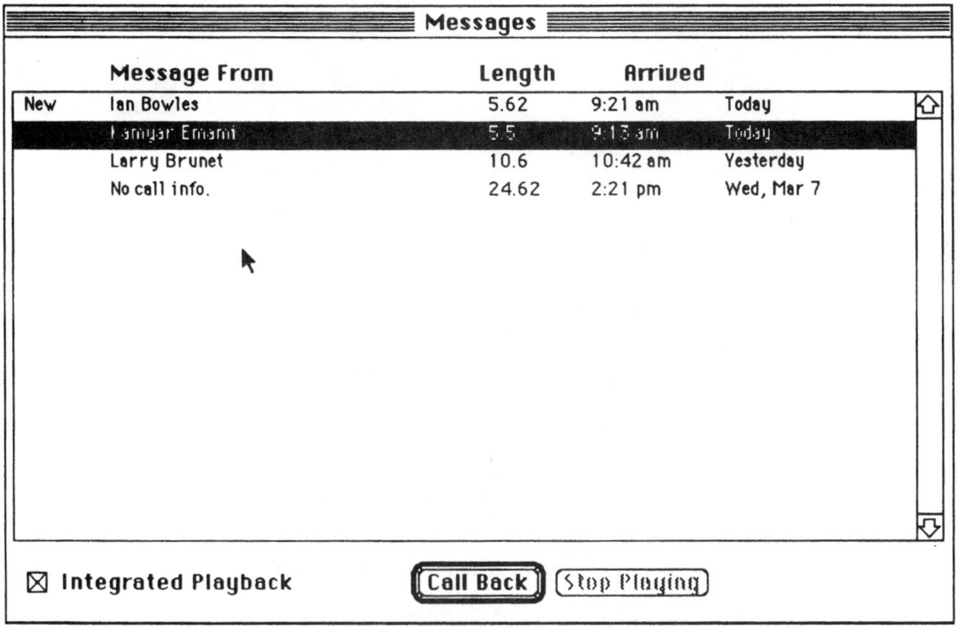

**Figure 11.6.** The display of a PX answering machine program. (Printed by permission of BNR.)

Except for the PBX, PX was a completely distributed environment. The connection management decisions were made on individual workstations. Each workstation implemented its own voice services and managed recorded voice locally. In addition to the speaker built into the computer, the local telephone set could be used as a speaker and microphone by the computer.

## Phonetool

Phonetool is a telephone dialing tool that allows users to place calls from their workstation; it was developed by Stephen Casner at the University of Southern California's Information Sciences Institute. Phonetool runs under the Sunview window system and uses a centralized telephone server to place calls. Phonetool provides a pop-up speed-dial menu (see Figure 11.7), can redial the most recently dialed number (which is displayed on the telephone icon), accepts numerical input from the keyboard, and can dial a number displayed in another window using mouse-based cut-and-paste interaction.

Phonetool places calls using a centralized server; a server is required because of hardware interface limitations for access to the telephone switch (a Rolm PBX). The server can place outgoing calls but it is not provisioned to receive them. Software was written to allow a personal computer equipped with a special PBX interface card and an Ethernet controller to function as a centralized server, i.e.,

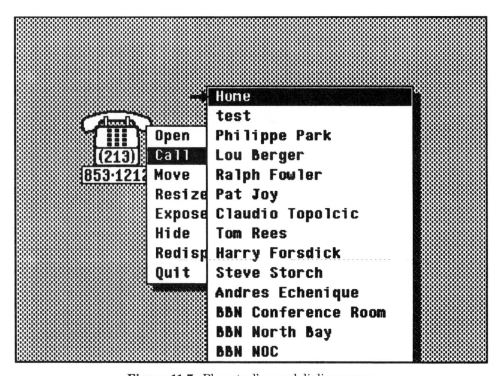

**Figure 11.7.** Phonetool's speed dialing menu.

by dialing on behalf of the numerous workstations (see Figure 11.8). In order to dial, the user's workstation sends a message over the Ethernet to the server specifying the number to dial. The server then dials the call on its own outgoing phone line. At this point, the server puts the outgoing call on hold and dials the user's intercom extension. Because the intercom is used, this call can go through automatically, putting the called party's telephone into speakerphone mode. At this

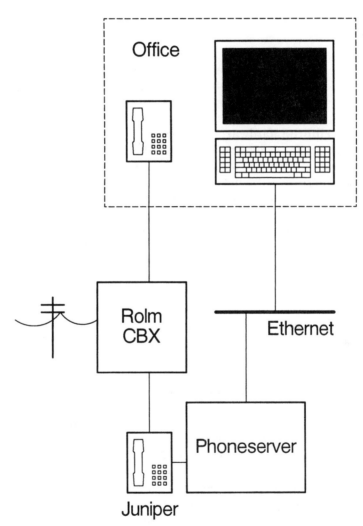

**Figure 11.8.** The I.S.I. phoneserver utilizes a personal computer with a specialized interface card to control the PBX. Workstations make requests of this server over a local area network. (From Schmandt and Casner, "Phonetool: Integrating Telephones and Workstations." Reprinted with permission from *IEEE Global Telecommunications Conference* © 1989, IEEE.)

point, the server puts the intercom call and the outgoing call together as a conference call and proceeds to drop out of the conversation. The server is now ready to service another request.

Phonetool was the starting point for Xphone described later in this chapter. Separating call control functions from the user interface allowed Xphone to be configured for both centralized and distributed architectures in a number of implementations.

# ARCHITECTURES

Several different system architectures can provide telephone functionality to workstations. It is useful to differentiate the *hardware* interface, which physically connects the computer to the telephone switch, from the *functional* interface, whereby applications on the desktop implement telephony services. A **distributed** hardware architecture requires each computer to have a hardware interface for communication with the switch. A **centralized** architecture uses a single link to the switch from one workstation; other workstations access this hardware over the network by communicating with a server process on the specially equipped workstation. Even when a hardware interface is found on each workstation, a local server may be used to allow multiple client applications to share hardware access. All these architectures could offer identical functional interfaces to clients for call control; what differs is the mechanism whereby client requests are communicated to the switch.

## Distributed Architectures

Enhanced telephone sets on every desk constitute the most direct implementation of a fully distributed telephone hardware architecture (see Figure 11.9). Advanced telephones may include improved displays, keyboards, touch screens, or speech recognition. These telephones provide superior user interfaces to traditional telephone functionality provided by the switch, and may implement new services, such as electronic mail storage within the telephone. This is not a new concept; in the early 1980s a number of "teleterminals" appeared providing small CRT displays and keyboards. More recent teleterminals use LCD or plasma displays with features such as programmable function keys, stylus input for hand writing, and local voice and text storage for messages. The most recent generation of enhanced telephones is ISDN-based; the ease of data communication between telephones allows for a range of new message services such as digital facsimile and screen-based remote data access.

This approach sidesteps the problem of computer integration, making the telephone powerful enough to obviate the need for the computer. But such devices have not proven popular beyond such consumer products as the combined telephone and answering machine. When made powerful enough to provide support for sophisticated teleservices, such stand-alone telephones become too expensive. Business users already use personal computers or workstations at their desks,

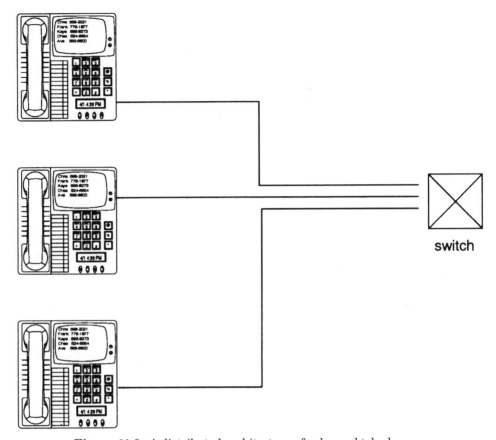

**Figure 11.9.** A distributed architecture of enhanced telephones.

and the general-purpose computer provides for more efficient resource allocation. Although much can be done to improve the design of telephones, they are not destined to push computers off the desktop. However, in environments where computers are not found, the introduction of ISDN may create a niche market for enhanced telephones.

The teleterminal provides a completely distributed architecture with one telephone per office. A completely distributed architecture can also be used for workstation-based telephony. For example, an inexpensive modem wired in parallel with a telephone can be used with autodialing software; the computer places the call and the user picks up the handset if the call is answered. Similarly, new consumer products plug into an analog phone line and decode calling-line ID information; when this information is available, the calling number is transmitted over a serial line to a host computer. Such approaches are practical on analog lines because modems are inexpensive and computer serial ports ubiquitous, but they provide only limited signaling functionality. For the computer to talk or listen to the voice circuit during a call, a higher degree of integration is necessary.

One means of providing both call control and telephone audio to a personal computer is a specialized telephone interface board. Such a board includes the required electrical interface to allow it to be connected to the telephone network, touchtone generator and decoder integrated circuits, a codec, and perhaps a digital signal processor or an integrated circuit for speech compression. Telephone interface boards are currently available for as little as a few hundred dollars.

Many workstations and personal computers now support audio digitization and playback. Telephone functionality can be added using simple external electronics. An external unit provides a telephone jack, a serial interface for call control, and analog audio input and output to be connected to the workstation. The computer sends commands and receives notification of events such as an incoming call over the serial interface. When the phone line is off hook, the computer's audio input and output are connected to the line. Touch tone dialing can be accomplished by playing prerecorded touch tone sounds once the telephone has been taken off hook. Tone decoding can be performed in the workstation by software (if the workstation is powerful enough) or by an integrated circuit in the external hardware.

ISDN is very attractive for workstation integration of telephony because it provides finer-grained call control due to its richer signaling protocol. The appropriate electrical hardware interfaces are beginning to appear as standard equipment on workstations, with ISDN call control protocols implemented in software. Once a telephone connection is established, the voice channel is already digital so further hardware is not required for voice interaction. Current advanced workstations can easily run Layer 3 ISDN protocols in software under multitasking operating systems. But less powerful computers or operating systems require separate microprocessor-based peripheral hardware to handle the real-time requirements of ISDN. Such peripherals are currently selling in the $800 range, which may represent a significant portion of the cost of the computer itself.

## Centralized Architectures

In the distributed architecture just described, telephone interface hardware is located on every computer. Such an arrangement may be impractical or inadequate for some applications, however. For either proprietary or ISDN digital switches, telephone interface hardware may be prohibitively expensive. Computer reliability is also an issue; when the workstation is down, does the telephone still work? Although it is easy to configure an analog line control card with a second telephone jack to let an adjunct telephone function when power is turned off, this is much more difficult under ISDN signaling. Some PBXs offer sophisticated computer interfaces but are equipped to connect only a single computer (usually through a serial interface); this precludes direct switch access from each workstation.

For any of these reasons, a centralized hardware architecture may be preferred or required. Figure 11.11 illustrates an example of this approach; using a telephone server provides distributed access to a network of computers. One computer, the server, includes the required hardware and software to communicate with the telephone switch on behalf of its clients. Clients are distributed over a

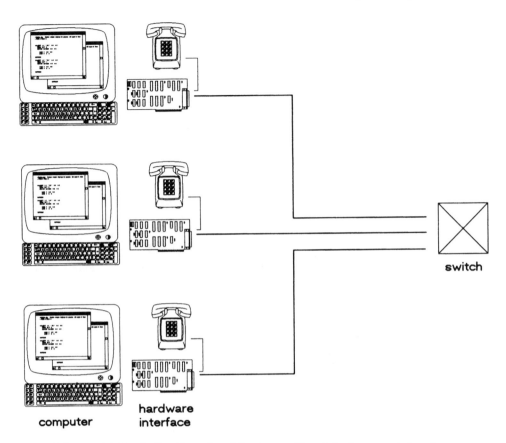

**Figure 11.10.** A distributed architecture with a telephone peripheral on each workstation.

local area network, sending requests and receiving events (such as notification of an incoming call) from the server. In this centralized architecture, application requests are translated into messages for the server and sent over the computer network; the server, in turn, translates these into commands to its local hardware and thence onto the telephone network. The centralized approach requires that one computer interact with many telephone lines so that a single server can act on behalf of a number of clients. This can be accomplished in several ways: each line can be connected to the server or the server can communicate directly with the telephone switch.

With analog telephony, each line has its own independent circuit for signaling and voice. A multiline analog telephone or key set has a pair of line wires for each line and selects between them with buttons. Similarly, interfacing a computer to multiple analog lines requires the use of one telephone line interface board per line. A single board can be made to handle multiple lines by replicating the interface circuits, which reduces the per-line expense; consequently, such boards are often used in voice mail systems, serving four to sixteen lines per board.

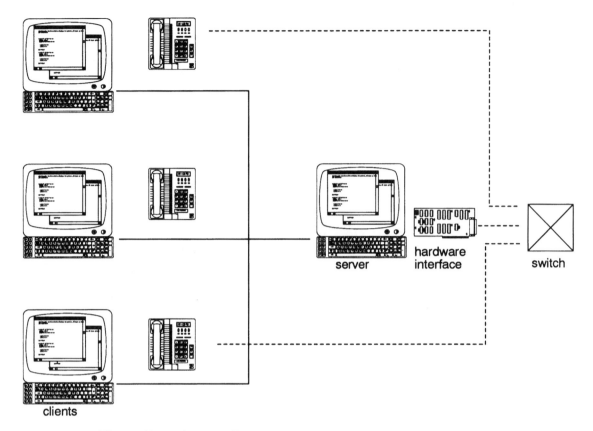

**Figure 11.11.** A server allows centralization of some resources with a network interface to each workstation.

An alternative arrangement is for the server to communicate with the switch directly through a custom interface. Some experimental systems, such as MICE, use small PBXs designed to be controlled by a host computer. Larger PBXs are less flexible but may still provide a simple computer interface. For example, some switches support a message set called SMDI (Simple Message Desk Interface), which carries selected signaling information from the switch over a serial line. Interfaces such as SMDI are often used by voice mail systems in the following fashion: When a call gets transferred to voice mail, the switch identifies the originally dialed number and a trunk line switches onto that which the call has been transferred so that the voice mail system can record a message into the proper mailbox. The signaling interface is bidirectional so the voice mail system can control the telephone's message waiting light via the switch. Such a PBX interface can extend call control to a single workstation, which communicates with the PBX and acts as a server to other workstations. SCAI (Switch-Computer Application Interface) is a proposed standard for external switch control. It is currently under study by the T1S1 committee of ANSI (the American National Standards Institute).

For digital telephone systems, particularly ISDN, multiple telephone numbers can appear on a single phone line if the switch is configured to support key set style telephones.[5] The sole D channel for the ISDN line carries signaling information in both directions for all numbers appearing on the line. So if in addition to each user's personal telephone line another line is configured with appearances of each user's number, it can be used by a server to control calls on those numbers. The D channel on the server's line can be used to allow a server to answer, transfer, or place calls by proxy at the request of client applications running on other workstations not equipped with ISDN interfaces. If the server ceases to function, the user's office telephones are unaffected.

## Comparison of Architectures

The ISI Phoneserver described earlier is an example of the server approach with centralized hardware. The choice of architecture was dictated by the PBX interface board; this board was expensive and incompatible with the users' workstations in their offices. Both MICE and Berbell used centralized telephone switching because the switching hardware supported a single serial interface. MICE stored call control tables in the server; instead of routing each call, clients programmed the call control tables and the server routed calls on its own. By contrast, Berbell allowed clients to dynamically route calls. MICE and Berbell also used centralized speech resources such as codecs and speech synthesizers. Although this provided adequate support for services to interact with remote callers, a user in an office also had to pick up the telephone to access these devices, e.g., to hear a voice message.

An ISDN-based telephone server similar to Berbell yet lacking built-in voice storage has been built at the MIT Media Lab. This server, used by applications described later in this chapter, allows access to a cluster of phone numbers using normal D channel signaling, obviating special hardware access to the telephone switch. In this environment only call control is centralized; audio services are provided locally at each workstation. Several servers provide specialized services such as a voice mail server to answer calls using the telephone server's B channel interface.

Both PX and Etherphone used fully-distributed architectures that took advantage of additional centralized services. In PX the telephone switch broadcasted information about every call, and the appropriate workstation requested that the switch complete the voice circuit. Although the switch was a central resource, it was designed to support fully-distributed call management, and most importantly the digitized voice was routed directly to the workstation. Similarly, in the Etherphone project, a central conversation manager connected digital audio streams from separate workstations for internal calls, whereas each workstation had complete local control to place outgoing calls and receive incoming calls from

---

[5]Unfortunately, these features are not published as any ISDN standard, so for now they remain vendor specific.

the public telephone network. PX stored sound locally on the workstation, while Etherphone digitized it and then stored it via a centralized voice storage server utilizing the voice ropes database described in Chapter 4. PX workstations shared a centralized speaker verification service, and Etherphone allowed workstations to have access to a central text-to-speech synthesis service.

From the point of view of hardware and system maintenance, the centralized and distributed architectures differ radically. These hardware differences can be made largely transparent to applications by means of a software library that shelters an application from details of communicating with the remote server. If implemented in such a network-transparent manner, the user is not concerned with whether the server process is on a local or remote workstation.

The server approach is attractive for device sharing and resource arbitration even if hardware devices and application processes are located on the same workstation. Device sharing promotes the development of environments with multiple small applications rather than a single monolithic application: a server allows each application to operate without knowledge of other applications that may require sporadic access to limited resources. Multiple applications may receive simultaneous notification of an incoming call; one application might alert the user using speech synthesis to name the caller or displaying the caller's name in a window on the workstation. Concurrently, an answering machine (voice mail) application waits a specified amount of time after the call is announced and picks up if the called party does not answer. Another application may keep a log of all calls, incoming or outgoing. A server architecture promotes such sharing of hardware resources, whether local or remote.

The differences between centralized and distributed architectures is more significant for voice storage, transmission, and presentation to the user in an office. If the telephone line terminates in the workstation, then when the workstation answers a call the voice circuit terminates locally. Under this architecture, an application might allow an incoming voice message to be monitored on the local workstation speaker for call screening and also permit the called party to pick up the phone in the middle of taking a message. Locally stored voice messages[6] can be played through the speaker without needing to re-establish an audio link to the server.

When the telephone line terminates in a remote location, monitoring message recording is more difficult and call pickup may not be possible. Losing the ability to screen calls is a common complaint among users when voice mail replaces answering machines. If voice is stored on a central resource, then it can be transmitted over the computer network (as was done in Etherphone) in order to be played. MICE used the existing telephone wiring to playback voice messages by first placing a local call from the central storage manager to the telephone in the office. This required the user to answer the phone to hear the message, making

---

[6]The actual disk drive on which the voice is stored may be in another location remotely mounted over the local area network. But this is transparent to the application and the sound appears as a local file system.

message playback much less spontaneous. Although we are used to the telephone as the means to retrieve voice mail, when stored voice permeates many desktop applications such as described in Chapter 12, audio playback through local speakers is much more desirable at least for use in a private office.

## CASE STUDIES

This section describes several sample projects from the MIT Media Lab. These case studies are intended as examples of the services and user interfaces that can result from the integration of telephony applications with computer workstations. Some of the case study examples contain similarities to the work on integrating computers and telephones discussed earlier in this chapter as many of the ideas have been explored across multiple research labs.

### Phone Slave

Phone Slave was an early (1983) integrated telephone management system developed by the MIT Architecture Machine Group (predecessor to the Media Lab) [Schmandt and Arons 1985, Schmandt and Arons 1984]. Phone Slave provided a variety of telephony functions including message taking, personal outgoing message delivery, a telephone number and address database, speed dialing by name, and remote access to both voice and text mail. With the breadth of functionality it supported, Phone Slave attempted to provide a complete interface to telephony functions from a general-purpose computer.

Phone Slave included both graphical and telephone-based user interfaces. It did not run in concert with any window system as window systems were not in general use at that time. Phone Slave was a monolithic process; in subsequent work at the Media Lab, many of Phone Slave's functions were implemented as separate applications (two examples, Xphone and Xrolo, are described later in this chapter). In the absence of a window system, Phone Slave shared the single graphics screen between three different display views: one for message retrieval, one for dialing on a telephone keypad, and the last for the name, address, and number database.

Phone Slave adopted a conversational approach to taking a telephone message. It asked a series of questions and recorded each response in a separate file. During recording, an adaptive pause detection algorithm determined when the caller was finished; the algorithm was adaptive with respect to the background noise level as well as the speech rate of the caller. The sequence of Phone Slave's questions was as follows.

- "Hello, Chris's telephone, who's calling please?"
- "What's this in reference to?"
- "I'm sorry, he's not available now, but he left this message . . ." followed by the owner's outgoing message and then "At what number can he reach you?"
- "When will you be there?"

- "Can I take a longer message for you?"
- "Thanks, I'll give him your message, goodbye."

Some naive subjects did not realize that they were speaking to a computer (note the wording of the initial greeting). Of course, there were instances when the conversational model would break down, which most commonly occurred when the caller responded simply with "yes" to the last question. The caller proceeded to wait for an anticipated prompt to leave a message and was surprised by the closing sign-off announcement. Each recorded comment with the exception of the last had a maximum anticipated response duration; once this was exceeded, Phone Slave would interrupt, saying "Excuse me, I'm just an answering machine, and it would be helpful if you could answer my questions directly."

Phone Slave's conversational format served several purposes. The first was to make it easier for the caller to leave a complete message. At the time when Phone Slave was implemented, answering machines were uncommon and seldom found in business situations so not all callers were accustomed to them. The second purpose was to provide segmentation of the messages for the sake of the recipient, Phone Slave's owner. Finally, during the caller's response to the first question (*"Who's calling please?"*), the telephone line audio output was routed to a speaker-dependent speech recognizer that attempted to identify the caller. The caller had to speak a consistent greeting to be recognized as the recognizer merely detected the familiar pattern of words.

A caller might be identified by Phone Slave, either by speech recognition or by entry of a touchtone password at any point in the conversation because speech recognition over long-distance telephone lines tended to be unreliable. If recognized, the caller was greeted by name, informed if Phone Slave's owner had listened to any recent messages from the caller, and possibly received a personalized outgoing message. After this, Phone Slave would say "If you'd like to leave another message, I'll record it now. Otherwise, just hang up and I'll tell him you called again."

When the owner called in and logged in, he could take advantage of a number of Phone Slave options including hearing messages, deleting messages, changing the outgoing message, and recording personal messages for known callers. Commands (e.g., Play, Delete) were entered either by speech recognition or touch tones. Because the incoming messages were segmented by the conversational recording method, several novel review options were available. For example, messages could be scanned quickly by asking "Who left messages?"; the system responded by playing back the initial recorded segment for each message in which the callers would have identified themselves.

Unlike conventional voice mail, Phone Slave integrated voice and text (electronic mail) messages. Text messages were presented by speech synthesis using the user interface described in detail in Chapter 6. Synthesized and recorded messages were intermixed, as Phone Slave sorted messages according to the sender (rather than the conventional time-sequential order) to facilitate complete responses.

In addition to taking messages, delivering personal messages, and providing mixed-media message retrieval over the telephone, Phone Slave provided screen-

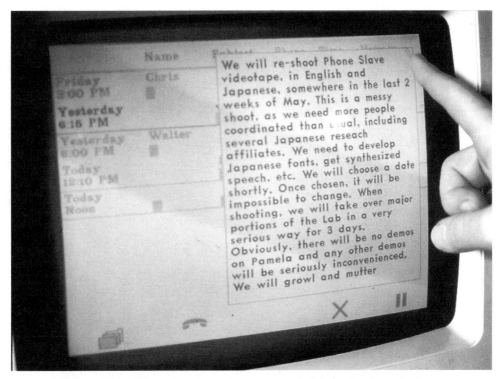

**Figure 11.12.** Phone Slave used a pop-up window to display a text message. From Schmandt and Arons, "Phone Slave: A Graphical Telecommunications System." Reprinted with permission from the *1984 SID International Symposium Digest of Technical Papers, edited by Jay Morreale. Vol. 25, New York: Palisades Institute for Research Services, Inc. June, 1984. pp. 146–149.*

based message access as well as other telephony functions using a color display and a touch-sensitive screen. Phone Slave implemented a limited set of window system functions, sharing the screen between a number of "views" and using pop-up windows for email display (see Figure 11.12). The message access view, for example, displayed each message with text fields to indicate the caller (if known), date and time, and subject field (for a text message). Each recorded sound segment appeared as a bar (see Figure 11.13), whose length indicated the duration of sound. Each message was displayed as a row of sounds; touching the left edge of the row would play each message segment in sequence. The bar changed color during playback from left to right in synchronization.[7] Touching a text message would pop up a text display window that could page through the message (see Figure 11.12).

---

[7] This sound bar was a direct predecessor of the SoundViewer widget for the X window system described in Chapter 12.

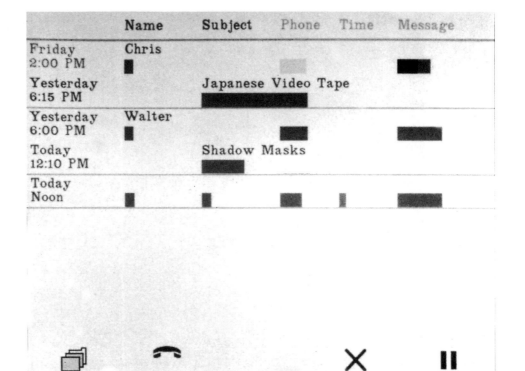

|  | Name | Subject | Phone | Time | Message |
|---|---|---|---|---|---|
| Friday 2:00 PM | Chris ■ |  |  |  | ■ |
| Yesterday 6:15 PM |  | Japanese Video Tape |  |  |  |
| Yesterday 6:00 PM | Walter ■ |  | ■ |  | ■ |
| Today 12:10 PM |  | Shadow Masks |  |  |  |
| Today Noon | ■ | ■ | ■ | ▮ | ■ |

**Figure 11.13.** Phone Slave's message access view. From Schmandt and Arons, "Phone Slave: A Graphical Telecommunications System." Reprinted with permission from the *1984 SID International Symposium Digest of Technical Papers, edited by Jay Morreale. Vol. 25, New York: Palisades Institute for Research Services, Inc. June, 1984. pp. 146–149.*

Phone Slave could place calls in several ways. The simplest method involved bringing up the telephone dialing view by pressing the telephone icon at the bottom of any other view (see Figure 11.14). The dialing view was modeled after a telephone keypad with an area for dialed-digit display. As with Phonetool discussed earlier in this chapter and Xphone introduced in the next section, Phone Slave accumulated the appropriate set of digits for a complete telephone number before commencing to dial, which allowed the user to delete digits without needing to hang up and restart from the beginning. While a call was in progress, the handset in the dialing view was raised to indicate the off-hook state; to hang up, the user would touch the handset, which would drop it back in place.

Phone Slave also included a simple name, address, and telephone directory, which was displayed in a view that listed each entry as an alphabetized card. This database was created in a text editor; Phone Slave allowed read-only access to it. In addition to the expected fields on the card, such as address and telephone number, any personalized outgoing messages were indicated by the presence of a

**Figure 11.14.** Phone Slave's telephone dialing view. From Schmandt and Arons, "Phone Slave: A Graphical Telecommunications System." Reprinted with permission from the *1984 SID International Symposium Digest of Technical Papers, edited by Jay Morreale. Vol. 25, New York: Palisades Institute for Research Services, Inc. June, 1984. pp. 146–149.*

sound bar on the card. The owner could review the outgoing message by touching the bar or create new messages by touching on the "reel of audio tape" icon. Depending on the time of day, either the home or work number would be highlighted in red. Touching the telephone icon on the card would switch to the telephone keypad view and automatically dial the number.

A special card was dedicated to choosing the generic outgoing message for an unknown caller (see Figure 11.16). The owner could select from a number of previously recorded messages suitable to particular occasions (out to lunch, out of town, etc.) or record a new temporary message. This option was included as part of the overall project goal of maximizing the information content of a transaction with an answering machine; as much information as possible was provided to both known and unknown callers.

Phone Slave was a direct predecessor of several related projects that followed in the next seven years. The answering machine portion was included in the Conversational Desktop project described in Chapters 9 and 12. Screen-based voice mail has recently been resurrected in a multiprocess version running under the X Window system. Separate processes manage message taking, the graphical

**Figure 11.15.** Phone Slave's name, address, and telephone number directory view. From Schmandt and Arons, "Phone Slave: A Graphical Telecommunications System." Reprinted with permission from the *1984 SID International Symposium Digest of Technical Papers, edited by Jay Morreale. Vol. 25, New York: Palisades Institute for Research Services, Inc. June, 1984. pp. 146–149.*

user interface, and remote telephone access to messages; this is described in more detail in Chapter 12. Also, Xphone, a telephone dialer, and Xrolo, a telephone directory application, provide the functionality of two of Phone Slave's views.

### Xphone and Xrolo

Xphone is a telephone dialing tool based in large part on the Phonetool dialing tool developed by Stephen Casner and described earlier in this chapter. Xphone runs under the X Window system and offers increased functionality over the original Phonetool [Schmandt and Casner 1989]. The basic idea remains the same: a powerful telephone dialer that occupies minimal screen real estate.

Xphone is displayed as a small window showing the most recently dialed telephone number (see Figure 11.17). There are a number of different methods of

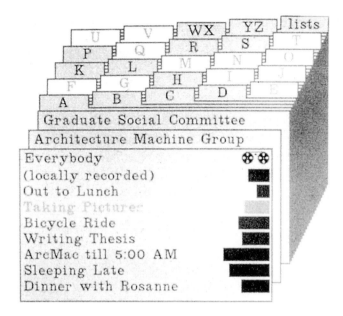

**Figure 11.16.** The outgoing message was selected using a special card. From Schmandt and Arons, "Phone Slave: A Graphical Telecommunications System." Reprinted with permission from the *1984 SID International Symposium Digest of Technical Papers, edited by Jay Morreale. Vol. 25, New York: Palisades Institute for Research Services, Inc. June, 1984. pp. 146–149.*

dialing a number with Xphone. The most recently dialed number can be redialed by clicking the left mouse button on the window. A number can be selected with the mouse from a different text window; when it is pasted into Xphone, the number is dialed. Alternatively, the user can type a number into the tool using either the number keys or numeric keypad on the computer keyboard. The keyboard-entry method is not as comfortable for dialing as the telephone keypad because the keys are arranged in a different order, but once the number has been entered, it can be dialed again much more quickly either via redial or the phone log described shortly.

Holding down the right mouse button pops up the speed-dial menu (see Figure 11.18). This menu displays the names found in a simple text file. A submenu reveals a log of recently dialed numbers (see Figure 11.19). Note that an entry in the log may appear as either a name or a number depending on how it was dialed.

**Figure 11.17.** The Xphone window displays the most recently dialed telephone number.

**Figure 11.18.** The Xphone speed-dial pop up menu. Selecting an entry places a call to the associated number.

An associated name, address, and phone number database tool, Xrolo, provides several other means of dialing. As with Xphone, Xrolo occupies limited screen space until activated, which is done either by typing a name into the small window or by holding down a mouse button to pop up a menu of names (see Figure 11.20). Once chosen, a card appears with relevant information in various fields, each of which can be edited (see Figure 11.21). The search may be based on personal name, computer login, or company. Related applications can generate facsimile cover sheets, long and short address lists, and mailing labels. There is also a text-based version of the tool for use over dialup lines.

Although the lines of text on an exposed card are independent objects and may each be edited individually, the application understands that there is a relationship among them. For example, an address usually consists of a name, a company

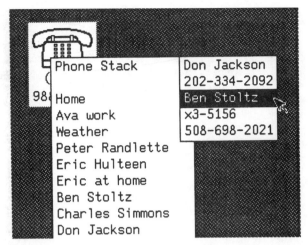

**Figure 11.19.** The Xphone call-log pop up menu allows recently called numbers to be redialed.

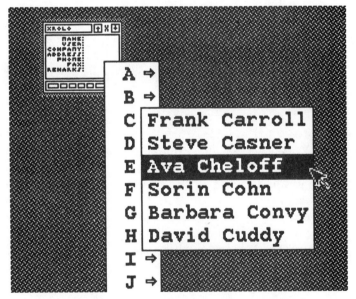

**Figure 11.20.** Pull down menu of names in Xrolo.

name (if it is a work address), street location, city, state, and postal code. A mouse click on the *work address* button selects all the relevant lines and highlights them appropriately for feedback to the user (see Figure 11.22). This selection may then be deposited by mouse click into another application.

Xphone and Xrolo interact with each other in several ways; the simplest and most common interaction is generating a phone call from the number on a per-

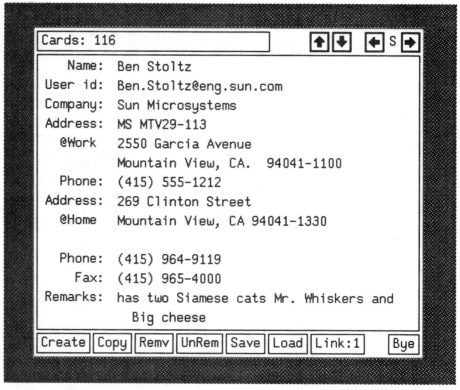

**Figure 11.21.** A name and address "card" from Xrolo.

son's Xrolo card.[8] Clicking the middle mouse button on a phone number sends a message to Xphone and dials the requested number. A number dialed in this manner would appear as a name in Xphone's phone log menu. A person's name or email address can be stuffed into Xphone just as easily as a phone number, which presents a more involved method of dialing by name. When Xphone parses the string containing a name, it fails to find a valid number and consequently sends a request to Xrolo to search for an entry that matches the string. If a match is found, Xphone obtains the associated telephone number and dials it and the name of the called party is noted in the call log.

## Flexible Call Routing

This case study describes a series of interrelated, small-scale Media Lab projects that have a common theme of flexible management of incoming calls. At

---

[8]Xphone and Xrolo communicate via the X selection mechanism, which provides a rendezvous point and data exchange through the X server.

```
    Name:  Ben Stoltz
 User id:  Ben.Stoltz@eng.sun.com
 Company:  Sun Microsystems
 Address:  MS MTV29-113
  @Work    2550 Garcia Avenue
           Mountain View, CA.   94041-1100
   Phone:  (415) 555-1212
 Address:  269 Clinton Street
  @Home    Mountain View, CA 94041-1330

   Phone:  (415) 964-9119
     Fax:  (415) 965-4000
 Remarks:  has two Siamese cats Mr. Whiskers and
           Big cheese
```

**Figure 11.22.** Highlighted text of the fields associated with *work address*.

**Figure 11.23.** Placing a phone call by name.

issue is the potential for computers through their participation in call setup to more effectively connect parties who need to speak to each other. At the same time it is essential to minimize the degree to which users are interrupted by unwanted calls if subscribers are to fully embrace the emerging mobile telephone technologies.

There is little doubt that although nearly all of us view the telephone as an essential part of our lives, we all also experience its annoying aspects as well. We resent unsolicited telemarketing calls at home during dinner or misdialed wrong-number calls in the middle of the night. We are annoyed when a face-to-face conversation in an office is interrupted for a call and are frustrated to wait in line in a hotel lobby while the reception clerk at the front desk takes a message for a guest. When we work alone in our offices, we may resent the interruption of the phone "ringing off the hook" all day; at home we often use answering machines to screen calls (a feature which disappears with centralized voice mail). Yet we rarely disconnect our phones, zealously play phone tag with those we wish to contact, and are disappointed with our few friends who still do not have answering machines.

The popularity of pocket cellular telephones[9] lends credence to the telephone operating companies' dreams of personal communication networks (PCNs) in which we each carry a phone and are always accessible via a universal personal number. Although some intense telephone users are ready for such services today, most of us shy away from the concept of always being reachable. If computers can become involved in call setup, how can they personalize and filter calls to make such services more attractive? This case study discusses some techniques that try to answer these questions based on alternate means of announcing incoming calls, user interfaces allowing manual intervention by either the caller or called party to route calls more effectively, and finally, automatic call filtering and routing by means of a personalized user agent.

The ring of the telephone is pervasive and penetrating, yet conveys only the minimal information that someone dialed a particular telephone number. With the gradual acceptance of calling party identification, consumer devices have become available that display the number of each caller, and many business PBX telephones similarly indicate this information on a small display. Unfortunately, the display built into the telephone is usually difficult to read, and it requires us to remember the phone numbers of all the people we wish to speak with. By the time our gaze is diverted to the telephone set, we have interrupted whatever task we were performing when the call came in. At MIT, telephones may ring differently for on-campus and off-campus calls, but this too is only marginally useful (contrast this with Etherphone's caller-specific ring tunes, for example.) Computer-based visual or audible alerting may minimize the interruption.

---

[9]In early 1993 the number of cellular telephone subscribers in the United States passed 10 million. There have been suggestions that poorly wired regions of Eastern Europe should bypass the local loop and go directly to universal cellular service.

Alternate alerting at the Media Lab is performed by a variety of workstation programs that act as clients of a centralized telephony server. This server uses a single ISDN interface to send notifications to clients (e.g., incoming call attempts) and can route calls at their request by performing call transfer operations. On-campus calls include calling number information, which the server translates to a name from a database.

One client performs visual alerting, and several others announce calls using synthesized speech. Visual alerting pops up a window on the user's display; as shown in Figure 11.24, this window indicates the caller's name (or "unknown") and disappears when the call is answered or the caller hangs up. Audible alerting in the office consists of a speech synthesizer announcing the caller's name. Additional audible alerting is provided in a large common lab work space where the synthesizer announces both the called and calling parties over a public address system; a similar service was provided under BerBell. Someone with an office near the lab space who is paged may be able to reach the telephone in time to take the call. But a workstation user can also take advantage of a variant on the visual call alert service by sending the call to the nearest telephone. This form of alert window shown in Figure 11.25 includes buttons that will route the call if the user selects one with the mouse.

Finally, some students and staff wear "Active Badges" that include several buttons. The Active Badges from Olivetti Research Laboratory use infrared signals to periodically transmit their identity to a network of sensors in strategic positions around the building [Want and Hopper 1992]. By pressing one of the buttons, a person is also able to route the call to the nearest telephone; this service has the advantage of being accessible even if the called party is not logged on to a workstation. Badges can also receive messages from the sensors to sound a tone or illuminate an LED (this provides yet another means of alerting a mobile

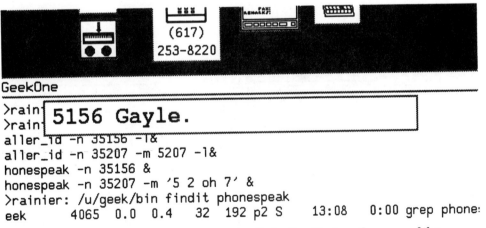

**Figure 11.24.** Window-based visual call alerting displays the name of the calling party.

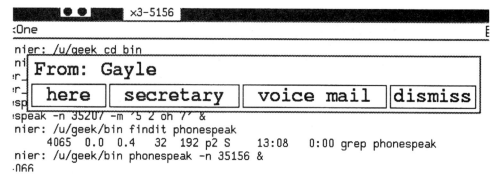

**Figure 11.25.** When routing buttons are added to the visual alert window, the called party can dynamically forward calls when working in another office.

user to an incoming call). At the Media Lab, an Activity Server combines badge-sighting reports with information about which users are logged in to which workstations on the local network (the "finger" command) to track users' activities and locations even when they are not wearing badges. The Activity Server also receives events from the telephone server and is notified when any lab telephone is in use.

Knowing colleagues' locations and activities helps local lab callers judge whether to interrupt someone with a phone call and know that person's location if they do proceed to call. A graphical user interface, Watcher (shown in Figure 11.26) displays users' physical locations and states, e.g., "alone in own office," "on the phone," or "in a meeting" (with other badge wearers) along with the number of the nearest phone. Clicking on the *phone* button sends a message to Xphone causing it to call the displayed number.

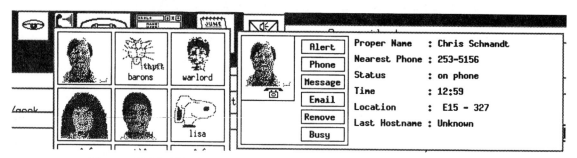

**Figure 11.26.** *Watcher* shows the location and activity of members of a workgroup. Buttons in the detail windows choose different means of sending messages to the selected person.

An interface such as Watcher helps the caller decide whether and where to phone, but it is available only to someone who is calling from a workstation in the lab.[10] The flexible alerting and call forwarding mechanisms just discussed enable the called party to manually intervene in call routing in response to the stimulus of an incoming call but depend on the availability of additional hardware such as a nearby workstation screen or a badge. A similar style of hardware-based remote intervention using pager technology is described in [Kramer *et al.* 1993]. Ideally one's personal workstation would make routing decisions automatically based on knowledge of the identity of the caller, the time of day, the location and activity of the called party, and whether a secretary or receptionist was available to take the call if it otherwise went unanswered. A person's location and activity may be derived from the dynamic information gathered by an entity such as the Activity Server, but personal calendars also give clues as to travel plans and meetings scheduled in advance.

A Media Lab thesis project [Wong 1991] explored the feasibility of call forwarding based on user-authored rules conditioned on the routing factors just mentioned. The graphical user interface shown in Figure 11.27 was used to create rules. A rule was defined by clicking with the mouse on icons representing four classes of conditions shown on the left of the figure; at this point, text-based dialog boxes appeared that allowed the user to complete the condition, e.g., specifying the time of day or name of the calling party. Each rule routed calls to destinations depicted on the right; these could be either a predefined phone number (e.g., a secretary's desk), voice mail, or a more dynamic location (e.g., the nearest available telephone). A knowledge-based "electronic receptionist" (from Bellcore) without a graphical interface is described in [Gifford and Turock 1992], which presents usage data supporting the position that automatic routing of some telephone calls may provide a valuable service.

Although initially promising, this method of defining call routing actions was problematic for several reasons. The graphical user interface was designed to shield users from the syntax and other details of the text-based rule language used to specify call routing. Although it was fairly effective for creating rules, the interface turned out to be unwieldy for modifying or deleting rules; it was difficult to graphically display a rule, especially one with multiple conditions for activation. The graphical interface did not provide capability for testing and debugging rule sets.

It may also be difficult for users to match their mental models of how the phone should behave with the operation of such an explicitly rule-based approach. Rules may conflict. For example, if I have one rule that says that after 5 P.M. calls forward to voice mail and another which says that calls from my daughter always forward to the nearest phone, then what should happen when my daughter calls

---

[10]Actually through the Phoneshell service described in Chapter 12, a knowledgeable subscriber can phone in, discover where other users are located, and then transfer the call to that location.

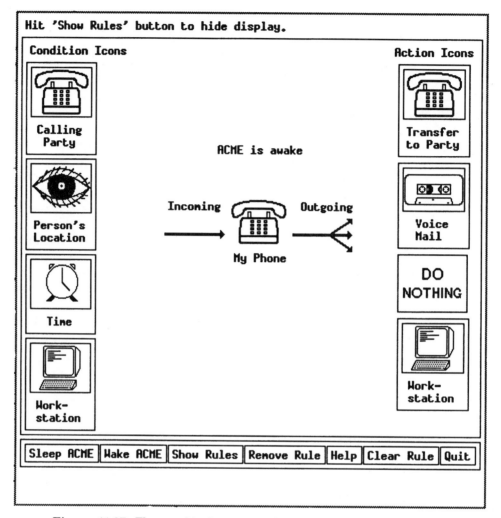

**Figure 11.27.** The graphical user interface to a rule-based call router. The user selected conditions on the left and associated them with routing destinations on the right.

at 5:30? This might be resolved by saying that rules involving the identity of the calling party take precedence over rules based on other conditions as telephone calls are more highly associated with the person calling than the time of day, for example. But what should happen if I also have another rule that says that I am never to be disturbed when in the conference room and when my daughter calls at 5:30 that is my location? Flexible call routing may be better performed by software that learns my preferences by observing my behavior over time, and this requires a feedback mechanism to retrain such software whenever it makes an incorrect decision.

## SUMMARY

This chapter was about computers performing telephone management tasks. Computers can place calls on behalf of a user, answer the telephone, or decide how to route an incoming call. This chapter began by making the case for computer-mediated telephony on the basis of its providing superior user interfaces than telephone sets, facilitating a more integrated overall electronic communications perspective, and extending the variety of call management services to which users may subscribe.

To place, receive, and route telephone calls, computers require hardware interfaces capable of communicating with the telephone switch. In some circumstances it may be appropriate to place such hardware on each computer in every office; this is a fully-distributed architecture. If telephone interface hardware is excessively costly or not compatible with the workstation in each office, a centralized approach may be preferable. With a centralized architecture, a single server computer with appropriate hardware manages telephones for many client computers. In either hardware scheme, centralized or distributed, a software-based server approach allows multiple client applications to participate in telephone management and effectively insulates application software from the details of the physical arrangement of hardware.

The concept of computer management of telephone calls was illustrated by a number of example projects discussed in different levels of detail. Etherphone and PX utilized distributed architectures to control flexible call switching entities, while MICE and BerBell explored the potential for client-based call control using centralized hardware similar to a telephone company's central office switch. Phone Slave presented a unified call management user interface including sophisticated answering machine capabilities. Xphone and Xrolo are examples of more modern software architectures and illustrate how multiple applications may coordinate with each other to provide enhanced access to multiple communication functions. Finally, a variety of small applications were discussed together under the theme of computer routing of incoming calls, either manually or automatically, and with or without the cooperation of the calling party.

The variety of functionality computers may bring to telephone management motivates and underscores the research projects discussed in this chapter. Some examples included enhanced message-taking features as well; once messages have been recorded, computer users can benefit from improved user interfaces to voice mail and may use these messages in other applications as well. This theme is continued in the next chapter, which discusses uses and interfaces for managing stored voice on the desktop.

# 12

# Desktop Audio

Because of limitations in speech technology, its successful deployment has been limited to certain situations in which voice offers unique advantages over visual interfaces or in which no other interface modality was practical. This bias has been reflected in the case studies as well, with their emphasis on hands-and-eyes busy environments or tasks oriented around managing voice communication with other people. This chapter instead focuses on applications of voice in an ordinary desktop computing environment used for day-to-day office activities. To continue the theme from the end of the last chapter, once computers manage our telephones and take voice messages for us, what else can we do with this stored speech?

Although nearly every office is equipped with a computer as well as a telephone, desktop voice processing is only beginning to become a reality. This gap is due in large part to the lack of a convincing argument for desktop audio; much office work is handled effectively with the use of keyboard and mouse to access text-based applications. To appreciate the potential of voice applications in the office we must first understand how speech can benefit office work as well as the synergy of using voice across a range of applications instead of in an isolated niche.

For decades computers were used to perform one task at a time; now window systems and multiprocessing operating systems give the user the ability to interact with many applications simultaneously. What is true with text-based software will be even truer with voice: no single application will dominate computer usage or provide sufficient benefit to warrant the purchase of voice processing capabilities. Rather in the future we can expect families of voice-capable applications running on the desktop sharing data and interaction techniques. Equally important to the need to share data among voice applications are the means to interchange information between voice and text databases and utilize presentation methods that allow telephone access to the desktop and other portable devices.

This chapter describes the concept of **desktop audio,** an environment that supports multiple voice applications on a single desktop computer and remote voice access to office databases. These ideas have already been touched upon in previous chapters: Xspeak (see Chapter 8) used speech recognition at the desktop to coordinate window-based interaction with multiple applications, Phone Slave (see Chapter 11) included a variety of telephone-related functions in a single application, and Voiced Mail (see Chapter 6) provided an integrated remote interface to voice and text messages.

This chapter considers several aspects of desktop audio. It first explores strategies that can smooth the transition from text-only to multimedia computing in the office and then presents a variety of graphical user interfaces to stored voice, which can help overcome its slow and serial nature in the desktop environment. The text advocates a client-server based software architecture to support multiple voice applications simultaneously. The notion of voice as a means of capturing much of our normal office conversations for later retrieval is discussed. In closing, the chapter presents a number of case studies to illustrate these desktop audio concepts.

## EFFECTIVE DEPLOYMENT OF DESKTOP AUDIO

Most new workstations[1] are now equipped with a speaker and a microphone and increasingly fast processors allow software-based implementations of speech recognition, text-to-speech synthesis, audio compression algorithms, and time-scale modification to intelligibly play voice back in less time than originally spoken. Yet deployment of voice applications has proceeded slowly and lags behind the underlying technology. This delay is due in part to the inability of software developers to target applications for which voice offers a benefit to the user, in part due to the difficulty of developing user interfaces that overcome the slow and serial nature of voice as data, and in part due to software architecture constraints interfering with the development of applications to be portable across a variety of hardware platforms.

From the desktop audio perspective, much of the difficulty lies in the lack of any single ideal voice application. To date the most prevalent speech application is voice mail, but current stand-alone implementations of voice mail are deployed and efficiently managed as part of the telephone system, not a networked com-

---

[1]The term "workstation" is used in this chapter to refer to any desktop computer. With ever-increasing microprocessor speeds, the distinction between "workstation" and "personal computer" is becoming increasingly blurred.

puter resource. The delay in proliferation of voice applications is exacerbated by the lack of integration between new voice-capable software and existing applications. If each speech application uses its own distinct user interface, it is harder still on the user to access multiple applications. The absence of a single "killer" desktop voice application does not mean speech will not be useful but it does suggest that it is essential to consider how speech applications will work with each other, how voice will enhance existing workstation applications, and what unique new capabilities voice will enable.

To succeed voice must offer supplemental value to the existing productivity tools on workstations rather than replace those tools. Users have not been willing to give up functionality or applications that they are already using for the sake of adding voice; voice capability must instead augment these applications as well as introduce additional new ways in which to use the computer. Augmenting instead of replacing functionality can be accomplished by maintaining compatibility with current text-based databases and applications wherever possible. For example, the multimedia mail system developed as part of Carnegie Mellon University's Andrew project [Morris *et al.* 1986] added the ability to include nontextual enclosures such as animations within Email messages. Users of a non-Andrew system could view the text portion of the message simply as conventional email without the animation, enabling Andrew users to continue to exchange messages with the non-Andrew Email users. But Andrew multimedia messaging never caught on in the larger non-Andrew world because it was so tightly embedded with the rest of the Andrew environment and hence not very portable. Recently, the MIME message format [Rose 1993] has been proposed for use in the Internet community to allow a broader exchange of multimedia messages in a heterogeneous operating environment. MIME is based on the desire to make multimedia capabilities available across the Internet without any modification of mail transport protocols or software and includes software to add minimal multimedia support to many mail reader programs across many operating systems. Rather than the all-or-nothing approach of Andrew (and similar multimedia mail systems), MIME attempts to add new media ability while minimizing disruption to traditional text-based mail. Desktop voice applications must do the same.

But even if voice can be added to the desktop with minimal disruption, what new capabilities will it provide? Chapter 4 already discussed the expressive richness of voice and its useful role as a document type in and of itself. With an appropriate graphical representation, voice can be mixed with media such as text and image as well and even moved between applications. Ordinary office conversations and meetings can be recorded for future use allowing this important record of decision-making activity to be archived and shared. Perhaps most powerful, speech user interfaces will allow computers to be accessed in new, nontraditional work environments.

Integrating telephone access with a unified voice application environment can result in a synergistic increase in the utility and need of voice as data. Speech synthesis can translate text into voice, enabling access to many text databases over voice telephone connections. This functionality will prove most valuable for retrieving timely personal information while traveling or working away from the office; databases may include telephone numbers and addresses, one's personal calendar, and electronic mail. Although voice access will not eliminate the use of modems, it is an attractive alternative in that it provides rapid access from any telephone obviating the need for additional hardware.

Perhaps even more significant will be the resulting changes in existing applications for dynamic support of stored voice as a data type. When users can access databases over the telephone some will wish to update them concurrently. If a caller wishes to enter data such as an entry in a calendar or the reply to an email message, recording a voice snippet is much easier than trying to type text with the telephone keypad. However, since we cannot yet reliably translate voice into text, the new entry must remain a voice file, and the underlying database becomes multimedia. The combination of voice and text data, in turn, has repercussions on the graphical interfaces of desktop applications accessing that database. And screen-based voice mail with audio cut and paste allows all the user's telephone messages to become data for manipulation by other applications as well.

Voice interfaces allow the telephone to be used as a computer terminal, and with the advent of highly portable cellular telephones, users can access their desktop from almost anywhere. But other portable technologies will utilize voice, and, in turn, contribute to the role of voice as a data type on the desktop. As laptop computers shrink to palmtops and smaller, the display and keyboard become limiting factors to further size reduction. Voice interfaces require little space; hand-held computing appliances may soon be used to record voice notes for later inclusion in other desktop applications [Stifelman *et al.* 1993]. For example, one may use a hand-held digital recorder to gather thoughts for a presentation while taking a walk or driving to work and later organize the recorded ideas at the office. Once uploaded into a desktop computer, graphical tools could allow the user to further edit, organize, and annotate the spontaneously spoken ideas into a coherent outline or a multimedia document.

## GRAPHICAL USER INTERFACES

Although the previous section pointed out that nonvisual user interfaces could enable computer use in novel situations, most applications of voice as data also benefit from visual interfaces when used on the desktop. Graphical representations of audio cue the user to the presence of voice data in an application as well as allow control of playback. Richer graphical interfaces allow direct manipulation of the stored voice by providing a means of positioning playback at random points throughout the sound as well as offering visual cues to a sound's overall length.

Simple "sound button" graphical interfaces (see Figure 12.1) use an icon such as a sketch of a speaker to alert the user to the presence of a sound. The user can click on the icon to play the sound and then click again to stop. Buttons are advantageous because they require little screen space, allowing many of them to be used by an application or to be mixed with text (see Figure 12.2). Buttons are

**Figure 12.1.** An assortment of "button" representations to indicate the presence of sound in a visual user interface. These representations are from (left to right) NeXT, Digital's Xmedia, and Sun's OpenWindows.

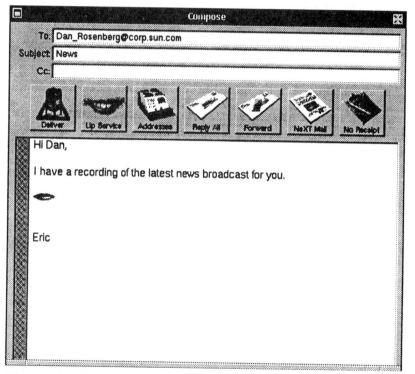

**Figure 12.2.** Because they are small, buttons can be easily mixed with text. This figure shows voice embedded in a text email message, on a NEXT computer.

intuitive to operate for most users familiar with graphical interfaces. The chief disadvantages of buttons are that the user has no sense of how long a sound will last once it starts and must listen to the entire sound sequentially. The lack of any sense of the duration of a sound while it plays makes it difficult to quickly search a number of sounds for desired information and shows many difficulties associated with similar graphical interfaces [Myers 1985]. The inability to skip around within an audio segment renders buttons useful only when they are used to control very short sounds.

An alternate form of graphical user interface displays additional information about the sound file and allows greater playback control; such visual representations of sound map time to the horizontal dimension, showing a bar the length of which indicates sound duration. The user plays the sound by clicking on the bar, and as playback progresses a cursor moves in synchronization to indicate temporal position. With many of these interfaces the user can change the playback position by clicking to reposition the cursor. Chapter 4 illustrated a variety of time bar representations, many showing speech and silence intervals. The Sound-Viewer is a more recent example of such an interface; it is described below as a case study.

The time bar representation has several advantages over the simple sound button by indicating the duration of the sound and providing finer control over playback. Its main disadvantage is the amount of screen space it requires. This difficulty has led to implementations in which the presence of a sound within an application is indicated by a small icon; when this icon is clicked on or dragged to another location a larger control panel opens up for playback, sound editing, and other functions (see Figures 12.3 and 12.4). Such an interface affords many of the advantages of the time bar display while saving screen space (especially useful if multiple sounds are visible), although it does require additional effort on the part of the user, and more importantly requires the user to shift gaze to the location where the control panel appears.

## AUDIO SERVER ARCHITECTURES

An appropriate software architecture is required to support access to desktop audio by multiple applications. Current audio servers support digitization and playback of voice, but future servers will also incorporate software implementations of the speech processing technologies discussed throughout this book. Software-based speech recognition, speech synthesis, audio data compression, time-scaling, and other signal manipulation algorithms are feasible on today's workstations; products to perform these operations are already becoming available. When recognition and synthesis required additional external hardware devices or add-in cards, they were costly and unwieldy. When available as software, these technologies can be considerably less expensive and more widely available and hence attractive to application developers.

Audio servers allow voice resources (speaker, microphone, voice processing algorithms) to be made available to multiple applications running simultaneously on one workstation. A server-based approach allows distributed audio processing and resource management among a variety of client applications. The relationship between an audio server and its clients is similar to that found in a server-based window system; instead of directly manipulating audio devices, clients make requests to the server, which controls devices on behalf of the clients. Because clients do not manipulate hardware directly, each client can operate without knowledge of the other clients. The server, or a separate policy agent operating in concert with the server, arbitrates conflicting requests (for a window system, the policy agent is the window manager). For example, if one client requests the server to play a sound while another client is already in the

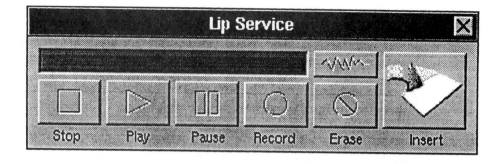

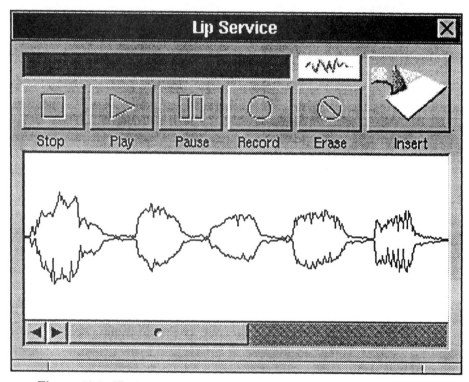

**Figure 12.3.** The NeXT audio control panel. In the top form sound is represented only as a bar; by clicking a button the user can invoke the waveform envelope display shown at the bottom.

midst of playing a different sound, various policies might be: make the new client wait, make the first client stop playing, or mix the sounds and play them simultaneously.

Because the server approach divides client and server into separate processes that communicate via a well-known protocol, several additional benefits are realized. An application need not be recompiled to execute with a different version of

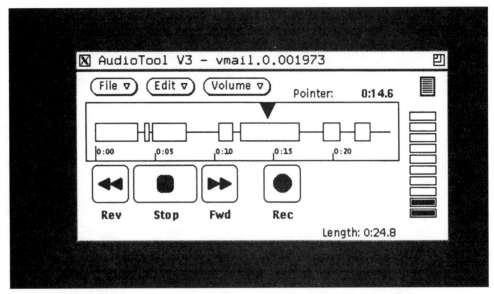

**Figure 12.4.** Sun's audiotool control panel displays speech and silence segments and provides editing capabilities.

the server; the same application binary file can run on different workstations with different audio hardware, simplifying software distribution. Additionally, because the server implies an interprocess communication path between client and server, a client can be made to communicate transparently with servers on its local or remote workstations across the network.

Another advantage of an audio server is that it frees the client application from the time-critical task of reading and writing data between the audio devices and disk files. The server also shelters the application from the detailed programming sequences that control the audio devices; the audio protocol is device independent. These characteristics lead to more modular and portable application software.

The client-server approach is evident in many of the projects described elsewhere in this book, such as Etherphone and MICE (see Chapter 11). An early audio server was developed at the M.I.T. Media Lab [Schmandt and McKenna 1988] in 1984; as with the two examples just mentioned, this server executed on separate hardware from the client. The availability of inexpensive add-in hardware and the real-time nature of the server's DOS operating system allowed the audio server to be implemented on a personal computer that communicated with a Unix host over a serial interface. This early server was motivated largely by the difficulties of managing the real-time audio data stream on early slow Unix workstations. Once playback of a sound begins, it must continue to completion without interruption; stops and starts in the audio medium are much more jarring to the user than an interrupted window refresh on a display.

All audio data was stored on a dedicated disk within the server hardware. The server incorporated a request **queue;** a client could ask the server to prepare for a series of play and record operations (e.g., the prompts and message-taking for an answering machine) and then let the server execute them without further intervention. By queuing requests, an application allowed the server to perform some time-consuming operations in advance such as creating and opening files and ensured that back-to-back play requests could be performed with no silence in between. The client received asynchronous events notifying it of completion of each task.

This server was later extended to include speech recognition, speech synthesis, and several audio compression algorithms, but never fully supported multiple clients' access to the server simultaneously. To do so would have required the server to associate requests with clients and maintain the correct state of devices for each client. For example, one client may set the output gain high, while another sets it low; the server would need to reset the gain of the audio device to the appropriate client-dependent level.

The Olivetti VOX audio server [Arons *et al.* 1989] provided more sophisticated protocols and implemented resource management for multiple simultaneous clients. It digitized and played sounds back from files managed by the server, but VOX also included external computer-controlled analog mixing and switching equipment to route audio to several speakers located in the same or different offices. To support multiple clients, VOX allowed clients to build hierarchical *CLAUDs* (Composite Logical Audio Devices) as server-side constructs. A CLAUD defined all the audio resources needed by a client, much as a window hierarchy specifies all of the graphical objects belonging to a client of a window system server. Again, as with window systems, clients could request that a CLAUD be **mapped** (activated) or **unmapped** (deactivated). Mapping would fail if resources were unavailable because they were currently utilized (mapped) by another client. A CLAUD contained a *Logical Audio Device* (LAUD) for each physical device it included; a LAUD stored the desired state of the physical devices for a particular client. When a CLAUD became active, the physical devices were set to the state appropriate for the client as contained in its LAUDs.

The Digital Equipment Corporation's Xmedia audio server [Angebranndt *et al.* 1991] incorporates the server-side client resource constructs of VOX (the composite audio device hierarchy), but the mixing and routing of audio paths are completely digital. The protocol for this server is more heavily influenced by that of the X window system, including a more sophisticated protocol than VOX for allowing a "media manager" to implement resource management policy. The Xmedia server also provides audio data paths to the client; in addition to recording or playing from a file, the client can provide or access audio data directly. Its internal logic for mixing and synchronizing multiple simultaneous data streams extends to control digital video as well as audio.

The Xmedia server was originally designed in a framework including an audio toolkit to free clients from the need to directly interface to the low-level audio server protocol, but only a minimal toolkit has been developed to date. A recently published audio server architecture from Hewlett-Packard shows a design very similar to that of the Xmedia server [Billman *et al.* 1992].

Because of the limited availability of any of the audio servers described so far, a new server has recently been developed at the M.I.T. Media Lab; it is used by many of the applications described later in this chapter [Arons 1992b]. This server does not contain any of the server-side resource management constructs from VOX or the Xmedia server but does implement a simple priority-based resource management policy. Clients can send audio data to the server or have it play from files and receive asynchronous notification of audio events. This server includes software for time-scale modification (as well as touch tone detection) making it simple for any application to vary playback speed. Other servers, e.g., for speech recognition and synthesis, are designed to work in concert with the audio server by using its ability to route copies of audio data streams. For example, a recognition server will always get copies of audio input while recognition is enabled. If some other client requests the server to record a sound, the same audio data will be copied into a file. Finally a recording-level client (e.g., to display a graphical "VU meter") would request its own copy of audio data whenever another client activates audio recording.[2]

The Media Lab's audio server is motivated primarily by the need for effective resource management because many applications share the audio device as well as audio data itself. In the absence of a policy agent, or audio manager, this server implements a simple priority scheme. Clients may declare themselves to be of high (urgent), medium (normal), or low (background) priority; higher priority requests supersede lower priority ones, whereas lower or equal priority requests are queued until the server is idle. When a play operation is superseded by another of higher priority, playing pauses and the client is notified; when the new request finishes, the interrupted one resumes. An interrupted record operation does not resume without client intervention.

One component of a software architecture missing from the servers just discussed is an **audio toolkit.** Graphical user interfaces are usually implemented in conjunction with software toolkits consisting of a set of direct manipulation objects such as scroll bars, sliders, and dialog boxes.[3] Audio toolkit objects might include constructs such as a **menu,** which speaks the user's choices and awaits a selection via touch tone, or a **form,** which speaks, prompts and records replies. Resnick's Hyperspeech project implemented a comprehensive set of telephone interaction objects to facilitate rapid development of telephone-based community bulletin boards [Resnick 1992b, Resnick 1992a, Malone *et al.* 1987]. Another such toolkit is described in [Schmandt 1993]; it is heavily used by Phoneshell, described below.

---

[2]Actually the meter client would request audio level events whereby the server provides periodic updates as to the audio energy level and thereby minimizes the data being transmitted from server to client.

[3]These are the *widgets* of the X-windows community.

Arons describes another hypothetical set of "audgets"—audio widgets—in [Arons 1991a]. An audio toolkit should be distinct from a graphical toolkit as some audio applications have no graphical interfaces. Graphical audio controllers, such as the SoundViewer described later, are best implemented as a separate toolkit layer, as shown in Figure 12.5, so as to free nonvisual or nonaudio applications from the added baggage of the unused media.

## UBIQUITOUS AUDIO

Most applications of desktop audio involve explicit invocation of recording activity; the user clicks the mouse or presses a touch tone key to digitize a short snippet of audio. Such recordings comprise but a small fraction of the speech we produce during a work day. We hold meetings, converse on the telephone, chat with visitors, and catch up on news at the water cooler. All of this talk has so far been beyond the reach of computer applications, but desktop audio configurations could allow recording and subsequent retrieval of much of this previously evanescent "ubiquitous audio."

Assuming 10:1 data compression of telephone-quality speech with half of the day spent in conversation of which 80% is speech and the remainder silence, a year's worth of office conversation would require slightly over 2 Gigabytes of storage. Although this quantity would have seemed outrageous as recently as several years ago, such storage capacities are rapidly becoming feasible. The combination

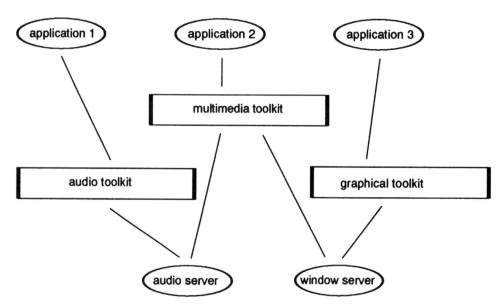

**Figure 12.5.** Audio and graphical toolkits shield applications from details of communication with their respective servers. Multimedia toolkits can be built on top of single-medium toolkits.

of audio-capable workstations, plentiful storage, and computer-mediated telephony hardware could allow us to record all the conversations that occur in our offices and meeting rooms. There is certainly no doubt that this audio record would contain a wealth of useful information and a valuable archive of business or engineering design decisions, but it would also include a plethora of social or otherwise irrelevant conversations of little archival value.

How could we access the important portions from such a vast quantity of stored voice, which is such a difficult medium to summarize or search? A variety of information sources come into play. Situational information specifies the circumstances in which a recording was made, but nothing about its contents; this includes dates, location, and participants in the conversation. It has been suggested that situational information may be adequate for retrieval of otherwise poorly structured multimedia records such as audio or video recordings [Lamming and Newman 1991]. If users are identified by wearing locator devices, by face recognition from a video record, or by initiating or receiving a call placed by a computer or the telephone network, the audio archive could store a list of talkers with each recording session. Applying situational constraints to form queries such as "Find all long telephone conversations with Eric last spring" can narrow the search immensely.

Because of the slow and serial nature of speech, playback of monolithic audio files is tedious regardless of their length. If structure can be added to the recording, it could provide a means of breaking the recording into segments, which indicate reference locations identifying conversational landmarks to assist random access techniques. Structure to aid audio retrieval can be created explicitly by user activity during recording or derived after the fact based on acoustic analysis.

For example, participants in a meeting may take notes on laptop computers; these text entries can be time-stamped and synchronized to the audio recording. Later a graphical conversation browser could tag the visual representation of the recording with the text from the notes or alternatively a text viewer could allow the user to click on a sentence and hear the associated audio. Acoustic analysis can break a conversation into segments delineated by pauses, and this can be incorporated into the visual browser as well. A more powerful method is to identify which speaker is talking at any moment, and visually differentiate the display of each speaker.

In some situations more explicit user activity could trigger recording, which would yield smaller units to archive, but this action must be unobtrusive. A Media Lab project shown in Figure 12.6 displays a graphical interface on the workstation while a user is engaged in a telephone call [Hindus 1992]. Speaker turns are detected and each scrolls across a small viewing panel showing the recent history of the conversation; each box represents the audio of a single turn. The user's hands and eyes are free during a phone call, and the mouse can be used to start or stop recording at any point. Several portions of the call might be recorded, and each is grouped into a "paragraph," or series of consecutive turn segments. Text annotation can also be added to the speech display. A similar graphical interface can be invoked at a later time for browsing completed telephone calls.

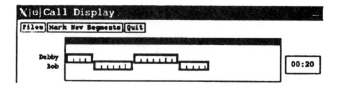

D: Hello, this is Debby Hindus speaking.
B: Hi Deb, it's Bob. I'm just getting out of work, I figured I'd call and see how late you're going to stay tonight.
D: Well, I think it'll take me about another hour, hour and a half, to finish up the things I'm doing now.
B: OK, I'm just going to head on home, I'll probably do a little shopping on the way.

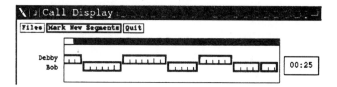

D: Well, if you think of it, maybe you could get some of that good ice cream that you got last week.
B: OK. By the way, somebody, uh...
B: mentioned an article you might be able to use

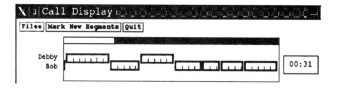

B: in your tutorial. Debby: Oh really? [Debby's very short turn is ignored.]
B: Yeah, it's by Graeme Hirst, in the June '91 Computational Linguistics.

**Figure 12.6.** A telephone recording tool shows the recent history of a conversation. Each box represents one turn; position differentiates speakers. Reprinted with permission from proceedings of the *ACM 1992 Conference on Computer-Supported Cooperative Work,* © 1992, ACM.

Another Media Lab application, Xcapture, records ambient sound in an office into a circular buffer or "digital tape loop," which serves as a short-term auditory memory aid. The archetypical situation for its use is a collaborative writing session; one person suggests an alternate wording for a sentence while the other hurries to write it down, but neither can repeat the revision word-for-word and it is lost. Xcapture records in the background, displaying a small animated icon with a moving bar. When the user clicks on this icon, recording stops and a SoundViewer widget appears in a popup window (see Figure 12.7); the Sound-Viewer allows interactive playback of approximately the last five minutes of recording (the precise amount depends on available system memory). The user can review this recording, scan it at a faster speed, save it to a file, or cut and paste it into another application.

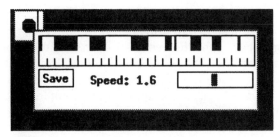

**Figure 12.7. Xcapture** displays a recording of recent conversation in a pop-up window.

Both these projects demonstrated potential but are limited in capability [Hindus and Schmandt 1992]. Xcapture is barely adequate for even short-term retrieval of a recent conversation because the SoundViewer lacks any cues of turns, pauses, or other structural landmarks in a conversation; even five minutes is a long duration of sound to navigate. Tools which are more sophisticated need to take advantage of multiple sources of structure and acoustic processing to enhance interactive retrieval of archived conversations. A requirement for the user is that it must take much less time to find the desired information than it would to listen to the entire recording sequentially. Playback speed is variable, using the time scale modification techniques described in Chapter 3. A recording can be scanned by playing small segments in sequence, skipping over larger intervening segments. Pauses in the conversation [O'Shaughnessy 1992] or emphasis detected using intonational cues [Chen and Withgott 1992] may suggest segments that are more likely to contain semantically significant utterances or mark the introduction of fresh topics. When coupled with an interactive user interface, such as one based on a touch pad, to scan through a recording at several levels of granularity [Arons 1993], none of these techniques need to work perfectly. Instead, they can act as an aid to the intelligent user, who may have even participated in the conversation being searched and have some memory of its overall structure.

Although recording the ubiquitous audio at work may be straightforward, retrieval from audio archives is difficult. Special capture applications unique to particular recording situations may be useful in the short term. In the long term, more research is needed into techniques to supply structure to recorded sound based on acoustic analysis. Additionally, development of interaction techniques, based in part on the acoustically derived structure, will facilitate retrieval from the audio archive. Whether such factors will impart real value to large audio archives remains to be demonstrated.

## CASE STUDIES

This section presents four case studies emphasizing various aspects of desktop audio. The first case study describes the iterative design of a visual representation of stored voice. The second highlights Conversational Desktop, an eight-year-old project designed to provide functionality spanning many desktop audio application areas. The third case study is of a telephone interface to many common desktop utilities, which is in use today. The final study returns to visual interfaces by examining more recent work in screen interfaces to audio applications such as voice mail; these applications complement the telephone interface in the third case study and are also in use today.

## Evolution of a Visual Interface

Visual interfaces to stored audio have been a recurring theme in this book. Chapter 4 pointed out the role of a visual user interface for an audio editor. Earlier in this chapter we returned to the utility and possible functionality of such an interface, presenting two extremes of graphical control of audio playback. A button-style interface requires very little screen space but offers minimal functionality; its small size allows it to be used repeatedly on the computer display by whichever applications contain audio data. These buttons were contrasted with more elaborate interfaces which offer visual representations of the stored voice, provide random access through voice files, and may even support limited editing functionality (but at the cost of size and complexity). In the control-panel style interface, sounds are represented iconically and the control panel appears when a user activates an icon.

This section considers a case study of the Media Lab's SoundViewer, a graphical interface which attempts to provide on-the-spot interactivity combined with small size so that the interface can be used in place by many applications [Hindus *et al.* 1993]. The SoundViewer uses horizontal size and time marks to convey the duration of a sound before a user decides to play it. It provides for direct manipulation at the place on the display where the user's attention is already focused, instead of in a separate control panel. Finally, a SoundViewer can operate in conjunction with other SoundViewers in the same or other applications to facilitate sharing voice data. Because the SoundViewer is an X widget, it can be controlled via X window resources and any change to the widget is inherited by all applications using it (after compilation). An application is required only to set the location of the SoundViewer and specify the sound file it is to control; all other graphical and audio interactions are managed by the widget.

The initial design of the SoundViewer was based heavily on earlier M.I.T. visual interfaces, including the Intelligent Ear (Chapter 4) and Phone Slave's graphical interface (Chapter 11). As with these earlier projects, the visual object's size indicates the length of the sound and its representation changes appearance in synchrony with audio playback. The basic SoundViewer action is shown in Figure 12.8; as the sound plays, a bar of contrasting color moves along left to right. The left mouse button is used to start and stop playback, while the middle button moves the position of the bar. Moving the bar during playback skips to a new location in the voice recording. Repeated clicking on the middle button repeats a segment over and over, which is particulary useful for tasks such as transcribing a phone number from a voice mail meassage. The right mouse but-

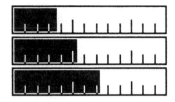

**Figure 12.8.** As a SoundViewer plays its associated audio file, a bar moves left to right in synchrony.

ton can be used to specify a portion of the SoundViewer, which then becomes the audio *selection* (see Figure 12.9); the selection can be moved to other applications using the standard X protocols.

One issue with visual display of audio data is the mapping between time and pixels, or width, which can provide both relative and absolute indications of sound length. The SoundViewer uses an internal algorithm (or one supplied by the application) to determine the interval at which to display tick marks; indicating time with too much temporal detail would just blur the marks. Although the heights of the tick marks are meant to differentiate them (e.g., those at every second are shorter than those at five-second intervals), no users have ever understood this without instruction. SoundViewer width is a very good indicator of relative length, however. But scale becomes a problem when short sounds are mixed with much longer sounds; the time-to-pixels ratio which just allows a 7 minute sound to fit on a screen would likely result in a 5 second sound being so short as to be rendered almost invisible. The SoundViewer therefore was made to support a mode in which sounds less than a specified threshold length are displayed at a constant scale to allow relative length comparisons, while longer sounds are "crunched" into allocated space by changing the time scale. Although this also changes the spacing of the tick marks appropriately, and the time bar moves more slowly as a result of greater time-to-width compressions, this duration cue is also poorly understood by users.

The tick marks provide useful navigational cues. For example, while listening to voice mail, users often watch to note the location of the time bar when the caller speaks a phone number; this makes it easy to return to the number at the conclusion of the message. But the ticks convey nothing of the *content* of the sound so an alternate representation was developed to display speech and silence intervals (see Figure 12.10) similar to Etherphone's visuals. More recently, "dog

**Figure 12.9.** Horizontal streaks provide visual feedback when a portion of a SoundViewer's associated sound is selected with the mouse. This SoundViewer shows less temporal detail than those in Figure 12.8.

**Figure 12.10.** The addition of speech and silence marking and "dog ears" to a SoundViewer.

ear" markings were added to the SoundViewer. A spot can be marked (using the keyboard) during playback, and the location of the mark, which appears as a caret symbol, is saved with the sound and appears whenever it is displayed.

After speech and silence intervals had been added, the SoundViewer was made to allow the user to jump ahead to the next speech segment or back to repeat the current or previous segments also under keyboard control. Pauses in the speech correspond to breath groups and are usually deliberate, semantically meaningful speech segments. The SoundViewer also has for some time supported audio time-scaling to play back sounds faster or slower than they were recorded (time-scaling algorithms were discussed in Chapter 3). Because this is a widget "resource," users can set default time scales for all SoundViewers or for those of just a particular application; when users become accustomed to time-scaled speech they begin to prefer it over normal rate speech. A more recent addition provides improved random access; while moving the location bar by hand back and forth across the width of the SoundViewer, it plays small chunks of sound in synchrony. This feedback provides surprisingly useful navigational cues although the proper presentation style is the subject of further research.

The SoundViewer breaks down for very long sounds. When time is mapped to width so as to allow a 10 or 15 minute sound to fit into a reasonable portion of the screen, time is so compressed that the sound bar barely moves as it plays, and it can be positioned only very coarsely. Also, the speech and silence markings interfere with each other when most pauses are shorter than the audio duration represented by a single pixel. Although these effects are not noticed on short sound snippets characteristic of voice mail or calendar entries, they have become problematic for longer sounds such as recordings of meetings or newscasts. A new variant of the SoundViewer provides a global and a detailed view of the sound as shown in Figure 12.11. The lower representation presents a close-up view and is a window into the entire portion of the sound,which appears above. The user can start playback, set a position, or make a selection from either view; as the sound plays, both views get updated simultaneously.

The SoundViewer has been used in all the recent Media Lab desktop speech applications, some of which are described later in this chapter. It has been effective at providing a direct manipulation interface to stored voice files while consuming minimal screen space. Its visual representations have evolved to better facilitate navigation, and additional audio processing enhances the SoundViewer with time-scaling and auditory feedback during random access. Maintaining consistent visual time scales has been a problem from the beginning, and an auxiliary view seems essential for managing very long sounds.

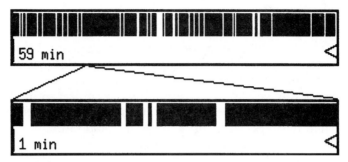

**Figure 12.11.** For very long sounds two representations are provided. The lower view is a close up of the entire sound shown above.

## Conversational Desktop

Conversational Desktop was an early (1985) effort at the Media Lab to present a vision of the possible range of desktop audio applications [Schmandt and Arons 1986]. It emphasized integrated telecommunication management combined with extensive use of voice both as a data type and as an element in the user interface. In addition to spoken language, Conversational Desktop included a touch-sensitive graphical interface which, in anticipation of window systems, allowed the user to quickly switch between displays of the calendar or voice messages. Conversational Desktop's dialogue system and parsing techniques that cope with fragmentary and error-prone speech recognition were described in Chapter 9; this case study focuses on its functionality and integration of multiple application areas.

Conversational Desktop operated across multiple workstations. Each workstation included speech recognition, speech synthesis, audio digitization hardware (implemented on separate dedicated computers acting as servers), and a telephone interface. This project spanned telephone management, voice mail, scheduling, remote database access, and audio reminders triggered by external events. From the standpoint of this chapter, Conversational Desktop's most interesting aspect was the synergy arising from the interaction among these functions.

Conversational Desktop emphasized the role of the workstation in managing both remote data access as well as voice communication through local and wide area networks. The workstation acted as a communication agent, contacting external databases (a traffic information service and simulated access to airline reservation systems) as well as negotiating with agents of other users (scheduling meetings and call setup negotiation). Although services were implemented over analog telephone lines and Ethernet, this project was designed in anticipation of ISDN; calling another Conversational Desktop user established a data connection as well as a voice circuit so the users' agents could communicate while users were conversing.

Conversational Desktop placed telephone calls through voice dialing and incorporated the conversational answering machine approach first implemented in Phone Slave (see Chapter 11). Calls between Conversational Desktop workstations were set up using the local computer network before an analog telephone circuit was established; as the calling party was therefore known, the answering machine could play personalized messages and inform callers of the status of earlier messages just as Phone Slave had.[5] Because the Conversational Desktop maintained the user's schedule, outgoing messages could be automatically selected to account for current activity (in a meeting, out to lunch, out of town, etc.). In addition, microphones in the office monitored audio levels to determine when visitors were present, and could automatically take messages from unknown callers without interrupting a conversation in progress.

Because it utilized early connected speech recognition, Conversational Desktop users were required to wear a head-mounted noise-canceling microphone. This microphone was also used during telephone conversations; its noise cancellation allowed use of full-duplex speakerphones. Additional microphones mounted by the walls were used to detect when other people were speaking; speech present at the background microphones but not at the noise-canceling microphone indicated that a visitor was speaking. When the user spoke, a comparison of audio levels in the background microphones could determine the direction he was facing; direction of speaking was used to model user attention and enable recognition. While the user was facing away from the monitor, speech was ignored, but when the user faced the workstation, audio from the microphone was switched to the recognizer. Turning towards the workstation also muted audio to the telephone, so the user could have a private conversation with the computer during a phone call.[6]

Conversational Desktop also allowed its users to record short audio reminders for later playback. When issuing the command to record a reminder, the user specified the situations or activities that would prompt playback such as "when I come in tomorrow." Playback of a single reminder could be triggered by multiple events: a "when I talk to Barry" reminder would be played when Barry called, when the user placed a call to Barry, or when the application announced that it was time for a scheduled meeting with Barry. Reminders were not played, however, when another person was detected in the office as the reminder might contain private information.

This project was an early example of applications of desktop audio. It used speech recognition and a dialogue system to address multiple application functions simultaneously and allowed each function access to stored voice. It explored issues in dynamic routing of audio paths among applications and combinations of speakers, microphones, and voice processing hardware. By incorporating a range of functions, Conversational Desktop demonstrated the synergistic interactions among disparate computer applications dealing with what might appear to be a single operation by the user, e.g., being reminded of something when placing a

[5]Where available, telephone network provided calling party identification and it could serve the same function today.

[6]An unfortunate disadvantage of this arrangement was that the user could not simultaneously read the computer screen and talk on the telephone.

phone call or automatically updating the outgoing voice mail message depending on one's schedule. Finally, Conversational Desktop demonstrated the personalization of call setup, depending on factors such as the calling party and activity in one's office.

Conversational Desktop also had a number of limitations. It was written as a monolithic application, which eliminated the need for interprocess communication but interfered with its modularity and hampered its extensibility. It also side-stepped some important considerations in managing the focus of speech recognition input across multiple applications; if the user is running several programs at once, which is being addressed at any moment? This project utilized custom-built or expensive peripherals, and a good deal of the computing resources of a laboratory group, which relegated it to the role of a demonstration system instead of one to be used in daily work. The audio switching based on direction of speech worked well in a single, sound-treated room, but may not extend well to noisy offices or open cubicles.

Despite these limitations, Conversational Desktop was valuable as an early, visionary system that later motivated much of the work described in several other projects described as case studies in this book; a remaining case study is described in this chapter. Although desktop audio required many exotic peripherals in 1985, all the functionality of Conversational Desktop can be implemented without additional hardware on workstations recently introduced by several vendors.

## Phoneshell

Phoneshell [Schmandt 1993] is a family of applications that allows telephone and facsimile access to common desktop utilities including voice mail, electronic text mail, name and address database, and calendar. Phoneshell illustrates the utility of the telephone as a remote link to the desktop, and the enhanced role voice can play as a data type motivated in large part by the difficulty of entering text with a telephone. The telephone interface stimulates the use of voice as a data type and places new requirements on the screen-based applications that must provide access to the stored voice at the desk.

Phoneshell consists of a set of applications loosely linked together under a top-level menu, which allows the user to invoke applications sequentially during a session. The applications share many aspects of their user interfaces, for consistency, and depend on common lower-level utilities, but each application has been developed independently. Figure 12.12 summarizes the functions embedded in Phoneshell.

The voice mail application is similar to many commercial voice mail products with several additional features. Voice messages can originate as telephone messages, from other voice mail users sending a voice message from their workstations, or via digitized voice attachments encapsulated in email arriving over the computer network. In addition to replying to a voice message or recording a message for another user, a caller can record "memo" messages. A memo is intended for screen access only; instead of cluttering the voice mailbox during telephone

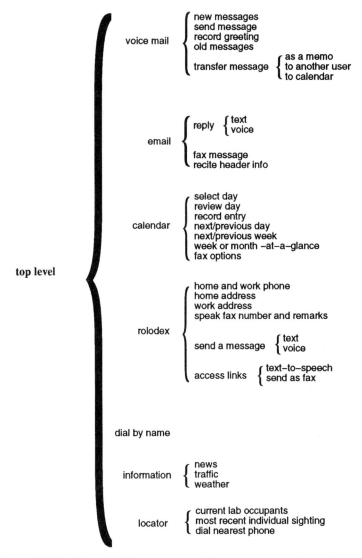

**Figure 12.12.** Phoneshell's menus provide access to a variety of personal information management functions.

access, a separate graphical things-to-do application absorbs the memo messages into its own database. Finally, in addition to being able to transfer a voice message to another user, a Phoneshell user can save an entire message to her calendar by specifying a date; this is the nongraphical equivalent of audio cut and paste.

The email-reading application is similar in many ways to Voiced Mail described in Chapter 6 in that it uses touch tone input to control the reading of email messages using speech synthesis. As with Voiced Mail, Phoneshell carefully pre-

```
Date: Tue, 30 Mar 93 21:01:55 PST

From: Ben.Stoltz@Eng.Sun.COM (Ben Stoltz)

Message-Id: <9303310501.AA13979@denwa.Eng.Sun.COM>

To: geek@media.mit.edu

Subject: Re: your schedule

Status: RO


> From geek@media.mit.edu  Tue Mar 30 15:17:50 1993

> Delivery-Date: Tue, 30 Mar 1993 15:17:53 -0800

> Date: Tue, 30 Mar 93 18:17:44 -0500

> From: Chris Schmandt <geek@media.mit.edu>

> To: stoltz@denwa.Eng.Sun.COM, stoltz@Eng

> Subject: your schedule

>

> What's the possibility of getting together Tuesday?

>


Dinner would be fun. Tuesday evening.
```

**Figure 12.13.** An email message that contains parts of other messages.

processes text such as email addresses so that they are pronounced correctly and breaks a message into sentences so the caller can skip forward and backward in the message and repeat the sentence currently being spoken. In addition, while reading a message included messages and their mail headers (see Figure 12.13) are detected; headers are summarized ("Header of message from 'Chris Schmandt' in reply to 'your schedule'") and included text can be skipped over by a "jump ahead" button. A message can be faxed as well as read; this is especially useful if reviewing mail about subjects such as an agenda or schedule from a remote telephone.

The user can also send replies using either voice or text. Voice replies are recorded and then returned to the original sender as a voice attachment to an email message using formats from a number of vendors. With voice being supported on a growing number of workstations, such attachments have become a convenient means of reaching many correspondents directly; this had been impossible a decade earlier under Voiced Mail. If the user does not know what message format to use or has no reason to believe the sender uses an audio-capable workstation, text replies can be typed with touch tones. Two keypresses specify each character; the first indicates the group of three letters and the second selects one of the three depending on whether it is from the left, middle, or right column of keys. Punctuation and digits are also available. Whenever the user completes a word ("*" is the space key), it is echoed. When the user pauses, the current word is spelled out. The most recent word can always be deleted. The message includes an automatically generated addendum explaining that it was entered using touch-tones and the author's "signature" information.

Mail reading is facilitated by the addition of **filtering.** Messages can be sorted into categories such as "urgent," "important," "personal," and "other" based on keywords found in the subject line or on the basis of the author of the message. Phoneshell users can specify arbitrary filtering categories and determine their presentation order. A user who receives large quantities of mail is likely to "read" only the more important categories using speech synthesis simply because this method is so much more time consuming than reading text on a terminal.

Some aspects of Voiced Mail were not carried over into Phoneshell. Because users now get many more email messages, they are less likely to want to hear all their messages so Phoneshell speaks the sender and subject of each message but does not recite the message itself unless requested. The repetition strategy of Voiced Mail (slow down, spell mode) was also abandoned.

The calendar application, Caltalk, lets users scan their calendars and add new entries. A date can be specified with touchtones, and users can hear calendar entries for that day item-by-item; text entries are synthesized and voice entries are played. New entries are recorded and stored as voice annotations. Portions of the calendar can also be faxed if requested.

Although reciting each entry for a day is effective in describing a particular day, in many ways using an auditory calendar interface is more difficult than a graphical interface. Earlier versions of the application provided a "week-at-a-glance" function that merely recited each entry day by day; this ineffectively conveys the overview available from scanning a graphical representation: "The first part of the week is rather free, Wednesday and Thursday have some appointments, and Friday is packed." A more recent version of Caltalk includes new week-at-a-glance and month-at-a-glance functions that attempt to better summarize the calendar and recognize keywords such as "important" in calendar entries as well as entries that span multiple days or are regularly scheduled each week. Caltalk might say, e.g., "Nothing scheduled Monday or Wednesday, important meeting with British Telecom and the usual meetings on Tuesday, you are in Palo Alto Thursday and Friday." Terse summarization is difficult to do well and illustrates some of the problems in converting a tool which usually is accessed visually to a voice-only interface.

A fourth application, Rolotalk, provides access to a personal name and address database. The caller spells a name using touch tones, one tone per letter, to select a "card" from the database; the user can also specify alternate search criteria, such as company name. Once selected, the user can request telephone numbers, postal addresses, electronic mail addresses, and additional information about the selected person. Most useful is Rolotalk's ability to communicate with the selected person; it can place a phone call to either the home or work number or send a voice or text message. When placing a call, Rolotalk dials the destination party and creates a three-way conference call including itself, the user, and the called party. Rolotalk remains on the line for several minutes; if it hears a "#" tone, it drops the onward call and returns to normal user interaction. This allows the user to remain connected to Rolotalk after dialing a busy number or leaving a message on an answering machine. Message transmission, either voice or text, is accomplished by the same mechanisms employed to respond to electronic mail.

In addition to information stored in explicit fields, the underlying Rolotalk database allows users to specify **links** to other files. Typical links contain maps to the homes or offices of people in the database or driving directions as text. When a user calls in, Rolotalk can try to recite any text file links using speech synthesis or can fax all the links to a nearby fax machine. A user can also fax email messages; this is especially useful for long formatted messages such as a meeting agenda or conference schedule.

Phoneshell also provides several simple communication utilities. A dial-by-name directory enables a caller to spell out the name of a Media Lab staff member and transfer the call to that person's number. Phoneshell can also report the locations of Speech Group members using the activity information described in Chapter 11. The caller can find out who is currently in the lab or logged in from home, call on site users at the nearest telephone, or inquire when a specific user was most recently detected. A Phoneshell user can forward either stored fax messages or an item selected from a small archive of frequently faxed documents (e.g., a map to one's office) to another number.

Although it is currently considered to be in developmental stages as a research project, Phoneshell has been deployed for several years at two locations with as many as 20 users. Its design has benefited from iterative improvements to its user interface due to users' varying requirements and levels of expertise. It has demonstrated the effectiveness of speech as a means of remote access for the mobile user by turning any telephone into a terminal. Although some of the Phoneshell databases are more easily accessed by a laptop computer and a modem, it is often inconvenient to hook up such hardware at a pay phone, to a cellular phone, or in a host's office or home.

Key to the success of Phoneshell has been its integration of multiple communication applications. Reading email over the telephone without any ability to reply would be very frustrating; the recent surge of support for voice encapsulated in email messages facilitates on-the-spot voice replies. It is sometimes useful to send a copy of an email message to someone who appears in one's rolodex. The necessity of calling separate voice mail and text mail applications to retrieve incoming messages would be inconvenient. The ability to query one's calendar while hearing messages about upcoming meeting dates makes it possible to coordinate schedules more effectively. In short, Phoneshell presents a work environment wherein a user can easily switch between as many applications as are required to complete a particular task.

## Visual User Interfaces to Desktop Audio

Earlier in this chapter visual user interfaces were extolled as the means of providing the user with random access to voice as data, thereby overcoming some of its slow and serial nature. The visual user interface also acts as a spatial representation, providing a navigational aid for applications presenting multiple snippets of audio. In the desktop audio context, some applications are intrinsically linked to stored voice, such as a graphical interface to voice mail messages. But with the increased availability of audio recording hardware on workstations plus remote telephone access through interfaces such as Phoneshell, many other applications may benefit from stored voice snippets. Both classes of applications require graphical user interfaces to stored speech.

This section describes a family of applications developed in recent years at the Media Lab which operate in concert with Phoneshell as well as some of the telephone management utilities described in Chapter 11. The intent of this case study is to illustrate this chapter's claims about visual interfaces and interapplication communication with actual examples. The SoundViewer widget described earlier in this chapter is used across all of these applications.

The first application to consider is a visual user interface to voice mail, seen in Figure 12.14. When not in use, this application is reduced to a small icon; when new voice mail arrives, the icon blinks, serving as a "message waiting" light. If the user clicks a mouse button on the icon, the message window opens, displaying messages as a column of SoundViewers with indication of the calling party's name or number if known. Vmail also accepts email messages containing voice attachments in several vendor formats; for these the sender's email address is displayed instead of a phone number. When the mouse is moved into the label identifying the caller, text in the upper-right corner of the window shows the date and time at which the message was recorded.

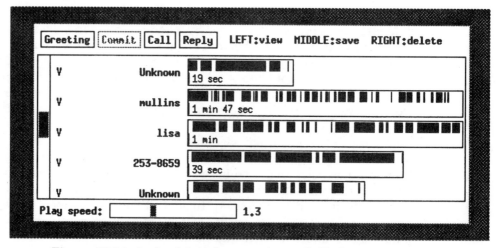

**Figure 12.14.** A visual interface to voice mail. Each row represents a message, and displays the caller's name or number, if known.

Clicking on a message causes it to play, with the SoundViewer bar moving left-to-right synchronously. While playing, the bar can be manipulated to move around within the message. If a second message is selected, the current message stops and the new message begins playback; this makes it easier to scan through a number of messages looking for one in particular, as messages typically can be identified by playing their first three or four seconds. Playback speed can be changed dynamically by a speed slider at the bottom of the window, and the user can specify a default playback speed for all messages.

After playback, a **V** appears to the left of the message indicating that it has been viewed; messages remain until they are explicitly deleted. Messages can also be saved to a file, in which case the user specifies a file name. If the caller's phone number is known, a return call can be placed by clicking on the "call" button; this sends a call request message to Xphone (described in Chapter 11). If the caller's name or email address is known, the "reply" button sends a request to Xmemotool (see below) to record a voice message in response.

This visual user interface to voice mail has proven very popular among the small community of users at the Media Lab. The direct manipulation Sound-Viewer interface makes it easier to play portions of the sound repeatedly, specifically while writing down a telephone number. The ability to increase playback speed lets users save time listening to messages, and some of them take advantage of this.[7] Because the application allows multiple users to access the same voice mailbox, a group secretary manages four mailboxes with 20 to 30 messages a day. Although many users delete messages immediately after they have been read, some leave 10 or 20 messages in their mailbox because the visual interface makes it easy to navigate between them and quickly find a particular old message; this is cumbersome with a tone-based telephone interface.

Users can also move messages or portions of messages to other applications. Holding down a mouse button and dragging the cursor across a SoundViewer selects a portion of sound, which can then be pasted into one's calendar, for example, or into the Sedit editor (described in Chapter 4) for further annotation. After editing, the resulting sound file can be forwarded to another user by pasting it into Xmemotool.

Xmemotool (see Figure 12.15) is a window-based utility for recording voice messages. Messages can be composed for other local voice mail subscribers or sent to remote users as email messages, in which case one of several sound file formats must be selected. Xmemotool can also receive the current audio selection instead of taking a new recording; this allows a segment to be cut from a SoundViewer in any application and pasted in as a voice message to be sent.

Xcal (see Figure 12.16) is a visual user interface to a calendar database. In many respects it is similar to a variety of calendar applications with the difference being that Xcal also supports voice annotations. Voice annotations may be recorded directly into Xcal but are more likely to be recorded over the telephone via Phoneshell. Voice entries can also be made by cutting and pasting from other

---

[7]A playback speed of 1.4 times faster than the original seems popular.

**Figure 12.15.** Xmemotool, an on-screen voice message taker.

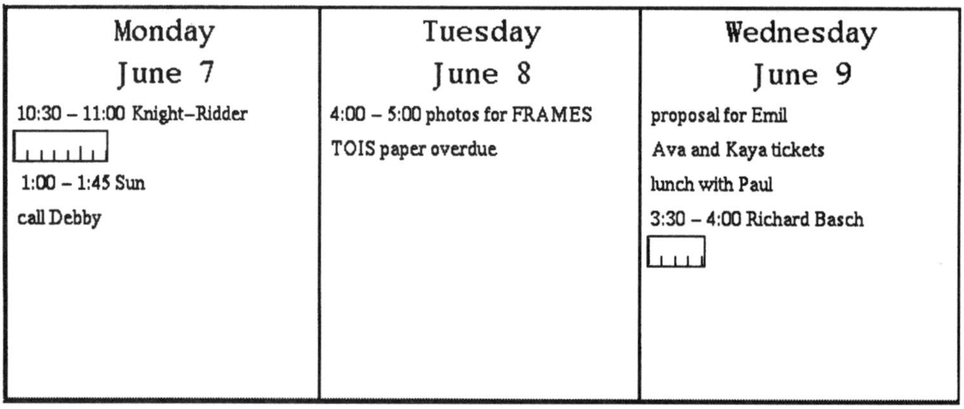

**Figure 12.16.** A personal calender containing voice and text entries.

applications; e.g., a user may select a portion of a voice message from a caller who will visit in a few days and paste that into the calendar as a reminder of the visit or to suggest topics for discussion during the visit.

Another application, ToDo, shown in Figure 12.7, combines voice and text in a things-to-do list. A user can enter voice or text notes while at the workstation, but voice notes more frequently originate from telephone interactions with Phoneshell. While accessing voice mail in PhoneShell, a user records a "memo"; this sound file is then incorporated into the ToDo database.

While each of these applications is fairly basic in isolation, it is their combination on a single workstation screen that renders them most powerful. In practice, little of the audio data used in these applications is recorded at the workstation; text is usually preferred simply because it is easier to retrieve at a later date. Instead, voice annotations arrive over the telephone into the databases used by these applications, either in the user's own voice via Phoneshell or as portions of voice messages from other people through audio cut and paste. Although none of

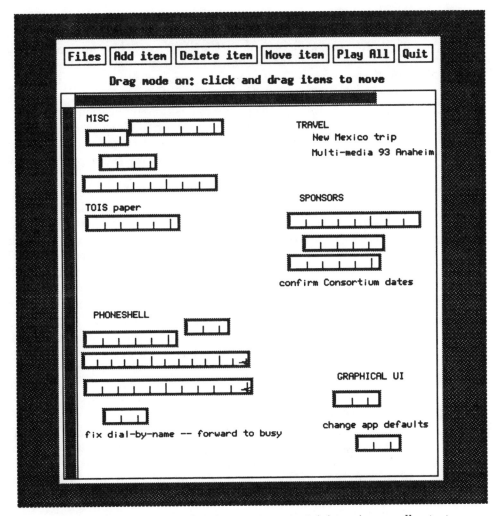

**Figure 12.17.** A personal project manager containing voice as well as text entries. Voice entries are most often recorded over the telephone using Phoneshell.

these applications is overwhelming in isolation, the appropriateness and ease with which they can be used in combination hints at the ultimate utility of desktop audio.

## SUMMARY

This chapter builds on the previous chapter's point of view of unifying telephones and computers by presenting the concept of Desktop Audio, the integration of voice processing into screen-based desktop computing. It started by arguing that the successful deployment of voice applications depends on a number of factors. The most important factor for success is that voice must add value to existing work practices, as it is unlikely that any single new application is going to radically change the ways in which office computers are being used. But it can enhance current productivity tools, e.g., by providing better user interfaces to current voice systems such as voice mail. Desktop voice processing can enable remote access over the telephone to desktop applications and their databases as was described in the case study on Phoneshell. The case study on Conversational Desktop was meant to illustrate this broad range of potential Desktop Audio functionality, and how it benefits from the integration of multiple voice processing technologies.

Desktop Audio requires graphical user interfaces to indicate the presence of stored voice within an application and to control its playback. Graphical interfaces can also support cut-and-paste of stored voice between applications. Common interfaces are the "button," which implements click-to-play while requiring little screen space, and more elaborate audio playback control panels which may also provide a temporal representation of of the stored voice. The SoundViewer, described as a case study, attempts to provide the enhanced functionality of control panels while minimizing its screen space requirements. The SoundViewer was shown in use in an array of applications discussed in the final case study.

Desktop Audio also benefits from a client-server architecture, which enables multiple applications to make use of digital audio resources simultaneously without interfering with each other. Audio toolkits should insulate clients from details of the audio server's protocol and provide convenient user interface building blocks to enable rapid application development. A number of server architectures were discussed in detail.

Desktop Audio has become a reality only very recently, driven primarily by the increased speeds of workstations. Issues with appropriateness of speech applications as well as the techniques to employ voice processing technologies effectively all come to bear on this integrated approach. With proper integration, voice can be used seamlessly across a range of tasks we perform in our daily work lives.

# 13

# Toward More Robust Communication

This book has discussed a variety of speech technologies including digital audio coding, speech recognition, text-to-speech synthesis, and the telephone. Intermingled with chapters explaining the algorithms that provide these capabilities to computers have been chapters devoted to applications and interactive techniques whereby speech may be employed effectively in a computational environment. The emphasis has been on *interaction* and *responsiveness* of voice applications; the case studies expand on these obvious surface features of conversation. But, despite the themes of higher-level discourse presented in Chapter 9, no specific application is capable of conversing at the level of a four-year-old child even when limited to a single topic.

Major constraints to conversational interactions are the limited ability of current speech recognition technology and the marginal fluency of synthetic speech. Chapters 10 and 11 temporarily overlooked these limitations by discussing the role of computers as *facilitators* of unconstrained conversation among people over the telephone. This led to Chapter 12's discussion of the role of audio as data captured on the desktop from sources such as voice mail and recordings of a meeting or telephone call. In some ways these later chapters are disjoint from prior chapters in that they describe situations in which the computer makes no pretense at conversational ability, understanding nothing about the content of the audio it is routing or recording while it assists with setting up a conversation or archiving it. But from the end user's perspective, this disjunction may not be so apparent. We converse in diverse situations and for many purposes; we introduce strangers, initiate conversations, and often listen to others more than we speak. For the user, speech is about getting something done, and the tasks we already perform among ourselves are more important in defining how we will utilize speech than the limitations of current technology.

This final chapter returns to the issue of increased computer participation in conversation and poses several domains in which computers woefully lag our conversational abilities beyond hearing words or stringing them together into spoken sentences. One component of improved computer support for conversations is a better appreciation of the interactive techniques we employ to ensure robust communication while talking. Another is tighter coupling between the acoustic and conceptual phases of language understanding. Finally, prosody is an essential element of human speech largely overlooked in computational speech systems. However, these are not presented here as unsolved problems but rather as encouraging avenues that may lead to more productive voice interaction between people and computers.

## ROBUST COMMUNICATION

In our use of language we employ a variety of techniques to confirm that the other party understands our message. When the other party is a computer communicating via technology of marginal ability, such robustness is even more essential. Most current applications of speech technology are extremely brittle; if they succeed it is mostly due to the cooperation of the user and our remarkable ability to adapt to conversations under conditions of extreme noise or very thick accents. If conversational computers incorporate our own communication protocols, they can become much more capable partners in conversation. This section describes some aspects of our conversational ability that have been largely left out of the design of dialogue systems to date, although many of these ideas were briefly introduced in Chapter 9.

In a seminal and lengthy journal article, Hayes and Reddy note a number of important elements of conversational protocols and identify some additional behaviors that a conversational system might employ [Hayes and Reddy 1983]. They identify the principle of *implicit confirmation:* if the speaker believes that the listener received the message, then the speaker also believes that the listener understood the message in the absence of any response. This places a huge burden on the listener who must indicate any difficulties understanding the message at the proper time or else the speaker may continue and the conversation will rapidly break down. Such expectations imply that speech recognition applications, which may be thought of as a listener at the end of a very noisy communication channel, must always respond in a timely manner to recognition errors.

Clearly it is a violation of the listener's side of conversational protocol to detect that recognition failed and not say anything as this constitutes an explicit acknowledgment that the message was understood. What should be said in response? Humans concisely communicate what has been understood and what information is lacking through a process of progressive clarification. This may be accomplished by asking a series of short, specific questions rather than more general requests for the speaker to repeat or rephrase the original utterance. The nature of questions that we ask strongly influences the speaker's response, and we should guide the conversation to a successful conclusion. By echoing portions of what has been thought to be understood, the listener also invites correction by the speaker. The principle of implicit confirmation suggests that an echoed statement can be assumed to be correct unless it is contested by the original speaker.

We often describe an object partially, identifying only its salient features. Grice's maxims support this behavior; they indicate that we should speak only as much as is necessary, i.e., if a complete description is not necessary to identify an object, then we should not elaborate. Humans excel at understanding each other from fragmentary utterances, but these sentence fragments can wreck havoc on computational parsers and semantic analyzers. "Conceptual" parsers operate on the basis of keyword detection, e.g., by placing keywords into slots with appropriate roles in a frame. But simply detecting keywords may be insufficient for identifying their role even in a syntactically simple utterance such as "The lion roared at the elephant in the tiger's cage"; here we must identify the syntactic relationships between the animals if we are to infer their roles in the activity described.

A conversational speech system should have the ability to answer questions that may fall into several categories. Hypothetical questions like "If I were to go on Tuesday could I get a lower fare ticket?" are often a prelude to further transaction and establish the basis of the next request. Questions about ability like "Can you pass the salt?" are often indirect speech acts. But other times answering questions about ability is essential as speech systems are not omnipotent but perform in a limited domain. In a graphical user interface, the user can pull down menus and read options in the process of deciding how to make a choice. In a speech system, this is not possible: the application would need to continually recite all possible options because of the transient nature of speech. Instead, the user must be able to ask the system what its capabilities are, and it must be able to reply in a rational manner.

Combining clarifying protocols with the various aspects of discourse described in Chapter 9, we begin to appreciate the complexity of conversation. There may be a round of clarifying discourse to resolve ambiguities about what one party has just said. This contributes to subgoals—mutual understanding on an utterance-by-utterance basis—in the context of the discourse. But discourse is usually not about simply understanding each other; certainly in the case of a human speaking to a computer, the human wishes the computer to perform some action or service. The computer must track the discourse focus and understand the user's goals at each step while formulating its own subgoals to understand the utterance. This is very difficult, yet it provides a powerful basis for graceful conversational interaction.

## SPEECH RECOGNITION AND ROBUST PARSING

One disturbing trend in speech recognition research is putting more and more linguistic knowledge into the word recognition process (this is good) but then using this knowledge to excessively constrain recognition, which leaves little room for speaker or recognizer error. Linguistic constraints, most prominently rules of syntax or word combination probabilities, limit the perplexity of the recognition task and this results in both significantly improved accuracy and the potential for much larger recognition vocabularies. Such constraints are certainly necessary to understand fluent speech and humans use them as well. But once a language is completely specified, what happens when the human errs?

In the majority of current, experimental, large-vocabulary connected speech recognizers, omission of a single word is likely to result in no recognition result reported at all. If the recognizer is configured to hear seven or ten digit telephone numbers and the talker stops after six digits, the recognizer may report nothing or possibly only the occurrence of an error without any hint as to its nature. But consider the conversational techniques discussed earlier in this chapter as well as in Chapter 8. It is extremely unproductive for the application to remain mute or to utter unhelpfully "What was that?" A preferable alternative might be to echo the digits back to the user either in entirety or in part. Another might be to use back-channel style encouragement ("Uh-huh" spoken with a somewhat rising pitch) to indicate that the application is waiting for more digits and anticipates that the user has not yet completed his or her turn. Further misunderstandings might cause the application to explain what it thinks the user has requested and why the request is not yet complete, e.g., "I can dial the phone for you but you must specify at least seven digits for a valid number."

In the above scenario, the human made a clear mistake by speaking only six digits. But a cooperative system will not castigate the user, rather it will try to help complete the task. Perhaps the user accidently missed a digit or cannot decipher a digit in someone else's handwriting, or paused to obtain reassurance that the system was still listening and realized that a call was being placed. Such occurrences are not even limited to situations in which the human makes such an unequivocal mistake; spoken language is ripe with false starts, ill-formed grammatical constructs, and ellipsis. When these happen, is there any hope for an application using speech recognition to recover gracefully and cooperatively?

One approach, similar to that used by Conversational Desktop and described in Chapter 9, is to define the recognizer's grammar so that all possible sentence fragments appear as valid utterances. When used during the recognition phase of discourse, such an under-constrained grammar would lead to reduced recognition accuracy due to increased perplexity. But humans are effective at conversing to attain a goal and, to the extent that we can engage in question-answering, we are capable of getting acceptable performance even in the face of recognition errors [Hunnicutt et al. 1992] so letting some errors occur and then negotiating with the user may be more productive than insisting on near-perfect recognition before reporting any results.

Two approaches from MIT's Spoken Language Systems Group illustrate practical hybrid solutions. One approach reported by [Seneff 1992] employs conventional parsing based on syntactic rules, but when a well-formed parse is not found, the parser switches to a more semantically oriented mode based on analysis of keywords in the context of the task domain. Additionally, conventional syntactic parsing can be improved by weighting word choices with probability measures. Under this approach, a grammar is augmented with word-sequence probabilities based on analysis of a corpus of utterances spoken by naive subjects attempting to access the chosen task [Hirschman *et al.* 1991].

But in natural speech these probabilities are dynamic and depend on the current state of the conversation as well as the listener's expectations of what the talker may be up to. In a fully integrated conversational application, pragmatic information such as identification of a partially completed plan or detection of elements of a script could tune word probabilities based on expectations of what is likely to follow. Similarly a focus model could suggest heightened probabilities of words relevant to attributes of entities recently discussed in addition to resolving anaphoric references. Domain knowledge plays a role as well, from simplistic awareness of the number of digits in telephone numbers to knowledge of the acceleration and turning capabilities of various types of aircraft in an air traffic control scenario.

Part of the difficulty with flexible parsing is the excessive degree of isolation between the application, its discourse system, and the speech recognition component. For many current systems the recognizer is given a language model in whatever form it requires; it then listens to speech and returns a string of text to the application, which must parse it *again* to know how to interpret the words meaningfully. Not only has syntactic information been needlessly lost when reporting the recognized speech as a string of words, but it also may be detrimental to strip the representation of any remaining acoustic evidence such as the recognizer's degree of certainty or possible alternate choices of recognition results. How can partial recognition results be reported to the parser? Perhaps several noun phrases were identified but the verb was not, confounding classification of the nouns into the possible roles that might be expressed in a framed-based representation.

These observations are intended to suggest that despite this book's portrayal of the various layers of language understanding and generation as distinct entities, they still must be tightly woven into a coherent whole. Isolation of the word identification portion of discourse understanding into a well bounded "speech recognizer" component cannot in the long run support sophisticated conversational systems. Knowledge must be communicated easily across components, and analysis must be flexible and based on dynamic conversation constraints.

## PROSODY

Prosody refers to the spoken style of discourse independent of lexical content, and it includes several aspects of how we speak. *Intonation* is the tune of an utterance: how we modulate F0 to change the pitch of our speech. Intonation operates at a sentence or phrase level; the rising tune of a yes-or-no question immediately differentiates it from the falling tune of a declarative statement. Intonation also helps to convey the stress of words and syllables within a sentence as stressed syllables are spoken with a pitch higher or lower than normal, and specific words are emphasized—an important aspect of communicating intent—by stressing their stressed syllables even more. *Phrasing* is the breaking of speech into groups, how many words we squeeze into an utterance before stopping for breath, or how we may speak a few words much more slowly for emphasis. *Meter* is carried largely by the duration of individual syllables, stressed syllables being generally longer than unstressed ones. Among stressed syllables, some syllables are more stressed than others resulting in a meter scheme across an entire phrase. Syllabic stress is also reinforced by intonation, and intonation helps convey phrasing as well, so all these elements intermingle during speech production.

In a nutshell, prosody encompasses the majority of information lost when comparing an utterance to its transcription, and much of the richness of speech is conveyed by exactly this nonlexical means of expression.[1] Although a back alley in the field, intonation has been explored extensively by linguists attempting to categorize it and understand how it is systematically and predictably used in spoken language [Ladd 1978, Bolinger 1982]. Pierrehumbert and Hirschberg suggest a grammar relating pitch accents to aspects of meaning [Pierrehumbert and Hirschberg 1990]. In their interpretation, intonation indicates factors such as the salience of an utterance, the speaker's degree of involvement or belief in the facts being proposed, and paths of inference the speaker wishes to emphasize. Although prosody is what differentiates spoken from written language, few conversational speech systems have attempted to exploit its expressiveness.

We notice the prosody of synthetic speech mostly by its absence or occasional misplaced syllabic stress. In Chapter 5 intonation was discussed in two contexts: differentiating alternate syntactic forms of words spelled identically but stressed distinctly and differentiating declarative and interrogative sentences by overall pitch contours. This analysis did not extend beyond individual sentences. The difficulty with applying prosodic cues to human-authored text lies chiefly with the fact that intonation conveys so many levels of meaning. Each sentence would need to be parsed to identify the syntactic role of some of the confusing forms, e.g., "live," "elaborate," and "conduct." But without understanding the semantic structure of a sentence, it is difficult to identify which word should be most stressed. And a sentence must be considered in a discourse context to correctly use prosody to convey the difference between given and new information (new is more heavily stressed).

Better use of prosodic cues for speech synthesis can be made by applications employing synthesis-from-concept techniques, i.e., generating utterances in a discourse based on internal models of the discourse and an associated task domain. Witten's Telephone Enquiry Service allowed application programmers to explicitly program intonation into text to be synthesized by marking it with special codes [Witten and Madams 1977]. Davis and Hirschberg used intonational cues to improve the expressiveness of the Direction Assistance program described in Chapter 6 [Davis and Hirschberg 1988]. They used intonational cues to convey given and new information and to cue listeners to shift the focus of discourse by

---

[1]Other information lost by the transcription are the speaker's identity (carried in part by the timbre or spectral characteristics of one's speech), accent, and emotional state.

increasing pitch range. Cahn explored the use of prosody and other acoustical cues to convey affect using synthesized speech; such prosodic cues included pitch range and speech rate as well as variations in how phonemes are realized and acoustical parameters of the synthesizer's vocal tract model [Cahn 1990]. Similar work was also reported by [Murray et al. 1988].

Attempts to employ prosodic cues for language understanding have likewise been limited. Lea proposed a wide ranging framework to take advantage of prosody during speech recognition, including, in part, the observation that stressed syllables are more phonetically invariant than unstressed ones (unstressed syllables are subject to reduction, e.g., to a schwa) [Lea 1980]. More recently, Waibel investigated the role of prosody in speech recognition suggesting that it could be used as a cue to word boundaries [Waibel 1988].

Grunt, described in Chapter 9, detected monosyllabic questions and responded to them according to its discourse model. Daly and Zue analyzed longer utterances' pitch contours in an attempt to differentiate questions of the sort which expect yes-or-no answers from Wh- questions [Daly and Zue 1990]. They achieved significant (though imperfect) results largely by looking at the final boundary tone or pitch excursion at the end of an utterance.

These are but small steps into the realm of intonation. The role of intonation in language is far from completely understood, and detection of prosody may be acoustically difficult especially in the absence of clear lexical analysis of an utterance. Nonetheless, prosody is an essential and powerful component of both speaking and listening and key for more natural dialog systems.

## WHAT NEXT?

This brief chapter has suggested some ways in which we have only begun to tap into the richness and robustness of conversation as a potential means of interacting with computer systems. But this is meant to be an optimistic note not a pessimistic one. The very richness of the human voice and its pervasiveness across so much of our expression mean that any ability to exploit it has potential for rewards.

Although the speech technologies described in this book are feeble when compared with human capabilities, the case studies demonstrate that with careful matching of technology to task and careful crafting of interaction techniques successful voice applications are already a reality. Speech is so powerful that even applications of very limited ability can be extremely effective in specific situations.

Speech technologies are improving rapidly, assisted by ever-increasing computer power. Raw technologies are an enabling factor and guarantee success only with careful consideration of how and when to apply them. That modern technologies impinge on only the most basic aspects of our attempts to converse clearly shows the power that conversational computing systems are one day destined to achieve.

# Bibliography

Ades, S. and D. C. Swinehart. "Voice Annotation and Editing in a Workstation Environment." In *Proceedings of the 1986 Conference,* pages 13–28, San Jose, CA: The American Voice I/O Society, September 1986.

Allen, J. *Natural Language Understanding.* Benjamin/Cummings Series in Computer Science. Reading, MA: The Benjamin/Cummings Publishing Co., Inc., 1987.

Allen, J., M. S. Hunnicutt, and D. Klatt. *From Text to Speech: The MITalk system.* Cambridge University Press, 1987.

Allen, J. "Overview of Text-to-Speech Systems." In S. Furui and M. M. Sondhi, editors, *Advances in Speech Signal Processing,* pages 741–790. New York: Marcel Dekker, Inc., 1992.

Allen, R. B. "Composition and Editing of Spoken Letters." *International Journal of Man/ Machine Studies,* 19:181–193, 1983.

Allport, D. A., B. Antonis, and P. Reynolds. "On the Division of Attention: a Disproof of the Single Channel Hypothesis." *Quarterly Journal of Experimental Psychology,* 24:225–235, 1972.

Angebranndt, S. R. L. Hyde, D. H. Luong. N. Siravara, and C. Schmandt. "Integrating Audio and Telephony in a Distributed Workstation Environment." In *Proceedings of the Summer 1991 USENIX Conference,* pages 419–435, Berkeley, CA: USENIX Association, June 1991.

Arons, B., C. Binding, C. Schmandt, and K. Lantz. "The VOX Audio Server." In *Proceedings of the 2nd IEEE Comsoc International Multimedia Communications Workshop,* New York: IEEE, April 1989.

Arons, B. "The Design of Audio Servers and Toolkits for Supporting Speech in the User Interface." *Journal of The American Voice I/O Society,* 9:27–41, March 1991.

Arons, B. Hyperspeech. "Navigating in Speech-Only Hypermedia." In *Proceedings of Hypertext '91,* pages 133–146. New York: ACM, December 1991.

Arons, B. "Techniques, Perception, and Applications of Time-Compressed Speech." In *Proceedings of the 1992 Conference,* pages 169–177, San Jose, CA: The American Voice I/O Society, September 1992.

Arons, B. "Tools for Building Asynchronous Servers to Support Speech and Audio Applications." In *Proceedings of the ACM Symposium on User Interface Software and Technology.* New York: ACM, November 1992.

Arons B. "Speech Skimmer: Interactively Skimming Recorded Speech." In *Proceeding of the ACM Symposium on User Interface Software and Technolgy.* New York: ACM, November 1993.

Austin, J. L. *How to do Things with Words.* Oxford, England: Clarendon Press, 1962.

Beasley, D. S. and J. E. Maki. "Time- and Frequency-Altered Speech." In N.J. Lass, editor, *Contemporary Issues in Experimental Phonetics,* pages 419–458. Academic Press, 1976.

Biermann, A. W., R. D. Rodman, D. C. Rubin, and F. F. Heidlage. "Natural Language With Discrete Speech as a Mode for Human-to-Machine Communication." *Communications of the ACM,* 28(6):628–636, 1985.

Billman, R., R. Hammond, P. McElbatton, E. N. Brandt, F. Sung, and N. Yost. "Workstation Audio in the X Environment." *The X Resource,* 1(4):137–158, October 1992.

Bly, S. A. and J. K. Rosenberg. "A Comparison of Tiled and Overlapping Windows." In *Proceedings of the Conference on Computer Human Interface,* pages 101–106, New York: ACM, April 1986.

Bolinger, D. "Intonation and Its Parts." *Language,* 58(3):505–533, 1982.

Bolt, R. A. "'Put-That-There': Voice and Gesture at the Graphics Interface." *Computer Graphics,* 14(3):262–270, 1980.

Bowles, I., R. Kamel, *et al.* "PX: Integrating Voice Communications With Desktop Computing." *Journal of The American Voice I/O Society,* 9:1–19, March 1991.

Briley, B. E. *Introduction to Telephone Switching.* Reading, MA: Addison-Wesley Publishing Co., Inc., 1983.

Cahn, J. E. "The generation of affect in Synthesized Speech." In *Journal of the American Voice I/O Society,* pages 1–19. San Jose, CA: American Voice I/O Society, July 1990.

Chalfonte, B. L., R. S. Fish, and R. E. Kraut. "Expressive Richness: A Comparison of Speech and Text as Media for Revision." In *Proceedings of the Conference on Computer Human Interaction,* pages 21–26. New York: ACM, April 1991.

Chen, F. R. and M. Withgott. "The Use of Emphasis to Automatically Summarize Spoken Discourse." In *Proceedings of the 1992 International Conference on Acoustics, Speech and Signal Processing,* pages 229–233. New York: IEEE, 1992.

Chorafas, D. N. *Telephony: Today and Tomorrow.* Prentice-Hall Series in Data Processing Management. Englewood Cliffs, NJ: Prentice-Hall, Inc., 1984.

Clark, H. H. and C. R. Marshall. "Definite Reference and Mutual Knowledge." In Webber Joshi and Sag, editors, *Elements of Discourse Understanding,* 10:63. Cambridge University Press, 1981.

Clark, H. H. and D. Wilkes-Gibbs. "Referring as a Collaborative Process." *Cognition,* 22:1–39, 1986.

Clark, H. H. and E. F. Schaefer. Contributing to Discourse." *Cognitive Science,* 13:259–294, 1989.

Clark, H. H. and S. E. Brennan. "Grounding in Communication." In L. B. Resnick, J. Levine, and S. D. Behrend, editors, *Socially Shared Cognition.* American Psychological Association, 1990.

Cohen, P. R., J. Morgan, and M. E. Pollack, editors. *Intentions in Communication.* Cambridge, MA: MIT Press, 1990.

Crowley, T. "Voice in a Multimedia Document System." *Journal of The American Voice I/O Society,* 9:21–26, March 1991.

Daly, N. A. and V. W. Zue. "Acoustic, Perceptual, and Linguistic Analyses of Intonation Contours in Human/Machine Dialogues." In *Proceedings of the International Conference on Spoken Language Processing,* November 1990.

Davis, J. R. *Back Seat Driver: Voice assisted automobile navigation.* Ph.D. thesis, MIT Media Arts and Sciences Section, September 1989.

Davis, J. R. and T. F. Trobaugh. Direction Assistance. Technical Report 1, MIT Media Laboratory Speech Group, December 1987.

Davis, J. R. and J. Hirschberg. "Assigning Intonational Features in Synthesized Spoken Directions." In *Proceedings of the Association for Computational Linguistics,* pages 187–193, 1988.

Davis, J. R. and C. Schmandt. "The Back Seat Driver: Real Time Spoken Driving Instructions." In *Vehicle Navigation and Information Systems,* pages 146–150, 1989.

Davis, J. R. and C. Schmandt. "Discourse Strategies for Conversations in Time." In *Proceedings of the AVIOS 1990 Conference,* pages 21–26, San Jose, CA: The American Voice I/O Society, September 1990.

Davis, J. R. "Let Your Fingers Do the Spelling: Implicit Disambiguation of Words Spelled With the Telephone Keypad." *Journal of The American Voice I/O Society,* 9:57–66, March 1991.

Denes, P. B. and E. N. Pinson. *The Speech Chain: The physics and biology of spoken language,* 2nd edition. New York: W.H. Freeman, 1993.

Dixon, N. R. and T. B. Martin, editors. *Automatic Speech & Speaker Recognition.* IEEE Press Selected Reprint Series. New York: IEEE Press, 1979.

Duncan, S., Jr. "Some Signals and Rules for Taking Speaking Turns in Conversations." *Journal of Personality and Social Psychology,* 23:283–292, 1972.

Duncan, S., Jr. "On the Structure of Speaker-Auditor Interaction During Speaking Turns." *Language in Society,* 2:161–180, 1974.

Egan, J. P. "Articulation Testing Methods." *Laryngoscope,* 58:955–991, 1948.

Englebeck, G. and T. L. Roberts. "The Effect of Several Voice-Menu Characteristics on Menu-Selection Performance." Technical report, U.S. West Advanced Technologies, Boulder, CO, 1989.

Fairbanks, G. "Test of Phonemic Differentiation: The Rhyme Test." *Journal of the Acoustical Society of America,* 30:596–600, 1958.

Fish, R. S., R. E. Kraut, M. D. P. Leland and M. Cohen. "Quilt: a Collaborative Tool for Cooperative Writing." In *Proceedings of the Conference on Office Information Systems,* pages 30–37, New York: ACM 1988.

Flanagan, J. L. "Analog Measurements of Sound Radiation From the Mouth." *Journal of the Acoustical Society of America,* 32(12), 1960.

Flanagan, J. L. *Speech Analysis Synthesis and Perception.* Springer Verlag, 1972.

Flanagan, J. L., M. R. Schroeder, B. S. Atal, R. E. Crochiere; N. S. Jayant, and J. M. Tribolet. "Speech Coding." *IEEE Transactions on Communications,* 27(4):710–737, April 1979.

Fletcher, H. and W. A. Munson. "Loudness, Definition, Measurements and Calculation." *Journal of the Acoustical Society of America,* 5, 1933.

Fry, D. B. "Experiments in the Perception of Stress." *Language and Speech,* 1(2):126–152, 1958.

Fujimura, O. and J. Lovins. "Syllables as Concatenative Phonetic Elements." In A. Bell and J. B. Hooper, editors, *Syllables and Segments,* pages 107–120, North Holland, New York, 1978.

Furui, S. and M. M. Sondhi, editors. *Advances in Speech Signal Processing.* New York: Marcel Dekker, Inc., 1992.

Gifford, W. S. and D. L. Turock. "The Electronic Receptionist: A Knowledge-Based Approach to Personal Communications." In *Proceedings of the IEEE Conference on Selected Topics in Wireless Communications.* New York: IEEE, June 1992.

Goffman, E. *Forms of Talk.* University of Pennsylvania Press, 1981.

Gould, J. D. "How Experts Dictate." *Journal of Experimental Psychology: Human Perception and Performance,* 4(4):648–661, 1978.

Gould, J. D. and S. J. Boies. "How Authors Think About Their Writing, Dictating, and Speaking." *Human Factors,* 20(4):495–505, 1978.

Gould, J. D. "Writing and Speaking Letters and Messages." *International Journal of Man/Machine Studies,* 16(2):147–171, 1982.

Gould, J. D.; J. Conti, and T. Hovanyecz. "Composing Letters With a Simulated Listening Type-writer." *Communications of the ACM,* 26(4):295–308, April 1983.

Gould, J. D., S. J. Boies, S. Levy, J. T. Richards, and J. Schoonard. "The 1984 Olympic Message System: A Test of Behavioral Principles of System Design." *Communications of the ACM,* 30(9):758–769, September 1987.

Grice, H. P. "Logic and Conversation." In Cole and Morgan, editors, *Syntax and Semantics: Speech Acts,* volume 3, pages 41–58. Academic Press, 1975.

Grosz, B. J., A. K. Joshi, and S. Weinstein. "Providing a Unified Account of Definite Noun Phrases in Discourse." In *Proceedings of the 21st conference of the Association for Computatonal Linguistics,* pages 44–50, 1983.

Grosz, B. J. and C. L. Sidner. "Attention, Intentions, and the Structure of Discourse." *Computational Linguistics,* 12(3):175–204, 1986.

Grosz, B. J.; K. S. Jones, and B. L. Webber, editors. *Readings in Natural Language Processing.* Los Altos, CA: Morgan Kaufmann Publishers, Inc., 1986.

Handel, W. S. Listening: *An Introduction to the Perception of Auditory Events.* Cambridge, MA: MIT Press, 1989.

Hauptmann, A. G. "Speech and Gestures for Graphic Image Manipulation." In *Proceedings of the Conference on Computer Human Interface,* pages 241–245, New York: ACM, May 1989.

Hayes, P. J. and R. Reddy. "Steps Towards Graceful Interaction in Spoken and Written Man-Machine communication." *International Journal of Man/Machine Systems,* 19:231–284, 1983.

Hindus, D. "Semi-Structured Capture and Display of Telephone Conversations." Master's thesis, MIT, February 1992.

Hindus D., C. Schmandt, and C. Horner. "Capturing, Structuring, and Presenting Ubiquitous Audio." *Transactions on Information Systems,* New York: ACM Ocotober 1993.

Hindus, D. and C. Schmandt. "Ubiquitious Audio: Capturing Spontaneous Collaboration." In *Proceedings of the Conference on Computer-Supported Cooperative Work,* pages 210–217 New York: ACM, 192.

Hirschman, L., S. Seneff, D. Goodine, and M. Phillips. "Integrating Syntax and Semantics Into Spoken Language Understanding." In *Proceedings of the Fourth DARPA Speech and Natural Language Workshop,* February 1991.

Hodges, M. E., R. M. Sasnett, and M. S. Ackerman. "A Construction Set for Multimedia Applications." *IEEE Software,* pages 37–43, January 1989.

Hunnicutt, S., L. Hirschman, J. Polifroni, and S. Seneff. "Analysis of the Effectiveness of System Error Messages in a Human-Machine Travel Planning Task." In *Proceedings of the Second International Conference on Spoken Language Processing,* October 1992.

Jacob, R. J. K. "The Use of Eye Movements in Human-Computer Interaction Techniques: What You Look at is What You Get." *ACM Transactions on Information Systems,* 9(3):152–169, April 1991.

Jelinek, F. "The Development of an Experimental Discrete Dictation Recognizer." In *Proceedings of the IEEE,* volume 73, pages 1616–1624. New York: IEEE, November 1985.

Kamel, R., K. Emami, and R. Eckert. "PX Supporting Voice in Workstations." *IEEE Computer,* 23(8):73–80, August 1990.

Klatt, D. H. "Software for a Cascade/Parallel Formant Synthesizer." *Journal of the Acoustical Society of America,* 67(3):971–990, March 1980.

Klatt, D. H. "Review of Text-to-Speech Conversion for English." *Journal of the Acoustical Society of America,* 82:737–783, September 1987.

Klatt, D. H. "Review of Text-to-Speech Conversion for English." *Journal of the Acoustical Society of America,* 82:737–793, September 1987.

Koons, D.B, C.J. Sparrel, and K.R. Thorisson. "Integrating Simultaneous Input from Speech, Gaze and Hand Gesture." In T.M. Maybury, editor, *Intelligent Multi-Media Interfaces,* Menlo Park: AAAI Press, 1993.

Kramer, M., G. Ramirez, D. L. Turock, and R. S. Wolff. "Use of Two-Way Wireless Messaging for Personal Telephone Management." In *Proceedings of ICUPC '93,* October 1993.

Kraut, R. E., S. H. Lewis, and L. W. Swezey. "Listener Responsiveness and the Coordination of Conversation." *Journal of Personality and Social Psychology,* 42(4):718–731, 1982

Kraut, R. E. and S. H. Lewis. "Some functions of feedback in conversation." In H. E. Syphers and J. L. Applegate, editors, *Communication by Children and Adults,* Chapter 9. Sage, 1984.

Ladd, D. R. *The Structure of Intonational Meaning.* Indiana University Press, 1978.

Ladefoged, P. *Elements of Acoustic Phonetics.* Chicago:University of Chicago Press, 1962.

Lamming, M. and W. Newman. "Activity-Based Information Retrieval: Technology in Support of Human Memory." Technical Report 91–03, Rank Xerox EuroPARC, February 1991.

Lea, W. A. "Prosodic Aids to Speech Recognition." In Wayne A. Lea, editor, *Trends in Speech Recognition,* Chapter 8. Prentice Hall, 1980.

Lee, K. *Large-Vocabulary Speaker-Independent Continuous Speech Recognition Using Hidden Markov Models.* Ph.D. thesis, Carnegie-Mellon University, 1988.

Lee, K. and H. Hon. "Large-Vocabulary Speaker-Independent Continuous Speech Recognition Using HMM." In *International Conference on Acoustics, Speech, and Signal Processing.* New York: IEEE, April 1988.

Lee, K. and F. Alleva. "Continuous Speech Recognition." In Sadaoki Furui and M. Mohan Sondhi, editors, *Advances in Speech Signal Processing,* pages 623–650. New York: Marcel Dekker, Inc., 1992.

Leland, M. D. P., R. S. Fish, and R. E. Kraut. "Collaborative Document Production Using Quilt." In *Proceedings of the Conference on Computer-Supported Cooperative Work,* pages 206–215, New York: ACM, 1988.

Levinson, S. C. *Pragmatics.* Cambridge University Press, Cambridge, Great Britain, 1983.

Lison, H. and T. Crowley. "Sight and Sound." *UNIX Review,* 7(10):76–86, October 1989.

Luce, P. A., T. C. Feustel, and D. B. Pisoni. "Capacity Demands in Short-Term Memory for Synthetic and Natural Speech." *Human Factors,* 25(1):17–32, 1983.

Mackay, W. E., T. W. Malone, K. Crowston, R. Rao, D. Rosenblitt, and S. K. Card. "How do Experienced Information Lens Users Use Rules?" In *Proceedings of the Conference on Computer Human Interface,* pages 211–216, New York: ACM 1989.

Malone, T. W., K. R. Grant, K. Lai, R. Rao, and D. Rosenblitt. "Semi-Structured Messages are Surprisingly Useful For Computer-Supported Coordination." *ACM Transactions on Office Information Systems,* 5(2):115–131, 1987.

Martin, G. L. "The Utility of Speech Input in User-Computer Interfaces." *International Journal of Man/Machine Studies,* 30:355–375, 1989.

Maxemchuk, N. F. "An Experimental Speech Storage and Editing Facility." *The Bell System Technical Journal,* 59(8):1383–1395, October 1980.

McPeters, D. L. and A. L. Tharp. "The Influence of Rule-Generated Stress on Computer-Synthesized Speech." *International Journal of Man/Machine Studies,* 20:215–226, 1984.

Medina-Mora, R., T. Winograd, R. Flores, and F. Flores. "The action Workflow Approach to Workflow Management Technology." In *Proceedings of the Conference on Computer-Supported Cooperative Work,* New York: ACM, November 1992.

Mermelstein, P. "Automatic Segmentation of Speech into Syllabic Units." *Journal of the Acoustical Society of America,* 58(4):880–883, October 1975.

Mermelstein, P. "G.722, a new CCITT coding standard for digital transmission of wideband audio signals." *IEEE Communications Magazine,* 26(1), 1988.

Minneman, S. L. and S. A. Bly. "Managing a Trois: a Study of a Multi-User Drawing Tool in Distributed Design Work." In *Proceedings of the Conference on Computer Human Interaction,* pages 217–224. New York: ACM, April 1991.

Minsky, M. "A Framework for Representing Knowledge." In P. Winston, editor, *The Psychology of Computer Vision,* pages 211–277. McGraw-Hill, New York, 1975.

Morris, J. H., *et al.* "Andrew: A Distributed Personal Computing Environment." *Communications of the ACM,* March 1986.

Muller, M. J. and J. E. Daniel. "Toward a Definition of Voice Documents." In *Proceedings of the 1990 Conference on Office Information Systems,* 1990.

Murray, I. R., J. L. Arnott, and A. F. Newell. "Hamlet—Simulating Emotion in Synthetic Speech." In *Speech '88; Proceedings of the 7th FASE Symposium.* Institute of Acoustics, Edinburgh, 1988.

Myers, B. A. "The Importance of Percent-Done Progress Indicators for Computer-Human Interfaces." In *Proceedings of the Conference on Computer Human Interface,* pages 11–17, New York: ACM, 1985.

Nakatani, L. H., *et al.* "TNT: a Talking Tutor 'n' Trainer for Teaching the Use of Interactive Computer Systems." In *Proceedings of the Conference on Computer Human Interaction,* New York: ACM, 1986.

Nicholson, R. T. "Usage Patterns in an Integrated Voice and Data Communications System." In *ACM Transactions on Office Information Systems,* volume 3, pages 307–314. New York: ACM, July 1985.

Nusbaum, H. C., M. J. Dedina, and D. B. Pisoni. "Perceptual Confusions of Consonants in Natural and Synthetic CV Syllables." Speech Research Lab Tech. Note 84–02, Indiana University, 1984.

Nye, P. W. and J. Gaitenby. "The Intelligibility of Synthetic Monosyllabic Words in Short, Syntactically normal sentences." *Haskins Lab. Status Report on Speech Research,* 38:169–190, 1974.

Nyquist, H. "Certain Factors Affecting Telegraph Speed." *Bell System Technical Journal,* 3:324–326, 1924.

Ochsman, R. B. and A. Chapanis. "The Effects of 10 Communication Modes on the Behavior of Teams During Co-Operative Problem-Solving." *International Journal of Man/Machine Studies,* 6:579–619, 1974.

Olive, J. P. "Rule Synthesis of Speech from Diadic Units." In *Proceedings of the International Conference on Acoustics, Speech, and Signal Processing,* pages 568–570. New York: IEEE, 1977.

O'Neill, E. F. "TASI—Time Assignment Speech Interpolation." *Bell Laboratories Record,* 37:83–87, March 1959.

Orr, D. B., H. L. Friedman, and J. C. Williams. "Trainability of Listening Comprehension of Speeded Discourse." *Journal of Educational Psychology,* 56:148–156, 1965.

O'Shaughnessy, D. *Speech Communication.* New York: Addison-Wesley Publishing Company, 1987.

O'Shaughnessy, D. "Recognition of Hesitations in Spontaneous Speech." In *Proceedings of the International Conference on Acoustics, Speech, and Signal Processing,* pages 1521–1524. New York: IEEE, March 1992.

Oshika, B. T., V. W. Zue, R. V. Weeks, H. Neu, and J. Aurbach. "The Role of Phonological Rules in Speech Understanding Research." *IEEE Transactions on Acoustics, Speech, and Signal Processing,* ASSP-23(1):104–112, 1975.

G. Peterson, W. Wang, and E. Sivertsen. "Segmentation Techniques in Speech Synthesis." *Journal of the Acoustical Society of America, 30*:739–742, 1958.

Pierrehumbert, J. and J. Hirschberg. "The Meaning of Intonational Contours in the Interpretation of Discourse." In P. R. Cohen, J. Morgan, and M. E. Pollack, editors, *Intentions in Communication,* chapter 14, pages 271–311. Cambridge, MA: The MIT Press, 1990.

Pisoni, D. B. and S. Hunnicutt. "Perceptual Evaluation of MITalk: The MIT Unrestricted Text-to-Speech System." In *Proceedings of the International Conference on Acoustics, Speech, and Signal Processing,* pages 572–575. New York: IEEE, 1980.

Pisoni, D. B. "Speeded Classification of Natural and Synthetic Speech in a Lexical Decision Task." *Journal of the Acoustical Society of America, 70*:S98, 1981.

Pisoni, D. B., H. C. Nusbaum, and B. G.Greene. "Perception of Synthetic Speech Generated by Rule." *Proceedings of the IEEE, 73*(11):1665–1676, November 1985.

Rabiner, L. R. and R. W. Schafer. *Digital Processing of Speech Signals.* Englewood Cliffs, NJ: Prentice-Hall, Inc., 1978.

Rabiner, L. R. and B. H. Juang. "An Introduction to Hidden Markov Models." *IEEE ASSP Magazine, 3*(1):4–16, January 1986.

Rabiner, L. R. and B. H. Juang. "An Introduction to Hidden Markov Models." *IEEE Transactions on Acoustics, Speech, and Signal Processing,* pages 4–16, January 1986.

Resnick, P. Hypervoice: "A Phone-Based CSCW Platform." In *Proceedings of the Conference on Computer-Supported Cooperative Work,* pages 218–225, New York: ACM, November 1992.

Resnick, P. *Hypervoice: Groupware by Telephone.* Ph.D. thesis, MIT, September 1992.

Resnick, P. and R. A. Virzi. "Skip and Scan: Cleaning Up Telephone Interfaces." In *Proceedings of the Conference on Computer Human Interface,* New York: ACM, 1992.

Roberts, T. L. and G. Engelbeck. "The Effects of Device Technology on the Usability of Advanced Telephone Functions." In *Proceedings of the Conference on Computer Human Interface,* pages 331–337, New York, May 1989. ACM.

Root, R. W. and C. R. Koster. "Experimental Evaluation of a Mnemonic Command Syntax for Controlling Advanced Telecommunications Services." In *Proceedings of the Conference on Computer Human Interaction,* pages 809–813, 1986.

Root, R. W. and C. Chow. "Multimode Interaction in a Telecommmunications Testbed: the Case of Memory Dialing." In G. Salvendy, editor, *Cognitive engineering in the design of human-computer interaction and expert systems,* pages 399–406. Elsevier Science Publishers, 1987.

Rose, M. T. *The Internet Message,* Chapter 6. Prentice Hall Series in Innovative Technology. Englewood Cliffs, NJ: P T R Prentice Hall, 1993.

Rosson, M. B. and A. J. Cecala. "Designing a Quality Voice: An Analysis of Listeners' Reactions to Synthetic Voices." In *Proceedings of the Conference on Computer Human Interface,* pages 192–197, New York: ACM, April 1986.

Roucos, S. and A. M. Wilgus. "High Quality Time-Scale Modifications for Speech." In *Proceedings of the International Conference on Acoustics, Speech, and Signal Processing,* pages 493–496. New York: IEEE, 1985.

Rudnicky, A. I. and A. G. Hauptmann. "Models for Evaluating Interaction Protocols in Speech Recognition." In *Proceedings of the Conference on Computer Human Interface,* pages 285–291, New York: ACM, 1991.

Rudnicky, A. I.; J. M. Lunati, and A. M. Franz. "Spoken Language Recognition in an Office Management Domain." In *Proceedings of the International Conference on Acoustics, Speech, and Signal Processing,* pages 829–832. New York: IEEE, May 1991.

Sacks, H., E. A. Schegloff, and G. Jefferson. "A Simplest Systematics for the Organization of Turn-Taking for Conversation. Language," 50(4):696–735, 1974. Reprinted in *Studies in the Organization of Conversational Interaction,* J. Schenken, ed., Academic Press 1978.

Sakoe, H. and S. Chiba. "Dynamic Programming Algorithm Optimization for Spoken Word Recognition." *IEEE Transactions on Acoustics, Speech, and Signal Processing,* 26:43–49, February 1978. Reprinted in Dixon and Martin.

Schank, R. C. and R. Abelson. *Scripts, Plans, Goals and Understanding.* Hillsdale, NJ: Lawrence Erlbaum, 1977.

Schmandt, C. "The Intelligent Ear: A Graphical Interface to Digital Audio." In *Proceedings IEEE Conference on Cybernetics and Society,* pages 393–397, New York: IEEE, October 1981.

Schmandt, C. and E. Hulteen. "The Intelligent Voice Interactive Interface." *Human Factors in Computer Systems,* pages 363–366, 1982.

Schmandt, C. "Speech Synthesis Gives Voiced Access to an Electronic Mail System." *Speech Technology,* 2(3):66–69, 1984.

Schmandt, C. and B. Arons. "A Conversational Telephone Messaging System." *IEEE Trans. on Consumer Electr.,* CE-30(3):xxi–xxiv, 1984.

Schmandt, C. and B. Arons. "Phone Slave: A Graphical Telecommunications Interface." *Proc. of the Soc. for Information Display,* 26(1):79–82, 1985.

Schmandt, C., B. Arons, and C. Simmons. "Voice Interaction in an Integrated Office and Telecommunications Environment." In *Proceedings of the 1985 Conference,* pages 51–57. San Jose, CA: *American Voice I/O Society,* September 1985.

Schmandt, C. and B. Arons. "A Robust Parser and Dialog Generator for a Conversational Office System." In *Proceedings of the 1986 Conference,* pages 355–365. San Jose, CA: *American Voice I/O Society,* September 1986.

Schmandt, C. "Employing Voice Back Channels to Facilitate Audio Document Retrieval." In *Proceedings of the ACM Conference on Office Information Systems,* pages 213–218., New York: ACM, 1988.

Schmandt, C. and M. McKenna. "An Audio and Telephone Server for Multi-Media Workstations." In *Proceedings of the 2nd IEEE Conference on Computer Workstations,* pages 150–159. New York: IEEE, March 1988.

Schmandt, C. and S. Casner. "Phonetool: Integrating Telephones and Workstations." In *Proceedings of the IEEE Global Telecommunications Conference,* pages 970–974. New York: IEEE Communications Society, November 1989.

Schmandt, C., D. Hindus, M. Ackerman, and S. Manandhar. "Observations on Using Speech Input for Window Navigation." In *Proceedings of the IFIP TC 13 Third International Conference on Human-Computer Interaction,* pages 787–793, August 1990.

Schmandt, C. "Phoneshell: the Telephone as Computer Terminal." In *Proceedings ACM Multimedia 93,* pages 373–382. New York: ACM, 1993.

Schmandt, C., M. S. Ackerman, and D. Hindus. "Augmenting a Window System With Speech Input." *IEEE Computer,* 23(8):50–56, August 1990.

Schwab, E. C., H. C. Nusbaum, and D. B. Pisoni. "Some Effects of Training on the Perception of Synthetic Speech." *Human Factors,* 27(4):395–408, 1985.

Searle, J. R. "The Classification of Illocutionary Acts." *Language in Society,* 5:1–24, 1976.

Seneff, S. "A Joint Synchrony/Mean-Rate Model of Auditory Speech Processing." *Journal of Phonetics,* 16:55–76, 1988.

Seneff, S. "Robust Parsing for Spoken Language Systems." In *Proceedings of the International Conference on Acoustics, Speech, and Signal Processing.* New York: IEEE, March 1992.

Sivertsen, E. "Segment Inventories for Speech Synthesis." *Language and Speech,* 4:27–90, 1961.

Snell, J. "The Lucasfilm Real-Time Console for Recording Studios and Performance of Computer Music." *Computer Music Journal,* 6(3):33–45, Fall 1982.

Spiegel, M. F. "Pronouncing Surnames Automatically." In *Proceedings of the 1985 Conference.* San Jose, CA: American Voice I/O Society, September 1985.

Spiegel, M. F. "Using a Monosyllabic Test Corpus to Evaluate the Intelligibility of Synthesized and Natural Speech." In *Proceedings of the 1988 Conference,* San Jose, CA: The American Voice I/O Society, 1988.

Spiegel, M. F. and M. J. Macchi. "Synthesis of Names by a Demisyllable-Based Speech Synthesizer (Orator)." *Journal of The American Voice I/O Society,* 7:1–10, March 1990.

Spiegel, M. F., M. J. Macchi, M. J. Altom, D. Kahn, N Jackson, and K. D. Gollha rdt. "State-of-the-Art Name Pronunciation Accuracy: Preparing the ORATOR Synthesizer for Applications." In *Proceedings of the 1991 Conference,* pages 119–123, San Jose, CA: The American Voice I/O Society, September 1991.

Stallings, W. *ISDN: An Introduction.* New York: Macmillan Publishing Company, 1989.

Starker, I. and R. A. Bolt. "A Gaze-Responsive Self-Disclosing Display." In *Proceedings of the Conference on Computer Human Interface,* pages 3–9. New York: ACM, April 1990.

Stifelman, L. J., B. Arons, C. Schmandt, and E. A. Hulteen. Voice Notes: "A Speech Interface for a Hand-Held Voice Notetaker." In *Proceedings of INTERCHI '93,* New York: ACM, April 1993.

Streeter, L. A., D. Vitello, and S. A. Wonsiewicz. "How to Tell People Where to Go: Comparing Navigational Aids." *International Journal of Man/Machine Systems,* 22(5):549–562, May 1985.

Talley, D. *Basic Carrier Telephony.* Rochelle Park, NJ: Hayden Book Company, Inc., second edition, 1966.

Terry, D. B. and D. C. Swinehart. "Managing Stored Voice in the Etherphone System." *ACM Transactions on Computer Systems,* 6(1):3–27, February 1988.

Thomas, R. H., H. C. Forsdick, T. R. Crowley, R. W. Schaaf, R. S. Tomlinson, V. M. Travers, and G. G. Robertson. "Diamond: A Multimedia Message System Built on a Distributed Architecture." *IEEE Computer,* 18(12):65–78, December 1985.

Treisman, A. and A. Davies. "Divided Attention to Ear and Eye." In *Attention and Performance,* volume IV, pages 101–117, 1973.

Vitale, T. "An Algorithm for High Accuracy Name Pronunciation by Parametric Speech Synthesizer." *Journal of Computational Linguistics,* 17(1):257–276, 1991.

Waibel, A. *Prosody and Speech Recognition.* Morgan Kaufmann, 1988.

Waibel, A. and K. Lee, editors. *Readings in Speech Recognition.* San Mateo, CA: Morgan Kaufmann Publishers, Inc., 1990.

Want, R. and A. Hopper. "Active Badges and Personal Interactive Computing Objects." *IEEE Transactions on Consumer Electronics,* 38(1):10–20, Feb 1992.

Weimer, D. and S. K. Ganapathy. "A Synthetic Visual Environment With Hand Gesturing and Voice Input." In *Proceedings of the Conference on Computer Human Interface,* pages 235–240, New York, ACM, May 1989.

Weimer, D. and S. K. Ganapathy. "Interaction Techniques Using Hand Tracking and Speech Recognition." In M.M. Blattner and R.B. Dannenberg, editors, *Multimedia Interface Design,* ACM Press frontier series, pages 109–126. New York: Addison-Wesley, 1992.

Wickens, C. D., S. J. Mountford, and W. Schreiner. "Multiple Resources, Task-Hemispheric Integrity, and Individual Differences in Time-Sharing." *Human Factors,* 23:211–230, 1981.

Wilpon, J. G., L. R. Rabiner, C. Lee, and E. R. Goldman. "Automatic Recognition of Keywords in Unconstrained Speech Using Hidden Markov Models." *IEEE Transactions on Acoustics, Speech, and Signal Processing,* 38(11), November 1990.

Winograd, T. *Language as a Cognitive Process - Syntax.* New York: Addison-Wesley, 1983.

Winograd, T. "A Language/Action Perspective on the Design of Cooperative Work." *Human Computer Interaction,* 3(1):3–30, 1988.

Witten, L. and P. Madams. "The Telephone Inquiry Service: A Man-Machine System Using Synthetic Speech." *International Journal of Man/Machine Systems,* 9:449–464, 1977.

Witten, I. H. *Principles of Computer Speech.* Academic Press, 1982.

Wong, C. C. "Personal Communications". Master's thesis, MIT, June 1991.

Yost, W. and D. Nielsen. *Fundamentals of Hearing*. Holt, Rinehart, and Winston, 1977.

Yngve, V. H. "On Getting a Word in Edgewise." In *Papers from the Sixth Regional Meeting*, pages 567–578. Chicago Linguistic Society, 1970.

Zellweger, P. T. "Scripted Documents: a Hypermedia Path Mechanism." In *Proceedings of Hypertext '89*, pages 1–14. New York: ACM, 1989.

Zue, V., J. Glass, M. Phillips, and S. Seneff. "The MIT SUMMIT Speech Recognition System: A Progress Report." In *First DARPA Speech and Natural Language Workshop*, pages 166–178, February 1989.

Zue, V., N. Daly, J. Glass, *et al.* "The Collection and Preliminary Analysis of a Spontaneous Speech Database." In *Proceedings of the DARPA Speech and Natural Language Workshop*, pages 126–134, October 1989.

# Index